To the memory of Betsy Crowder
(1926–2000)

Black Rock Falls, Uvas Canyon Park

SOUTH BAY TRAILS

OUTDOOR ADVENTURES IN & AROUND SANTA CLARA VALLEY:
From the Diablo Range to the Pacific Ocean

Jean Rusmore · Betsy Crowder · Frances Spangle

WILDERNESS PRESS
BERKELEY

FIRST EDITION November 1984
SECOND EDITION August 1991
THIRD EDITION October 2001

Copyright © 1984, 1991, and 2001 by Frances Spangle and Jean Rusmore

Design and production by Margaret Copeland/Terragraphics
Maps by Ben Pease
Cover design by Larry Van Dyke

Library of Congress Card Catalog Number 00-053427
International Standard Book Number 0-89997-284-5

Manufactured in the United States
Published by   Wilderness Press
1200 Fifth Street
Berkeley, CA 94710 -1306
(800) 443-7227
FAX (510) 558-1696
mail@wildernesspress.com

Contact us for a free catalog
Visit our website at *www.wildernesspress.com*

Front cover photo: Jean Rusmore, *Joseph Grant County Park*;
Inset, *Wind Poppy*
Frontispiece: Jean Rusmore, *Black Rock Falls, Uvas Canyon Park*

 Printed on recycled paper

Library of Congress Cataloging-in-Publication Data
Rusmore, Jean.
    South Bay Trails : outdoor adventures around the Santa Clara Valley, from the Diablo Range to the Pacific / Jean Rusmore, Frances Spangle, Betsy Crowder.—3rd ed.
      p. cm.
    Spangle's name appears first on the earlier editions.
    Includes bibliographical references and index.
    ISBN 0-89997-284-5
    1. Hiking—California—Santa Clara Valley (San Benito County and Santa Clara County)—Guidebooks. 2. Parks—California—Santa Clara Valley (San Benito County and Santa Clara County)—Guidebooks. 3. Santa Clara Valley (San Benito County and Santa Clara County, Calif.)—Guidebooks. I. Spangle, Francis. II. Crowder, Betsy, 1926– III. Title.

GV199.42.C22 S319957 2000
917.94' 73—dc21

00-053427

Table of Contents

Foreword

During our daily routine, it is easy to forget about the natural beauty of the hills and baylands around the South Bay. Traffic congestion, air conditioned offices, and deadlines fill our work week, and often our weekend.

Yet, in the mountains east and west of the Santa Clara Valley and along its creeks and baylands are parks and open spaces that offer visual, spiritual and recreational respite from our daily rigors. An invigorating walk through Santa Teresa County Park in the early evening or a full day of bicycling through Henry W. Coe State Park provides an opportunity to connect with nature and to recreate. Our open spaces also provide habitat for wildlife. Deer, snakes, birds and other animals make their home here. By protecting open space, we have not only an opportunity to ensure that wildlife has a place in our community, but also a chance to see and understand more about nature itself.

South Bay Trails is a friendly reminder of the spark of a new-found interest in the beauty just beyond the tract homes and commercial buildings of the Silicon Valley. This book provides the reader with the guidance, advice and direction to experience our protected open space in the South Bay. In its third edition, *South Bay Trails* benefits from two earlier editions, as well as the vast knowledge and experiences of Jean Rusmore, Betsy Crowder and Frances Spangle who have hiked all of the trails in this book. *South Bay Trails* reflects their passion for trekking through diverse terrain and climate zones. Their appetite for hiking also drives their even stronger desire for preserving more open spaces for future generations to enjoy.

As you take this book as your guide to trails in the South Bay, consider the value of our endangered open spaces and the importance of saving these natural habitats for our future generations. With you, we can, as my old friend Wallace Stegner once said, "...try to save for everyone, for the hostile and indifferent as well as the committed, some of the health that flows down across the green ridges from the Skyline, and some of the beauty and refreshment of spirit that are still available to any resident of the valley who has a moment, and the wit, to lift up his (or her) eyes unto the hills."

Byron D. Sher
Senator, State of California
11th District

Preface

In the sixteen years since the first edition of *South Bay Trails* was published we have seen an incredible increase in the acreages of public parklands. Over these years, voters created a new district, the Santa Clara County Open Space Authority, and public agencies bought new parklands and open space preserves, expanded existing parklands, carried out new park plans, and built many miles of new trails.

This third edition of *South Bay Trails* is greatly expanded as well. We now cover all the trails in Castle Rock and Big Basin Redwoods state parks, as well as the Skyline-to-the-Sea Trail that joins them. In addition, we included several trails from the new southwestern entrance to Henry W. Coe State Park. Including this expanded area, *South Bay Trails* now covers almost 200,000 acres with 568 miles of trails.

On revisiting the parks and preserves and adventuring through the two parks newly added, and while walking all the existing trails, we met increased numbers of hikers, runners, equestrians and bicyclists along the way. We discovered improved park facilities, innovative displays at visitor centers, and many trail events led by trained docents. We found that increased numbers are turning out to help with trailbuilding, maintenance and trail activities. Now many hiking and bicycle patrols, and even an occasional companion dog patrol, are joining longtime horse patrol volunteers. Helpful for trail information and interpretations, as well as emergency assistance, these patrols provide a valuable service to the public and the park agencies.

Progress, too, has been made on the three regional trails that wind through these public parklands. The Bay Area Ridge Trail is now 225 miles long, 48 miles in the area covered by this book. The Bay Trail, with 205 miles in place, follows a circuitous route around the South Bay where three new segments bring its total to 22.5 miles in our book. The Anza National Historic Trail route has been established, and signs are appearing along the trail, which traverses 51 miles in the area of this book. On the bicentennial of the expedition costumed equestrians reenacted the long trip from Mexico and followed the segments of this trail in present-day Santa Clara County.

The hundreds of miles of trails in this book cover terrain of remarkable diversity—from the rugged, western slopes of the Diablo Range and the creeksides and baylands of the Santa Clara Valley to the wooded eastern flanks of the Santa Cruz Mountains and its forested summit and then down the western conifer-clad slopes to the Pacific Ocean.

To help the hiker, runner, equestrian, and bicyclist explore these many trails, we arranged *South Bay Trails* by trips, often combining several trails to form loops. This distinctive feature suggests outings that vary from short easy strolls to long, strenuous expeditions, some with overnight camping at park campgrounds or backpack camps.

Of special interest is Appendix A, *Guide to Choosing a Trail*, which groups trails so readers may choose those that fit their inclinations and abilities. Here is a wealth of recreational opportunities for every ability.

Frances Spangle and Jean Rusmore authored the original *South Bay Trails* in 1984. In 1995 Betsy Crowder joined the partnership, and Frances Spangle retired to the North Bay. From 1995 through most of 2000, we hiked through every park and preserve, Bayland marsh, and creekside park chain, on loop and roundtrips, exploring and marveling at the rich variety of landscape and the magnificent heritage of natural beauty showcased in the South Bay's public parklands. We hoped that our readers would also come to enjoy the first-hand experience of exploring these trails and would come to appreciate, treasure, and care for these public open spaces. Here are almost 200,000 acres of public parklands at the fringes of bustling urban centers, yet wild enough to offer solitude, majestic views, and opportunities to re-create.

Unfortunately, a tragic freak automobile accident ended Betsy Crowder's life on September 29, 2000, not more than a mile from her home in Portola Valley. Her death is a terrible loss to the Bay Area environmental community, to the Midpeninsula Regional Open Space District, to the trail organizations, to her family and many friends and to me. I miss her good humor, her determination, her dedication to our books and her company on the trail. May her spirit prevail in protecting our wild and natural places, and may she rest in peace.

Jean Rusmore
October 2001

❖ Introduction ❖

The South Bay Setting

Geography

A 100-mile-long valley flanked by two arms of the Coast Range mountains lies at the southern end of San Francisco Bay. Through this valley flow tree-lined creeks that drain the steep, forested mountains and oak-dotted foothills of the Santa Cruz Mountains and the grassy and wooded heights of the Diablo Range. When the streams reach the Bay's edge, they widen into sloughs and meander through what were once broad marshes but are now diked salt ponds. On the western flanks of the Santa Cruz Mountains are heavily forested ridges creased by deep canyons through which lively streams flow into Monterey Bay and the Pacific Ocean. This is the setting for this third edition of *South Bay Trails*.

The eastern mountains, the Diablo Range, extend from Contra Costa County south to Pacheco Pass at the extreme southern end of Santa Clara County. The highest point in the range, 4372' Copernicus Peak, is near Mt. Hamilton, which is a few feet lower and better known for its observatories. Other tall Diablo Range mountains are Mission Peak and Monument Peak in the north and Mt. Sizer and Pacheco Peak in the south.

These mountains, dry and grassy on their west- and south-facing slopes, are broken into parallel ridges with steep sides separated by narrow, intervening wooded valleys. The general trend of ridges and valleys is northwest-southeast, following the direction of major earthquake faults in the region. The Diablo Range separates the Santa Clara Valley from the San Joaquin Valley, coaxing moisture from the clouds that brush against its tall peaks.

Across the valley on the west side are the Santa Cruz Mountains and their foothills, slightly lower in elevation than the Diablo Range. This range extends south from Montara Mountain near San Francisco along the ridges topped by Mt. Umunhum and Loma Prieta to Mt. Madonna, and then slopes to the valley of the Pajaro River, which flows west to Monterey Bay. A shallow notch in the Santa Cruz Mountains called Saratoga Gap has long been the route from the valley to destinations along the Skyline ridge and to the west. This gap is now the authors' entree to the state parks and trails leading to the ocean.

South from Saratoga Gap the Santa Cruz Mountains are interrupted by a low pass where Los Gatos Creek cuts through on its northeastward course to the Bay. The Spaniards called the northern mountainous area the Sierra Morena (dark mountains) and the southern area the Sierra Azul (the latter, perhaps, because of the blue haze that often hangs over its forested heights). The tallest mountain, Loma Prieta, is 3791'. Just north, other landmark peaks include Mt. Umunhum, Mt. Thayer and El Sombroso; farther south is Mt. Madonna.

The Santa Clara Valley lowlands enclosed by the two ranges consist of a number of alluvial fans and floodplains formed by deep deposits of material eroded from the surrounding mountains. The relatively smooth valley floor ranges in elevation from 150' to 400'. The valley rises from the Bay to a low, almost imperceptible divide at Morgan Hill, south of which the drainage flows to the Pajaro River.

Fifteen miles wide in the north, the valley tapers at the Santa Teresa Hills to a passage 2 miles wide, sometimes called the "Coyote Narrows," through which Coyote Creek flows.

Coyote Creek is the longest stream flowing out of the Diablo Range. Joined by tributary creeks, San Felipe and Silver, in the foothills, then by Penitencia, Berryessa, Calaveras, and Scott on the valley floor, it empties into San Francisco Bay northeast of Alviso. The waters of Alameda Creek, now contained in a flood-control channel, flow into the Bay just north of Coyote Hills. Pacheco Creek in Henry Coe State Park flows south, gathering waters from its many tributaries, then turns west and is impounded in San Felipe Lake, after which it merges with the Pajaro River, which forms the Santa Clara/San Benito County boundary, and then it flows into the Pacific Ocean at Monterey Bay south of Watsonville.

Major creeks that course down the east side of the Santa Cruz Mountains are Stevens, Calabasas, Saratoga, and Los Gatos, which joins the Guadalupe River, all of which flow into San Francisco Bay. Streams rising in the mountains southeast of Loma Prieta—Uvas, Llagas, Little Arthur and Bodfish creeks—also join the Pajaro River on its way to the ocean.

Few creeks flow freely across the valley. For purposes of flood control or ground-water recharge most are dammed at some point, diverted to percolation ponds, or channeled. Nevertheless, many stretches of these creeks flow toward the Bay, still bordered by the oaks, alders, sycamores and bay trees that have always lined their banks.

On the west side of the Santa Cruz Mountains in the area of this book, Waddell Creek, which drains most of Big Basin Redwoods State Park, flows directly into the Pacific Ocean at Waddell State Beach, just south of Año Nuevo State Reserve. The headwaters of the San Lorenzo River rise in Castle Rock State Park and, joined by several tributaries, its waters flow due south to Santa Cruz on Monterey Bay.

Plants and Animals

The great variety of South Bay terrain from mountains to plains accommodates a corresponding variety of plant communities—conifers on the mountains, chaparral on dry slopes, maples and ferns in damp stream

Coe Park, magnificent Quercus Lobata

canyons, grasses and occasional oaks in the meadows and distinctive salt-tolerant plants in Bay marshes.

Grasslands cover the foothills on both sides of the valley as well as the south and west slopes of the Diablo Range. The familiar golden hills of summer and the sometimes brief green of winter and spring come from the predominant European oats and other annual grasses. In the grasslands are found the most spectacular wildflower displays. At times the low hills, even seen from a distance, are colored for miles with goldfields, tidytips and poppies.

Grasslands on the west-facing slopes of the Diablo Range are studded with magnificent open stands of deciduous valley oaks. In the bare hills of this range are canyons lined with live oak, California bay, maple, alder and sycamore. In both the Diablo and Santa Cruz ranges great areas of brushland or chaparral clothe dry hillsides with woody plants in various combinations—coyote bush, toyon, chamise and the ubiquitous poison oak. Occasional stands of knobcone pine adapt to the dry, rocky terrain and protrude over the chaparral—sometimes in thick young forests where they have sprung up after fires. On much of the Santa Cruz Mountains stands of live oak, madrone, canyon oak and black oak form a dense canopy. In the damp canyons bay trees proliferate.

In the area of this book coniferous forests are found chiefly in the Santa Cruz Mountains. From the valley you can see the silhouettes of Douglas firs and redwoods. On the lower western slopes redwoods predominate until you are close to the seacoast. Some of the world's largest and tallest trees grow in Big Basin Redwoods State Park. Associated with these forests, where sunlight filters through the trees, an undergrowth of black-berries, huckleberries and other shrubs and numerous fern species flour-ishes. Though most of these areas were logged in the past century, they now have maturing forests of good-sized trees; some immense virgin red-woods remain.

One can see the jagged outlines of another conifer on the hilltops of the Diablo Range in and near Coe Park, where the ponderosa pine has found a niche far from its usual Sierra habitat.

Gray, or foothill pines, formerly called Digger pines, grow in elevations ranging from two to three thousand feet in Henry W. Coe State Park and Joseph Grant County Park in the Diablo Range and on Mt. Umunhum in Sierra Azul Open Space Preserve in the Santa Cruz Mountains.

A special plant community borders the Bay where cordgrass, salt grass, pickleweed and other salt-tolerant plants grow in tidelands, wetlands and marshes.

Dark-green bands of trees still persist along the banks of creeks where they thread through the built-up cities on the valley floor. The alders, sycamores, oaks, maples, willows, shrubs and vines that make up the riparian vegetation provide a valuable habitat for wildlife.

In large parks and preserves where the land is relatively undisturbed, many animals that lived here before the coming of Europeans can still be found. Gone are the antelope and the bear, but deer in numbers and coy-otes and foxes, as well as many smaller mammals, still live here. You will see their tracks on and off the trails. Even a bobcat or a mountain lion is occasionally sighted in a remote part of a mountain park. A relative new-comer to Bay Area parks is the feral pig, descendant of European wild boar and escaped domestic pigs, which is proliferating throughout the region.

South Bay woods and fields contain myriad birds—over 300 species have been counted. Some more easily identifiable ones are mentioned in this guide because the authors saw them. The Baylands, reservoirs and percolation ponds are teeming with shorebirds and waterfowl. Resident birds that have long lived by the sloughs and marshes are finding new habitats by percolation ponds and salt ponds. Joining them in winter months are migrating birds by the thousands using the Pacific Flyway.

In deep, dark redwood forests few birds can be seen, but the marbled murrelet, an endangered species, nests in the upper branches of the coast redwoods. It spends its days feeding at sea and returns to its nest only at night. Although rarely observed, knowledgeable birders can identify it by its call.

The South Bay's Past

In the years since the arrival of the Spanish in 1776, three distinct periods have together seen the changes that transformed the valley and the foothills at the south end of San Francisco Bay into today's densely urban scene.

For thousands of years before 1776 Ohlone Indians lived here, possessing a stable culture that had relatively little impact on the land. After the founding of Mission Santa Clara in 1777 and Mission San José in 1797, the Indians were baptized and taken into these establishments. They left their villages, and their lands were divided into huge ranches that raised cattle for their hides and tallow.

The second transitional period began after nearly 100 years of Spanish and Mexican rule. The discovery of gold and the admission of California to the United States were followed by the break-up of the ranches into farms producing wheat, fruits, vegetables and dairy products to supply the rapidly growing city of San Francisco. To build housing and commercial development for the burgeoning population, logging of the immense redwoods began. By the end of the 19th century many of the forests had been clearcut, on both sides of the Santa Cruz Mountains.

In the last half of the 19th century large dairy farms prospered along the southern San Mateo and northern Santa Cruz coasts. Today, many of these are in public open space. However, vast stretches of the coastal terraces are still in private agriculture—especially artichokes, broccoli, brussels sprouts and pumpkins.

Then, a century after the Gold Rush, came a third major change. The postwar boom ushered in the most profound alterations of the valley landscape as industry and housing swept away orchards, vineyards and truck farms. In less than two decades this agricultural valley became urban—home to more than a million people.

However, concern for the impact of unrestrained growth led to programs that created today's remarkable parks, open space preserves and trail systems. As present-day trail-users traverse these trails, they can still find much that evokes the earlier periods in South Bay history. See "Hikes into History" in Appendix A.

The Ohlone Indians

Of the earliest settlers, the Ohlone people, few remain, but we value the records we have of their lives and treasure the artifacts of their culture. They lived well on the abundance of this fertile, well-watered land, depending on the plentiful supplies of acorns, seeds, fruits, game, fish and shellfish. Their villages, circles of huts made of rushes over frameworks of bent willows, have disappeared, but traces remaining around their shell mounds have been studied by archeologists.

The Ohlone had no pottery, but their baskets of extraordinary fineness served every purpose. Of the very few that survived, some may be seen at the Los Altos Library, at Coyote Hills Regional Park, and at the Cantor Arts Center at Stanford.

The Ohlone were runners of great speed and endurance. There are no time records to compare them with the runners who follow our trails today, but an 1898 account testifies to their speed and endurance: ". . . one would run from my ranch at Edenvale to Santa Clara keeping up with the fastest horse, and laugh when he got there. . . ."

When Gaspar de Portolá came through the Santa Clara Valley, he described the people he found in large villages by the Guadalupe River as "generous affable heathen." Other early explorers commented on their curiosity and hospitality and noted that they were well-formed and come-ly. (Later reports on the Ohlone, when they were living in the missions, were not so complimentary. They were sometimes described as uncoop-erative—but perhaps their behavior was just a reaction to the frequently harsh discipline they faced.)

In a sad chapter in our history, the Ohlone population was greatly reduced and their culture destroyed as they were christened and taken from their villages to live in the missions. There they succumbed to dis-eases against which they had no resistance. After secularization of the missions under Mexican rule, they were dispersed to work on ranches. By 1810 only a few Ohlone were living an aboriginal life. Under U.S. rule too, they were often badly treated.

Spanish and Mexican Rule

Soon after the founding of Mission Santa Clara and the establishment of the Pueblo de San José, Spanish and then Mexican governors of California granted ranches of thousands of acres as rewards for service or simply to settle the land. The economy was based on raising cattle and exporting hides and tallow. From this period Spanish place names abound. Streets, cities, creeks and mountains carry the names of Spanish families and patron saints. Spanish words survive in today's terms *chap-arral, manzanita, arroyo, embarcadero* and *plaza*, among others.

The most visible heritage from these times covers our hills, which are colored golden in summer by the imported European oats that replaced the native bunchgrasses.

The supporting Pueblo de San José beside the Guadalupe River, at first just a double row of mud huts, has remained the focus of civic and cul-tural activity for the valley.

Neither Mission Santa Clara nor Mission San José has come down to us intact; floods, fires and earthquakes destroyed the early buildings. But fragments of old walls remain from an early Mission Santa Clara, and the museum of Mission San José occupies the surviving building of the old mission. A fine reconstruction of the 1807 mission is now completed. A few adobe buildings are still standing around the valley, some lived in today.

Many of the big parks in the hills are parts of former Spanish and Mexican ranches. Some have been used for grazing since those days, and grazing is still carried on. Mission Peak Preserve was a part of Mission San José lands; a part of the Higuera family's Rancho Tularcitos is now Ed R. Levin Park; in Santa Teresa Hills we can walk or ride over José Bernal's lands.

The Coming of the American Settlers and a Century of Agriculture

Even before the discovery of gold in California a steady trickle of immigrants from the east was arriving in the Bay Area. The first American settlers from an overland expedition reached San Jose in 1841. The war between United States and Mexico broke out in 1846. In the "Battle of Santa Clara," engaging only about 100 soldiers on each side, U.S. forces prevailed and the Bear Flag was raised over San José.

When California was admitted to statehood in 1850, San Jose became its first capital. The town soon changed from a sleepy Mexican village to a bustling center for the farms that supplied Gold Rush San Francisco. Stage lines and steamers made regular runs between San Francisco and Alviso, and by 1864 the San Francisco-San Jose Railroad was completed.

Bringing an exotic touch to valley life by the mid-1850s was the astoundingly productive New Almaden Quicksilver Mine. Seemingly inexhaustible supplies of cinnabar, mined from miles of tunnels through the hills, were processed in giant reduction works. The mines supplied needed mercury to California's goldfields and to international trade, chiefly with China.

But agriculture remained the basis of the South Bay economy. Fruit trees thrived in the valley, watered by creeks and irrigation ditches. Rich alluvial soil 30-40' deep overlaid clay and waterbearing gravel substrata. For a while artesian wells gushed from the Bay plain.

Orchards and vineyards soon covered the valley floor and the foothills. Stock imported by French nurserymen produced the country's finest fruits, and Santa Clara Valley wines won awards in Paris. In the "wine boom" of 1880 grapevines were planted in thousands of acres across the valley and up to the summit of the Santa Cruz Mountains. But soon after came a glut of grapes, falling prices and a deadly root disease. As a result, vineyards were interplanted with prunes and apricots.

The valley continued to be one of the most productive agricultural areas in the U.S. Each spring, from the foothills, one looked down on a pink-and-white mosaic of fruit blossoms. This was indeed, the "Valley of Heart's Delight," as Santa Clara County people fondly called it. They made excursions out into the beautiful foothills surrounding the valley. Wagon trips to Lick Observatory were popular. As early as 1872 Alum Rock Park was set aside as a park by the State Legislature. Spas flourished around mineral springs and hot springs—at Congress Springs above Saratoga (which took its name from the New York resort), Gilroy Hot Springs and Warm Springs, near Mission San José.

In 1888 San Jose's Dashaway Stables advertised a large string of "useful, careful animals of fine appearance." It urged patrons to "revel in delights of spring through Santa Clara Valley, its foothills and adjacent mountains behind a Dashaway team."

The exuberance of these times took form in spacious farmhouses, great mansions, luxurious estates, and even a few villas scattered through the foothills. Many of these handsome structures have disappeared, but thanks to recent interest in historic preservation many notable buildings have survived. Among those in the parks are the Bailey House in Calero Park, the Gallegos Mansion at Ohlone College near Mission Peak, Villa Montalvo in Saratoga, the Rengstorff House now in Shoreline at Mountain View, and La Casa Grande at New Almaden.

Expanding agriculture and a growing urban population increased demands on the valley's water supply. As water was pumped from wells to augment the once-ample supplies from creeks, the water table fell drastically. In consequence, the land around San Jose suffered massive subsidence. Periods of drought, with water shortages, and years of heavy rainfall, with disastrous floods, plagued the valley. In response, water-conservation districts were formed. They built dams to retain winter rains, control floods and replenish underground water supplies, and they constructed levees along creek banks to protect lands in floodplains.

These water-conservation measures have brought opportunities to create parks and trails beside reservoirs and ponds. The levees beside creeks and near the Bay have become routes for trails and bicycle paths. Streamside park chains along Coyote, Guadalupe, Los Gatos, Alamitos/Calero, Penitencia and Stevens creeks have expanding systems of trails.

From Agriculture to Industry

With World War II came the beginnings of the transformation of the Santa Clara Valley and the East Bay south of Fremont. In a few decades the area changed from a balanced agricultural community to a metropolitan area of more than a million people.

During the war, scientific expertise around Stanford University was developing electronic equipment for the military. A major naval air station was installed at Moffett Field and other military facilities sprouted on major peaks around the South Bay. Then after the war came a spurt of urban growth as electronic plants offered employment in what we now call "Silicon Valley." Santa Clara County became one of the principal magnets for migration into California. Cities around the South Bay grew until their boundaries merged. Now housing developments and industrial plants creep up the mountainsides and fill the once-fertile valley floor.

Progress Toward Parks, Preserves and Trails

By the mid-1960s valley residents began to realize that this phenomenal growth was eroding the quality of their environment. Since then, citizens, non-profit groups and public agencies have moved to restore some of the amenities lost in the fast pace of postwar building and the high-tech electronic boom and to protect what was left.

Park Plans and Acquisitions

In the area covered by this book, the East Bay Regional Park District, formed in 1934 in Alameda and Contra Costa counties, acquired Coyote Hills Regional Park in 1967, adding to its earlier holdings. The Alameda Creek Regional Trail was developed on each side of the flood control channel from the Bay to Niles. Mission Peak Regional Preserve was acquired in 1974, bringing the acreage covered in this book to more than 4000.

In Santa Clara County a far-sighted plan for regional parks was spearheaded by Ed R. Levin, a planning commissioner. Adopted in 1972, it called for major parks throughout the valley and recreational corridors along the creeks. In the next year a policy plan for the Santa Clara County Baylands was adopted and implementation is nearly complete. Santa Clara County's tax allocations for parks have supported acquisitions and park improvements. Today, there are more than 45,000 acres of Santa Clara County Parks. The county adopted a comprehensive Trails Master Plan in November 1995 to guide future trail connections between county parks and those of other agencies.

The citizen-initiated Midpeninsula Regional Park District (now the Midpeninsula Regional Open Space District) was established in 1972 in northern Santa Clara County. It now includes southern San Mateo County, and has over 45,000 acres of open-space preserves, more than 16,000 in the area covered by this book. The District's Mission Statement is "To acquire and preserve a regional greenbelt of open space land in perpetuity; protect and restore the natural environment; and provide opportunities for ecologically sensitive public enjoyment and education."

In 1994 the voters in Santa Clara County formed the Santa Clara County Open Space Authority (SCCOSA), a special district with a purpose similar to that of MROSD. Its boundaries are the entire southern part of Santa Clara County from Santa Clara south to the county line, with the exclusion of Gilroy. A major property under its jurisdiction west of Henry W. Coe State Park is the Palassou Ridge. Recent purchases in the Coyote Creek watershed eventually will provide a continuous open space corridor from the Santa Clara Valley floor to Henry W. Coe State Park. In 2000 additional properties adjoining northern Alum Rock Park were acquired as well as parts of Rancho Cañada de Oro near Calero Creek County Park.

The state of California Parks and Recreation Department's three parks covered in this guide—Castle Rock, Big Basin and Henry W. Coe state parks—add up to more than 100,000 acres.

The Don Edwards San Francisco Bay National Wildlife Refuge in the South Bay now protects more than 22,000 acres of water, marsh and slough. Additionally, EBRPD Coyote Hills Regional Park, Palo Alto's Baylands Preserve, Shoreline at Mountain View and the Sunnyvale Baylands encompass vast acreages of shoreline, slough and marshland.

New Trails and Campgrounds

Of particular interest to trail users is Santa Clara County's Trails Plan, approved in 1998 after several years of public hearings. This plan sets up a complete trail system and details methods for its implementation.

In the 21st century a new generation is joining veteran hikers and equestrians: a veritable army of runners and bicyclists is out on the trails. The Trail Center, organized in 1983, coordinates volunteer activities in trail building and maintenance, prepares trail maps and provides information to interested hikers, riders, bicyclists and runners, particularly on its Website. See Appendix B.

Many parks and preserves now have active organizations of supporters and volunteers who train to become docents, to assist rangers, to staff visitor centers, to publish newsletters and in many ways to enrich the experiences of park visitors and trail users. A list of these groups is in Appendix B.

Nine parks included in this guide provide overnight camping facilities. With an early start from a campsite the trail user can take long day trips through beautiful foothill and mountain parks. Then at day's end campers can watch for wildlife emerging at dusk and observe stars in the clear mountain air.

Grant Park's extensive trail system offers possibilities for a week of day trips exploring its 50 miles of trails. Mt. Madonna Park's forest camps and Uvas Canyon Park's oak-shaded camping areas are cool retreats from summer valley heat and bases for leisurely exploration of the trails.

Sanborn County Park's overnight campgrounds and the AYH Hostel there are good starting points for hikes. Henry W. Coe State Park has thousands of acres of wilderness to explore from camps near headquarters and from backcountry backpack campsites.

Coyote Hills Regional Park offers camping for groups, Castle Rock State Park has backpack campsites and Big Basin Redwoods State Park has both organized campsites and backpack trail camps.

Long Distance Trails Beckon Backpackers in the 21st century

Of the parks included in this guide, Henry W. Coe and Big Basin Redwoods state parks offer backpacking campsites which provide ample scope for a week's trip into remote canyons, to hidden lakes, or through redwood groves, to campsites near springs, flowing streams, lakes or waterfalls.

Several South Bay trails connect with other trail systems that provide opportunities for extended backpacking trips—west to trail camps on the forested slopes of the Santa Cruz Mountains and to the coast, north to Monte Bello Open Space Preserve, to Pescadero Creek County Park,

Portola Redwoods State Park and Long Ridge Open Space Preserve, and east on the Ohlone Wilderness Trail in the eastern Diablo Range.

Early interest in trail connections between Castle Rock State Park on the Skyline ridge and Big Basin Redwoods State Park near Santa Cruz led to the construction of the Skyline-to-the-Sea Trail. With the support of the Sempervirens Fund and the State Parks Department this famous 25-mile route descends through woodlands in Castle Rock Park on a trail easement beside Highway 9 into deep forests in the heart of Big Basin State Park, then continues over ridges and along creeks to the mouth of Waddell Creek at the Pacific Ocean. Backpack camps are spaced at a distance of a day's walk or less. For information and reservations call the ranger at Big Basin State Park—831-338-8860. Excellent trail maps may be purchased from the state parks, the Sempervirens office and other map outlets, such as the Map Center in Berkeley.

Some day another crossing into the western Santa Cruz Mountains may lead to the Forest of Nisene Marks State Park near Aptos on Monterey Bay. Trail camps midway down the park's western ridge would provide stopovers for long-distance trail users. However, until the status of intervening unimproved roads is clarified, this trip is not recommended.

The East Bay Regional Park District's 28-mile Ohlone Wilderness Trail from Mission Peak Regional Preserve extends across oak-dotted hills and through forested canyons to Del Valle Regional Park south of Livermore. The route crosses San Francisco Watershed lands and the Sunol and Ohlone Regional Wilderness areas (see Mission Peak Preserve, Trip 4, page 30). Hikers, backpackers and equestrians can stop at backpack and equestrian camps along the way. For information, a map and the permit required for the trail, call the East Bay Regional Park District: 510-635-0135.

Three Long Distance Trails

Three regional trails are in the making—the Bay Area Ridge Trail and the San Francisco Bay Trail—one on the ridges and the other at water's edge. A third route, the Anza National Historic Trail, is marked with handsome signs to indicate where Juan Bautista de Anza and his stalwart band crossed the Diablo Range in today's Henry W. Coe State Park and his route northward to San Francisco, some segments traversing other South Bay parks.

The Ridge Trail for hikers, equestrians and bicyclists, well on the way to its 400-mile goal, has already dedicated 220 miles of trail. In a cooperative effort, public agencies and citizen organizations in the South Bay are working to complete a route south along the Diablo Range and north along the Santa Cruz Mountains. At this writing approximately 48 miles of Ridge Trail traverse the lands covered in this guide. These segments are identified in the text and on the maps of each park.

A plan to circle the shores of San Francisco and San Pablo bays with a paved trail for hikers and bicyclists, the San Francisco Bay Trail, is also being realized. Around the South Bay more than 16 miles of nearly continuous trail are in use at this writing and more segments are in the planning stage.

Between October 1775 and May 1776 a Spanish expedition led by Captain Juan Bautista de Anza made a remarkable trip from Tubac, Mexico (now southern Arizona) with a party of 240 people to explore and settle the area around San Francisco Bay. Anza's trail now has become a National Historic Trail, and about 51 miles of the route are in the area covered by this book. Signs marking the route already have been placed in Henry W. Coe State Park; others are planned for the route roughly paralleling El Camino Real throughout Santa Clara County.

Using This Guide

Each of the 31 parks and preserves in this guide is numbered on a locator map at the beginning of the book to correspond with its numerical listing in the Table of Contents. The Diablo Range parks and the Santa Cruz Mountain parks are listed from north to south; the Baylands parks are numbered around the Bay from east to west, as are the creekside parks and trails.

The bulk of this guide contains descriptions of trips on trails in the public lands of the South Bay. Short hikes from park entrances are described, as well as longer and more extensive trips. Sometimes a car shuttle is suggested for long hikes. Where possible, trips are planned to end on a downhill stretch. Many trips are loop hikes which begin and end at the same place. Tips for planning hikes include times of day and seasons of the year when hiking is best—important on South Bay trails.

You will find a handy reference in Appendix A—*Guide to Choosing a Trail*—which lists trips for a variety of circumstances and degrees of difficulty. Trips on shady trails for hot summer days, hikes to high places, trails for wheelchair users, and long expeditions are some of the categories that may help you find the right trip for a special occasion or remind you of old favorites.

The time required for a trip is based on the authors' moderate walking pace—two miles an hour. This allows time for enjoying views, admiring flowers, examining animal tracks and taking short rests along the way. Bicyclists and equestrians, who may travel faster, can use these times to estimate their trip's duration.

Figures for elevation change tell the net vertical footage gained or lost over the whole trip. To help estimate the time required for a trip where the cumulative gain is more than 1000 feet or there are steep climbs within a short distance, the authors used an old hiking rule, helpful to other users also: for every 1000 vertical feet gained, add one-half hour. When the outward leg of a trip is uphill, the elevation change is given as a gain; then, of course, the return is an elevation loss. Conversely, when the outward leg is downhill, the elevation change is given as a loss.

The authors aimed for accuracy in reporting, but enthusiasms for particular features are the authors' subjective responses. Sightings of birds and animals, the presence of individual flower species in bloom, good weather on a certain day—all depend on the fortunate combination of being in the right place at the right time.

They have attempted also to include all public trails currently open in the South Bay area, but new park lands are being added yearly and new trails will undoubtedly be added as enthusiasm for walking, hiking, running, bicycling and horseback riding continues.

How to Get There

Directions from the nearest major road to the parks are given. Although the car remains the quickest and easiest way to get to the trails, a few buses with adequate schedules can take you to several parks in the South Bay. The guide notes bus service where bus stops are within a few blocks of park entrances. AC Transit permits bikes on some buses on weekends. For up-to-date schedules call Valley Transportation Authority, 800-894-9908, for Santa Clara County, or AC Transit, 510-817-1717, for East Bay parks, or Santa Cruz Metro District, 831-425-8600, for bus service from Waddell Creek to Big Basin Park Headquarters via Santa Cruz.

Bike lanes and some separate bicycle paths lead to the creekside park chains, the Baylands and some of the foothill parks. In Alameda County a long bicycle path leads from Niles Canyon to Coyote Hills Park, and there are bike lanes to the Wildlife Refuge and across the Dumbarton Bridge.

Information and Maps

The maps in this guide show all the trails for trips described in South Bay parks, preserves, creek chains and baylands. Although most jurisdictions offer park maps, they are not always available at the trailhead. You can call or write the public agencies listed in Appendix B for maps and further information. The Map Legend (on page 17) depicts the symbols used on the maps. Trails are indicated by line values distinguishing between foot trails, horse trails and bicycle trails. A number of trails are for hikers only and some are for hikers and equestrians only. The text treats these distinctions for each trip. Many of the trails are old, unsurfaced ranch roads, powerline service roads or fire roads. Unless the road is also used for public vehicular access, it is shown as a trail.

Excellent topographic maps for all the parks in this guide are available at the United States Geological Survey headquarters at 345 Middlefield Road in Menlo Park. Some outdoor equipment stores also carry them, as does The Map Center at 2440 Bancroft Way, Berkeley, and at 63 Washington Street, Santa Clara, and by mail or online from Wilderness Press—see Appendix B.

The specific topo map(s) for each park is listed at the beginning of its section. The quadrangles of the 7.5-minute series, on a 1" = 2000' scale, are excellent for all trail users. Many local trails and old ranch roads are marked on these maps. There are symbols for natural features, such as vegetative cover, streams, lakes and mountaintops. Elevations and contour lines give information about the steepness of the terrain you will cover.

Some parks and preserves offer hikes, nature walks, and guided field trips led by staff naturalists or trained volunteers and docents. The interpretive centers and science and history museums at park headquarters are well-worth a visit.

Trail Rules, Etiquette And Safety

Park and open-space preserve regulations are few, but they are important. Based on common sense, they are necessary for your own safety and the protection of the parklands. To preserve the beauty of the natural setting, all plants, animals, natural features and archeological artifacts are protected. Leave them undisturbed for others to enjoy. Stay on the trail. Short-cuts across trail switchbacks break the trail edge and accelerate erosion. Don't smoke on the trail, and build no fires except where permitted in established fireplaces. Firearms and bows and arrows are prohibited.

Hours: Generally open 8 A.M. to dusk; MROSD preserves open dawn to dusk. Fees collected for some state and county parks; subject to change.

Trail closures: In wet weather trails often are closed to bicyclists and equestrians. Newly constructed trails are temporarily closed until treads harden.

Dogs: In Santa Clara County dogs are prohibited except in some parks that permit dogs on a short leash in picnic areas, but never on trails. Midpeninsula Regional Open Space District permits dogs on leash in some preserves; call for information. State parks allow dogs on leash in campgrounds but not on trails. Dogs are not allowed in the Don Edwards San Francisco Bay National Wildlife Refuge. In East Bay Regional Parks dogs are allowed in certain posted areas on a 6-foot leash; they may be off-leash in open space and undeveloped areas of parklands, if under voice control at all times. Owners must dispose of dog waste in containers.

Sharing the trail

Hikers and runners: Yield to equestrians.

Bicyclists: Observe closure signs; ride on designated trails only. Helmets required in all parks and preserves. Speed limit in MROSD preserves, Santa

Clara County parks, East Bay Regional Parks, and the State parks is 15 m.p.h—5 m.p.h. when passing and on blind curves. Yield to equestrians and hikers. Big Basin Redwoods and Castle Rock state parks allow bicycles on park service roads only; Henry W. Coe allows bicycles on most trails, except those for hikers only.

Equestrians: Observe closure signs. Indicate to other users when it is safe to pass.

Safety: Travel with a companion rather than alone. List of organizations offering group trips is in Appendix B.

These basic rules are common to all parks and not repeated in the individual park sections.

Some Hazards for Trail Users

Poison Oak: This plant, *Toxicodendron diversilobum*, is widespread through most of the South Bay parks. You don't need to remember its Latin name, but you should learn to recognize this ubiquitous plant with its three-lobed leaves. A pretty cream-colored flower cluster is followed by white berries. It looks different according to the season and the environment where it is growing. In spring its gray branches send out reddish buds, then shiny, young, light-green leaves. In autumn it has rosy red leaves that are brilliant in the woods and along the roadsides. To touch the twigs or leaves is to court the outbreak of an uncomfortable, itchy, blistering, long-lasting rash. Avoid it! Wear long sleeves and long pants for protection; bathe with cool water and soap when you get home. If you have unavoidably brushed against some poison oak, wash that area in the nearest stream or even use water from your canteen.

Rattlesnakes: Another, and far less common, hazard is the rattlesnake. It has a triangular-shaped head, diamond markings or dark blotches on its back, and from one to ten or more rattles (segments) on its tail—it is said that it adds a new rattle each time it sheds its skin. It is the only poisonous snake native to Bay Area hills; it inhabits many hillside parks, though it is rarely seen. The rattlesnake will avoid you if it possibly can. Just watch where you put your feet and hands, and stay on the trails.

Lyme Disease: A potentially serious illness can result from the bite of the Western Black-Legged tick, a .25-inch-diameter insect. Ticks brush off onto you from grasses and trailside bushes. Wear long pants, tucked into boots or socks, and a long-sleeved shirt. Check yourself for ticks when your finish your hike.

Mountain Lions: Sighting of these shy, native resident of wild lands have become more frequent due to increased use of their habitat by people. A mountain lion is about the size of a small German shepherd, with a thick tail as long as its body. It is recommended that trail users stand facing any mountain lion they encounter, make loud noises while waving their arms, and not run away.

Bobcats: Not hazardous to humans, they are about twice the size of a house cat with whiskers on their ears and with six-inch-long tails.

Feral Pigs: Imported from Europe, these animals have spread over many acres of wild lands since their introduction for hunting in the 19th century. While generally not dangerous to humans, they can be fierce when cornered.

Remember, wild animals, including coyotes, normally avoid humans, if possible. Trail users must be careful not to entice them closer by giving them food, as they may lose their natural fear and cause problems.

Thirst and heat exhaustion: Although many days in summer are fine for trail use, sometimes the temperature rises above 100°. On these days avoid long trips on steep, sunny hillsides. Always carry plenty of water— at least a quart per person per day. There are no drinking fountains on the trails, and stream and pond water is not potable. Wear a wide-brimmed hat to protect your face and head. With a little forethought you can plan your trip to avoid these hazards.

Climate And Weather

The South Bay's generally moderate climate makes good hiking possible throughout the year. Even the coldest months have unseasonably mild days to lure you out on the trails, and there are shady hillsides for those hot summer days.

In general, choose your trip to match the season and the day's weather. On hot summer days the western slopes of the Diablo Range have little shade and are unbearably warm; try instead the shady trails in the Santa Cruz Mountains among the coastal redwoods, or take trips along tree-bordered creeks. Start early in the morning or take an early-evening supper trip. Remember that ocean breezes blowing down the Bay keep summer temperatures cooler on the Baylands.

Hot weather inland draws fog from the cold water of the Pacific Ocean, sometimes spilling over the Santa Cruz Mountains. So you may plan a trip on the western side of the mountains, only to find that fog drip from the redwood forest dampens more than your spirits.

In spring and fall you have unlimited choices. For winter days try short hikes by the Bay or on sunny south- and west-facing slopes. After a winter storm, when skies clear, try an exhilarating peak or ridge climb for superb views of the Bay or even a glimpse of the distant Sierra Nevada.

What To Wear And Take Along

Hiking is not an expensive sport. The only special equipment you need is a pair of well-fitting shoes that give good support and have a raised tread. The authors have found running shoes to be very satisfactory except on the more rugged, rocky trails. For these trails lug-soled hiking boots are better.

Wearing several layers of outer garments topped by a windbreaker traps the heat when the day is cold and lets you peel off as you and the day warm up. On trips to higher elevations in winter, you will need a warm wool sweater and an insulated jacket. A cap or hat also helps reduce body heat loss. Sudden showers or downpours can make an outing miserable, so be sure to carry appropriate rain gear and good footwear for possibly muddy trails.

Summer hiking calls for sun protection—the earlier-mentioned hat with a brim, sunscreen and dark glasses. Even when the day is hot, a sweater or windbreaker is good insurance against freshening breezes or afternoon fog, especially in the redwoods.

A small day-pack will hold your extra garments and the few necessities for your trip—lunch, water and this guide. If you have room, a bird book and binoculars can add interest to your trip.

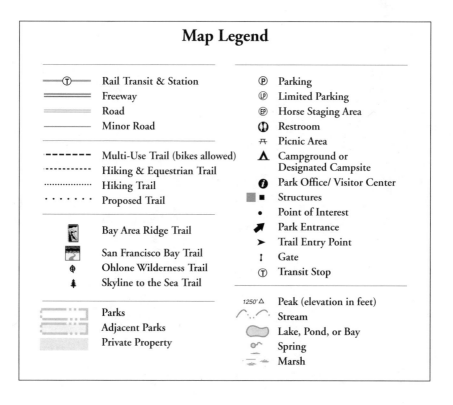

Map Legend

Rail Transit & Station	Parking
Freeway	Limited Parking
Road	Horse Staging Area
Minor Road	Restroom
	Picnic Area
Multi-Use Trail (bikes allowed)	Campground or Designated Campsite
Hiking & Equestrian Trail	Park Office/ Visitor Center
Hiking Trail	Structures
Proposed Trail	Point of Interest
	Park Entrance
Bay Area Ridge Trail	Trail Entry Point
San Francisco Bay Trail	Gate
Ohlone Wilderness Trail	Transit Stop
Skyline to the Sea Trail	
	Peak (elevation in feet)
Parks	Stream
Adjacent Parks	Lake, Pond, or Bay
Private Property	Spring
	Marsh

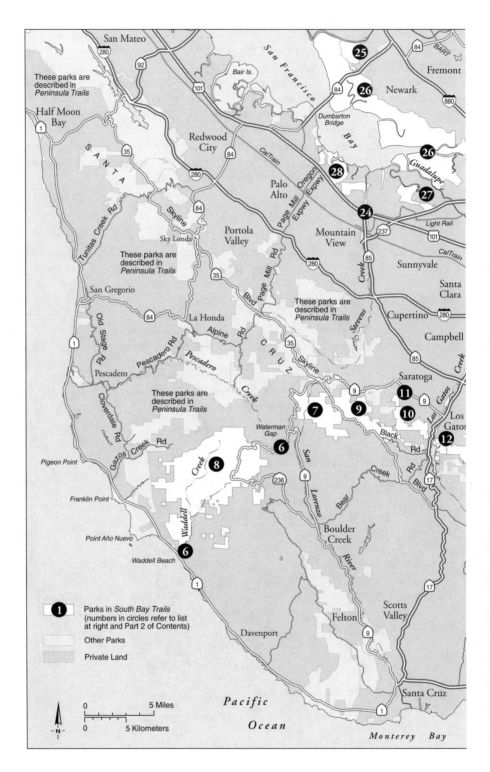

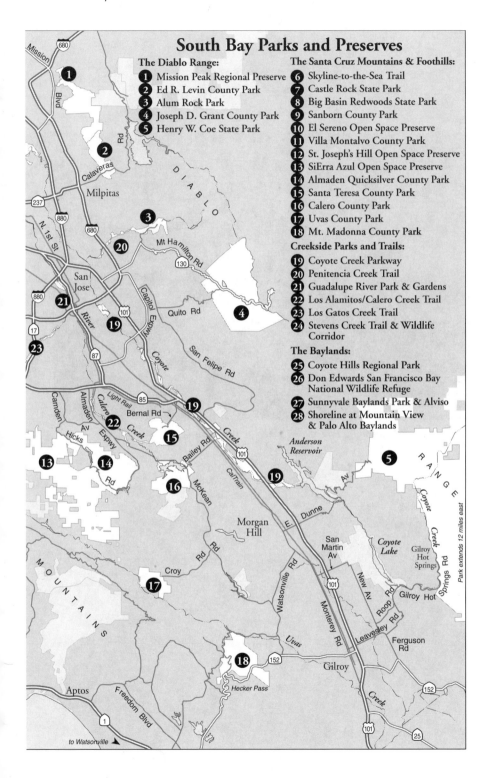

South Bay Parks and Preserves

The Diablo Range:

1. Mission Peak Regional Preserve
2. Ed R. Levin County Park
3. Alum Rock Park
4. Joseph D. Grant County Park
5. Henry W. Coe State Park

The Santa Cruz Mountains & Foothills:

6. Skyline-to-the-Sea Trail
7. Castle Rock State Park
8. Big Basin Redwoods State Park
9. Sanborn County Park
10. El Sereno Open Space Preserve
11. Villa Montalvo County Park
12. St. Joseph's Hill Open Space Preserve
13. SiErra Azul Open Space Preserve
14. Almaden Quicksilver County Park
15. Santa Teresa County Park
16. Calero County Park
17. Uvas County Park
18. Mt. Madonna County Park

Creekside Parks and Trails:

19. Coyote Creek Parkway
20. Penitencia Creek Trail
21. Guadalupe River Park & Gardens
22. Los Alamitos/Calero Creek Trail
23. Los Gatos Creek Trail
24. Stevens Creek Trail & Wildlife Corridor

The Baylands:

25. Coyote Hills Regional Park
26. Don Edwards San Francisco Bay National Wildlife Refuge
27. Sunnyvale Baylands Park & Alviso
28. Shoreline at Mountain View & Palo Alto Baylands

Ponderosa pines surmount live oaks in a canyon in Henry W. Coe State Park

◆ The Diablo Range ◆

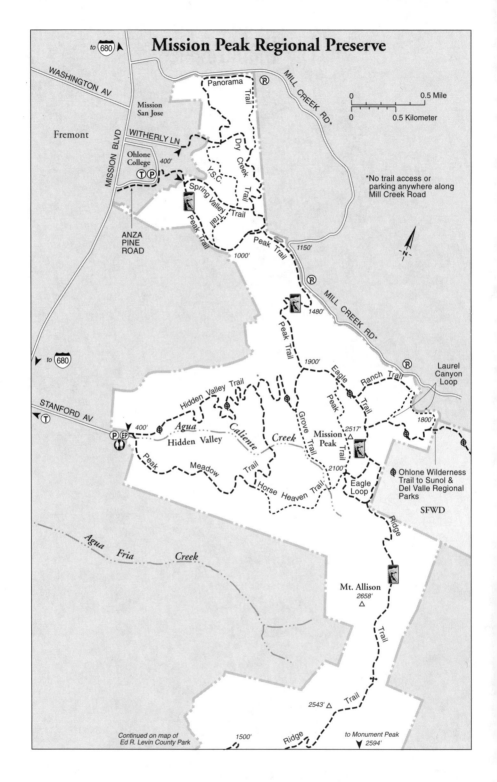

Mission Peak Regional Preserve

to 680

WASHINGTON AV

Panorama Trail

MILL CREEK RD*

0   0.5 Mile

0   0.5 Kilometer

Mission San Jose

Fremont

MISSION BLVD

WITHERLY LN

Ohlone College

400'

Dry Creek Trail

Y.S.C.

Spring Valley Trail

*No trail access or parking anywhere along Mill Creek Road

T P

ANZA PINE ROAD

Peak Trail

Peak Trail

1150'

1000'

1480'

MILL CREEK RD*

to 680

Peak Trail

1900'

Eagle Peak Trail

Ranch Trail

Laurel Canyon Loop

STANFORD AV

T

400'

Agua

Hidden Valley Trail

Caliente   Creek

Grove Trail

Mission Peak

2517'

1800'

P EP

Hidden Valley

Meadow   Trail

2100'

Mission Trail

Ohlone Wilderness Trail to Sunol & Del Valle Regional Parks

Peak

Horse Heaven Trail

Eagle Loop

SFWD

Agua   Fria   Creek

Ridge

Mt. Allison 2658'

Trail

Continued on map of Ed R. Levin County Park

1500'

Ridge

2543'

Trail

to Monument Peak 2594'

◆ Mission Peak Regional Preserve ◆

Mission Peak, that austere East Bay landmark, is more approachable than its steep west face reveals. In the Mission Peak Regional Preserve 18 miles of trails take you through wooded canyons, gently rolling hills, hidden valleys, sheltered glens and up to its summit. As well as the spectacular panorama from the top of Mission Peak, there are fresh vistas at each turn of its trails.

Mission Peak and the East Bay Regional Park District's 2999-acre preserve surrounding this landmark were part of the vast holdings of Mission San José, founded in 1797, whose lands once extended north almost to Oakland and east to the Livermore Valley. The mission's broad lands grew olives, fruits, grapes and wheat, and grazed 12,000 head of cattle. Soon after its founding, this became one of the most prosperous of California's missions. From what is now Washington Boulevard a road led to the mission's embarcadero on Newark Slough. Later known as Jarvis Landing, this embarcadero remained a port for Bay traffic until early in the 20th century.

When the mission was secularized in 1836, its lands were divided into ranches, and a settlement grew up around the mission and its supporting enterprises. During Gold Rush days the community became a bustling

Looking west over Bay from Santa Cruz Mountains

provision center, as it was on the route to the southern mines. Later, bypassed by the railroad, it again became a quiet village.

The 1806 adobe mission, handsomely reconstructed, and the adjoining museum in one of the original mission buildings are well worth a visit. In the community of Mission San José many buildings of the late 19th century remain, and they make a good walking tour. The valuable architectural heritage of this community, within the Fremont city limits, is protected by designation as a historic district. Ohlone College, on Mission Boulevard, is on the hills once covered by the mission's vineyards. Palm and pepper trees are left from the site of an old park and estate. The double row of olive trees along Mission Boulevard marks the old road that ran from Mission Santa Clara to Mission San José.

In Mission Peak Regional Preserve, 18 miles of trails lead to the summit of the peak through the rolling hills behind Ohlone College. Trails also reach the peak from Stanford Avenue, a few miles farther south. Another network of trails over college property behind the campus is open to the public. The East Bay Regional Park District's 28-mile Ohlone Wilderness Trail extends east to Del Valle Regional Park from Mission Peak Preserve. The regional Bay Area Ridge Trail now connects Mission Peak with Ed Levin County Park in Santa Clara County and will some day go north from Mission Peak to Garin Regional Park near Hayward.

Jurisdiction: East Bay Regional Park District.

Facilities: Trails—hiking, equestrian and, on designated service roads, bicycle. Equestrian staging area at Stanford Avenue with water, restroom.

Park Rules: Hours: Trails open daily. Curfew, Stanford Avenue staging area 10 P.M. to 5 A.M. Dogs under control allowed off leash only in undeveloped areas; leash required in parking areas.

Maps: EBRPD *Mission Peak Regional Preserve;* USGS quad *Niles.*

How To Get There: *By Car:* For Trips 1, and 6—From I-680 in Fremont go north on Mission Blvd. 2.5 miles to Ohlone College. On weekdays, when classes are in session, a parking fee is charged for lots D and H, payable at collection boxes in general parking lots; on weekends, free parking. For Trips 1 and 6 park on south side of campus; walk to swimming pool—trailhead just beyond. For Trip 5 go to northeast side of Anza Pine Rd., which circles the parking areas. For Trips 2, 3 and 4 up the west side of the peak—From I-680 go north on Mission Blvd. 0.5 miles, then turn right (east) on Stanford Ave. and go 0.5 mile to trailhead staging area.

By Bus: AC Transit buses from Fremont Bart Station, Dixon Landing.

Mission Peak Regional Preserve
PEAK TRAIL TO THE SUMMIT FROM OHLONE COLLEGE

An exhilarating trip takes you to spectacular views, reaching the peak from its north side.

Distance: 6.1 miles round trip

Time: 4 hours

Elevation Gain: 2100'

Trail Notes

From the parking lots on the south side of semicircular Anza Pine Road on the Ohlone College campus, take the Ohlone Trail and walk uphill past the swimming pool to the eucalyptus grove, where you will see a sign for the Mission Peak Regional Preserve. The Peak Trail starts from a stile by a locked gate on the right, and the Spring Valley Trail starts uphill, veering to the left. Go over the stile to the Peak Trail, an old ranch road that goes steadily up the side of the mountain, rising about 600' to a saddle in less than 0.5 mile. The trail surface is well-compacted sandstone, making this a good trip in winter even shortly after rains.

More than halfway up the hill, note a trail junction to the left (north). Here a narrow footpath, the Y.S.C. Trail, leaves the broad trail to cross over the hill to the Spring Valley Trail.

As you climb on the Peak Trail, the Bay plain comes into view, including Fremont and Milpitas, and beyond, the patterns of salt ponds and sloughs. In a half hour's walk the trail enters a wooded canyon. Just before you go into the woods, look back to catch the sweep of the Bay—from Mt. Tamalpais in the north down to Mt. Umunhum and Loma Prieta in the south.

For a short time you walk in one of the wooded canyons under oaks found in the folds of these otherwise bare East Bay hills. Then the trail comes out onto open grasslands in a saddle, passes a shallow pond reserved for watering cattle, and turns toward the northeast boundary of the preserve. You see the Dry Creek Trail turning north, uphill, through a cattle gate to pastures beyond. Instead of going to the peak you could take this trail for a short trip back, turning down the Spring Valley Trail at the next junction.

To continue to the peak, bear right on the Peak Trail, following the preserve-boundary fence. Mill Creek Road also follows the fence and then leads to a subdivision. There is no public access to the preserve from Mill Creek Road, and as you will see, there is no parking whatever along the road.

Your path leads into an oak grove, welcome shelter from the wind that funnels through the pass by the reservoir. The path along the fence rises gently through the trees and soon comes out into a small meadow. Beyond, you meet an intermittent stream lined with alders, where you turn away from the boundary to come out onto an open pasture. Here you pick up an old ranch road going uphill through a handsome buckeye grove.

Now the climb to the peak begins in earnest, and you gain 520' in elevation in the next 0.5 mile. Your trail winds out of some oak woods, then veers south in a steady pull up a broad ridge. On a saddle below the peak you meet the Hidden Valley Trail coming up the west side from Stanford Avenue.

At the Hidden Valley Trail junction, 2.5 miles from the college, bear east for 0.25 mile to the summit approach. Up a draw where the wind can be fierce, is a junction with the Eagle Trail, which loops around the high hilltops east of the summit. It connects with the Laurel Canyon Loop, which descends to a canyon below and continues to the northeastern boundary of the park. From the Eagle Peak junction it is a steady 0.5-mile climb up the rocky footpath to the top of Mission Peak. Below you is the craggy face of the peak's west side. Stay on the trail. It is unsafe to explore the precipitous hillside below; a fence is there to deter the foolish.

One last clamber and you are on the 2517' summit. Here is a tall wooden post with directional sighting holes that point to other landmarks in the Bay Area. Stop for lunch here to enjoy the breathtaking view around the compass. Mt. Diablo stands out to the north. Southwest is Monument Peak, on the Alameda/Santa Clara county line, less than 2 miles away as the crow flies. South of Monument Peak is Ed Levin Park, in Santa Clara County, 4.7 miles away on the spectacular Bay Area Ridge Trail route.

On clear days the peaks of the Sierra are visible across the San Joaquin Valley. Due east, you can see the lands where the Ohlone Wilderness Trail goes over high, rolling hills studded with oaks.

You may find yourself sharing the crags with a herd of goats that pose picturesquely on the pinnacles right below. This herd has gone wild, apparently finding the rocky summit to their liking.

The trip back from the summit is downhill all the way. You have alternate return routes of about the same length via the Hidden Valley or Horse Heaven/Peak Meadow trails west to Stanford Avenue, but they require a shuttle.

Mission Peak Regional Preserve
PEAK CLIMB FROM THE WEST

A 2100' climb on the Hidden Valley Trail to the craggy summit offers views of landmarks from the Santa Cruz Mountains to the Sierra.

Distance: 6.3 miles round trip

Time: 4¼ hours

Elevation Gain: 2100'

Trail Notes

This is a strenuous climb, to be taken in cool weather and with an early start up the exposed west slope. From the staging area at the end of Stanford Avenue go over a hiker/equestrian stile or through a gate, and then take the road to the left. This Hidden Valley Trail, a ranch and fire road, winds up a low ridge toward the peak. Its sign posts, marked with red dots, indicate the Ohlone Wilderness Trail route.

You walk with the sounds of Agua Caliente Creek rushing down the canyon below the trail and the song of meadowlarks in the grass. It is likely that Ohlone Indians occupied campsites in these pleasant foothills away from their permanent villages near the Bay. Archeological evidence from freeway excavations nearby suggests that Indians camped by streams in such sites to process bulbs and corms in the spring and acorns in the fall.

With the wooded depths of Hidden Valley indeed out of sight, your trail climbs out of the north side of the canyon, leaving the creek far below. As you gain elevation, the urban scene comes into view—suburbs, freeway arteries, the spreading manufacturing plants, and to the north the blue waters of Fremont's Central Park Lake and its civic center. Bayward, the straight lines of salt-pond levees are intersected by curves of sloughs entering the Bay.

As the mountain steepens, your trail proceeds via switchbacks, three times approaching small streams shaded by bays and live oaks, then veering away over the bare hills. The shade and cool sounds of running water are welcome if the sun has risen high. At an elevation of about 1400' is a junction with the Peak Meadow Trail, which winds south across Hidden Valley. You can take this trail back to the staging area for a 3.7-mile loop trip on the lower slopes of this beautiful mountain.

Continuing on the Hidden Valley Trail, in two more switchbacks you approach the rocky face of the peak, where uptilted layers of rock laid bare by landslides and erosion tower 700' above, looking like the jagged spines of huge prehistoric animals.

The McClure Ranch House

During the severe storms of 1998, Mission Peak lost a sizable piece of its western face. Eyeing these awesome cliffs, you walk up to a gate and through a stile and are suddenly in a gentle little valley at the foot of the crags.

Tucked behind a low ridge on the west are fields, a farmhouse and barns. This fertile valley, the McClure Ranch, homesteaded in the mid-1850s, was long an enclave of private property in the preserve, held in a life estate. The ranch came to the park district in 1982, when the last member of the McClure family died at age 93. Today, the old house serves as a ranger residence and a reminder of the stalwart pioneers who lived in this pretty valley. By special arrangement, the area can be used as a backpack camp on the route of the Ohlone Wilderness Trail.

From the Hidden Valley Trail the 0.75-mile Grove Trail passes beside the fenced off house and adjoining buildings and continues through the A. A. Moore Memorial Grove to McClure Spring and a junction with the Eagle Trail. This Moore Grove of magnificent live oak trees, dedicated to the mountain's original settler by his descendants, is nourished by the waters gushing from hillside springs that you would pass on the Eagle Trail. The authors found this trail impassable on a winter hike.

Continuing on the Hidden Valley Trail turn north to leave the little valley, and find a trail marker pointing to your route up around the north side of the peak. Soon you have climbed out onto a grassy saddle to overlook the valleys and mountains on the east side of the peak—Mt. Diablo and the Livermore Valley. Right below are Mill Creek Road and the houses that edge the east side of the preserve. Here the wind blows with the force expected on such exposed heights, bending the grass in shining ripples with every gust.

In this windy saddle is the junction with the Peak Trail, which starts from Ohlone College; you can see the trail as it comes up the broad ridge from the north. From this junction continue on the Peak Trail. Then, at the Eagle Trail junction take the footpath, the Peak Trail, to the mountain top.

To complete the trip back to Stanford Avenue when you have come down from the peak, retrace your steps past the little hidden valley and continue down a couple of switchbacks to the Peak Meadow Trail junction. From here you could turn left (south) on this trail (see description in Trip 3, below) or descend on the Hidden Valley Trail to the Stanford Avenue staging area.

Mission Peak Regional Preserve
Horse Heaven Trail to the Peak and down the Hidden Valley Trail

A stiff climb from the Peak Meadow Trail on the steep Horse Heaven Trail crosses the headwaters of Agua Caliente Creek to ascend the peak on its south side, returning by the Hidden Valley Trail. The Horse Heaven Trail is for hikers and equestrians only, and can be impassable in wet weather.

Distance: 5.5-mile loop

Time: 4 hours

Elevation Gain: 2100'

Trail Notes

From the Stanford Avenue staging area, start up the Hidden Valley Trail and almost immediately take the Peak Meadow Trail right, downhill, to cross Agua Caliente Creek. Your route is above the course of this sycamore-bordered stream as it winds up the canyon. The trail, on a ranch road, makes wide swings up grassy meadows where cattle graze. As the trail rounds a broad swale at an elevation of about 1200', the Horse Heaven Trail turns right (south) up a draw to a little pass. From this point you can see into the ranch lands south of the preserve.

For the next 1.5 mile this trail for hikers and equestrians only climbs an open ridge. Views are spectacular to the rocky face of Mission Peak, rising from the deep gorge cut by Agua Caliente Creek. Below the peak you will often see the herd of white goats that make this craggy outcrop their home.

Watch for a bedrock mortar of grinding holes made by the Ohlone Indians. This outcrop, with two holes worn by pestles, is on an open slope on your right beside the trail. There are no oak trees nearby, but it is believed that the Indians collected acorns elsewhere and ground them at sites with fine views such as this.

After 1.5 miles on the Horse Heaven Trail you reach a small wooded canyon, sheltered by great outcrops, where Agua Caliente Creek cascades over rocks, enters a culvert under the trail and splashes into a rocky ravine. A low stone wall offers a place to sit and enjoy the sounds of falling water.

Another 0.25 mile brings you to the 2200' shoulder of the peak, where your trail meets the Eagle Trail. From this point you look east over the Diablo Range. From the Eagle Trail junction, hikers can turn north on the Peak Trail, a relatively easy climb from here, or continue over the peak and down the other side to meet the Hidden Valley Trail which leads back to the start of your trip. If you have climbed the peak before, you can take the Eagle Trail, joining equestrians and bicyclists, and bear right to circle a hilltop to the south, then turn north to traverse the hill below the peak on its east side. You can then swing left to take the Hidden Valley Trail downhill to the trailhead at Stanford Avenue.

Mission Peak Regional Preserve
THE OHLONE WILDERNESS TRAIL ROUTE

This route is the beginning of the 28-mile Ohlone Wilderness Trail for hikers, backpackers and equestrians, which extends to Del Valle Regional Park south of Livermore. The first segment, through Mission Peak Preserve, takes you over the north shoulder of the peak and down to the trailhead at the preserve's eastern boundary. From there the trail continues through San Francisco's Watershed lands, Sunol and Ohlone Wilderness and on to Del Valle Regional Park. Red disks on the trail intersection signs mark the route all the way.

A permit/map is required. Send $2.50 and your name, address and telephone number to Ohlone Wilderness Trail, East Bay Regional Park District, 2950 Peralta Oaks Court, PO Box 5381, Oakland, CA 94605. With the permit come a fine map, trail regulations for the trip and a detailed description of this wilderness route through the Diablo Range.

Distance: Within the Mission Peak Preserve, 4.75 miles one way to the backpack camp in Sunol Regional Wilderness, 11.8 miles; to Del Valle Regional Park, 28 miles

Time: 2½ hours within the preserve

Elevation Gain: 1500'

Trail Notes

The route starts on the Hidden Valley Trail from the Stanford Avenue staging area (see Trip 2, page 27). After you cross the north shoulder of the peak, turn east on the Peak Trail to the Eagle Trail. Follow the Eagle Trail 0.5 mile, passing the Ranch Trail, to the Laurel Canyon Loop, where you turn left, downhill. Very soon you bear right when the Laurel Canyon Loop branches, keeping on the ranch road rather than the path down the creek canyon. After about 0.75 mile the trail veers west as it reaches the preserve boundary fence. Continue to the gate, where you start on the trail along the route across San Francisco Watershed lands. To continue on the Ohlone Wilderness Trail you must have a permit, even for day use, and must sign the register at this trailhead.

Del Valle Regional Park is 24 miles east, on the red-disk-marked trail, over the oak-dotted hills of the Diablo Range. Camping at the backpack camps requires a permit and reservation from the East Bay Regional Park District.

5

Mission Peak Regional Preserve
A Loop around the North Highlands

Try this easy walk over high grasslands behind the campus on a winter or spring day; for hikers only.

Distance: 5-mile loop

Time: 3 hours

Elevation Gain: 400'

Trail Notes

Park free during weekends in one of the college lots near Witherly Lane. On weekdays park in one of the lots and pay the parking fee.

Starting from Witherly Lane north of Ohlone College, go through a cattle-guard gate above the campus. On the way up Witherly Lane you pass one of the town's handsomest old houses, the Gallegos mansion, still occupied and well kept. Continue on the road around the bend beyond Campus Building 29, an old house. There you will see the Dry Creek Trail going uphill. A short way up it, you turn left (north) on the Panorama Trail, which traverses the pasture lands and stays above a row of old eucalyptus trees. The trail for the most part is an old ranch road going in and out of small wooded ravines. Sandstone boulders dot the hillside and, above the trail, standing out against the sky, is a battlement of these huge boulders. Lichen as bright orange as the poppies that cluster nearby encrusts the rocks on this hillside.

Your trail rises on a gentle grade through pasture lands to meet the fenced northern boundary of the preserve, where you bear right and climb the trail by the fence, above a wooded canyon that drops steeply to Mission Creek, 400' below. The pattern of vegetation here is common in the East Bay hills—grassy slopes bare of trees on the warm south- and west-facing slopes, like those across the canyon, and a cover of oaks, bays and buckeyes on the shadier north slopes and in the canyons, like the wooded hill below the trail. At your eye level turkey vultures ride updrafts in the canyon, close enough for you to see their red heads and the spreading black feathers on their wingtips.

Soon your trail cuts across the north tip of the preserve, then zig-zags up through the edge of some woods and chaparral to emerge on a grassy flat at the high point of this route. From here you have the panorama promised by the trail's name—views east to a succession of ridges of the Diablo Range and west across the Bay, with Mission San José below. Continue around and up the hill on the trail, which now roughly parallels the eastern boundary of the preserve. You soon drop to a small reservoir in a cleft in the hills. On a windy day (and wind is more usual than not on these hills), take shelter here for a snack or a rest stop.

Pick up the trail on the far side of the reservoir, where lupines and poppies bloom in a long spring season. From these high pasture lands you can fly kites, watch the soaring hawks and turkey vultures and perhaps catch sight of a hang-glider overhead. At the next junction, take the Dry Creek Trail, on which you continue southeast, and cross under powerlines to a plateau. Then follow the trail south of the powerlines, again on an old ranch road.

After skirting the head of a canyon, the trail continues over a low hill. At the head of the next canyon, you leave the boundary fence and the Dry Creek Trail to go down the Spring Valley Trail in a streambed through the woods. (The Dry Creek Trail continues southeast, climbing out of the canyon to join the Peak Trail over the hill.)

A 10-minute walk on the Spring Valley Trail under the oaks, coffeeberries and bays in this narrow ravine brings you to the spring, which gushes into a rocky basin by the trail. In a pleasant oak glade often filled with cattle coming to the watering trough fed by the spring is a crossing of the Y.S.C. Trail, for hikers only. One branch of it goes south through the woods and uphill to join the Peak Trail. You take the branch to the right (north), which climbs the bank between the spring and the watering trough. For the next 0.75 mile your trail goes along grassy slopes, descending gradually to the Dry Creek Trail, where you turn left in a grove of eucalyptus above the road where you started, and ramble downhill to your car.

Mission Peak Regional Preserve
THE BAY AREA RIDGE TRAIL
TO ED LEVIN COUNTY PARK

This top-of-the-world route brings views of the east and west sides of the Diablo Range from three of its highest peaks.

Distance: 9.7 miles, with car shuttle

Time: 6+ hours

Elevation Gain: 2220'

Trail Notes

This trip over high, exposed grasslands can be very hot in summer and winds are often strong. So carry plenty of water and get an early start to enjoy this wonderful trip. Acres of springtime wildflowers, glimpses of bald eagles and isolated clumps of bay and oak trees await you en route.

Begin your trek as in Trip 1 and follow the Bay Area Ridge Trail signs up to the Hidden Valley, Peak and Eagle trails junction. If you haven't been to Mission Peak's summit, turn off right here and make the 0.5-mile ascent. After admiring the fantastic Bay Area, descend the south side of the peak and pick up the Eagle Trail in the high grasslands. Drainage from Mission Peak and these high meadows collects in Agua Caliente Creek and flows down its west side. During the Mission era, warm water from this creek was carried by an aqueduct to the Mission San José settlement for bathing and laundering.

Bay Area Ridge Trail signs along the fence line east and then shortly south guide you to a wide road/trail across the high plateau which you will traverse for the next 3 miles. At first you are on the east side of Mt. Allison's private 2658' summit property. Looking out over the vastness of high ridges and intervening valleys that are largely uninhabited can give you a feeling for what Juan Bautista de Anza and his company encountered on their westward trek. Today, the Ohlone Wilderness Trail traverses some of these ridges, including almost reaching the summit of 3817' Rose Peak, on its way to Del Valle Regional Park.

About a mile from the Eagle Trail you enter the land acquired from the Wool family, who still own a nearby ranch. This Wool property formed the connection between the public parklands at each end of this trail. "Sandy", Mr. E. O. Wool, a prominent 1900s family member, once farmed the valley in Ed Levin Park, where the lake is named for him.

After traveling for more than a mile through the saddle between Mt. Allison and Monument Peak, both bristling with tall radio and TV towers—a veritable communications pincushion piercing the sky—you trend west to surmount a small rise, and there the Bay view unfolds below you—salt ponds, the Bay's open waters, the expanding communities of Fremont, Milpitas and Newark below; the South Bay cities where more parklands offer open space to relax and more trails to follow; the Peninsula Bayside cities and forested ridges; the San Francisco skyline and bridges; north in Marin, Sonoma and Napa counties; and south along the Contra Costa and Alameda counties' high ridgeline. The route of the Bay Area Ridge Trail, now more than half complete, traverses the ridgetops that enclose this beautiful Bay.

To continue, follow the wide ranch road that drops 2000' in elevation down the very steep prow of these East Bay Hills. Rocky knobs dot the hillside, reminders of this ridge's position between the Hayward and Calaveras faults. These sedimentary deposits were uplifted through the eons by fault movement as the Pacific Plate slid northward along the North American Plate some 15 million years ago.

Where the trail makes wide switchbacks, there is welcome shade under clumps of bay and live oak trees growing up through piles of rocks. Though the trail demands close attention, pause occasionally to look skyward for the turkey vultures, the red-tailed hawks whose cries pierce the air, or the bald eagles that are known to nest in high aeries here.

In spring the multitudes of wildflowers that blanket these hillsides will delight the eye and brighten the trailside. From the gold of California poppies to the magenta of clarkia "farewell-to-spring" there is a colorful succession of blooms. By summer the golden oat grass waves in the breeze (strong wind at times). In fall the tawny grasses contrast with the dark green of oaks that hug the ravines where creeks tumble down the mountainside.

Continuing your rapid descent, you reach the wooded banks of Scott Creek, the boundary between Alameda and Santa Clara counties, and enter Ed Levin Park. The Ridge Trail follows the Agua Caliente Trail and then reaches the Calera Creek Trail, lined with lofty sycamore trees that cast welcome afternoon shade. Soon leaving the sound of the lively creek, you follow the fence line of the once-vast Tularcitos Ranch, granted to the Higuera family in 1821.

Several right-angle turns take you beside the fenced enclosure used as a landing for hang-gliders, those colorfully winged craft that descend from the flanks of Monument Peak, from which you took the earthbound route. Then, almost 2 miles from Scott Creek, you sight the parking areas beside Sandy Wool Lake, where your car-shuttle friends await with a picnic lunch or supper at a lakeside table.

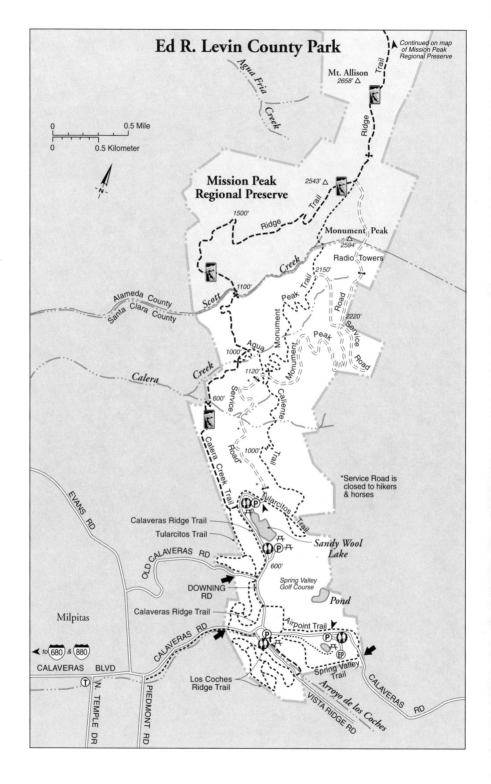

Ed R. Levin County Park

Continued on map of Mission Peak Regional Preserve

Mt. Allison
2658'

Ridge Trail

Agua Fria Creek

0   0.5 Mile
0   0.5 Kilometer

N

Mission Peak Regional Preserve

2543'

Ridge Trail

1500'

Monument Peak
2594'

Radio Towers

Scott Creek

2150'

Peak Trail

Alameda County
Santa Clara County

1100'

Road

2220'

Service Road

Peak

Monument

Monument

Agua

1000'

Caliente

Calera   Creek

1120'

600'

Service

Road

1000'

Trail

*Service Road is closed to hikers & horses

Calera Creek Trail

Tularcitos

EVANS RD

Calaveras Ridge Trail

Tularcitos Trail

Sandy Wool Lake

Tularcitos Trail

OLD CALAVERAS RD

600'

Spring Valley Golf Course

DOWNING RD

Pond

Milpitas

Calaveras Ridge Trail

Airpoint Trail

to 680 & 880

CALAVERAS RD

EP

CALAVERAS BLVD

T

W. TEMPLE DR

PIEDMONT RD

Los Coches Ridge Trail

Spring Valley Trail

Arroyo de los Coches

VISTA RIDGE RD

CALAVERAS RD

◆ Ed R. Levin County Park ◆

Ed R. Levin Park, east of Milpitas, extends from low hills sheltering a 2-mile-long valley up to a high ridge rising to 2500' Monument Peak. The 1544-acre park's activities are focused in the valley, where lakes, ponds and spacious lawns draw crowds of weekend picnickers. An 18-hole golf course is busy every day. Rental stables and parking for horse trailers make the park popular with equestrians. Steady winds and good thermals make the park's hang-gliding launch sites some of the finest in the Bay Area.

Ed Levin Park is part of the 4000-acre Tularcitos Ranch, granted in 1821 to Juan Higuera, the mayor-domo of Mission San José, by the last of the Spanish governors in Alta California. This ranch extended from the confluence of Calera and Penitencia creeks to Calaveras Road and to the ridges at the headwaters of Calera Creek and Arroyo de los Coches. The large Higuera family built haciendas on its lands and were for years a dominant force on this side of the Bay. Of their seven adobe houses, one remains. It was rebuilt by the Curtner family, who later owned the Tularcitos Ranch. Recently restored, it stands surrounded by ancient fig, olive and pepper trees as the feature of charming little Higuera Adobe Park at Wessex Place and Park Victoria Drive, just east of Highway 680.

The little valley was considered as a reservoir site but was found to have poor geologic formations for holding water. The entire site is dotted with springs, which now fill the lakes and ponds and water the Spring Valley Golf Course.

Santa Clara County acquired the park in 1967, owing in good measure to the efforts of Ed R. Levin, the remarkable man for whom it was named—geologist, explorer, teacher, athlete and county planning commissioner. In 1979 the Minnis Ranch, on the north, was added to the park, taking in the hills rising above the valley up to Monument Peak. Under a lease agreement, cattle from the ranch continue to graze the hillsides. Aside from the communications installations on their heights and the hang gliders soaring above, these hills are much the same as when Juan Higuera's cattle ranged the slopes. European oats have taken the place of native bunchgrasses, however, and the beef cattle from the Minnis Ranch that you meet on the trails are quite different from the Higuera cattle, which were raised for hides and tallow.

As you leave the flatland subdivisions and shopping centers, driving on Calaveras Road, you slip through a cleft in the ridge, following the little stream in Arroyo de los Coches for a mile into a narrow canyon. Notice a paved path on the south side of the narrow road, installed from Evans Road to the park boundary. This path was installed at the instigation of

Artemas Ginzton (now deceased) of the Santa Clara County Trails and Pathways Committee. Shortly past an old quarry on the left the canyon opens up into the hidden valley that is the heart of Ed Levin Park. Directly ahead are the new red clubhouse and greens of the Spring Valley Golf Course, operated by a concessionaire. At the junction of Downing Road on the left, go right to reach park headquarters and a series of picnic grounds, the start of Trip 1. From Downing Road you reach pretty little Sandy Wool Lake, weeping willows trailing into its waters and ducks and geese bobbing on its surface. This is the start for Trips 2 and 3.

Fine weekends draw crowds to the picnic tables by the lake. Anglers line the shores to try for bluegill, crappie and bass. If the winds are right, you will find the meadow beyond the lake bright with hang gliders soaring above, alighting, testing their colorful wings. Graded launch sites range from 40' bunny hills for learners to the heights of the ridge for those who are Hang III. Hang gliders share the skies with red-tailed hawks, turkey vultures and an occasional golden eagle. The pilots watch the soaring birds to check the wind currents; some of them feel that the birds eye them in return.

The bare, grassy heights of the park are characteristic of East Bay hills. However, even on these slopes, so sere-looking in summer, are ravines lined with oaks, bays and sycamores watered by spring-fed streams. In contrast are the well-wooded east-facing slopes of the ridge above Arroyo de los Coches.

Although many of Ed Levin Park's trails have been laid out with equestrians in mind, a number of its trails offer fine trips for those on foot. Only the Bay Area Ridge Trail route, the northern leg of the Agua Caliente Trail and the Calera Creek Trail, is open to mountain bicyclists. The long but exhilarating hike to Monument Peak over much treeless hillside is a trip to take in the cool weather of spring or fall, but the trails on Los Coches Ridge are walks for all seasons, with shade on the east side and breezes on the hilltops.

Jurisdiction: Santa Clara County.

Facilities: Trails: hiking, equestrian and bicycle. Park headquarters. Lake for fishing and boating. Picnic areas: family and group. Restrooms. 18-hole golf course. Horse-rental stables, horse-trailer parking.

Park Rules: Hours: 8 A.M. to one-half hour after sunset. Fees. Dogs allowed only in Elm Group Picnic Area, on leash. Swimming and wading prohibited. Phone 408-262-6980.

Maps: Santa Clara County *Ed R. Levin Park;* USGS quads *Milpitas, Calaveras Reservoir.*

How to Get There: Turn east from I-680 on Calaveras Blvd. exit. After 2 miles Calaveras Blvd. becomes Calaveras Rd. which you follow to park entrance.

Ed R. Levin County Park
LOS COCHES RIDGE TRAILS

*For fine walks in all seasons on shady hillsides and sunny hill-
tops, try the network of trails on this ridge.*

Distance: 4 miles round trip

Time: 2 hours

Elevation Gain: 200′

Trail Notes

This trail system loops back and forth along the wooded east slopes of
the ridge and circles its 740′ heights. Views from the hilltop stretch in all
directions, and breezes from the west are cooling even on bright, sunny
days. You can walk the entire Los Coches Ridge in a morning or an afternoon.

Starting from the main (second) parking lot on Calaveras Road near the
picnic areas, those who do not want a long hike can circle the small Spring
Valley Pond on the Spring Valley Trail, which goes uphill past the horse-
trailer parking and staging area to the fence bordering the southern
boundary of Ed Levin Park. Bearing right, you can parallel the fence to the
west and then take a descending branch down toward the Oak Knoll picnic area and go right to your starting place.

The main Los Coches Ridge trail system continues left (southwest)
from the upper part of the Spring Valley Trail and drops to cross the
Arroyo de los Coches (Creek of the Pigs) on a small bridge. The trail then
crosses paved Vista Ridge Drive leading to a subdivision of large homes
on the southwest side of the park.

Bearing left and crossing another small drainage, you pass through a
shady live oak and bay tree forest, the bays with multiple trunks appearing to have stump-sprouted after a long-ago fire.

As you climb, the high hills on the east side of the park come into sight.
Take the first intersecting trail uphill, leading to the open ridgetop. As this
is a popular route for riding, you may be joined by groups of equestrians
from the park's rental stables. The trails are not wide so it is important to
observe trail etiquette: stand quietly beside the trail until the horses have
passed.

When you reach the hilltop, you will want to take in the sweeping
views. In the north Mt. Tamalpais rises above the frequent ocean fogs and
valley smogs. The Santa Cruz Mountains fill the western horizon. To the
east, the park's golden (sometimes green) hills rise to Monument Peak.
You may see bright-winged hang gliders drifting gently down from the

rocky point above the big green water tank on the hillside above and north of Sandy Wool Lake.

After circling the knolls on the ridgetop, you have several choices for your return. A good route is the trail around the boundary, going north through the woods and making a loop above Calaveras Road where it enters the park. In early fall you will still find wildflowers on these slopes, such as clarkia and goldenrod. In the woods, the banks above the trail glow with colorful poison oak, which you can admire without touching; in April and May the whole hillside is flowery.

As the trail through the woods turns east, take the left fork for a lower and shadier trail back to Vista Ridge Drive and cross it to the trail back to the Oak Knoll group area and continue to the parking lot.

Ed R. Levin County Park
CLIMB TO THE HEIGHTS OF MONUMENT PEAK

For fine walks in all seasons on shady hillsides and sunny hill-tops, try the network of trails on this ridge.

Distance: 8-mile loop trip

Time: 6 hours

Elevation Gain: 2000'

Trail Notes

Start from the upper parking lot at Sandy Wool Lake at the Tularcitos Trail trailhead, and cross through a cattle gate to the Agua Caliente Trail. You pass under a rocky promontory, one of the launch sites for hang gliders who use this park in great numbers when the wind is right. Go through several more cattle gates as you zig-zag upward through open grasslands. Leave the gates as you find them; this is active cattle range. Here you meet a service road which takes off uphill to a vista point and hang-gliding launch site 400' above you. This makes a good destination if you do not want to make the long climb to Monument Peak. The 0.8-mile round trip to the rocky promontory of this vista point offers a brisk climb up a zig-zag trail. On a day with propitious winds you can watch the hang gliders taking off.

Immediately below, tucked into a small valley against a hill, is the Minnis Ranch. As though looking through a window onto the past, you see the old ranch houses with the palm trees that were a popular accent to gardens of the 19th century. A small orchard surrounds the barns. The ranch still manages the herds you have been meeting along the trail. In

Monument Peak Trail, looking toward hang-glider takeoff

contrast to the condominiums, subdivisions and shopping centers on the west side of the hill, the ranch seems a century removed.

As you climb you cross a branch of Calera Creek, dry in summer but bordered with oaks, bays and a few sycamores testifying to underground water. Turn right on the Monument Peak Trail, while the Agua Caliente Trail goes northwest. You may see some bubbling springs along the way. The trail here is close to the Monument Peak Road, which soon veers east toward the ridge. Where your trail crosses the main Calera Creek, running merrily in the fall, look for two huge, leaning sycamores in a riparian grove. Here might be a good place to pause for lunch in the shade.

After leaving Calera Creek the climb begins in earnest, switchbacking steeply upward, with loose gravel underfoot making the going difficult. Finally around a bend is a gently sloping high plateau. Right above is the peak, a gleaming moonscape in summer when covered with pale yellow oatgrass, and surmounted with antennas and various communications installations.

The trail becomes a road as it enters lands of the East Bay Regional Park District's Mission Peak Preserve and crosses west of 2594' Monument Peak to join the Bay Area Ridge Trail route. This trail traverses a long "skyway" through ridgeline grasslands from Mission to Monument peaks. At this junction you are 3.8 miles from your starting point at Sandy Wool Lake. You could retrace your upward route, or you could follow the Ridge Trail and head southwest on a long descent over steep terrain in East Bay Regional Park District lands. Here the road-width trail winds around ridges, with views as far as Mt. Tamalpais in the north. A large stand of bay trees on a knoll is evidence of springs under this apparently dry hillside.

After descending almost 1500 vertical feet, you cross Scott Creek, often still running in fall after a long, dry summer, and pass from Alameda County into Santa Clara County. Now again in Ed Levin Park, and despite some confusion in signs, follow the Agua Caliente Trail across Calera Creek (bicyclists turn right to take the Calera Creek Trail) and down past the Minnis Ranch to reach Sandy Wool Lake. If you are lucky, you will have seen soaring red-tailed hawks, golden eagles, and perhaps some humans gliding above you with the aid of hang-gliders or para-sails.

3

Ed R. Levin County Park
THE CALERA CREEK TRAIL TO THE PARK'S NORTHWEST BOUNDARY

This trail, the only one designated for mountain bicycles in the park, follows the western park boundary past open pasturelands, then climbs beside Calera Creek to turn west on the Agua Caliente Trail to the park's north boundary near Scott Creek.

Distance: 5 miles round trip

Time: (hikers) 2 hours

Elevation Gain: 1000'

Trail Notes

Bicyclists are required to wear helmets and to observe, for their safety and that of others, the trail rules granting right of way to hikers and equestrians, and to heed cautionary signs for steep sections of the trail.

From the parking lot at the northwest end of Sandy Wool Lake find the mountain bicycle trail just left of a gate for hang gliders' vehicles. The trail turns uphill, then goes right, through a cattle gate.

The trail then keeps near the park's boundary on the edge of a pasture and below low hills above which roofs of subdivision houses on the far side are beginning to appear. As a small ravine opens up, more of the sub-division is in view, as are the tees and greens of a golf course. Your trail turns uphill to follow an intermittent creek edged with cottonwoods, then crosses to the far side.

Toward the mountains an old, unmarked road, closed to bicyclists, leads to the Minnis Ranch buildings, now used by the Parks Department for meetings. The ranch, extending up the mountain, was added to the park, but cattle still graze the hills. The Calera Creek Trail turns down by a pasture fence into a remote little valley and soon passes under an

Trail through the velvety green hills of Ed R. Levine County Park

immense live oak. Just beyond you follow arrows pointing to a pasture gate and directing you down by the far side of the fence.

Ahead groves of trees mark Calera Creek, which your trail follows around a bend. Even in a dry year this spring-fed creek is running. You follow it for a short distance, then cross to the far side, where another gate ahead leads into an upper pasture.

The trail steepens and then climbs toward the Agua Caliente Trail above. Veering away from the creek, your trail passes two even steeper trails used by equestrians but closed to bicyclists. After a final stiff grade, where there is a warning for bicyclists heading down, you reach the Agua Caliente Trail.

The bicycle route turns left (west) on the Agua Caliente Trail. From these heights are views of the urban valley, San Francisco Bay and the Santa Cruz Mountains. The trail contours around the hill for about 0.5 mile to a vista point at 1000' elevation near Scott Creek. Now you can follow the route of Trip 2 in reverse, to the summit of Monument Peak.

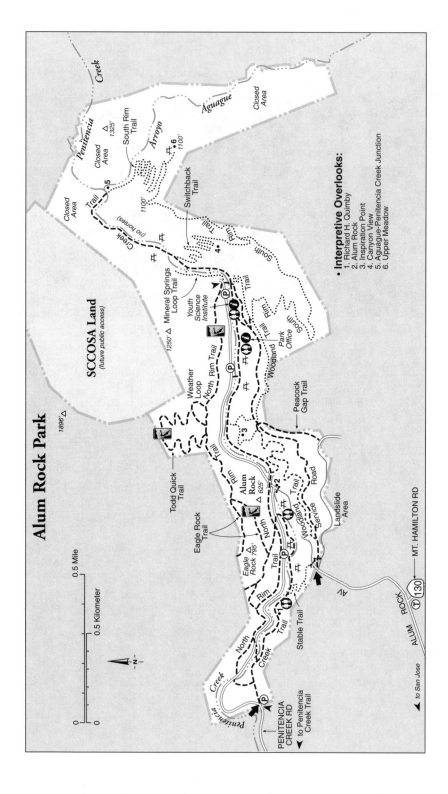

Alum Rock Park

0.5 Mile

0.5 Kilometer

–N–

SCCOSA Land
(future public access)

Closed Area

Penitencia   Creek

Closed Area

Aguague   Arroyo

Closed Area

South Rim Trail
△ 1325'

5

6 ·⊥
1100'

Switchback Trail

1100'

1100'

Creek
Trail
(no horses)

4

South Rim Trail

1250 △

1896'△

Mineral Springs Loop Trail

Youth Science Institute

North Rim Trail

Weather Loop

North Rim Trail

Todd Quick Trail

Eagle Rock Trail

South Rim Trail

Woodland Trail   Park Office

Peacock Gap Trail

3

Alum Rock
△ 625'

2

Eagle △
Rock 795'

North Rim Trail

Woodland Trail

Service Road

Landslide Area

North Rim Trail

1

Stable Trail

Creek Trail

North Creek Trail

Penitencia   Creek

PENITENCIA CREEK RD

to Penitencia Creek Trail

to San Jose

ALUM ROCK   AV

T 130   MT. HAMILTON RD

• Interpretive Overlooks:
1. Richard H. Quimby
2. Alum Rock
3. Inspiration Point
4. Canyon View
5. Aguague-Penitencia Creek Junction
6. Upper Meadow

◆ Alum Rock Park ◆

Although the storms of 1998 and 1999 caused severe damage to this park, repair work has been completed in an environmentally sensitive manner. In the upper creek canyon, failing walls were replaced with native rock and planted with native species. Every effort was made to protect the steelhead trout and red-legged frog that inhabit the creek and its environs.

The lovely canyon of Penitencia Creek has been a popular excursion spot since 1872, when the park was acquired. This canyon was called simply "The Reservation" in its early days. The special charms of the cool, shady flats along its ever-flowing creek and the acclaimed medicinal qualities of its mineral springs soon brought it national recognition. Its present name, which came into being around the turn of the 19th century, refers to a huge rock standing 625' above sea level on the north side of the canyon where the park's two entrance roads join. Both Alum Rock and the taller Eagle Rock nearby are of volcanic origin. The Calaveras Fault lies east of the park and a spur fault runs through Penitencia Creek Canyon.

After 1890 the park became widely known as a health spa. Its hot springs, containing seven minerals considered therapeutic, drew thousands. Stone grottos in the romantic European tradition gushed with a variety of supposedly healing waters. Mineral baths, an indoor swimming pool, a tea garden, a restaurant and a dance pavilion made this a fashionable retreat. A steam railroad brought visitors from San Jose on a 25-cent ride.

In the 1930s WPA workers added bridges built of gray stone from the canyon, and rock walls along the creek banks. With the advent of the automobile, the once-crowded train could not compete, and it discontinued service in 1931. After World War II throngs of visitors overwhelmed the park facilities, and cars overcrowded the parking lots. Eager explorers trampled the fragile plants and slid down the steep hillsides, eroding unstable soils.

To preserve this canyon required reorienting activities to ones emphasizing the natural setting. Now parking is limited, to control the number of visitors. However, parking restrictions do not apply to hikers, bicyclists and equestrians. Outdoor education programs at the Youth Science Institute are encouraging a better understanding of the park's ecology.

Gone are the baths, pavilions and restaurants, but Penitencia Creek still makes its way over the rocks in its shady canyon. You can still sample a mineral spring, stroll along the creek and relax on the lawns. Picnic tables and children's play areas invite you to enjoy family gatherings where San Jose society played in a former day.

A fine example of an ornate stone bridge which crosses Penitencia Creek

Thirteen miles of good trails give the visitor a chance to know the remarkable features of this 700-acre park. Some park trails climb the steep hillsides for fine views; the wide Creek Trail, now designated a National Recreation Trail, follows Penitencia Creek through the length of the park. Joggers and hikers can use all the trails, equestrians are welcome on the North Rim trails, and bicyclists may use the Creek Trail, the North Rim trails and paved roads. Following are four trips to help you discover the park's splendid features.

Jurisdiction: City of San Jose.

Facilities: Visitor Center, Youth Science Institute. *Trails:* hiking, equestrian and bicycle. *Picnic areas with barbecues:* family, group by reservation. Children's playgrounds. Day camps by arrangement. Wheelchair access to Visitor Center and to the paved Creek Trail from the Log Cabin to the Live Oak Area.

Park Rules: *Hours:* Park open every day in the year from 8 A.M. to one-half hour after sunset. Youth Science Institute open noon to 4:30 P.M. daily. No dogs. No hard liquor. No smoking or motorized vehicles on trails. Park phone: 408-277-4539. Reservations: 408-277-5561. Vehicle park entry fees are charged daily. Youth Science Institute phone: 408-258-4322. Fees: child 10 cents, adult 50 cents, $1/family.

Maps: City of San Jose *Alum Rock Park* and *Joggers' Guide*; USGS quad *Calaveras Reservoir.*

How To Get There: *By Car:* Main entrance: From Hwy. 101 or I-680 take Alum Rock Ave. east to parking near picnic areas in lower and mid-canyon. West entrance at Penitencia Creek Rd. closed to motor vehicles. There is room for 8–10 cars at park boundary. **Note: Severe winter storms caused major slides at the Alum Rock Ave. entrance. Until repair work is completed, temporary vehicle access is at the west entrance on Penitencia Creek Rd. Limited parking is available outside park at the Alum Rock Ave. entrance.**

By Bicycle: From Penitencia Creek Park at Mabury Rd. and Jackson Ave. take the paved bicycle path, sidewalks and trail along Penitencia Creek Rd. to the park's west entrance.

By Bus: County Transit 21 to Alum Rock Ave. and Miguelita Ave.

Alum Rock Park
SOUTH RIM LOOP

From the cool shade of the Penitencia Creek Trail climb through oak woodlands to the chaparral-lined south rim of the canyon and make an easy descent to the lawns and picnic areas near the Visitor Center.

Distance: 4 miles

Time: 2½ hours

Elevation Gain: 630'

Trail Notes

From the easternmost parking lot go across one of the park's many bridges and head upstream on the Creek Trail. Penitencia Creek's waters tumble musically over sandstone boulders, with willows, big-leaf maples and sycamores lining its banks. You pass little grottos where springs seep out of the hillside, leaving minerals encrusted on the rocks. Only the mineral spring near the lawn area is tested for potability. If you would like to see other ornate grottos and still-active mineral springs, pick up the self-guiding, interpretive leaflet at the Visitor Center and follow the 0.3-mile Mineral Springs Loop Trail.

Having been close to the high south-rim wall, your trail now crosses a stone bridge over the creek. Under spreading live oaks is an array of picnic tables pleasantly removed from the busiest recreation areas of the mid-canyon. At a sharp bend you see where the creek in its narrow gorge has cut through upended chert strata. Then your trail crosses the creek on a sturdy steel bridge faced with wooden planks colloquially known as the "no-horse bridge," (the title to be taken literally) to an overlook that invites a pause to enjoy the sight of Penitencia Creek cascading down over the rocks. Note the graceful circular stone steps, flanked by two sycamore trees, remaining from the original bridge.

Here Penitencia Creek is joined by Arroyo Aguague, whose waters originate in the mountains of Joseph D. Grant County Park, several miles south. (This creek's name, derived from the Spanish word aguaje meaning "a rush of water," is still appropriate today.) The Indians called Penitencia Creek "Shistuc."

From this cool retreat in summer you can look up to the hot, dry north canyon wall dotted with gray pines (also called foothill pines.) The rushing waters, quiet pools and dappled sunshine invite you to linger here. This place makes a good destination for an easy, short stroll and picnic, about a mile from the Visitor Center. Yellow blooms of monkey flower hang from a high stone embankment of the park's earlier days.

To continue, take the South Rim Trail, for hikers only, up the precipitous canyon for a half hour's climb to the top. A trail sign warns of the dangers of short-cutting corners, not only to the hiker but to those walking below, who may be hit by dislodged rocks. You can see the damage done along this trail by heedless hikers.

Ten switchbacks take you up the fern-clad and spring-flowered hillside. Bay and oak trees arch overhead, accented in late spring by light pink blooms of buckeye trees. As you near the summit, an unmarked 0.1-mile trail leads obliquely left (west) to reach the Upper Meadow Rest Area. In this shady, sloping glade in the woods a picnic table under the trees invites you to pause, have lunch, or enjoy the views of the heights of the northeast canyon.

From the meadow you can follow a narrow trail that leads uphill to the summit. Or continue on a few more feet to the last switchback of the South Rim Trail, where a jumble of rocks seems to hang over the canyon. Easy footholds beckon the adventurous to find a perch from which to see the views. Or from a nearby bench, you may hear the lively chorus of birds that inhabit this place. Hardly considered songbirds, the blue Steller jays call raucously from perches on limbs just above the trail. You can tell them from the scrub jays by their crest of deep-blue feathers. Chestnut-backed chickadees, with their sooty caps and white cheeks, may delight you with their acrobatics in the branches of a big foothill pine.

Leaving the woodlands, the trail continues along a narrow ridge through high chaparral of coyote bush, sagebrush and scrub oak. Soon tall buckeyes, toyons and bays begin to give shade. About 0.5 mile from the summit, the trail forks. You can turn right, downhill, on a shorter route, the Switchback Trail, back to the canyon floor. That trail takes you to the Canyon Viewpoint, then zig-zags many times until it comes out at the Creekside Picnic Area. From there it is less than 0.5 mile downstream to the Visitor Center.

If you stay on the South Rim Trail along the canyon heights, however, another 0.5 mile brings you to a sharp bend, from where you head north on a zig-zag descent to the canyon floor. At the Woodland Trail intersection, turn right for a few yards and then go left down the stone steps and walkways of former park days. You emerge just a few paces east of the Visitor Center. A stop here to see the nature displays, the relief model of the park and the photos of yesteryear is instructive and entertaining.

Or go on a bit farther east and visit the Youth Science Institute to see its collection of live birds, snakes and small animals. The creatures here have injuries or defects that preclude survival in the wild. Most impressive are the huge hawks and owls chained to perches above you. This is also your chance to see a live rattlesnake—safely behind the glass walls of a cage.

Alum Rock Park
CIRCLE HIKE TO EAGLE ROCK ON THE NORTH RIM

Hike up the north side of the canyon to Eagle Rock for an over-look of the park and the Santa Clara Valley. Return along the Creek Trail on the route of the old Alum Rock Steam Railroad.

Distance: 2.2 miles

Time: 1¼ hours

Elevation Gain: 336′

Trail Notes

It is best to take this trip from the east end of the park, for the trail goes up more gradually and the views out of the canyon expand as you walk. Start from the far end of the upstream parking lot where the North Rim Trail goes uphill. At the first intersection take the trail to the left; the other, a private road, is closed to all but service vehicles. A gentle climb brings you out above the steepest part of the canyon. Sounds of the creek and the cheerful cries of children from the playgrounds reach you from below.

In about 0.5 mile you reach a buckeye-shaded flat where the Weather Loop Trail turns off right, uphill. An extra 10-minute push reaches a high ledge studded with a few deciduous oaks. This is the area where the park staff takes the weather readings that help them advise visitors of fire con-ditions and other weather-related circumstances that may affect park usage. From the north side of this loop, look for the 0.9-mile, well-designed Todd M. Quick Loop that zig-zags up the hillside to a picnic table under tall eucalyptus and a viewpoint over the Santa Clara Valley. The other side of the loop rejoins the North Rim Trail farther west. The Todd M. Quick Loop, named in honor of a former park ranger, was built by volunteers from the Trail Center and sponsored by REI.

If you stay on the Weather Loop, it rejoins the North Rim Trail at a point where you'll find a few picnic tables beneath clumps of evergreen oaks. On the hillside above are old palm trees on a former ranch site. Although subdivisions creep up to the park boundary on both sides, the rustic charms of the wooded creek canyon remain for the public to enjoy.

The North Rim Trail heads west, undulating up and down till it meets the Eagle Rock Trail, on which you bear right, make a last short climb, and arrive at the overlook on the uphill side of Eagle Rock. On a clear winter day you can see for miles across the valley to the Santa Cruz Mountains. Looking northeast you see the high bluff lands recently purchased by the Santa Clara County Open Space Authority, which may someday be open for passive recreation consistent with its many natural resources.

Now retrace your steps to the first intersection, turn right, and take the trail below Eagle Rock. From the steep downhill side this upthrust of volcanic rock is impressively tall and rugged. Signs ask hikers to stay off this slope. The authors saw two deer grazing there, oblivious of signs and people.

To reach the valley floor, take the next left bend to meet the Creek Trail going east. This trail, open to bicyclists, passes right below Alum Rock and crosses over the main park-entrance road on the old bridge that once carried the Alum Rock Steam Railroad. On the south side of the bridge, a railroad tunnel went through rock, now crumbled away. A metal plaque on the rock walls tells the story of the old railroad.

The Creek Trail continues upstream on the railroad right-of-way. As you walk here, you can imagine the pleasant and exciting trip in the days when the railroad passed under the trees beside the creek. The sycamore trees, with gray-and-white mottled trunks, now tower more than 100' above the creek. On the grassy banks magenta farewell-to-spring blooms in June and July. Farther on, thickets of wild rose, snowberry and blackberry bushes cover the banks under the alder, cottonwood and bay trees.

The wide, slightly uphill Creek Trail is a popular stroll. On the way back to your starting point, you will find yourself in the company of many families enjoying this park and the pleasant picnic areas nearby.

"Walkie-Talkies" en route to Eagle Rock near the Weather Loop

Alum Rock Park
CIRCLE HIKE FROM THE PARK'S WEST END

Starting along the Penitencia Creek Trail, this trip climbs through an oak forest on the Woodland Trail and circles back on the open hillsides of the north canyon wall.

Distance: 3 miles

Time: 1½ hours

Elevation Gain: 360'

Trail Notes

Although the west entrance is closed to vehicles, there is room for 8 to 10 cars beside Penitencia Creek Road at the park's west entrance. However, bicyclists may use this entrance and can ride through the park on the paved road and return on either the Creek Trail or a service road on the south hillside.

Hikers will see the sign for the Creek Trail which goes east through the edge of a former quarry, created in the 1960s when the San Jose Airport runways were lengthened. Once past the quarry site, you come to year-round Penitencia Creek, its banks clothed with several species of fern and snowberry, wild rose and blackberry bushes. The bright red rose hips and waxy white snowberries are important food sources for birds and animals. On a quiet morning walk you may see a black-tailed deer coming down from the woods to drink. The ample waters of this creek sustain the park's plants and abundant wildlife and then flow west to percolation ponds to improve Santa Clara Valley's groundwater supply.

After about 0.5 mile you will note some steps on your right leading up the bank to a marker honoring Richard H. Quincy, an early San Jose wood and coal dealer who promoted the Alum Rock Steam Railroad. At first a narrow-gauge steam line, the train was electrified in 1901. It crossed the creek here on a trestle, which was completely destroyed by floods in 1911. Remnants of pillars supporting the trestle can be found along the creek at low water. This old trestle is commemorated here at an interpretive overlook and rest area.

Relaxing on this high, sunny platform above the alders and cotton-woods, you can look far up the wooded canyon to the hills on its north side. You may hear woodpeckers in the forest or see a brown red-shafted flicker showing its white rump patch and red wing and tail linings as it flies.

Return to the Creek Trail, continue upstream, and arc right on the Stable Trail, which is closed to bicyclists, and there is no longer a stable uphill. Now zig-zag up the south side of the canyon through oak wood-lands interspersed with occasional buckeyes and red-berried toyons. When you come to the park's main entrance road, cross over and go left a short distance on an old paved road, now a bicycle trail. Watch for a footpath on the left, the Woodland Trail, and take this winding path under the trees along the canyon side.

You could continue on the Woodland Trail all the way to the Visitor Center, but for this circle hike from the park's west entrance, after about 0.6 mile turn off to the left, downhill, toward the Creek Trail.

Here and there on the gentle descent you pass 3–6-foot conglomerate rocks—masses of rounded pebbles and clays cemented together by geo-logic forces. Probably once in the creek bed but now high above it, they are clothed with gray-green mosses and lichens.

The Woodland Trail is well-designed and has easy switchbacks, but short-cutting has badly eroded the turns. Park rules caution hikers to stay on the trail for their own safety and for protection of the hillside from scouring erosion.

At the Creek Trail go left (west) again for about 200 feet. Before the creek crossing, you find another remnant of the railroad. Once a tunnel went through the rock walls of the canyon, but, by 1909 the rock was crumbling and so the walls were removed. Now at this Alum Rock Rest Area explanatory plaques tell about the railroad and the early days of Alum Rock Park.

Back on the Creek Trail, bear west to cross over the park road and the creek, passing right under Alum Rock, towering 200' above you. On the far side you can see the Rustic Lands Picnic Area, reached by a small foot-bridge that is removed in winter. At the next trail junction veer right, tak-ing the Eagle Rock Trail, which shares the alignment of the North Rim Trail here. In 500 feet the trail to Eagle Rock turns right but you continue straight ahead (west) on the wide North Rim Trail, traversing the open hillside. At a slight rise the sawed-off top of Loma Prieta, standing tall in the distant Santa Cruz Mountains, appears framed in a notch in the hills.

In less than 0.2 mile a junction sign points right, to Lariat Lane, but you continue on a trail bearing left about 45 degrees. Follow this trail on a steep hillside past scattered large evergreen oaks, until you meet the other segment of the North Rim Trail, which more or less parallels the road below. Turn right (west) on this trail, contouring around the hill. The trail soon crosses Penitencia Creek Road and leads to the creek, which you can ford in the dry season to reach the Creek Trail. During the wet season, stay above the road; shortly an informal trail descends to the road by the maple-lined creek.

As the creek and the road continue west, bending around a hill, you cross the creek on a narrow bridge, built in 1909 and flanked by round pil-lars ornately set with fossil-bearing rocks, probably from this creek bed. On the other side of the road, you find a gated, wide entry to the service area. The barrier is for motor vehicles only; hikers go right on through. Tall big-leaf maples and willows line the creek side of this large flat. You head south, intersecting the Creek Trail in the quarry area where your trip began. Arc to the right, and over a little hillock you'll find the park's west entrance.

If you go west from here on Penitencia Creek Road, you will be following the creek for several miles. The City of San Jose and Santa Clara County are completing land purchases to form a chain of creekside parks. At this writing a tree-shaded, paved trail borders Penitencia Creek for several miles downstream. (See page 257, Penitencia Creek Trail.)

Alum Rock Park
LOOP TRIP TO INSPIRATION POINT

An easy, shady hike for the dry season on the Woodland and Creek trails features the interpretive overlook that explains the park's geologic origins.

Distance: 2.5-mile loop

Time: 1¾ hours

Elevation Gain: 400'

Trail Notes

This little trip, for hikers only, can be taken from any of the picnic areas in the park starting in either direction, but is not possible in winter because the portable bridge is removed. Since most of the trail segments are described in Trips 1 and 3, only brief directions are given here. Inspiration Point, the highlight of the trip, makes a pleasant destination for a picnic lunch.

Starting at the Visitor Center, go upstream on the Creek Trail to a spur of the South Rim Trail. Turn right on this hiker's trail, which goes abruptly uphill on the steep south canyon wall. After about 500 feet and several zig-zags, the trail turns west and levels off. At the junction of the main South Rim Trail you bear right, continuing west. In less than 0.5 mile and just after your trail crosses the surfaced bicycle path, take a trail to your right a few hundred yards to find the log-fenced overlook at Inspiration Point.

Wooden benches shaded by young oaks invite you to pause here to read the information panels and enjoy the views. A plaque on the overlook tells of the canyon's volcanic and seismic origins. It informs you that a Calaveras Fault branch cuts through the park and Penitencia Creek follows its alignment. From this vantage point you can see the tree-lined path of the stream through the canyon.

While enjoying the views from here, look out across the canyon to the opposite hillside, where Eagle Rock rises to 795', some 300' above the level of the creek bed. East of this rocky promontory you can see shelves, or ledges, probably formed by landslides following earthquakes in past centuries. Part of the North Rim Trail traverses one of these shelves (see Trip 2, page 50).

Refreshed and more knowledgeable after your stop here, retrace your steps to the Woodland Trail and resume your hike west. Where the trail intersects the main park-entrance road, cross over it and descend for the next 0.5 mile on the tree-canopied Stable Trail, for hikers only. In the fall acorns cover the trail underfoot. In winter and early spring you will also find large, shiny, orange-brown balls on the ground here—the seeds of buckeye trees. If you come in late spring, the fragrance of pink-and-white buckeye blossoms fills the air.

At the creek, turn upstream (east) on the Creek Trail and go past the Quail Hollow Picnic Area. You can ford the stream here at low water, but the Creek Trail stays on the south side and in the dry season crosses farther upstream on a portable bridge, removed in winter, to the Eagle Rock Picnic Area. The trail then weaves informally past parking areas and picnic places and eventually crosses the park road opposite the Rustic Lands Picnic Area.

Two switchbacks take you to the trail coming down from Eagle Rock, the North Rim Trail. You go right here, heading due east to the old railroad-bridge stream crossing. Now the wide Creek Trail, shaded by alders and sycamores, makes its way on the south bank past the Log Cabin and Tot Lot picnic areas back to the Visitor Center.

More than 100 years from its founding, Alum Rock Park, in the lovely, narrow valley of Penitencia Creek, continues to provide relaxation and pleasure in a rustic setting.

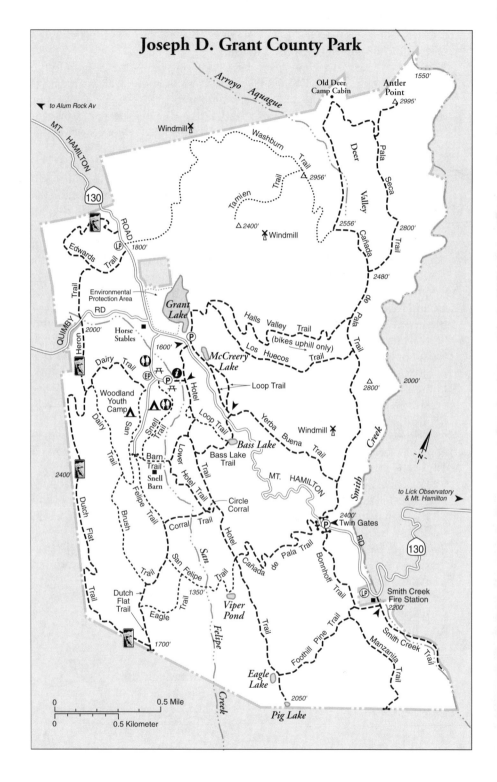

Joseph D. Grant County Park

◆ Joseph D. Grant County Park ◆

The 9522-acre Joseph D. Grant Park, in the Diablo Range, includes secluded Halls Valley, sheltered on the west by a high, wooded ridge and on the east by worn, rounded hills dotted with great oaks. The Grant Ranch was a part of Rancho Cañada de Pala, awarded to José Jesús Bernal in 1839. The entire 15,000-acre ranch was owned by the Bernal family until 1848 when the southern third of the ranch was sold. When Bernal had to file a claim to his land in 1851, he paid his attorney, Frederick Hall, with the land that is the present-day Halls Valley.

In 1880 a major owner sold the property, now the present park, to Adam Grant. Adam, who had moved to San Francisco in Gold Rush days, started a successful dry-goods store, and then became a banker and director of a number of corporations. His son, Joseph Donohoe Grant, born in 1858, was raised in San Francisco but was interested in the ranch and tried to raise polo ponies there. He was a patron of the arts, a trustee of Stanford University, and a founder of the Save-the-Redwoods League.

Josephine, one of Joseph's three children, eventually became the sole owner of the property, operating it as a cattle ranch and living there much of the time. After her separation from Captain Selby McCreery, she lived at the ranch year-round. At her death in 1972 the ranch, willed to the Save-the-Redwoods League and the Menninger Foundation, was offered for sale. Santa Clara County bought the ranch in 1975. Now Joseph D. Grant Park, the county's largest, is enjoyed by increasing numbers of visitors each year as its facilities expand.

The handsome old ranch house on the floor of Halls Valley, now park headquarters, contains a museum with early ranch artifacts and an interpretive center with fine displays of wildlife. The 40-acre Grant Lake and two small lakes are popular with anglers, who must abide by all State Fish and Game laws. Beside Grant Lake an environmental protection area in marshy land is set aside for research. Twenty two campsites are scattered under the trees on a wooded hill approximately 0.75 miles from the park entrance. One of these is for the handicapped. A 0.75-mile trail for the physically limited traverses the area around the ranch house. Camping in the park allows visitors a welcome, early start on the trails.

A group called Friends of the Grant Ranch Park, formed to stimulate interest in the park, trains docents who assist in interpretive programs. Contact the park staff for the current interpretive schedule.

Halls Valley slopes gently south for 2 miles from the old ranch house. San Felipe Creek meanders through its broad riparian meadows to the hills at its lower end, where it cuts through a narrow canyon on its way to San Felipe Valley, 5 miles downstream.

Trips on the park's almost 50 miles of trails range from short walks close to headquarters for picnicking or fishing to hikes around Halls Valley and into the hills. The adventurous will find challenging climbs out of the valley to the park's high ridges.

Trails in Grant Park are for the most part ranch and service roads, broad and well signed. With some exceptions they follow reasonably comfortable grades. Because so many of the trails are old ranch roads, they are clearly shown on the USGS map of the area—*Lick Observatory*—which gives detailed topographic information that cannot be shown on either the park map or the one in this guide.

For comfortable trips adjust your hikes to the weather and seasons. The open, west-facing hills are hot in summer and early fall, but trails on these hills make for good flower gazing in spring and fine walking on crisp fall days. Trails on the wooded western hills offer shady summer trips. Most park trails are multi-use trails, open to hikers, equestrians and bicyclists. Some trails have restricted use, such as the Halls Valley Trail, which is open to bicycles going uphill only. The Washburn Trail, most of the Dairy Trail, and the Brush Trail are for hikers only. Bicyclists are required to wear helmets.

Jurisdiction: Santa Clara County.

Facilities: Headquarters with interpretive center and museum. *Trails:* hiking, equestrian, and bicycle trails. Trail for the physically limited near park office and interpretive center. Picnic areas: family—first come, first served; groups by reservation. *Camping:* 22 drive-in sites for families; group sites by reservation; 1 site for handicapped use. An equestrian area offers both camping (9 sites) and day use.

Handicapped Facilities: ramps, restrooms, 1 campsite, 0.75-mile Whole Access Trail in ranch house area.

Park Rules: Hours: 8 A.M. to sunset. Dogs on 6' leash, but no dogs in primitive areas or on trails. Dogs allowed on Edward's Trail only. No fires except in designated areas and in provided stoves. No smoking on trails. Hikers must stay on trails. No swimming or wading. Fees: Vehicle fees are collected year-round seven days a week. Seniors (age 60 and over) and handicapped are exempt from day-use fees. Fees are required for camping, and for use of group picnic areas. Camping fees required for pets. Camping available 7 days a week, March through November. For information call 408-274-6121.

Maps: Santa Clara County *Joseph D. Grant Park;* USGS quad *Lick Observatory.*

How to Get There: From Hwy. 101 or I-680 in San Jose go east on Alum Rock Ave. to Mt. Hamilton Rd. (Hwy. 130), turn right, uphill, and go 8 miles to park entrance on south side of road. Several parking areas near the Visitor Center; more parking available on east side of Mt. Hamilton Rd. at Grant Lake trailhead and 2 miles farther southeast at Twin Gates.

Three Trips Exploring Halls Valley

The following three loop hikes are of varying length and reach special points of interest in the valley. Each trip's outbound route starts on the San Felipe Trail and each destination site and return route are described. On your way to the Snell Barn, Circle Corral, or Rattlesnake Pond you experience the rich landscape nourished by the park's major watercourse, San Felipe Creek, and its tributaries. Here you can enjoy the tranquillity of vast meadowlands and views of the park's surrounding ridges.

Joseph D. Grant County Park
To Snell Barn

An easy 1.75 mile walk down into tranquil Halls Valley goes over low hills and crosses the valley past old Snell Barn. This almost-level trip is just right for young hikers.

Distance: 1.75-mile loop

Time: 1 hour

Elevation Gain: 120′

Trail Notes

Leave the headquarters parking lot going west under the giant valley oaks toward the equestrian area ahead on your left. As the trail veers south at the corrals, pick up the San Felipe Trail for hikers and equestrians only, which borders the road to the family camping area. Continue past the campsites tucked among the trees on the low ridge to your left.

Watch for the Barn Trail in 0.4 mile from the corrals and turn left on it toward Halls Valley. Your trail passes the big white Snell Barn, built in the 1800s and still standing, but much in need of repair. In spring when the flower-strewn grass is green, when new leaves are coming out on the oaks, when the air is filled with songs of birds, and when watercourses are running, this trip is a delight. You pass patches of shooting stars, a whole field of buttercups, clumps of blue-eyed grass, and yellow Johnny-jump-ups accented by pink mallow and a scattering of lavender brodiaea.

After passing the Snell Trail on your left, the Barn Trail heads for the Lower Hotel Trail on the far side of San Felipe Creek. You will cross this creek and its tributaries on three fine bridges arching over streams lined with cattails and tall, graceful willows. Beyond the creek, you turn left (north) onto the broad Lower Hotel Trail, bordered with widely spaced, deciduous valley oaks. Skirting the base of a tall, tree-topped knoll, the Lower Hotel Trail soon joins the Hotel Trail. From a bench located on a little rise at this junction you see the route of your return.

For the next 0.75 mile, the Hotel Trail winds north through grasslands. Soon you see the old ranch house and its tank house on a little rise beside San Felipe Creek, where you bear left to cross the creek once more, and return to the parking areas.

Joseph D. Grant County Park
TO THE CIRCLE CORRAL

This leisurely excursion for hikers and equestrians goes halfway down Halls Valley to enjoy open fields and views up to the surrounding hills.

Distance: 3.7 miles

Time: 2+ hours

Elevation Loss/Gain: 210'/210'

Trail Notes

Start this trip on the San Felipe Trail, as in Trip 1, but continue past the Barn Trail turnoff. Your trail runs along the side of the valley, at the edge of the woodlands that clothe the western ridge of the park. As you walk through open meadows, the valley opens up, and the high eastern ridge of the park comes into sight. From some points you can see the white gleam of the Lick Observatory domes on Mt. Hamilton.

The fields in spring are busy with scampering ground squirrels, sitting on their hindquarters to nibble at grass seeds or parting the grass to scurry to their holes to avoid hawks sailing overhead. Later, as the grass dries and summer comes, ground squirrels disappear into their holes, seldom to venture out again until the grass turns green. A store of seeds "squirreled away" will last them until the next crop.

About 0.75 mile beyond the Barn Trail turnoff, you enter a copse of oaks where you turn left on the Corral Trail, the next trail across the valley. Descending a little to cross San Felipe Creek you then pass the Lower Hotel Trail and go between fences that could pen many head of cattle. On these fences you may see western bluebirds, the male's rosy breast accented by deep blue back and wings.

At the junction with the Hotel Trail you can lean on the Circle Corral fence, imagine round-ups of not too long ago, and reflect on the good fortune of Bay Area residents to have this spacious valley for relaxation and exploration. And remember the generosity of Josephine Grant McCreery and the wisdom of the Santa Clara County Supervisors who acquired this vast ranch for a park.

After turning left (north) on the Hotel Trail, you walk north through the rolling grasslands past trail turn-offs described later in this book. In 1.3 miles you are back at the ranch house area where you started your trip.

Joseph D. Grant County Park
To Viper Pond and Rattlesnake Rock

This longest of the Halls Valley trips for hikers and equestrians makes a circle around the valley to reach the ford at its end, with a way-stop by a pond.

Distance: 4.75-mile loop

Time: 2½ hours

Elevation Gain: 300′

Trail Notes

Although you can make this trip in a few hours, you will want to take your time to admire the flowers, catch a soaring eagle in your binoculars, watch deer at the edge of the woods and enjoy a long lunch under a spreading valley oak.

Start this trip as in Trip 2 but continue past the Corral Trail staying on the San Felipe Trail for 0.3 mile and passing the Brush Trail on your right. You climb to a meadow cut off from Halls Valley by low hills—a flowery garden in spring; in summer tawny grasses contrast with valley oaks.

After passing the Eagle Trail on your right, the San Felipe Trail veers due east and begins a steep descent around several switchbacks to San Felipe Creek. Swollen by the waters of many small tributaries, the creek is here a year-round watercourse, so in rainy months you may have to wade the ford. This is the lowest point in the trip; ahead is an elevation gain of 200′ to the Hotel Trail. Switchbacks on the east side of the creek take you into shady little ravines where the banks blossom with Chinese houses and shooting stars. After a long bend north in the trail, you come to Viper Pond, edged with reeds and, as its name suggests, a place where some passerby may have seen a rattlesnake. Across the trail from the pond is the rugged outcrop of Rattlesnake Rock.

Past the pond, the trail crosses under high powerlines and out to viewpoints that take in the entire length of this beautiful valley. Where the San Felipe Trail intersects the Hotel Trail, you turn left for your return north on the valley's east side.

For the next 0.5 mile the broad trail continues through sloping grasslands, goes over a little rise, and through a stony meadow where wildflowers flourish with particular intensity. It is worth a special trip in spring to see this garden of close-growing pink mallow, orange poppies, blue lupines, goldfields, blue-eyed grass, and johnny jump-ups. Serpentine soil in this meadow inhibits tall grasses but provides the conditions for such flowers to thrive.

The trail then leads to a little stream in the shade of cottonwoods, a welcome, cool place to stop on a warm day. Just beyond the stream you see the Circle Corral, from which you follow the Hotel Trail north to headquarters, as in Trip 2.

Joseph D. Grant County Park
THE LAKE LOOP

Footpaths take you to shady sites at Bass and McCreery lakes for fishing and picnicking.

Distance: 3-mile loop

Time: 1½ hours

Elevation Gain: 340′

Trail Notes

From the parking areas near the ranch house, take the trail that heads for the eastern foothills, go through a green park gate, cross San Felipe Creek and turn south on the wide Hotel Trail. After 0.3 mile pick up the Loop Trail on the left, which climbs grassy slopes and then follows a small stream up a rocky, wooded ravine. You will find a small reservoir, Bass Lake, in a bench on a hillside at the head of the stream. A picnic table under a tree invites you to make this your destination for lunch. The surrounding hillsides, dotted with great valley oaks that are silhouetted against grass and sky, make a fine backdrop for your repast.

Taking the path that leaves the west corner of Bass Lake, you make a steep climb that brings you to the side of Mt. Hamilton Road, where your trail turns left to parallel the road. Watch for a stile in the fence, where you cross to the stile on the opposite side and meet the broad Yerba Buena Trail going north and south. Here a footpath takes off downhill into a ravine leading to McCreery Lake.

Take the footpath and go down the ravine beside a stream. You are soon under the cool shade of oaks and buckeyes, and in spring the little stream ripples musically down its rocky course. The damp banks of the ravine are strewn with nearly every species of flower to be found in the park. Lavender Chinese houses cover the ground in sheets and blue larkspur's spikes blossom here against the intense magenta of clarkias. The

Bass Lake

uncommon wind poppies, with their pale orange, papery flowers, grow in the moist shade (in contrast to their not-too-close relatives, the California poppies, which thrive in the sun).

This pleasant, woodsy trail continues beside the stream to where it meets a larger stream; here the ravine opens up into a small meadow. Sheltered from wind and shaded by overhanging trees, this trail is a good one for either a warm or a blustery day. You soon come to McCreery Pond, popular with anglers, who catch bass here, and with picnickers, who enjoy a place by the water in the sun or in the shade of nearby sycamore trees.

To continue on the loop trip, take the path at the northwest end of the lake out to the Yerba Buena Trail. A stile across Mt. Hamilton Road leads to the Hotel Trail, which you take down to park headquarters, 0.3 mile away. If you would like to extend your hike, you can continue 0.2 mile north to Grant Lake on either the Yerba Buena or Lakeview trails. (A slightly longer route east of these trails follows the Canal Trail and turns left on the Los Huecos Trail to reach Grant Lake.) After enjoying the lakeside view of Grant Lake, take the Hotel Trail south back to park headquarters.

Joseph D. Grant County Park
AVENUE OF THE NOBLE GIANTS

Marvel at the ancient live oaks overarching this hillside trail.

Distance: 2.9 miles

Time: 1½ hours

Elevation Gain: 300′

Trail Notes

From the ranch house/park office go west toward the equestrian area under the shade of valley oaks. Across the park road that leads south to the campsites is the San Felipe/Dairy trails junction. Take the Dairy Trail uphill (west) through clumps of live oaks interspersed with patches of poison oak, honeysuckle vines, and coyote bush that fill openings between trees. If you hear quail calling in the woods, you may see a covey scampering ahead on the trail. When the trail levels off a bit, you can turn around to see the valley and campsites on a knoll above the San Felipe Trail.

After 0.8 mile and a steady elevation gain of 300+ feet, the trail levels off a bit at the Dutch Flat Trail junction where you turn left (south) continuing on the Dairy Trail (no bicycles). During rainy years little rivulets trickle down the sides of the trail nourishing clusters of deep pink shooting stars that nod on 6- to 8-inch stalks. With an oak-topped knoll on your left you walk through lush springtime grasslands bursting with buttercups and woodland stars. Here you can watch ground squirrels scurrying through the grass or hear their warning calls made from atop their underground nests.

In another 0.2 mile you begin what the authors term the Avenue of the Noble Giants—a long line of ancient live oaks on the east side of the trail. With trunks that measure 6 feet in diameter, some with hollowed-out trunks, they still support 6 or 7 huge limbs that spread out 40 feet from the base to shade the trail. The authors guess these trees were standing long before Sir Francis Drake sailed the California coast in the 1500s.

Farther on you may hear water running; you soon come to its source— a large marshy area with a rivulet merrily winding through it. Where the Brush Trail takes off on your right and the little stream tumbles directly downhill, you follow the Dairy Trail left around a wide bend and contour 0.6 mile gently north along a heavily wooded hillside. Descending quickly, you come out of the woods and see across to the Snell Barn and campgrounds on the other side of the San Felipe Trail. When the Dairy Trail intersects the paved campgrounds road, you turn right (south) on the wide, graveled San Felipe Trail, go south for less than 0.1 mile, and then turn left onto the Barn Trail.

As you meander through the grasslands with the old barn off to your right, watch for the Snell Trail on your left. If you take it north, you will pass the amphitheater on the hillside above and in 0.5 mile you will be back at the parking areas near the park office.

Joseph D. Grant County Park
HIKE TO THE PARK'S EAST RIDGE

The Halls Valley Trail, for hikers and uphill-bound bicyclists only, is fine at any time of the year, but don't miss it in spring, when leaf buds on the oaks are bursting in pale green and hillsides glow with sheets of wildflowers.

Distance: 4-mile loop

Time: 2½ hours

Elevation Gain: 1100'

Trail Notes

The Halls Valley Trail starts from the parking lot at Grant Lake on the north side of Mt. Hamilton Road, 0.75 mile east of the main park entrance. The lake is popular with anglers, who try for black bass and bluegill, and with birders, who find a wide range of birds, from orioles and magpies to great blue herons that nest by the lake.

The Halls Valley Trail leaves the lake on its east side, dipping below the earth dam and crossing a ditch carrying water from springs uphill. The trail turns north around a clump of tall eucalyptus that once surrounded an early ranch building. Golden eagles sometimes alight in these trees.

In May you will have a flowery walk to some of the Bay Area's finest displays. On the slope ahead great clumps of blue-eyed grass take over a meadow. Around the bend is the Los Huecos Trail, on which you will return. Continue on the Halls Valley Trail, which winds up a wooded canyon on an old ranch road above a deep creek canyon. Flowers line the shady banks in April and May—iris, shooting stars and pagoda-like Chinese houses. Splashes of buttercup gild the slope under the oaks.

As you gain altitude, leaving the canyon depths, you come out on an open, grassy hillside dotted with valley oaks. You look down on Grant Lake and across to the hills on the west side of the park and to the Santa Cruz Mountains beyond. The air is loud with cries of woodpeckers and jays in the canyon.

On up the hill in springtime are deciduous oaks whose dark branches are tipped with new leaves, young grass shimmers in the breeze and flowers are everywhere. As you approach the ridgetop, where soils are thinner, flower displays are even more lavish. Here the Halls Valley Trail meets the Cañada de Pala Trail at a 2400' saddle—a blaze of flowers in spring and a golden glow of oats against blue sky in summer.

From the saddle you look down into narrow Smith Creek Canyon and its east-facing slope edged with scrub oak, gray (or foothill) pine and buckeye. Turn right (south) onto the Cañada de Pala Trail (open to bicycles) and go uphill for 0.3 mile to the Los Huecos Trail intersection. Looking east from here, you see the white observatory buildings atop Mt. Hamilton. Established in 1888 through the gift of James Lick, the original observatory was the first permanently occupied mountain observatory in the world. The work begun in those early days is carried on by astronomers from the University of California at Santa Cruz.

Pause here for the fine views all around before you make the steep descent on the Los Huecos Trail. You may wish to return by the Halls Valley Trail to avoid sharing this downhill run with bicyclists. Go with care; the loose rock surface of the trail makes the footing treacherous. Down the trail 0.25 mile is a large-scale rock garden—a stunningly composed stone outcropping, weathered and lichen-covered, surrounded by a swath of orange poppies with accents of blue larkspur in spring.

The Los Huecos Trail continues steeply down to a lower ridge, where it levels off on a grassy hogback edged with oak woods on its north side. After a few more steep drops, the trail joins the Halls Valley Trail a short distance from your parking place near Grant Lake.

Joseph D. Grant County Park
BAY AREA RIDGE TRAIL ON THE WEST RIDGE

Views over the Santa Clara Valley alternate with panoramas of the Grant Ranch, its pasture lands, and Mt. Hamilton to the east. In October 1997 this route was dedicated as a new segment of the Bay Area Ridge Trail open to hikers, equestrians, and bicyclists.

Distance: 5.6 miles plus 2.6 miles to return to parking area and 1.5 miles to Edward's Trail north entrance on Mt. Hamilton Road, a total of 9.7 miles. With a shuttle to north parking the trip could be shortened to 8.2 miles.

Time: 5½ hours

Elevation Gain: 1000'

Trail Notes

On this trail you sample the environments of the full length of the park's west side—chaparral, oak woods, gentle meadows, wooded pasture lands and streamsides. The views from Dutch Flat alone are well worth the climb.

Begin this trip on the Edwards Trail on the west side of Mt. Hamilton Road about 1.5 miles north of the main park entrance. On the road's east side is limited parking. Do not block the gate. Leaving a car here entails a walk back to it after your 8.2-mile trip.

Leaving Mt. Hamilton Road you begin a fairly steady climb on an old ranch road, still used to tend cattle, which you may meet if you come here in late spring. Your way is shaded by occasional monarch live oaks and brightened by displays of blue lupines and large yellow mule ears in spring. At one of several wide switchbacks you can look back over Halls Valley to the ranch house complex, the former home of Joseph D. Grant. Beyond lie the steep hills of the eastern side of the park and on Mt. Hamilton the Lick Observatory domes glisten in the sun.

Soon you pass a spring which feeds a huge live oak with wide-spreading branches trimmed by the cattle. You will follow high powerlines for a good part of this trip. When you reach the highest point of this first one-mile leg of your trip, you turn south, intersect the other leg of the Edwards Trail, and pass a small pond shaded by a stand of black oaks. Shortly, you turn right onto the Heron Trail and proceed under the powerlines for 0.6 mile to the green-gated crossing of Quimby Road and reassuring Ridge Trail signs.

Still following the Heron Trail beyond Quimby Road, you continue south, undulating up and down. Now there is more shade—bay trees and willows grow in the ravines you cross and huge white oaks arch over the trail. Then, quite unexpectedly, you dip into a dense, cool grove of very large and mature bay trees, one with 14 trunks coming from its central bole.

With the Heron Trail, you pick up the Dutch Flat Trail, which you follow to the extreme south end of the park. You make a wide swing to the right, climbing in earnest through a fine stand of black oaks—deciduous in winter, bronze-red in spring when getting their new leaves, and tawny-gold and orange in fall.

As the trail turns south again, openings in the woods offer views of vast Halls Valley, the centerpiece of this park. Grant Lake shimmers in the sunlight and the park's many trails meander down the valley and up grassy hillsides indented by streamlets that nourish stands of oaks and sycamores.

From Dutch Flat, a broad lofty plateau that extends along the west boundary of the park, you can see across the Santa Clara Valley to the Santa Cruz Mountains with landmark Mt. Umunhum's blocky building atop it. Far south is the Gavilan Range. You are nearly at the level of the park's eastern ridge and can make out the wide fire road that is the Yerba Buena Trail.

From this point the undulating Dutch Flat Trail rises on gently rounded hills dotted with fine oaks, making this a lovely walk. For the next 2 miles you are near the fence line of the park's western boundary. The old wooden fence, still in good shape, was put up in the days when the Grant family operated the ranch.

This is a trail to linger on, to identify landmarks in the urban valley on the west or in the ranch on the east, and to watch hawks as they soar on the updrafts. At the trail's 2457-foot vista point is a picnic table—a place to pause for lunch, although there is no shade in summer. You can note how well the two arms of the Coast Range enclose the Santa Clara Valley. Mt. Umunhum and Loma Prieta lie in the southern part of the Santa Cruz Mountains—the Outer Coast Range—and to the east lie the lofty peaks of the Inner Range—Mts. Hamilton and Copernicus, as well as the trio of high points a bit north—Monument, Allison, and Mission peaks.

After a jog in the trail, it continues near the park boundary passing stock ponds on the right and then another on the left, this latter one nestled in the shade of lofty oak trees with ducks swimming on it. Bending east beyond the pond for more than 0.5 mile along the park's south boundary, the Dutch Flat Trail then turns north. Quail make their dignified way on the trail ahead until startled into whirring flight. Rabbits rest in the shade by the trail, leaping to safety only when you approach too closely.

You pass the Eagle Trail on the right, then pick up the Brush Trail and go right (north) on it. Continuing through more delightful meadows and woodlands, you bear left on the San Felipe Trail, which hikers and equestrians can take all the way north to the equestrian area and the road back to the parking areas. Bicyclists must turn east onto the Corral Trail from the San Felipe Trail and then go north on either the Lower Hotel or the main Hotel Trail back to headquarters.

If you would like to shorten this trip, you can start west from the headquarters parking lot on the road leading to the equestrian area and just after rounding it, turn off uphill, west, on the Dairy Trail. This trail ascends with pleasant changes in grade through familiar-looking oak woods and chaparral, crossing small meadows and climbing up wooded slopes. After approximately a half-hour climb, the Dairy Trail departs south at its junction with the Dutch Flat Trail, on which you then join the Ridge Trail route.

Joseph D. Grant County Park
THE CAÑADA DE PALA TRAIL
ON THE EAST RIDGE

Here is a dramatic trip for hikers, equestrians, and bicyclists that traverses the park's eastern heights to hidden Deer Valley.

Distance: 8 miles round trip

Time: 4 hours

Elevation Gain: 450'

Trail Notes

Although the ridge is beautiful in spring, when the grass is green and wildflowers bloom, it is most striking in early summer, when the oats are pale gold against a blue sky. Try for a day when the weather is not too hot, and make an early start. By leaving your car at the Grant Lake parking area, hikers and equestrians can shorten the trip by returning on the Halls Valley Trail, which is closed to bicyclists going downhill. Bicyclists can return on the Los Huecos Trail.

This trip on the Cañada de Pala Trail runs north along the park's east ridge from the Mt. Hamilton Road as far as Deer Valley, at the north edge of the park. The trail, on a ranch road, takes a sinuous route over high grasslands, winding around the smooth hilltops.

Start from the Twin Gates parking area at the crest of Mt. Hamilton Road before it descends east to Smith Creek, about a 10-minute drive from the main park entrance. Enter the trail through a gate on the north side of the road and go through a dense grove of oaks to climb to the hilltop, a rise of 200'. From this viewpoint you see down into Smith Creek Canyon, a steep 500' below, and up to the white domes of Lick Observatory. In the other direction you see Grant Lake at the head of Halls Valley and the wooded hills of the park's west boundary.

About 0.5 mile north is a junction with the Yerba Buena Trail, a wide fire road coming up from Mt. Hamilton Road. The ridge ahead is open grazing land, with a scattering of deciduous oaks. Grasses, now mainly European annual oats and some rye, grow fast to take advantage of the short "spring" after the winter rains. By April the hilltop blooms brilliantly with poppies, mallows, lupine, brodiaea and goldfields, followed in June by farewell-to-spring and mariposa lilies.

The oaks, fine specimens of the valley oak, *Quercus lobata*, depend not on rain falling around them but on deep water found by their long roots. In such dry areas they are spaced widely and are often found lining ravines, where there is more underground water. On this ridge the oaks are broad-trunked old trees. Here and there broken stumps and fallen dead branches remain where age has finally overtaken them. You see few young trees. More than a century of grazing has prevented the sprouted acorns' growth into young trees. The maximum life span of these giants is 500 years, so without a positive program to protect young trees, these hills will someday be bare.

Soon you cross the high point of this part of the ridge and descend past a junction with the Los Huecos Trail, open to bicycles. Then 0.3 mile farther, you reach a broad saddle where you meet the Halls Valley Trail, another route up from Grant Lake. Continuing on the Cañada de Pala Trail, you climb north along the ridge, passing no-longer-used corrals and cattle chutes. After 0.25 mile you come to a junction with the Pala Seca Trail, which leads east and then follows the ridge north to the far end of the park. Staying on the Cañada de Pala Trail, you descend the hillside past watercourses in each small ravine, where reeds and marshy spots mark springs, and enter the head of Deer Valley, which drains to the north.

Ringed with parklike oak groves, this mile-long valley is one of the wildest and most remote parts of the park. From the stately blue oaks, acorn woodpeckers swoop with flashing black-and-white wings, endlessly exchanging their sharp cries. Less visible, dark-blue Steller's jays call to each other from treetops. The stillness is sometimes further broken by the cries of golden eagles, whose voice the Audubon Society's field guide describes as "soft mewing or yelping notes." These magnificent raptors with wingspreads of 6–8′ can sometimes be seen soaring above the treetops and swooping down into the grasslands.

In this highland valley you will often catch sight of small bands of deer bounding out of the brush, and on rare occasions

Cañada de Pala Trail, looking south toward Pala Seca Trail junction

might even glimpse a mountain lion. These shy and rare animals pose little threat to deer populations; most of the deer they kill are weak or crippled.

Hikers who have left a car at Grant Lake can retrace their steps to the Halls Valley Trail and take it for 2.5 miles downhill to the car. Bicyclists can return on the Los Huecos Trail.

Joseph D. Grant County Park
EAGLE LAKE LOOP

Descending through open pasture lands to Eagle Lake, traversing a narrow creek canyon and then climbing through foothill pine and valley oak forests is a rewarding experience in the park's southeast corner.

Distance: 5.2-mile loop

Time: 3½ hours

Elevation Gain: 840'

Trail Notes

From the parking area at Twin Gates this trip starts downhill and ends uphill, no matter on which end of the loop you begin. It is described here ascending the Bonnhoff Trail because in very hot weather this route is shadier.

The Cañada de Pala Trail goes southwest from the Twin Gates parking area on Mt. Hamilton Road switchbacking down a rocky trail through chaparral country into Halls Valley. This route, a utility service road under tall powerlines, takes you over grassy slopes, here and there shaded with valley oaks, and into cool, wooded ravines where creeks run in winter and spring. In very wet years a small waterfall drops into a deep pool lined with reeds.

As you descend, Halls Valley opens up to view with the ranch house on its floor, Grant Lake beyond and Snell Barn across the valley. Over the wooded hills to the west you see the Santa Cruz Mountains and far south the mountains east of Monterey. The melodious songs of meadowlarks and the sharp calls of woodpeckers stand out in the general chorus of bird song.

After the last switchback the 1.7 mile Cañada de Pala Trail rises out of a small ravine to meet the Hotel Trail. Early in this century a popular inn (no longer extant) on Smith Creek near the fire station offered enterprising excursionists lodging before taking a wagon up Mt. Hamilton to Lick Observatory.

Bear left (south) on the Hotel Trail where a wooden bench invites a rest stop with a view. The trail rises gradually through gentle meadows rimmed with fine valley and blue oaks and past small reservoirs for watering cattle. After 1.2 miles you go through a small draw and come upon tranquil Eagle Lake, brimful in May. Frogs splash into the water at your coming. Here is a bench set under a spreading oak and fenced off from intruding cattle.

On a May visit the authors looked up to see large, dark gray animals moving through tall grass on a nearby hilltop. As they approached, they proved to be a small herd of the feral pigs that have become numerous in the park. A boar nearly 3 feet tall, with long, menacing tusks, accompanied by two sows and a piglet, trotted down the hill and out of our sight. These pigs, descendants of wild boars imported to the East Coast from Europe in the past century, were brought to California as game animals and have proliferated. They will avoid you if they can, but leave them alone; they might be dangerous if cornered.

Before you leave Eagle Lake go just beyond the south rim of the lake for a view down the San Felipe Valley. Mt. Misery is the tall peak you see at the south end of the valley, and beyond is a succession of hills and mountains all the way to the Santa Lucia Mountains near Monterey. Another pond, known as Pig Lake, lies 0.2 mile farther south. Rimmed with great oaks, it is the outlet for a creek you will cross later in the trip.

To continue your trip, take the well-signed 1.1-mile Foothill Pine Trail, once a footpath, now graded for service vehicles, from the northeast end of the lake. It descends abruptly into a narrow-walled canyon, then meanders beside an intermittent stream, which you cross and re-cross before starting uphill. In warm weather this stretch is a pleasant, cool interlude. Sycamores edge the stream, ferns drape the steep hillside, and delicate wind poppies with orange-red flowers blossom along its shady banks.

Your trail soon takes off straight uphill and climbs out of the canyon in a series of short, steep pitches mixed with easy grades shaded by bay and oak trees. Now about halfway along the Foothill Pine Trail and 2.5 miles from your starting point, you begin to see the blue-green, long-needled foothill (or gray) pines found on dry heights such as these. Their unusually large seeds were an important food for Native Americans, who sometimes traded with tribes farther west.

In a flowery, damp meadow where a pond catches runoff from surrounding hills, you meet the Manzanita Trail going off to the south. Then 0.1 mile farther at another trail junction, the Foothill Pine Trail goes right (east) 0.3 mile down a gentle slope to the Sulfur Creek Trail. There a short lane leads to a stile and a gated entrance from Mt. Hamilton Road.

But to complete the trip on the Bonnhoff Trail, turn left (north) on the trail named for the man who was for many years Josephine Grant McCreery's ranch manager. The climb from the meadow is one of several short, but steep, stretches without switchbacks on this trail. However, the route along the hilltops has magnificent wide views of Halls Valley. Widely spaced deciduous oaks—huge valley oaks and occasional black oaks—offer shade to trail users and to native grasses that flourish under their leafy canopy. After 0.8 mile, the Bonnhoff Trail rounds a high, tree-topped knoll and descends to the Twin Gates at Mt. Hamilton Road.

Joseph D. Grant County Park
THE WASHBURN TRAIL TO DEER VALLEY

A stiff climb, for hikers only, to the high, remote northeast corner of the park takes you to lush Deer Valley, to hilltops of flowers, to forests of great oaks and to breathtaking vistas.

Distance: 9.7 miles roundtrip to Grant Lake; 11.2 miles round trip to Washburn trailhead.

Time: 8 hours

Elevation Gain: 1800'

Trail Notes

This is a challenging, spectacular trip with long uphill climbs, one for cool weather and an early start. The Washburn Trail starts from the east side of Mt. Hamilton Road about 1.5 miles north of the main park entrance, and the trip ends on the Halls Valley Trail at Grant Lake, 0.2 mile south of the park entrance. The distance between the two will seem long at the end of the day, so try to arrange a car shuttle.

A stile by a gate on the east side of the road leads to a wide private ranch road/trail passing north of the Washburn Barn. Head down the ranch road straight toward the hills. You can look up from here at the 2900' heights you will cross on the Washburn Trail. A 20-minute walk through a pasture brings you to oak woods, then a quick descent to the banks of Arroyo Aguague. Sycamores and alders arch overhead where two branches of the stream join by a small flat, then flow west to Alum Rock Park. This makes a pleasant destination for a picnic in late spring before the creeks dry up. Children would be happily occupied here.

For those who continue, the trail crosses the creek and climbs steadily up a ravine beside a branch of the creek. Leaving the ravine, you climb around bend after bend for 0.8 mile. The trail is now out in open pasture lands dotted with the valley oaks that are a constant delight in this park. The ranch road you have been following approaches the northern boundary of the park and then crosses it through a locked gate into a ranch beyond. You stay in the park, turning right on a jeep track going uphill, which the Washburn Trail now follows.

Here in a draw by the trail one of Grant Park's windmills pumps water to fill a cattle trough. You are at an elevation of 1800', with more than 1000' to go before reaching the high point of the trail. It is a steady, steep climb now, up hillsides bright with yellow mariposa lilies, lavender brodiaea and magenta clarkia, to reach a narrow ridge shaded by a grove of blue oaks. Then the trail continues in a series of steep rises mixed with level stretches. Repeatedly, the feeling that surely the brow of the hill ahead is the summit gives way to dismay that another climb is beyond, and then still another. However, you can stop along the way to look off to the Bay far below and to admire the grassy slopes, where silvery-headed blow-wives glisten and more mariposa lilies and brodiaeas blossom. At last you reach the high point of the Washburn Trail at an elevation of 2956'.

From the south side of the trail a series of hogbacks, or shoulders, extends from the ridge down to Grant Lake. Along these heights the 0.9-mile Tamien Trail (named for an early Ohlone tribelet) takes off to a wind-mill on a hilltop.

Continuing on the Washburn Trail, you follow a fence to a gate, where you turn sharply downhill. The trail goes through a grove of magnificent oaks—some of the finest in the park. A long arc of the trail brings you to the south end of Deer Valley and the Cañada de Pala Trail. A leisurely lunch here will give you time to enjoy this beautiful setting.

Remote Deer Valley is a place of eagles and deer herds. Mountain lions have been seen here too, but that is little cause for alarm; their shyness keeps them out of your way. Cattle no longer graze in this valley, thus removing the excitement of meeting an errant bull.

This almost 2-mile-long valley is enclosed on the west by a ridge forest-ed with blue and black oaks; on the east by rounded, grassy hills rising above 2900', dotted with valley oaks and furrowed by wooded ravines. Here and there are great outcrops of lichen-covered rocks.

From the junction of the Washburn and Cañada de Pala trails, you have alternate routes for your return trip. The shortest way is by the Cañada de Pala Trail south for 1.0 mile to the Halls Valley Trail for an easy trip down to Grant Lake. A longer, more circuitous and more spectacular route for energetic hikers is to follow the Cañada de Pala Trail north down the val-ley, then take the Pala Seca Trail over the east ridge to join the Cañada de Pala Trail going south to the Halls Valley Trail.

If you choose the long way, take the Cañada de Pala Trail 1.3 miles down the marshy valley. Its waters gather into a meandering stream through some sycamores before it descends to join a branch of Arroyo Aguague. As Deer Valley narrows at its lower end, you see the remnants of the Old Deer Camp Cabin above the trail. It is said that a group of doc-tors leased this part of the park for hunting and used the cabin for overnight stops.

Turning east you continue 0.7 mile to climb the rocky, enclosing hills near the park's north boundary. At the junction with the Pala Seca Trail, where you turn south to complete the loop around Deer Valley, you can take a side-trip north to Antler Point, the park's highest at 2995 feet and the best around-the-compass views.

Returning to the Pala Seca Trail you start south along the broad, grassy ridge that overlooks the narrow canyon of Smith Creek, the east boundary of Grant Park. A highlight of this trail is a profusion of yellow mariposa lilies, which makes the trip very much worthwhile in spring. These exquisite blossoms grow in such surprising numbers that the ridgetop sparkles with glints of pale gold. Patches of dwarf lupines echo the blue of the sky in April and early May. If you hear the lilting song of meadowlarks, you may see them too, as they fly close, trying to distract you from their nests in the grass or from their fledglings.

After 1.6 miles along the high grasslands of the Pala Seca Trail, you descend to the Cañada de Pala Trail junction, where an immense lone oak tree casts its generous shade. From this intersection the Cañada de Pala Trail descends 0.4-mile to the Halls Valley Trail junction, where you turn right for a "downhill-all-the-way" trip to the parking lot at Grant Lake.

Deer Valley

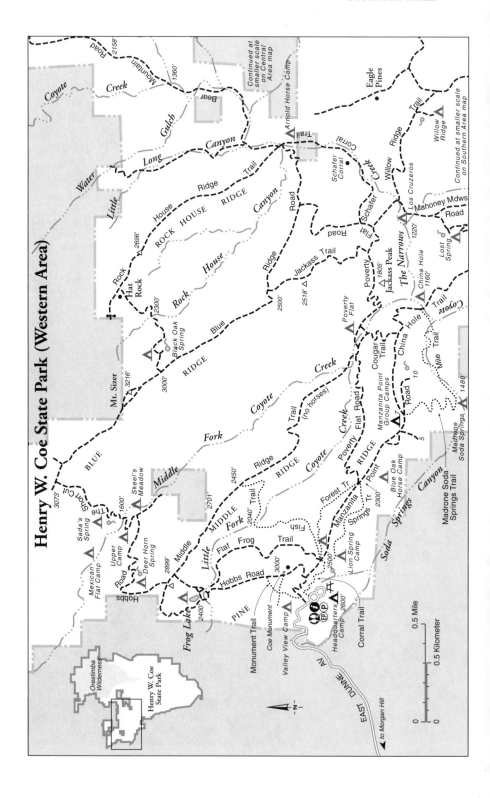

Henry W. Coe State Park (Western Area)

Road 2158'

Coyote   Creek

Mountain   '1360'

Bear

Arnold Horse Camp

Eagle Pines

Continued at smaller scale on Central Area map

Gulch

Water

Long   Canyon

Corral

Schafer Corral

Willow   Ridge   Trail

Willow Ridge

Continued at smaller scale on Southern Area map

Little

House   Ridge   Trail

ROCK   HOUSE   RIDGE

Canyon

Road

Schafer   Flat

Creek

Los Cruzeros

Mahoney Mdws Road

Rock   House

Canyon

2696'

Road

Jackass   Trail

Flat   Road

Poverty

'1220'

Lost Spring

Rock

Hat Rock

2300'

Rock

Ridge

2500'

2518 △

Poverty Flat

Jackass Peak '1805

China Hole 1160'

The Narrows

Black Oak Spring

Blue

Cougar   Trail

Coyote

Trail

China   Hole

Mile   Trail

Mt. Sizer

3216'

3000'

RIDGE

Coyote   Creek

Trail (no horses)

Manzanita Point Group Camps

Road   10

'1480

Madrone Soda Springs

BLUE

Fork

Poverty Flat Road

△7

5

3073'

Short Cut

Skeel's Meadow

Middle

Ridge   RIDGE

Coyote

RIDGE

Blue Oak Horse Camp

Madrone Soda Springs Trail

Sada's Spring

The

'1600'

2450'

Forest Tr

Point

2300'

Soda

Canyon

Mexican Flat Camp

Upper Camp

Deer Horn Spring

2701'

2040' Trail

Fish

Manzanita   Point

Lion Spring Camp

Spring Tr

Soda   Springs

Road

2899'

Little   MIDDLE   Fork

Flat   Frog   Trail

2500'

Hobbs

Middle

3000'

Lion Spring Camp

Hobbs Road

2400'

PINE

Frog Lake

Monument Trail

Coe Monument

Valley View Camp

Headquarters Camp 2600'

Corral Trail

DUNNE   AV

EAST

to Morgan Hill

Orestimba Wilderness

Henry W. Coe State Park

0.5 Mile

0.5 Kilometer

N

0

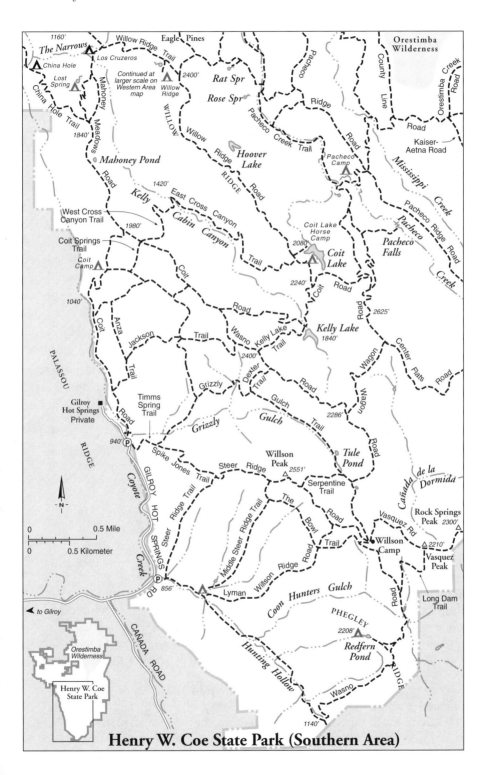

1160'
The Narrows
China Hole
Los Cruzeros
Willow Ridge Trail
Eagle Pines
Orestimba Wilderness

Lost Spring
Continued at larger scale on Western Area map
2400'
Rat Spr
Rose Spr
Pacheco Creek
County Line
Road
Orestimba Creek Road

China Hole Trail
Mahoney
Meadows
1840'
WILLOW
Willow Ridge
Willow
Road
Ridge
RIDGE
Road
Pacheco Creek Trail
Ridge
Road
Kaiser-Aetna Road

Mahoney Pond
Hoover Lake
Pacheco Camp
Mississippi Creek

Kelly
1420'
East Cross Canyon
West Cross Canyon Trail
1980'
Cabin Canyon
Trail
Coit Lake Horse Camp
2080'
Coit Lake
Pacheco Ridge Road
Pacheco Falls
Pacheco Creek

Coit Springs Trail
Coit Camp
1040'
Coit
Trail
2240'
Road
Coit
Road
2625'

Coit
Anza Trail
Jackson Trail
Wasno
Trail
Kelly Lake Trail
2400'
Kelly Lake
1840'
Wagon
Center Flats Road
Road

PALASSOU RIDGE
Gilroy Hot Springs Private
Timms Spring Trail
Road
940'
Grizzly
Dexter Trail
Grizzly Gulch
Gulch
Road
2286'
Gulch Trail
Wagon Road
Cañada de la Dormida

Spike Jones Trail
Steer Ridge
Willson Peak
2551'
Serpentine Trail
Tule Pond
Vasquez Rd
Rock Springs Peak 2300'

COYOTE HOT SPRINGS RD
Steer Ridge Trail
Middle Steer Ridge Trail
The Bowl Road
Road
Trail
Willson Camp
2210'
Vasquez Peak

856'
Lyman
Willson Ridge
Coon Hunters Gulch
Road
Long Dam Trail

to Gilroy
CAÑADA ROAD
PHEGLEY 2208'
Redfern Pond
RIDGE

Orestimba Wilderness
Henry W. Coe State Park
Hunting Hollow
Wasno
1140'

0   0.5 Mile
0   0.5 Kilometer

Henry W. Coe State Park (Southern Area)

◆ Henry W. Coe State Park ◆

Rising to over 3500' on the southeastern flank of the Santa Clara Valley, this wild, undeveloped region is California's largest mountain state park. Its more than 87,000 acres of ridges, deep canyons, upland meadows and flowing streams beckon the ambitious visitor to days of long hikes and rides or a week's extended backpacking trip through nearly untrammeled wilderness.

The original park of 13,000 acres was a gift of Sada Coe Robinson to Santa Clara County in 1953. Subsequent additions of several cattle ranches brought the size of the park to over 81,000 acres. Following the acquisition of these ranches, the California State Parks Department reclassified a large area of Henry W. Coe State Park as the Orestimba Wilderness. In the park's southwest corner recent acquisitions provide access to lands in the Gilroy Hot Springs area.

The park is open all year, although spring and fall are the most popular visiting periods. Temperatures can drop below freezing in winter, and summer maxima reach well above 90°. However, the variety of terrain provides opportunities to enjoy the park in any season. Sunny, south-facing slopes offer warm pockets in winter, and shady stream canyons are cool in the heat of summer.

Tens of thousands of people visit this vast and challenging park every year. Whether you hike to Sada's Spring in the northwest section of the park or climb to the monument honoring Sada's father, you can enjoy the beautiful setting of her ranch. Later acquisitions multiplied and extended her gift to the people many times.

History

The Ohlone Indians were the first inhabitants of the lands that now make up the western part of Henry W. Coe State Park. They made their homes on several sites near year-round streams where fish were plentiful. Acorns, the staple of their diet, were supplemented by berries, nuts, deer and an abundant supply of small animals. Recent research indicates that the Northern Valley Yokuts, a tall, light-complexioned, peaceful tribe, came to the eastern areas of the park (now the wilderness area) from their villages in the San Joaquin Valley. (Please note that all archeological artifacts are protected and should be left undisturbed. Visitors should report any such finds to a ranger.)

During the westward movement of the mid-1800s, among the many pioneers settling in the South Bay was Henry W. Coe, Sr., who bought a 500-acre ranch in the San Felipe Valley, north of today's park. In the 1880s Henry Coe's sons, Henry Jr. and Charles, homesteaded lands in this vicinity. By the early 1900s Henry Jr. had purchased the Pine Ridge Ranch and built a house there. He married Rhoda Sutcliffe in 1905, and they lived at the ranch with their two children, Henry S. and Sada Sutcliffe Coe, until 1913. Many years later Sada and her husband, Oscar Robinson, managed the ranch. At the death of Sada's father in 1943, it was sold to a cattle company. But Sada bought it back in 1947 and ran cattle there herself until she gave the ranch to Santa Clara County in 1953.

Sada Coe wanted to preserve the ranch from development and to give others the opportunity to experience the peace and tranquillity of its remote location. She dedicated it ". . . as a living memorial to those great and sturdy pioneers" of early California, as she wrote in *My Log from the Hearth*. Santa Clara County held the ranch until 1958, when the State of California took it over.

Sada Coe Robinson lived until 1979, 26 years after her generous gift of Pine Ridge Ranch to the people. During these years she followed the development of the park as the campgrounds and some trails were built. In 1971 Sada gave money to construct the museum, donating many of her family's furnishings as well. A collection of antique carriages is housed in one of her barns.

Natural Resources

This outstanding park provides a remarkable diversity of plant and animal life. With almost every ecological zone of the Coast Range represented, one can find all the usual plants of oak woodlands, grasslands, coniferous forests and riparian communities. Fields of wildflowers are spectacular in spring throughout the park, but there are exceptional displays on Pine Ridge near the monument, in Miller Field and in many remote wilderness areas. Giant manzanitas tower over trails, and stands of ponderosa pine give the park's western ridge its name.

The Pine Ridge Association volunteers and park rangers lead wildflower walks in the spring to the season's best displays. Saturday evening programs in spring and early summer highlight biological and natural features of the park. A stop at the charming farmhouse Visitor Center at park headquarters offers a glimpse of the region's cultural and natural history. Call the park office or write for the schedule of activities.

Seldom seen, but known to be inhabitants of the park, are mountain lions, bobcats, and wild boar. Golden eagles and red-tailed hawks patrol the skies. There is an abundant animal population of deer, fox, rabbit, squirrel, and many small rodents.

Geology

Coe Park presents an excellent cross section of the Diablo Range, stretching from the eastern foothills of the Santa Clara Valley to the low-lying hills and valleys west of the San Joaquin Valley. The mountains consist largely of Franciscan Formation rocks, a jumble of rocks that accumulated as the Pacific Plate slid under the North American Plate some 90 million years ago.

The southeast part of the park contains some of the largest blue schist blocks found in California. Compared with the surrounding sediments, crystalline blue schist is resistant to erosion. Consequently, isolated blocks of this schist stand out prominently on hillsides. In Coe Park some are as large as a half mile across. The park visitor can see some examples of well-preserved marine sediments in the chert layers on road-cuts near the park headquarters and on top of the Rooster Comb in the Orestimba Wilderness. With a hand lens one can see the tiny marine fossils whose shells make up this rock.

Most creeks in Coe Park run northwest-southeast, following the general trend of earthquake faults in California. Soda Springs Creek, following this alignment, runs through the canyon that contains the Madrone Springs Fault.

Trails in Coe Park

Within the original Coe Park area are some 40 miles of hiking and riding trails. These trails climb ridges to mountaintop views and descend to wooded canyons and secluded campsites beside streams. In the entire park there are 175 miles of trail, including many miles to explore in the remote, 23,000-acre wilderness. The southwestern area of the park lies on the east side of Coyote Creek and offers access to the most recently acquired ranch lands. Its two entrances, Coyote Creek and Hunting Hollow, are at lower elevations, thus offering immediate uphill challenges

Springs Trail, heading toward Visitor Center

to day hikers and backpackers. Here are grand views of the southern Diablo Range, new campsites, and opportunities to reach previously untrammeled regions.

Most of the park trails are old ranch roads, today used only by patrol vehicles and the few people with private inholdings in the park. These ranch roads are open to hikers, equestrians and bicyclists, but some trails are designated exclusively for hikers. Only hikers and equestrians are allowed in the Orestimba Wilderness. Trails that follow or cross creeks may be impassable just after heavy rains. Consult the ranger and park maps for an alternative route at these times.

Spring and fall are the best times for trips in this park, when the weather is usually cool and the skies clear. California's mild winters can also offer periods of excellent hiking or riding weather. The authors have even had pleasantly cool hiking in Henry Coe Park on summer days, but it is well to remember that on hot-weather backpack trips, you should plan to do the long uphill stretches in the early morning and reach your campsite by midday.

Although running streams and springs are found throughout the park, the water supply is undependable and may not meet state drinking water standards—so following the trails in Coe Park requires that you carry plenty of water or the means to purify the park's spring and stream water. Even though each campsite is located by a spring or flowing creek, most of the streams dry up in summer and many springs stop flowing. Therefore, you should carry water—at least a quart of water per person per day is recommended, more in hot weather.

The climbs up rugged ridges and descents into steep canyons present physical challenges that the user must recognize. The extra time required for such elevation gains is reflected in the time suggested for hikers on each trip.

Maps of Coe Park are available at the Visitor Center at park headquarters. A large-format map, covering the entire park, designates all the trails in the park's three main areas: (1) the Coe Ranch section from park headquarters, (2) the lands in the park's southwest corner, and (3) the Orestimba Wilderness. Most trails are open to all users; those with restrictions are clearly indicated on the map. New signs on the trails are keyed to this map. Designated campsites in the western area and those suggested in the southwest and wilderness areas are shown as well as the location of springs. In addition, there are a number of books and brochures about the park, including The Pine Ridge Association's *Trails of Henry W. Coe State Park*, by Winslow R. Briggs, and *South Bay Trails*.

Trips from the Coe Ranch Headquarters—Western Area

This guide details six trips from the park headquarters—short walks of about a mile up to the Henry Coe memorial monument and out over the gentle meadows to flowing springs. Beyond are trips of a few miles and one as long as 17 miles. Two other trips from the Manzanita Point Group Area save campers the 5.2-mile roundtrip from headquarters. Three loop trips from the Coyote Creek and Hunting Hollow entrances reach Kelly and Coit lakes and Redfern Pond and remarkable spring flower displays.

Backpack trips to outlying camps from park headquarters enable the hiker to explore the far reaches of the park's original area. All overnight park users must have a permit from the ranger and must get current information on routes and their seasonal limitations.

Climbing up rugged ridges and descents into steep canyons presents physical challenges. The extra time required for such elevation gains is reflected in the time suggested for hikers on each trip.

The Southwest Corner—From Coyote Creek and Hunting Hollow entrances—The Lakes Area

South and east of the headquarters area are three lakes, Coit, Mississippi, and Kelly, fine destinations for long and demanding hikes, and backpacking, equestrian, and bicycle trips. The north fork of Pacheco Creek drains most of this section of the park, fed by Mississippi, Coon, and other minor creeks. Along Pacheco Creek are some steep canyons and a spectacular but remote waterfall in rugged terrain. Between Coyote and Kelly Cabin Canyon creeks is the long slope of Mahoney Meadows with its high grasslands and oak savanna. Higher ridges covered with blue oak and live oak separate creeks to the north. Along streams are denser stands of bay, live oak, and sycamore trees. Gray pines and blue oaks are found on the dry, steeper slopes, and chaparral thrives on the dry, hot south- and west-facing ridges.

The Orestimba Wilderness

This area of relatively undeveloped land has retained its primeval character without permanent improvements or human habitation, other than a few structures that pre-date acquisition. This wilderness, affected primarily by the forces of nature, has outstanding opportunities for solitude and exploration. It contains natural features of scientific, educational, scenic, and historical value.

Steep ridges, high peaks, some broad flats, and wide gravel washes characterize much of this wilderness. Gray pines and blue oaks cover the hills, while grassland on the long Paradise Flat is dotted with magnificent oaks. Sycamore, live oak, willow, and bay trees flourish by the South Fork of Orestimba Creek and its tributaries, Red and Robinson creeks.

Ridgetop trips reward the visitor with immense vistas south to the Pacheco Pass peaks and west to Monterey Bay and its nearby mountains. The adventurous equestrian or intrepid backpacker who reaches the park's northern heights can look down into the wide San Antonio Valley and up to Mt. Hamilton.

Not included in the wilderness area is a vehicle access to Coe Park from Bell Station on the Pacheco Pass Highway (152), which may some day be an entrance to the vast backcountry and the Orestimba Wilderness. Bell Station was an important center of large cattle ranch operations in this part of the Diablo Range. The road from Bell Station follows a 6-mile, State-owned corridor through private property to the Dowdy Ranch. This former cattle ranch may some day provide a trailhead and staging area for trips into areas north and west. Beyond this ranch is a 6-mile dirt road to Orestimba Corral, where trailhead parking may provide access for day and overnight use by hikers and equestrians.

Each year on the last weekend in April the Pine Ridge Association offers the Coe Backcountry Weekend, an opportunity for a limited number of visitors to spend one or two days in this area. Lucky participants are chosen by lottery from applications submitted in March. Flyers and forms are available at sporting goods, equestrian, and bicycle shops, the Pine Ridge Association, and from the website listed in Appendix B.

From the Dowdy Ranch and the Orestimba Corral extends a network of unimproved roads, some now overgrown, that serve as trails along creek valleys and over ridges. The wilderness area just north of the corral is open to hikers, backpackers, and equestrians with permits, who have access to unimproved campsites. No bicycles are allowed in the wilderness area.

Camping and Backpacking in the Park

Coe Park offers many opportunities for camping: some for car campers, near the park headquarters on Pine Ridge. Each has a barbecue and picnic table; some have sun shelters. Water and latrines are nearby. Others, popular with youth and church groups, are the 10 group sites at Manzanita Point. Campers must walk the 2.5 miles in to the site, but one vehicle for each group may drive in with supplies and water and as a stand-by for emergencies.

Backpack camps scattered throughout the park in scenic places near water have one to five campsites each with fairly level bedsites. There are no prepared fire rings; in fact, fires are not allowed at backpacking sites, although you can carry a backpack stove, if you have a permit from the park office. The camps are no more than a day's hike apart and visiting a combination of these can make an extended trip of several days.

Equestrians can camp behind the ranch headquarters, and at several horse camps a day's ride from the park entrances. Camps lie north of Schafer Corral on the East Fork, along Mississippi Creek south of the lake, at Coit Lake, and at Coit Camp on Coit Road in the southwestern section of the park. One of the Manzanita Point camping areas, Blue Oak, can be used by equestrian groups. Equestrians may also camp in the Orestimba Wilderness.

Whether you plan an extensive backpack trip or just an overnight in one of the backpack camps, you must check in with the ranger to get a permit, pay fees, and obtain a campsite assignment. Day hikers and equestrians must also pay fees and check in with the ranger. For your safety the park staff should know your destination and estimated return time. No camping is allowed within 0.5 mile of the Coyote Creek or Hunting Hollow entrances.

Jurisdiction: State of California.

Facilities: Headquarters and Visitor Center. Trails: More than 175 miles; hiking, equestrian, bicycling, (more than 40 miles in area covered by this book.) Horse-trailer parking. Family picnic area. Camping: 18 backpack; 20 family drive-in; group camps—10 hike-in, by reservation; 5 horsemen's camps. Fishing under regulations of State Fish and Game. Handicapped access to one campsite. Headquarters family drive-in campsites may be reserved by calling 1-800-444-7275.

Park Rules: Hours: Open daily throughout the year. No open fires, except at headquarters camps and those designated in Manzanita Point Group Camps. Bicycles allowed on dirt roads and some trails, but not in the Orestimba Wilderness. Dogs not allowed on trails or roads; on leash in headquarters area only. Vehicle, campsite, backpack, dog fees charged year-round. Overnight campers must check in with ranger to get a permit. Phone: 408-779-2728.

Maps: State of California *Henry W. Coe State Park*; USGS quads *Gilroy Hot Springs, Mississippi Creek, Mt. Sizer, Mt. Stakes, Mustang Peak, Pacheco Peak,* and *Wilcox Ridge.*

How To Get There: *1. Coe Headquarters:* From Hwy. 101 near Morgan Hill take East Dunne Ave. for 13 miles to park entrance. *2. Southwest area—Coyote Creek and Hunting Hollow entrances:* From Hwy. 101 north of Gilroy and south of the main Coe State Park road—East Dunne Ave.—take Leavesley Rd. east about 1 mile to New Rd. and turn left (north.) Turn right (east) onto Roop Rd., which then becomes Gilroy Hot Springs Rd., and continue east beside Coyote Creek passing Coyote Creek County Park Rd. on the left. After the pavement gives way to gravel you reach the large Hunting Hollow parking lot on your right where you pay your State Park fee at the kiosk and register for overnight camping (if already reserved—see above.)

Henry W. Coe State Park
Lion Spring Jaunt

*A short, fairly level walk from the park office on the south side of
Pine Ridge visits a cool retreat—a delightful, fairly level trip for
a family picnic.*

Distance: 2.4 miles round trip

Time: 1+ hour

Elevation Gain: 480'

Trail Notes

When you leave the Visitor Center, cross the road near the stop sign
and enter the trail next to the cattle-loading chute. Take the hikers-only
Corral Trail going left, downhill, into a little ravine below the barn. In and
out of oak-wooded ravines, this trail gently contours along the hillside
where chaparral grows on the drier, south-facing slopes.

In 0.6 mile you come out into a tree-studded grassland, or savanna,
where tall oats, green and lush in spring and golden brown in summer,
provide food and shelter for small animals, which in turn, are food for
hawks, coyotes, and owls. Here is the junction where the Springs Trail
veers right and the Forest, Fish, and Flat Frog trails go left (north) just
across Manzanita Point Road.

You take the Springs Trail and follow it 0.3 mile through the area called
Arnold Field, where O. Arnold homesteaded in the 1870s and planted an
apple orchard. After 0.3 mile through shade of scattered gray pines and
oaks, look for a trail on the right which descends on a good grade down
to the Lion Spring campsite. If no one is occupying the site, you might
have your lunch at the table under the trees.

But first circle around the outcrop of big gray boulders to find Lion
Spring, originally developed to water the Coe Ranch cattle. Many years
ago its cool shade lured the ranch children here to spend hot summer
afternoons. Legend has it that sometimes they saw a lion crouching on the
shadowy ledge above the spring. Today, only a lucky and very observant
visitor would ever see a mountain lion in the park, although it is a known
inhabitant. This beautiful, shy creature is much too wary of humans, so
enjoy the children's retreat without trepidation.

Returning to the Springs Trail, you turn sharp left (west) and take the
Corral Trail back to your starting point. (See Trip 2, page 86 for a loop to
some more of the park's 100 springs.)

Henry W. Coe State Park
CIRCLE HIKE ALONG THE SPRINGS AND FOREST TRAILS

Another level hike visits the south and north sides of Pine Ridge.

Distance: 3.6-mile loop

Elevation Change: Relatively level, 80′ loss and gain

Time: 2 hours

Trail Notes

Begin this hike as in Trip 1, continuing past the Lion Springs turnoff on the Springs Trail. Although most of the springs are not marked, in spring and early summer you will cross their seeps along this trail. If you pause beside a moist area and listen carefully, you will hear, and perhaps see, the many birds who come to sip. Other creatures that inhabit this side of the ridge visit this spring, as you can tell by the tracks in the damp earth.

About half way along the Springs Trail you make a sharp bend into the head of a ravine under a canopy of beautiful, spreading oak trees. In wet years you can hear the sound of a merry stream below the trail, which is probably spring-fed.

After 1.9 miles you emerge on the wide Manzanita Point Road, cross it and the Poverty Flat Road, and pick up the well-signed Forest Trail. Heading west on this beautiful trail you contour through oak, bay, and madrone woods on the northeast side of Pine Ridge. In spring the wild-flowers will delight you with blossoms of every color. Early spring brings the deep red of Indian Warriors, a bit later mauve, three-petaled trillium peek out from moist hollows, and later larkspur and lupine appear in many shades of blue.

This is a perfect trail for a hot afternoon and for an exploration of the huge moss-covered boulders found along the way. Their intriguing shapes and great size are a source of wonder as you wend your way along this slope. When you leave the forest and round a bend to the south, you can see the wide Manzanita Point Road ahead, which you cross to reach the Corral Trail where you left it 2.4 miles earlier. Now you have a gentle return to the Visitor Center and its interesting displays.

Henry W. Coe State Park
A SHORT CLIMB TO HENRY W. COE'S MONUMENT

The spectacular views are worth the trip up Pine Ridge.

Distance: 1-mile round trip

Time: 1 hour

Elevation Gain: 640'

Trail Notes

When you leave the Visitor Center, go back up the entrance road 300' and take the gated road uphill for 0.1 mile. On your left is the well-marked, hikers-only Monument Trail, that goes up the grassy hillside. Equestrians and bicyclists can take the park road to the monument. Although the way is steep, a glade of oaks soon gives some shade. Deep blue lupines stand out in the grass, and drifts of shiny, yellow-petaled buttercups grace the shady places in spring. Even in fall the fields of golden oats are brightened with lavender asters and the purple spikes of vinegar curls.

After a couple of switchbacks the trail climbs straight up the south-facing ridge. (Do this early on a hot day.) You veer a bit to the right as you round a little ravine, and then gain a final 80' to a trail junction, just 0.3 mile from the park road. Here you detour 600' east and cross the ranch road to reach the monument to Sada Coe's father, Henry W. Coe, Jr. This monument is surmounted by some of the tallest ponderosa pines in the park, landmarks that are identifiable from other high points in the park and even from some places in the Santa Clara Valley.

Take the time to pause here on Pine Ridge among the towering ponderosa pines that give the ridge its name. These trees have grown to stately proportions—a little biological island found in only a few places outside their usual habitat, the Sierra Nevada.

The sounds of the wind in the pines and the birds singing give one the feeling of calm and peace that Sada Coe described in stories based on her life on this ranch. "Slowly the peace of the hills crept into her heart," she wrote in *My Log from the Hearth*.

Returning to the Monument Trail junction, you can take another little path west a few yards to Eric's Bench, a memorial to a young man who loved these mountains. When you have enjoyed the views and the stillness of the scene, go back to the main trail and wend your way down to the Visitor Center.

Henry W. Coe State Park
LOOP TRIP TO MIDDLE RIDGE VIA FROG LAKE

A good stiff climb on the outbound trip takes you to ridges capped with pines and tall manzanitas followed by a trip through a pretty valley.

Distance: 7.8-mile loop

Time: 4½ hours

Elevation Gain: 1400'

Trail Notes

Leave the Visitor Center on the Corral Trail as in Trip 1. At the first junction go across Manzanita Point Road to the Fish/Forest Trail junction, and almost immediately turn off left (northeast) on the Flat Frog Trail. This trail contours 2.3 miles along the east-facing hillside on a grade that surely befits its name.

After crossing the several tributaries of the Little Fork and then the main stem, you reach the marshy shores of Frog Lake, a little green reservoir, ringed with reeds, and a peaceful destination offering good picnic places under the trees. If you take time to explore the lakeside, the creatures for whom the lake is named may treat you to an unexpected leap into the water—or perhaps give you a croaking chorus when all is quiet.

After exploring the lakeside, take the 0.9-mile Frog Lake Trail ascent to Middle Ridge. A generous scattering of black oaks gives you shade on the way up the steep trail. Once you reach the ridgetop, you meet the Middle Ridge Trail, for hikers and, except after rain, for bicyclists. Turn to the right (southeast), traverse a grassy meadow and descend gently to a saddle before climbing again to 2700'. On this rise you enter an amazing stand of large, spreading manzanitas. Their shining mahogany-red trunks support a broad canopy of leaves that casts a deep shadow. On a still day you can hear the faint rustle of the little papery curls of bark peeling from the trunks and falling to carpet the ground. Here and there straight trunks of ponderosas pine trees grow up through the manzanita. From your vantage point on Middle Ridge you see northeast to 3000' Blue Ridge, which cuts diagonally northwest-southeast through the park for about 7 miles.

Then on a gradual descent along the ridge you arrive at the Fish Trail, for hikers only, and turn right (southwest.) (Bicyclists continue to Poverty Flat and follow the road back to headquarters.) Hikers make a couple of switchbacks down the south slope through chaparral and mixed woodland to cross the Little Fork once again. In 0.6 mile you are down at the boulder-strewn creekbed, usually dry in summer, but after heavy rains you may have to hop across on rocks or take off your shoes and wade.

Now the Fish Trail makes a few switchbacks through the woods and you soon arrive at a small, open, grassy valley. In summer and fall the magnificent specimens of valley oak here stand out darkly against the pale gold grass. In spring the new leaves unfolding on gnarled, bare branches shine light-green in the sun, and deep-blue heads of tall brodiaea wave above the emerging oats.

The trail bends around the hillside to enter a tight, shady little canyon and emerges on the open savanna of Pine Ridge, 1.3 miles from the creek. Across the Manzanita Point Road you pick up the Corral Trail going west, and wind through the woods back to your starting point.

Henry W. Coe State Park
POVERTY FLAT CIRCLE HIKE VIA MIDDLE RIDGE

This trip follows the route of Trip 4 as far as the Flat Frog Trail junction, then climbs up the Fish Trail to continue southeast down Middle Ridge (for hikers and bicyclists only) through its shady north-slope woods to the confluence of the two forks of Coyote Creek near Poverty Flat.

Distance: 9.3-mile loop

Time: 6 or 7 hours

Elevation Gain: 2280'

Trail Notes

From headquarters this is a full day's hike or an easy 2-day backpack trip. Follow the directions for Trip 4 to the Flat Frog Trail, but there take the Fish Trail up to Middle Ridge, reversing the descent on this trail described in Trip 4.

At the Middle Ridge junction, turn right (southeast) and follow this trail along the sloping plateau, at first through the shade of a dense growth of huge manzanitas. Then the narrow path emerges onto grasslands punctuated by occasional blue oaks and ponderosa pines. When the grassy area widens, you meander through a magnificent, broad, undulating savanna, with immense, widely spaced valley oaks and some blue oaks riddled with woodpecker holes.

As the trail slopes down on the south side of the broad ridge, you see across the canyon of the Little Fork to Pine Ridge. You can pick out the main ranch road winding up through the rugged woodlands of the ridge's north-facing slope, where this trip will eventually take you.

About a mile from the Fish Trail junction, the trail turns northeast, crosses the ridge, dips into a few ravines, and then drops down the north side. Here the forest deepens, and trees of many species crowd the steep slopes—madrones, tall ponderosa pines and gray pines, blue and black oaks interspersed with a few canyon oaks. Toyon, manzanita and poison oak fill the understory. Since the discontinuance of cattle grazing, the native bunchgrass is flourishing on this hillside.

The authors felt truly remote from civilization here. The only noises were the calls of many birds and the splashing of the creek in the canyon below. When a 2-foot-long animal (perhaps a fox) silently crossed the trail ahead of us, we sensed we were privileged humans in this wilderness.

On many switchbacks you continue east and down the steep slope for more than a mile. After 7.6 miles into your trip, you arrive at the confluence of the two forks of Coyote Creek at the foot of a narrow peninsula between them. Sunlight filters through the trees, and patterns of light dance on the waters of grass-edged pools.

If you are going to the Poverty Flat backpack camp, you will find the first site under the oaks on the broad flat just across the stream. Hop across on the rocks—no bridge here. At high water you may have to wade through the chilly stream.

If you are going back to headquarters, walk about 0.25 mile past the first campsite, then cross the creek at the ford (or wherever you can make it over the rocks) and pick up the ranch road, the Poverty Flat Road, going west, uphill. After two very steep climbs on a zig-zag route of slightly less than 2 miles and an elevation gain of 1200', you reach the open meadows on Pine Ridge. The spring flowers of the woodlands—white milkmaids, shooting stars, blue iris and pink-blossomed currant—bloom beside the trail. Scarlet flowers of the California fuchsia stand out on open road cuts late in the year. The authors found a striped racer snake sunning its 18 inches on the warm, dusty road.

At the Poverty Flat/Manzanita Point roads junction, the Springs and Forest trails leave the park road and branch out to the west and east sides of Pine Ridge. If the day is hot, take the shaded Forest Trail—the Springs Trail is sunnier, especially in the afternoon.

If you wonder what birds you saw perched in the trees beside the trail, stop in at the Visitor Center when you get back to headquarters and look over the many helpful pamphlets and books. The knowledgeable ranger or one of the trained volunteers will answer your questions or tell you where to look for the information.

6

Henry W. Coe State Park
THE BIG LOOP

From the heights of Blue Ridge to the cool waters of East Fork Coyote Creek, this hike samples most of the unique terrain of Sada Coe's original park gift. It is a very strenuous, long day's hike or a good weekend backpack trip.

Distance: 14.2-mile loop from headquarters over Jackass Trail cut-off; 17.1-mile entire loop.

Time: 10-12 hours; 2-day vigorous backpack trip.

Elevation Gain: 3940'

Trail Notes

Leave the park office as in Trip 2, and take the Flat Frog Trail toward Frog Lake. At the lake, drop down to the wide Hobbs Road and continue on it up Middle Ridge. Through oak woodlands this road then heads northwest and rounds a bend to reach Deer Horn Spring on the right—one of the park's many springs. Its waters are piped into a large trough, beside which a sign warns to purify before drinking this water. During the heat of a summer's day, the flow often stops, perhaps because of the high rate of transpiration from the trees, and then resumes in the evening.

Here too is the site of the Widow Hobbs' cabin, the intrepid woman for whom the road is named. The only remaining signs of her residence are the chimney stones and an apricot tree struggling to survive. In good years it bears fruit, enjoyed mostly by birds. Here you will find three campsites for today's adventurers. Whether you stop for the night or just for a moment in the shade of the big black oaks, you can enjoy the view across to the south face of Blue Ridge. Its grassy flats and chaparral-covered slopes do not look blue. From Henry Coe's first homesite north of the ridge, however, the heavier woods, blue oaks and manzanita on the north slope do in fact look blue—hence its name.

Continuing downhill the road switchbacks several times during its 600' descent toward the Middle Fork of Coyote Creek. In less than a mile you come to a right turnoff that leads to the Skeel's Meadow camps. In a grassy opening above the creek are three campsites, some of the choicest in the park. The year-round waters of the lovely Middle Fork form small pools. Bright green sedge grass edges pools between the rocks, giving a Japanese garden effect. If you made an early start from the park headquarters, this creekside will be a delightful place for lunch. Ringed by maples, oaks, and buckeyes, this appealing site drew Indians long before campers. Here and there on large boulders by the creek are grinding holes where they ground acorns into meal.

Middle Fork of Coyote Creek

Retrace your steps to the main trail and in a few hundred feet come to the left turnoff for Upper Camp. Big sycamores twine their roots around the boulders in the creek, and several little waterfalls splash into big pools, one large enough for swimming. Both Skeel's and Upper Camp by the Middle Fork of Coyote Creek are inviting enough for a few days' stopover for relaxing and exploring. Originating northeast of the park boundary, the Middle Fork swings around the northwest corner of the park and flows between Middle Ridge and Blue Ridge. At Poverty Flat the Middle Fork joins the Little Fork, and they continue down to the confluence with the East Fork at China Hole.

Along the creek banks or in the water, you might see a common amphibious snake, the California aquatic garter snake. You have to look carefully for it, as the single yellow stripe running the length of its dark back gives the snake the appearance of a twig lying on the rocks or floating in the water.

The next part of the trip on Hobbs Road takes you up a very steep mountainside on Short-Cut Road—something of a misnomer, as it is the only way to reach the crest of Blue Ridge, where you turn right. You will certainly want to make this 1.3-mile, steady 1500' climb while the day is young and you are fresh.

Your reward for this strenuous stretch lies at the top of Blue Ridge, crowned with a magnificent forest and open for sweeping views. On very clear days you can see the Sierra Nevada peaks, sometimes even identifying Half Dome. Pause awhile under the shade of a black oak or one of the fine specimens of ponderosa pines scattered along the ridge. This is a good vantage point from which to watch for golden eagles. You may see an eagle soaring on its 8' wingspread high above the ridge make a stunning dive of thousands of feet into the canyon. Also look for eagles perched in the top branches of a dead tree.

The Blue Ridge Road continues southeast, rising slightly for about a mile toward 3216' Mt. Sizer, near the north park boundary. Looking back northwest, you can see Mt. Hamilton. At the east boundary of the park is Mustang Peak, and beyond lie the peaks near Pacheco Pass. This remarkable country, relatively untouched by man's activities, is yours to explore. Notes from De Anza's diarist Pedro Font, exploring here two centuries ago, tell us that "on the ridges and at intervals there are seen strips and stretches of very white gravel." You too, can see them shining in the north.

A scattered canopy of large trees gives the impression of walking down a shady sky-lane with ridge after ridge of mountains falling away on every side. In less than a mile you pass the trail to Black Oak Spring on the left. This trail takes you to a backpack camp, just 0.5 mile down the mountainside. As a second-night stop on the Big Loop, this camp, considered an optional site with water at least half the year, makes a good base for exploring Hat Rock and Rock House Ridge farther east. You will find spectacular wildflowers here in the spring.

If you decide to investigate the Hat Rock area, consider that the trail to it and down Rock House Ridge may be overgrown and the route difficult to follow. Descending gradually southeast for 2.5 miles, it stays on the exposed ridgecrest most of the way. After you drop down into the canyon of the East Fork of Coyote Creek, you turn south and follow the fork downstream to Los Cruzeros.

Eschewing the Black Oak Spring alternate and staying on the Blue Ridge Trail for 1.3 mile more, you meet the Jackass Trail on the right, which offers a 5.2-mile shorter version of this trip, bringing you to the Poverty Flat Road, near Jackass Peak. There you turn west to Poverty Flat and follow the road of that name back to the park headquarters. This cutoff eliminates the Narrows-to-China Hole section, described later, which is impassable after storms.

To continue on the longer trip, stay on Blue Ridge Road past upper Poverty Flat Road, descending gradually in light shade for 1.8 miles to Miller Field. Named for a former cattle baron whose herds once grazed here, these grasslands are now noted for a spectacular display of spring wildflowers. (Note for early season and years of heavy rainfall—take the Poverty Flat Road, thus avoiding the likelihood of impassable East Fork and Narrows routes.)

The canyon of East Fork Coyote Creek lies below, and Blue Ridge Road drops quickly to meet it. Here you leave the road, which arcs north to Bear Mountain and the Orestimba Wilderness. However, you follow the creek downstream (south) in a wide, gravely wash, wherever you can find a good path. Passing Arnold Camp, a horsemen's campsite, and then

Mahoney Meadows Road to Jackass Peak on your right, you continue down the arroyo to Los Cruzeros. In April of 1776, when Juan Bautista de Anza and his men came from the San Antonio Valley along this creek, they named it "Arroyo del Coyote." At this point they crossed the creek—hence, perhaps, its name, "the crossing." (Literally, *los cruzeros* means "the crossbearers.") The backpack campsite at Los Cruzeros was marked with a plaque in 1976 honoring the 200th anniversary of de Anza's trip, which was missing when the authors hiked there.

The easiest way for hikers to return to park headquarters is to follow the creek route through The Narrows to China Hole. (This route, however, is impassable after storms.) Then climb to Manzanita Point on the China Hole Trail and take Manzanita Point Road till the turnoff for either the Forest or the Springs Trail, both of which join the Corral Trail and return to headquarters. Bicyclists and equestrians take the Manzanita Point Road all the way to headquarters.

Two Trips from Manzanita Point Group Area

For campers at Manzanita Point trips 7 and 8 will save the 5.2-mile round trip from headquarters.

Henry W. Coe State Park

LOOP TRIP FROM MANZANITA POINT TO POVERTY FLAT

This trip, for hikers only, features over 2 miles of shady stream-side trails, with a stop for lunch and swimming at China Hole, and a steep climb back from Poverty Flat through a forest of oaks, bays and manzanitas.

Distance: 5-mile loop

Time: 3½ hours

Elevation Gain: 1160′

Trail Notes

This trip is described starting down the Madrone Springs Trail from Manzanita Point (which is 2.6 miles from headquarters), because criss-crossing up this south-facing slope can be hot in late afternoon. On a cold spring day, however, you might enjoy climbing back to Manzanita Point with the warmth of the sun on your back. In winter or early spring, high water makes this trail impassable; be sure to check with the ranger.

The trail takes off to the right from the main road through the Manzanita Point Group Area, just opposite Camp 7. At first it goes through rolling grasslands marked by brilliant displays of wildflowers in the spring, including tall, purple Ithuriel's spear and deep orange poppies. Here and there are clumps of madrones and live oaks that offer shade to hikers zig-zagging down the nose of this ridge.

In half an hour you can be at Soda Springs Creek, the site of one of the park's backpack camps—Madrone Soda Springs. Cross the creek and explore the wide flat where Indians once lived. In 1879 Dr. Clinton Munson and Marshall Hunter bought Madrone Soda Springs and built a hotel offering the inducement of the springs' special healing properties. In 1881, at the height of the resort's popularity, a stage made four runs a week here from Madrone (Morgan Hill.) A wagon road led from the hotel up Soda Springs Canyon and then climbed the 1000' ridge on the southwest side of the creek.

Madrone Soda Springs was later operated as a hunting resort and was used into the 1940s. Except for a small rock house on the north side of the creek, not a trace of the old resort remains today. On this flat are two backpack sites, although the authors found too much yellow star thistle for comfortable late spring and summer camping here.

After exploring the area, cross the creek again and note the low rock house, possibly a stage stop, then head downstream on the "Mile Trail" to the junction of Soda Springs and Coyote creeks. This trail, for hikers only, goes through a narrow canyon, crossing the creek many times. It usually stays close to the water's edge among shade-loving plants—snowberry, mint and ocean spray—sheltered by evergreen bay trees and deciduous big-leaf maples and black oaks.

About one-third of the way down the trail you come to an abandoned, tumble-down cabin tilted out over the creek. Although trespassing is forbidden and completely unsafe, you can imagine how pleasant it was to live here with the sounds of water flowing over the rocks and with the deep shade of trees in summer. Continuing downstream, the trail follows the creek, crossing it several more times. In spring, new shoots of ferns uncurl their light-green fronds, and columbine, star flower, trillium, and woodland star thrive in this damp canyon. In fall the golden maple and ubiquitous red poison-oak leaves stand out against the dark green of bays and oaks, and the California fuchsia adds its scarlet touch to the rocky banks.

Emerging from this woodsy canyon, Soda Springs Creek flows into the wide streambed of Coyote Creek. You turn left, upstream, staying on this side of the creek for 0.3 mile. At China Hole deep pools and rocky beaches invite you to stop for a swim. On the far side of the creek you will find the China Hole backpack camp in the shelter of big boulders, a popular goal of weekend pack trips.

Continue upstream a few yards to the confluence of the Middle and East forks of Coyote Creek. Here you look right into the steep-sided canyon of the East Fork, aptly named "The Narrows." But your route, except when impassable after storms, lies north along the Middle Fork, following the stream to Poverty Flat. You may have to do some rockhopping or wading in the creek.

In less than ½ hour you clamber over big boulders to Poverty Flat Road, which comes in from the east side of the park. Follow this road west to broad Poverty Flat with backpack campsites under oaks and sycamores, an inviting base from which to explore this part of the park. You can understand why one of the park's largest Indian settlements was in this pleasant flat, which had water, abundant fish and game, and plentiful fruits and berries nearby. And you can sympathize with the reluctance of the homesteader who resisted Henry Coe's efforts to buy him out.

To return to your campground at Manzanita Point, cross the creek and zig-zag up the steep Cougar Trail under cover of handsome oak and bay trees, appropriate for the afternoon of a hot day. Former cattle fences were cut to let the trail go through, but no cattle have grazed here since the state took over these 13,000 acres for a park in 1958.

In 0.7 mile, at the China Hole Trail junction, you bear right along the spine of Manzanita Point through the chaparral and manzanita forest. Deep mahogany-red branches of the large manzanitas fanning out to leafy, rounded crowns of gray-green contrast sharply with the nearly white lichen frosting the branches.

After 0.9 mile on this trail a spur takes off left to Manzanita Point Camps 8, 9, and 10. Soon your trail levels out and enters the clearing at Camp 7. Nearby are Camps 4, 5, and 6. Return to your campsite and enjoy the views over the canyons of Coyote and Soda Springs creeks that you have just trod.

Henry W. Coe State Park
LOOP TRIP TO MAHONEY MEADOWS

A vigorous trip from Manzanita Point takes you to China Hole, out to the high, oak-dotted grasslands of Mahoney Meadows in the eastern sections of the old Coe Ranch, and back through The Narrows of East Fork Coyote Creek.

Distance: 6.2-mile loop from Manzanita Point; add 5.2 miles if starting from headquarters.

Time: 4½ hours; add 2½ hours if starting from headquarters.

Elevation Gain: 1560'

Trail Notes

Starting from the wide clearing at Manzanita Point Road near Camp 7, take the China Hole Trail that goes left (northeast) out along the north side of the ridge. Through a forest of giant manzanitas that grow as high as trees, traverse this narrow ridgetop on carpets of the manzanita's small, spent leaves.

As you come out of the manzanita forest, you find a fork in the trail. The left one, the Cougar Trail, goes to Poverty Flat, but you arc right, staying on the China Hole Trail, and begin your descent through thick chaparral on the east-facing ridge. In spring your path is brightened by the light pink, bell-shaped flowers of spiny gooseberry plants. The terrain soon becomes more open, with occasional clumps of oaks and an understory of poison oak, holly-leaved cherry and honeysuckle.

Several zig-zags interspersed with long, gentle traverses that skirt an open, grass-covered hillside carry you to the creek's edge. Right after heavy rains, crossing may require wading, but in summer and early fall it is easy to rockhop across the stream. Along the creek banks are clumps of wild roses bearing clusters of pink flowers and later, red rose hips. Native Americans who once lived along Coyote Creek dried the hips for tea.

Across the creek, the China Hole Trail rises on many switchbacks under a cover of bay trees, with an occasional black oak towering overhead. Large boulders on the hillside offer protection to clumps of bright-magenta-and-white shooting stars in spring. Moving out into rolling grasslands of the ridgetop, you intercept the trail from Lost Spring and step onto the Mahoney Meadows. These meadows, and the road, pond and backpack camp, are named for Mike Mahoney and his family, who homesteaded more than 200 acres here in the late 19th and early 20th centuries. Mike, who ran a large cattle ranch here, left his holdings to his nephew, who sold these magnificent lands to Henry W. Coe State Park. From here on a clear day, you too can see the view that Mike Mahoney enjoyed from his cabin—ridge after ridge of mountains to the south and southwest, as far south as San Benito County.

From this point you can look east across a steep canyon to Willow Ridge, chaparral-covered except for thick stands of bay trees filling its canyons. On its northernmost reach a clump of straggly-looking gray pines, known as the Eagle Pines, appear indeed to be perfect lookout perches for eagles. The canyon between you and Willow Ridge is Kelly Cabin Canyon, named for an early settler.

If you are on a backpack trip to campsites at Kelly or Coit lakes, continue southeast on Mahoney Road. See Trip 9, page 99 for the route to these lakes from the Gilroy Hot Springs entrance.

When you are ready to start back, head north to the junction with the Lost Spring Trail. Take this shady, gentle, downhill trail, which bypasses the steep graveled Mahoney Meadows Road to Los Cruzeros. In spring the grasslands are ablaze with wildflowers, the blue of lupines contrasting with the yellow of johnny jump-ups. Fall brings the brilliant scarlet California fuchsia blossoms and yellow- and white-flowered tarweed. About one-half mile down the Lost Spring Trail is a pleasant campsite, a picnic table, and a fairly steady spring flow—a fine place for your back-pack lunch.

Continuing downhill for 0.3 mile you meet the Mahoney Meadows Road and soon arrive at Los Cruzeros, marked by several California sycamores with gnarled white trunks. Their large leaves, golden brown in fall, make a bright contrast to the dark-green foliage of the oaks and bays on the canyon walls. This is the point where East Fork Coyote Creek enters the canyon called The Narrows, steep-sided in some places and impassable after heavy rains. At Los Cruzeros, along the banks of the creek under the shade of valley and live oaks, are three backpack camps.

Turn left, downstream, at Los Cruzeros, and walk on the dry, gravely streambed or step from rock to rock over the water, depending on the season. At some points, even in summer, you have to climb up the banks and around large boulders because the water is too high to cross on the rocks.

Shortly beyond the tightest place in The Narrows, you emerge at the confluence of the Middle and East forks of Coyote Creek—China Hole. Here are several popular swimming holes. In late spring and early summer of wet years, you can find many good and less crowded swimming holes back in The Narrows.

From here you retrace your steps uphill on the northwest bank toward Manzanita Point on the China Hole Trail. Take the left fork at the junction with the Cougar Trail from Poverty Flat, and go up through the manzanita forest. This 2.6-mile climb back to the trailhead at Camp 7 in the Manzanita Point Group Area gains 840', so allow a good hour and a half to negotiate it, especially if you are carrying a backpack. If you continue to park headquarters, about 2.5 miles farther on an easy grade, it takes another hour.

Two Trips In The Park's Southwestern Corner

Two long loop trips, numbers 9 and 10, from the Coyote Creek entrance and one from Hunting Hollow explore steep ridges and wooded canyons that lead to backpack sites, an old ranch and hunting camp, and two pretty lakes. Pine Ridge Association volunteers lead occasional weekend trips to both these popular destinations. Contact park headquarters to receive the association's program.

Henry W. Coe State Park
LOOP TRIP TO KELLY LAKE FROM THE COYOTE CREEK ENTRANCE

From creekside to ridgecrest to lakeside this trip in spring will reward you with fields of wildflowers and a shady rest stop beside Kelly Lake.

Distance: 12.1 miles

Time: 9 hours

Elevation Gain: 2676′

Trail Notes

Begin this trip from the Coyote Creek entrance by taking the short Timms Spring Trail north. Shortly you hop or wade across the sometimes-wide Grizzly Gulch Creek and then bear right on the trail of the same name. Here you begin a 3.9-mile, steady climb up Grizzly Gulch Canyon in the shade of verdant oak woodlands and out onto grassy meadows where spring wildflowers abound and deer graze. At about midway up the mountain you begin to see huge, blackish outcrops, some rounded as if cones of old volcanoes, others flattened like tables.

You cross several little tributaries of Grizzly Gulch Creek, which nourish the valiant live oak and bay trees clinging to the huge boulders that seem to have broken off from these outcrops. In a tight little canyon where two creeks come together, your narrow trail turns right and contours across an open hillside to reach a junction where the faint trace of a trail (called Rock Tower Trail on sign) takes off north toward a suggested backpack campsite. Just beyond this turnoff, the Grizzly Gulch Trail bends north and becomes a double-track route—marked Decker Trail on some maps, but not on the ground when the authors were here. If cars or trucks ever drive on it, they surely need four-wheel drive, as this route goes straight up the mountain for at least 0.33 mile. The pebbly surface is treacherous going downhill—hence the recommendation to do this trail going uphill.

After you reach a small flat, you can continue uphill over knolls, leveling off, then climbing again. Or, you can bear right from the small flat for 100 yards and then proceed left uphill on a trail that skirts the west side of a marsh known as Decker Pond. In either case, at 2400′ you will reach Wasno Road, on which you bear left (northwest) for a few minutes to the Kelly Lake Trail turnoff on your right.

From here it is a pleasant 1-mile descent, undulating up and down with a final drop to the bulrush-bordered lakeside shaded by great valley oaks and rangy, white-barked sycamores higher on its banks. Here is a place for your lunch and a rest under the trees before starting the return leg of this loop—almost all downhill.

Return to Wasno Road, gaining the 540' you lost getting to this pretty place, then turn right (northwest) and watch for the Jackson Trail on your left. From here your downhill starts on a patrol road, again a bit steep, but your way is through a field of shimmering, silvery balls waving atop 10-inch stems—the seed pods of an inconspicuous flower—blow-wives. Here too, are sheets of pink phlox and lavender linanthus, an unusual spring treat, and poppies and lupines amid sheets of low-growing deep yellow goldfields.

Descending through grasslands where huge, solitary oaks and California buckeyes spread a parasol of shade, the wide road/trail then rounds a tree-topped crest and becomes a narrower trail heading due west through lush grasslands. At a signpost where a right turnoff leads downhill to a little pond, you continue straight on the main Jackson Trail, winding through meadows and switchbacking downhill gently on the south side of Jackson Canyon.

Look for a dry wash full of lichen-encrusted boulders, probably fed by a spring uphill, and shaded by oaks—a great place to pause and savor the views. On the far tree-shrouded mountainside known as Palassou Ridge the straggly gray pines rise above the various greens of oaks and buckeyes. Part of this ridge above the Coyote Creek Canyon will some day become open space.

Traversing down the mountain and around several switchbacks takes you to the Anza Trail, where you veer left to reach Woodchopper Springs. Here in an oak forest is a horse trough, uphill is a suggested campsite, and downhill is a large sign describing this as the route that de Anza followed on his way west from the San Antonio Valley to the Santa Clara Valley. Descend a few steps to Coit Road, the unpaved park service road, which you follow south for about a mile, staying high up on the steep bank of Coyote Creek. Few vehicles traverse this road, unless there is a special equestrian event, and the banks above the road are ablaze with wildflowers in spring and shaded by overhanging buckeyes, bays, and live oaks in summer. The only sounds are the creek rippling over rocks, wild turkeys gobbling in the woods, and the calls of uncounted birds in the bushes and in the sky overhead. You'll pass a decrepit cattle chute just before you reach the parking area, then ford the creek and pass through the gated entrance to this splendid corner of Henry Coe State Park.

Henry W. Coe State Park
LOOP TRIP TO REDFERN POND FROM HUNTING HOLLOW ENTRANCE

Climb to high, steep-sided ridges above tree-shaded canyons to remote grasslands with around-the-compass views.

Distance: 11-mile loop; 6.4 miles to campsite.

Time: 7-hour loop; 3½ hours to campsite.

Elevation Gain: 1352'

Trail Notes

This trip in the recently opened southwestern corner of Henry W. Coe State Park takes the park visitor up high, steep-sided ridges above tree-shaded canyons and through remote grasslands dotted with oaks and punctuated by rocky outcrops. This area is heavily used by equestrians, as it has easy access for horse trailers, but its beauty deserves much wider acquaintance. Numerous small ponds are remnants of the cattle-grazing era, and an overnight stay at Redfern Pond is one of the most attractive.

Begin your trip through the gate at the southeast end of the Hunting Hollow parking lot. The first half-mile along one of the tributaries of Coyote Creek is on a dirt road, through a wide valley with magnificent sycamores growing in the creekbed and huge bay trees nearby. In the fall ground squirrels busy themselves in the meadow near the creek, gathering winter supplies. The road/trail crosses back and forth over the creek four times in the first half-mile. In a wet spring this can produce some soggy shoes; a hiking stick can help you leap across to dry ground.

After 0.5 mile, you reach the junction of Lyman Willson Ridge Road on the left, actually a wide trail that formerly was a ranch road. If you hear a squeaking noise here it will not be a worried animal but a windmill, pumping water into a horse trough nearby. Beyond the junction under a large oak is a small fenced camping spot with picnic table, cupboard and barbecue, a good starting place for an equestrian trip.

This trip follows the Lyman Willson Ridge Road through a gate and past a corral shaded by walnut trees, and then goes steeply uphill toward the east. Now you are in oak woodland country with typical Henry Coe open grassland visible on Middle Steer Ridge across the canyon to the left. In spring iris, brodiaea and buttercups are seen everywhere; in fall the smell of tarweed permeates the air. As you ascend the ridge you see to the south the tree-covered slope of the next canyon, part of Phegley Ridge, and at an open spot catch a glimpse of Pacheco Peak and Lovers Leap in the distance near the Pacheco Pass Highway. Look down the canyon to the west across the Santa Clara Valley to see Loma Prieta, the highest peak in the Santa Cruz Mountains.

After a mile of uphill some rocks under the shade of blue oaks provide a convenient rest stop. This is followed by a long stretch of open grassland before the trail contours right (east) into the shade of some black oaks. As you climb, watch the trail at your feet for tracks of deer, coyote, fox, and bobcat, plus an occasional horse or human tread.

After 1.5 miles the trail levels out a bit and crests a knoll on the ridge, where there are wide views to the east, south and west. Vasquez Peak to the east is the highest nearby point at 2210', from here a rounded grassy knob. Henceforth the trail crosses open grasslands for another mile to the junction with the Bowl Trail. At this writing there is no sign, but it is easy to identify using your map. The Lyman Willson Trail continues straight uphill; the northward branch of the Bowl Trail, apparently little used, contours left. Your route follows the eastward-trending branch of the Bowl Trail to the right. Yellow tarweed smells very strong in the fall. You see two dammed cattle ponds, one below to the right, one immediately to your left. There no longer is grazing in this part of the park, but the wild animals appreciate getting a drink.

Increasing numbers of rocky outcrops, part of the Franciscan Formation called blue schist, add interest to the scene. Oaks grow around these rocks picturesquely. After passing a small spring close to the trail, now a rough road, the high point of the trip at 2208', the trail begins to drop down to Willson Camp, the former cattle ranch of Lyman Willson. Nestled under the shade of a huge live-oak tree, the old house looks south across grasslands and canyons toward Pacheco Peak. It takes about 2½ hours to reach this place—3.5 miles from the Hunting Hollow entrance. Remains of the ranch include an old cow-shed, two derelict house-trailers, various shacks, and remnants of waterlines.

Lyman Willson was the son of an early Gilroy pioneer, Horace Willson, who emigrated from New Hampshire in 1853 to what was then known as San Ysidro. Horace accumulated large land holdings by homesteading and purchase in the Diablo Range east of Gilroy. Sons Edwin and Lyman ranched property of their own near Gilroy Hot Springs. In 1915 Lyman was thrown from his horse and killed on Middle Ridge while bringing a deer down to Hunting Hollow from the family hunting camp. His brother Edwin lived until 1937, but the ranch had been sold eight years earlier.

From Willson Camp continue a short distance southeast to a trail junction with Wagon Road, a graded dirt road that follows Steer Ridge. As you head right (south) along the ridge, note the sign at the junction that says it is 6.9 miles north to Pacheco Camp, and 1.8 miles north and then east to Vasquez Peak. Great views to the east, south and west stretch before you. Looking below the trail at another stock pond you may catch a glimpse of a wild pig and piglets quenching their thirst. These descendants of escaped domestic pigs crossed with wild European boars have proliferated in the Diablo Range and you can frequently see their rootings in the ground. Their tracks are similar to those of deer. Do not approach too closely, however. The boars can be aggressive, as can a sow with piglets.

At another trail junction, the Long Dam Trail leads off to the north curving eastward toward Vasquez Peak. But you continue south, alternately descending steeply to cross three creeks, then again struggling steeply uphill. At 5.8 miles an unsigned track cuts off right toward the Redfern Pond Trail. In some seasons this may be hard to find, so continue 0.2 miles on Wagon Road to the main junction. Here, next to a small stock pond, the Redfern Pond Trail takes off to the north, rising gently uphill across the open grasslands of Phegley Ridge.

When you crest the ridge, about 0.5 mile farther on, you are again at a high point of your hike, some 2200'. Below you lies a large linear pond about 1.5 acres in size, partly encircled by tall reeds. The small dam is at the far end, and the pond drains to the west. Songs of red-winged blackbirds rise from the inviting bowl, and you may hear the cry of a red-tailed hawk cruising high above. Blue- and live-oak trees dot the grassy knolls above the pond, providing many inviting campsites. The H.W.Coe map suggests a campsite above the pond to the right. The trail continues on for a short distance, but this is your welcome home for the night.

You have the option of camping here two nights and taking a 5.2-mile round trip day hike east to Vasquez Peak. This trip would be partly on roads, partly on a trail. To take this trip, return north on Wagon Road 1.4 miles and turn right on the Long Dam Trail. Curving around past a stock pond (Long Dam Pond), the trail climbs past Edith Pond, and 1.2 miles from Wagon Road it reaches Vasquez Road near Vasquez Peak.

When you continue on the loop trip from Hunting Hollow the next day, return from Redfern Pond to Wagon Road, which the route follows all the way to Hunting Hollow. First the road climbs steeply uphill, with very little shade until the ridgetop. Here you feel as if you were on top of the world (or at least on top of Henry Coe Park), before making your final descent south to the tributary of Coyote Creek along which you began your hike.

The final 3 miles of this hike are along the valley of Hunting Hollow, with numerous creek crossings as you head northwest. Here again are the ground squirrels and brush rabbits that like meadows and bushes. In the fall tarantulas emerge from their holes looking for mates; they aren't dangerous, but give them room to escape your tread. Among other tracks in the dust are linear grooves; these are made by snakes, occasionally rattlers, and you will want to watch your step.

At 10.5 miles you have completed your loop trip to the junction with the Lyman Willson Trail. Another half-mile takes you to the trailhead parking. While this entire loop trip can take 6 to 8 hours and can be done by strong hikers in a day, it makes a relaxing weekend trip to a little-visited part of our Bay Area wild lands.

◆ Santa Cruz Mountains, Foothills ◆ and West to the Pacific

In this third edition of *South Bay Trails* we have expanded west and south of the crest of the Santa Cruz Mountains all the way to the ocean. Connected by the Skyline-to-the-Sea Trail are two state parks, Castle Rock and Big Basin Redwoods. They extend from the heights of Skyline ridge to the shores of the Pacific.

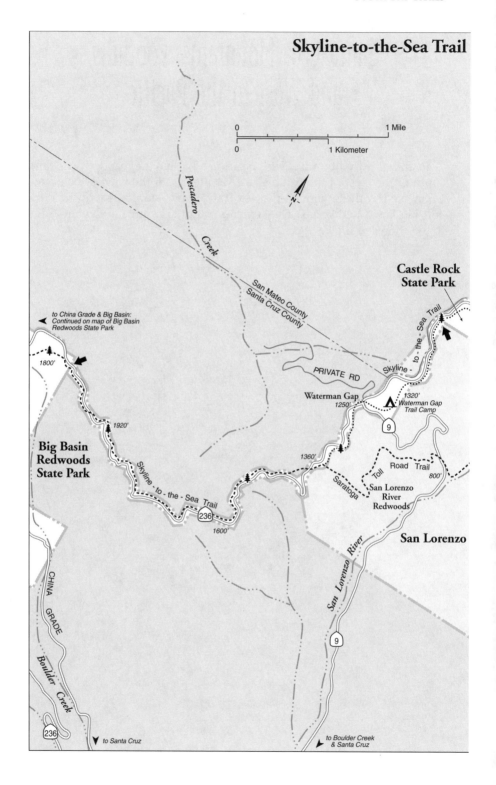

Skyline-to-the-Sea Trail

0 _____ 1 Mile
0 _____ 1 Kilometer

-N-

Pescadero Creek

San Mateo County
Santa Cruz County

Castle Rock
State Park

Skyline - to - the - Sea Trail

to China Grade & Big Basin:
Continued on map of Big Basin
Redwoods State Park

PRIVATE RD

1800'

Skyline -

Waterman Gap
1250'

1320'
Waterman Gap
Trail Camp

9

1920'

Big Basin
Redwoods
State Park

1360'

Road   Trail
800'

Skyline - to - the - Sea Trail

Toll

Saratoga

San Lorenzo
River
Redwoods

236

1600'

San Lorenzo

CHINA

San Lorenzo River

GRADE

9

Boulder Creek

236   ▼ to Santa Cruz   ▼ to Boulder Creek
& Santa Cruz

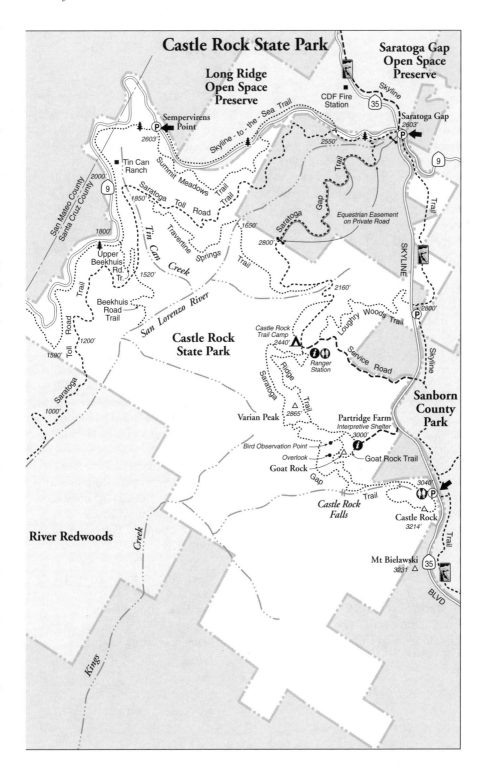

◆ Skyline-to-the-Sea Trail ◆

The Sempervirens Fund, formed in 1968 as a successor to the Sempervirens Club of 1900, has as its purpose "To preserve and protect the natural character of California's Santa Cruz Mountains and to encourage appropriate public enjoyment of this environment."

The non-profit fund seeks to achieve this by "...acquiring suitable land in a working partnership with the State of California and other public and private agencies by completing Big Basin Redwoods and Castle Rock state parks, by fostering public participation in activities such as reforestation and trail projects, and by linking parks and open spaces to provide an integrated parkland system."

In order to connect Castle Rock and Big Basin Redwoods state parks, the concept of the Skyline-to-the-Sea Trail was born. A strip of 150 feet along Highways 9 and 236 belonged to the state parks since completion of the highways as successors to the old Turnpike (or Toll Road). After it was surveyed by a State Parks engineer, the 25-mile trail was constructed entirely by 2500 volunteers under the direction of Dr. Maurice Tripp, Bob Kirsch of the Pioneer District, Boy Scouts of America, and Tony Look of the Sempervirens Fund, with a *grande finale* work weekend on April 15 and 16, 1969. Castle Rock and Big Basin Redwoods state parks were thus connected. In 1976 the trail was completed by virtue of Big Basin's purchase by the State Department of Parks and Recreation as far as Waddell Beach on the Pacific Ocean.

In several of this book's trips, in both Castle Rock and Big Basin Redwoods state parks, you will travel on portions of the Skyline-to-the-Sea Trail (open for hikers only, no equestrians or bicyclists). It is, of course, possible to hike the entire 25-mile trail, with potentially an overnight stay at either Waterman Gap Trail Camp or one of the camps in Big Basin, or one can use portions of the trail as part of a loop trip.

As we wind along this tree-shaded path, we all can thank the vision and dedication of those who conceived of this trail and those who constructed it.

Maps of the Skyline-to-the-Sea Trail are available from Sempervirens Fund, Drawer BE, Los Altos, CA 94023, phone 650-968-4509, from local REI stores, and from The Map Center in Berkeley and Santa Clara.

✦ Castle Rock State Park ✦

This park of over 3600 acres lies mostly on the ocean side of the crest of the Santa Cruz Mountains, beginning at the southeast corner of the junction of Highway 35 (Skyline Boulevard) and Highway 9 (Big Basin Way) in Santa Cruz County. The park is a semi-wilderness, with about 30 miles of trails and a primitive backpack camp. Heavily logged in the 1800s, much of the forest has re-grown, and now surrounds several spectacular sandstone rock outcrops, popular among climbers, and the lovely Castle Rock Falls.

The ancient Ohlone Indians used the area of this park as a through trail from the Santa Clara Valley to the coast. Europeans also found this a good route, and used it to haul out great redwood trees from the twenty-eight lumber-mill camps up and down the San Lorenzo Valley. Later the sandstone formations became a tourist attraction, and valley residents began to use the area for recreation rather than for profit. At the instigation of Russell Varian, an early supporter of land protection, Castle Rock was added to the State Park system in 1968. Strongly supported by the Sempervirens Fund, a nonprofit land conservation group responsible for establishing Big Basin as California's first state park in 1900, Castle Rock has grown from its original 513 acres to 3657 acres today.

Castle Rock is located between parks and open spaces managed by several other agencies. To the north and east are lands of the Midpeninsula Regional Open Space District (MROSD), largely undeveloped except for trails. Also to the east toward Saratoga is Sanborn County Park, managed by Santa Clara County. Directly south of Castle Rock, separated by some private lands along highways 9 and 236, is Big Basin Redwoods State Park, famous for its magnificent

Tafoni holes in sandstone rock

stands of virgin redwood trees. Castle Rock lies on the spine of the Santa Cruz Mountains, with its highest peak at 3200 feet.

The sandstone formations for which Castle Rock is famous were formed under an ancient sea, then lifted, folded and faulted in a mountain-building process that still continues. Loma Prieta, a 3791' mountain, approximate site of the 1989 namesake earthquake, lies on the San Andreas Fault only 15 miles to the southeast. The Vaqueros and Butano sandstones have been shaped by a process of chemical weathering, called Tafoni, into unusual caves and filigree shapes that fascinate visitors and lure climbers.

A large part of Castle Rock that is without trails was designated wilderness in the Master Plan approved on March 8, 2000 by the California State Parks and Recreation Commission. A citizens' advisory committee is at this writing working on a draft trail use plan. There are no virgin redwoods remaining, but there are some lovely areas of second-growth redwoods, plus forests of Douglas fir, madrone, tanoak, live oak, and bay trees. The campground is surrounded by knobcone pines, and there is an extensive stand of black oaks due south of the parking lot and near the Partridge Farm area. In winter visitors will enjoy the warm chaparral-covered slopes, and great views to the south are to be had from scattered meadows. Many of the trails follow former roads, often now reduced to trail width but on relatively gentle grades. Animals common to all the Santa Cruz Mountains live in the park.

Jurisdiction: State of California

Facilities: 30 miles of trails, backpack camps at Castle Rock Trail Camp near Park Office and at Waterman Gap; interpretive exhibit at Partridge Farm area.

Park Rules: Hours 6:00 A.M. to dusk; no firearms, dogs, glass containers or smoking; horses on designated trails only; bicycles on entrance service roads only; fires in fire-rings in off-season only; camping in designated areas only, by reservation.

Park Office: Castle Rock State Park, 15000 Skyline Blvd., Los Gatos, CA 95030; phone: 408-867-2952.

Maps: USGS quads *Big Basin, Castle Rock Ridge,* corners of *Mindego Hill* and *Cupertino; Castle Rock State Park* map; Sempervirens Fund *Trail Map of the Santa Cruz Mountains, map 1.*

How To Get There: From Saratoga follow Hwy. 9 (Big Basin Way/ Congress Springs Rd.) to Saratoga Gap at the intersection of Hwy. 35 (Skyline Blvd.). Park on east corner here at Caltrans vista point, or proceed south on Skyline to Castle Rock parking lot.

Castle Rock State Park
SANDSTONE FORMATIONS
AND CAMPGROUND

*A round-trip walk on the Ridge Trail and the Saratoga Gap Trail
past fantastic rocks and sparkling falls to park headquarters and
campgrounds and back to parking area.*

Distance: 6.7 miles round trip

Time: 3½ hours

Elevation Loss: 600'

Trail Notes

From Saratoga Gap drive 2.7 miles southeast on Skyline Boulevard to
Castle Rock parking lot (fee, restroom, phone).

You will find two routes on the south side of the parking lot. This trip
takes the left-hand one (more easterly) to pass by Castle Rock itself. You
wind uphill through a forest of Douglas fir, tanoak, hickory oak and
madrone. This trail is the main hiking route to the trail camps at park
headquarters, and a sign warns the visitors not to bring glass containers,
bicycles or horses on this trail. In June, look for white violets in the shady
carpet of needles and leaves under the forest canopy.

In less than 0.3 mile the trail reaches a junction where you turn right on
a road-width trail, a remnant of the old Summit Road that preceded
Skyline Boulevard. A schoolhouse once stood in this area. Shortly on your
left you see a wonderful sandstone formation that tempts one to scramble
on it. This can be very damaging to the delicate tracery that sometimes
can be seen on these rocks. At 0.5 mile an even larger rock looms up, surrounded by firs. This is the real Castle Rock for which the park is named.
The unusual shapes and caves of this Tafoni sandstone formation are fairly common all along the crest of the Santa Cruz Mountains, many of them
protected in parks and open space preserves.

The trail leaves the old road and winds down and around the north
side of Castle Rock through a fir forest growing on rocky ground. Because
of many unofficial side routes, the main trail is difficult to follow here. At
0.8 miles, as you approach trickling Kings Creek, you reach a junction
with the Ridge Trail which goes uphill to the right to skirt the upper side
of Goat Rock. Your route goes left on the Saratoga Gap Trail, and after a
while crosses Kings Creek on a small bridge. Leaves of wild ginger, round
and spotted, flourish in the dampness near the creek.

After you have gone a mile and a half from the parking lot you find
Kings Creek plunging over a sandstone cliff in Castle Rock Falls, which

Goat Rock, a popular climbing area

you can view from a wooden platform secured to the rock. The trail beyond skirts the hillside west and north along a steep, south-facing hillside with chaparral-like growth. Look back here for the best view of the falls—the water spills over its sandstone lip, narrow and dainty, about 80' high, looking, in winter, almost like Bridalveil Falls in miniature. Look further to the southwest from this slope to watch the ocean fog retreating before the sun's warmth in the San Lorenzo River headwaters basin. Along the trail, among other Tafoni rocks, chamise and yerba santa bloom in spring, and manzanita berries, enjoyed by the Ohlone people as well as by the local foxes, are ripening in the sun.

The trail contours over the rocky hillside, narrow and twisting, with some scrambling necessary. As you head more to the north and back into the trees you approach a saddle with small meadows beside the trail. Among the scattered blue oaks, yellow Mariposa lilies and blue brodiaea bloom in spring, and some black oaks unfurl their early leaves in flaming red.

At 2.4 miles on your right is a trail up to the Ridge Trail, but you continue straight on the Saratoga Gap Trail through meadows with scattered blue oaks. Crossing a small divide on a ridge, you get a great view of the main San Lorenzo River canyon to the north and west. Meadows near Sempervirens Point (see Trips 3 and 4, pages 117 and 120) and houses in the private Indian Rock Ranch subdivision can be seen beyond. Further to the west the top of Butano Ridge appears through the receding fog.

A surprise comes at 3.4 miles when the trail goes up a sandstone cliff on narrow steps. Your route is secured with a cable railing. Back in oak woodlands at 3.7 miles you meet a junction with the Ridge Trail, which will be your return route. Just ahead is the first of the trail camps, Oak Meadow Camp. There are 23 campsites in the three adjacent trail camps—this, and nearby Frog Flat and Main camps, each with picnic table, fire ring (firewood cannot be gathered, but is sold at the park office for use in off-fire season), vault toilets and piped water. Park headquarters and the ranger office are nearby, and the camps here are an excellent base for exploring the rest of Castle Rock State Park. While bicycles are not allowed in the park, they may access the trail camps via the service road (see map).

The trail camps are shaded by a forest of knobcone pines, a contorted species of pine that favors dry areas and tolerates thin soils, especially sandstone. Small tributaries of the San Lorenzo River run through the campground crossed by board bridges.

Your return route is on the Ridge Trail, which more-or-less parallels the Saratoga Gap Trail but is higher on the hillside. The Ridge Trail splits left from the Saratoga Gap Trail just beyond a bridge over a small watercourse. First, go gently uphill through beautiful madrone trees. This relative of the rhododendron and manzanita has a smooth reddish trunk which always feels cold to the touch, even on hot days. Large, shiny, oval leaves, and clusters of urn-shaped, white flowers in winter are followed by red berries ripening all year. Madrone wood is hard and dense.

The Ridge Trail continues through patches of chaparral and madrone forest. Note that the trees appear all the same size and age, and show signs of stump-sprouting (having grown from the stump of a larger tree). One madrone has as many as 10 sprouts in a circle. This is probably evidence of an earlier forest fire. Chaparral plants often grow in areas that have been burned. Soil erosion also can follow a fire, and a grove of scrawny knobcone pines just ahead have taken root in thin soils.

At about 5 miles you reach a side trail to the right leading to the Emily Smith Bird Observation Point. Even if no birds are visible, there is a great view here of Monterey Bay and the Gabilan Range nearly due south, and of nearby Butano Ridge to the west. The Ridge Trail route here is on the west side of the ridge going through oak meadows with black oaks and one huge hickory oak growing to the right of the trail.

The Ridge Trail splits at 5.3 miles, the right fork leading right to the bottom of Goat Rock and the left fork leading to the Partridge Farm interpretive shelter. In the lovely oak woodlands in spring grow lavender Chinese houses and yellow buttercups.

At the top of Goat Rock climbers lounge in the sun while awaiting their turn on the ropes. This is the most popular climbing rock in the park, and unfortunately has been treated carelessly. Unofficial trails have damaged the plants, and climbing hardware and chalk mar the sandstone slabs. A trail loop leading to the right (southwest) from the top of Goat Rock leads to a scenic overlook with benches and excellent interpretive panoramas showing important park animals and plants and identifying distant landmarks. By the summit of Goat Rock a trail takes off to the left, hidden between huge sandstone boulders. This is the Goat Rock Trail, leading to the Partridge Farm interpretive shelter.

To continue around to the lower side of Goat Rock, take the Ridge Trail, which switchbacks to the base of this huge formation. At this writing this trail was in poor condition, requiring some rock-scrambling (rope not necessary). From the lower side of Goat Rock you get a good view of climbers practicing their skills. Following the uneven trail eastward you descend several steps cut into the sandstone slope. At 6.2 miles, by Kings Creek, the Ridge Trail reaches the Saratoga Gap Trail, on which this trip started, and on it you continue uphill past the Castle Rock Trail on which you came to reach the parking lot at 6.7 miles.

Castle Rock State Park

Loop down the Skyline-to-the-Sea Trail and Back through Park

A quick route down to the park center, then a treasure of a trail back to the Skyline through a demonstration forest.

Distance: 6.0 miles round trip

Time: 3½ hours

Elevation Loss/Gain: 700'

Trail Notes

Start at Caltrans vista point parking lot at Saratoga Gap.

Cross Skyline Boulevard from the Caltrans parking lot at Saratoga Gap to the southwest corner of Highway 9 and Highway 35. There is a sign facing the corner, but it is hard to see and not visible from the Caltrans parking. You must walk on the shoulder of Highway 9 for about 500' until you reach the Saratoga Toll Road Trail on your left. A sign here advises hikers that they can reach the Loughry Woods Trail by following the Skyline Trail on the east side of Skyline Boulevard. This will be your return route at the end of this trip.

After 100' you reach a cut-off trail to the left, for hikers and equestrians, which leads to the Indian Rock Ranch subdivision. A sign tells you it is 4.3 miles to the trail camp. As you walk steeply down through a forest of Douglas fir and bay trees, you are now looking down on the headwaters of the San Lorenzo River, which runs into the Pacific Ocean at Santa Cruz.

After about another 1000' you reach Indian Rock Road, the private road leading to the housing subdivision. The State Park has an easement along this road, but you are asked to fill out a little permit form provided in a wooden box on a post. Here a sign tells you the trail campground is 2.7 miles ahead. You are now on the Saratoga Gap Trail. The road is paved, and at a junction with First Fork Road on the left you take Indian Trail Road to the right. No sign indicates this turn.

Reaching another junction, you again follow Indian Trail Road to the right. Soon leaving the woods the route enters a chaparral area, and you can see Pine Mountain on the horizon to the south.

Passing Madrone Place, a subdivision road, you go left and at the next intersection bear right, passing close to a residence. Here the pavement ends, but the wide dirt road continues downhill. On the shoulder next to the pavement there has been room along this road for horses to walk. Henceforth they can use the dirt road.

At 1.5 miles from Highway 9 you reach the gate to Castle Rock State Park. The sign tells you that no dogs, motorcycles, fires or cigarettes are permitted. Here is a good view of the Santa Lucia Mountains above Monterey Bay, as the trail now is in low-growing, open chaparral.

At 2.1 miles the Saratoga Gap Trail reaches a junction with the Travertine Springs Trail leading to the right (west). You will walk on this trail in Trip 3.

Continuing east downhill you shortly reach Twin Bridges on Craig Springs Creek. In winter there is much water running in this tributary of the San Lorenzo River, through a moss-draped open forest of Douglas fir and tanoak. You pass the Frog Flat Fire Road Trail leading to Frog Flat Trail Camp, and at 2.75 miles from your starting point reach a horse trough. Here is the rest of the trail camp complex, consisting of a trail shelter, 23 primitive campsites, a ranger station, and a ranger residence. Campsites are sheltered by knobcone pines and thick shrubbery.

Continuing east on the service road you soon reach a junction with the Loughry Woods Trail leading left. No bicycles or horses are permitted on this narrow trail, which reaches Skyline Boulevard in 1.7 miles. Loughry Woods Demonstration Forest was named after an early ranger who collected and planted many species of trees, not all native to the site. Few are now visible.

On the narrow Loughry Woods Trail you hike down along sandstone outcrops through chaparral and knobcone pine habitat. Unusual oaks, called maul or gold-cup oaks (for their very hard wood and yellow-backed leaves), are interspersed with madrone as the chaparral is left behind. Trail steps have been cut in the sandstone, and areas of Tafoni formation can be seen above the trail (see description in Trip 1, page 111).

Unfortunately, in Castle Rock Park the serenity often is disturbed by the sound of guns. The private Los Altos Rod and Gun Club owns a piece of land on the west side of Skyline Boulevard surrounded by the park, and members actively practice, especially on weekends. The club land is close by, east of your trail.

You continue up the Loughry Woods Trail through varying vegetation—sometimes chaparral, sometimes a forest of bay, oak and madrone—following switchbacks and crossing two branches of a stream on small bridges. The trail is narrow and the ground carpeted with needles and leaves.

After reaching Skyline Boulevard, just under 5 miles from the start, you cross the highway and walk north on the Skyline Trail, which is part of the Bay Area Ridge Trail, the planned 400-mile route around San Francisco Bay's ridgetops. The trail here is mostly road-width and can be used by equestrians. After 1.5 miles you reach the junction of Highway 9 and Highway 35 (Saratoga Gap) where this trip started.

Castle Rock State Park
A Trip Through the Center
of Castle Rock State Park

Meet the Skyline-to-the-Sea Trail and contour through woods past hidden springs.

Distance: 8.4-mile loop

Time: 4½ hours

Elevation Loss: 800'

Trail Notes

From Saratoga Gap drive southwest down Highway 9 two miles to the parking area at Sempervirens Point.

Sempervirens Point is a wonderful place to start a hike in Castle Rock. Situated on the left (south) side of Highway 9, the point is named for the Sempervirens Fund, the non-profit agency that has worked so diligently to add lands to Castle Rock and Big Basin Redwoods state parks. A paved parking area and nearby bench invite the visitor to view the ever-changing vistas to east, south and west. In winter a kaleidoscope of clouds hangs in wisps on the forested hills, changing with the wind. In summer the ocean sparkles in the distance, luring one to the coast. In the foreground lie the valleys and forests of Castle Rock State Park, which you will sample on this trip.

From Sempervirens Point start down the Skyline-to-the-Sea Trail, which begins at the right (west) side of the parking lot. You pass two huge Douglas firs, part of a nice fir forest that grows in this western part of Castle Rock. On foggy days be prepared to protect yourself from the moisture dripping from saturated tree branches. Needles surface the trail, which has little erosion, as horses and bicycles are prohibited.

After a quiet section, in which you barely hear the noise from the gun club, mentioned in Trip 2, or from busy Highway 9, the trail passes a paved driveway leading to Tin Can Ranch, a property now owned by the Park and used for meetings and a ranger residence. The Skyline-to-the-Sea Trail henceforth almost always parallels the highway, at this point nearly 100' above you. Several more driveways lead left to private property hidden in the fir forest, and some memorial groves have been dedicated by families to their deceased loved ones.

After a mile and a half from Sempervirens Point you reach a road-width trail cutting left (east) toward the Saratoga Toll Road Trail, and you take it. This is the Beekhuis Road Trail (pronounced "Beek-us"), and a sign says it is maintained by the Santa Cruz Mountains Trail Association,

A colossal bay tree thrives at Travertine Springs

a hard-working volunteer support group. Shortly you go by a cut-off trail leading back (right) to the Skyline-to-the-Sea Trail slightly further to its south, which you ignore.

Winding around the broad swings of the Beekhuis Trail you soon reach the Saratoga Toll Road Trail, about 1.8 miles from your starting place at Sempervirens Point, and go left (north) on it. The forest here is quite moist, and in winter the sound of the San Lorenzo River and its tributaries is loud.

The Saratoga Toll Road was built in 1871 to haul people, lumber and supplies between Saratoga and the logging camps all down the western slopes of the Santa Cruz Mountains. When Highways 9 and 236 were built in 1915 and 1930 the Toll Road became obsolete, but it has been used as a recreational trail for many years. Parts of this trail are wide, like the original road, but many sections have been eroded or blocked by slides or trees, so that vehicles no longer can traverse it. It is one of the few trails in Castle Rock that is open to equestrians (but not to bicyclists).

Hiking north on the Toll Road Trail you must climb around a high bridge that is badly damaged and closed, working your way across a dam and then a culvert. The trail narrows here. At 2.7 miles you reach a junction with the Travertine Springs Trail, which you take to the right (east). No bicycles, horses, dogs or cigarettes are permitted. This trail segment is also an old road.

The forest opens up as you walk the Travertine Springs Trail, and soon you cross a small wooden bridge with railings. Here is evidence of past human activity: near a colossal bay tree are a 3-rail fence and an acre-wide flat, open area. Some *equisetum* (horsetails, an ancient plant from the Cretaceous Period) suggests moist habitat, and indeed here is a sign announcing Travertine Springs. Nearby two derelict shacks, some buckets, a ladder, and a patch of the escaped alien plant *vinca major* remind you that you are not the first to admire this spot. Who did what here?

Beyond Travertine Springs the forest gives way to chaparral, and then widely spaced madrone and tanoak trees, with occasional small firs, evidence of past fires. When you have gone 3.3 miles a view opens up to the south through chaparral across the canyon of the San Lorenzo. The river's roar echoes in the valley, and across to the south is Ben Lomond Mountain. A high-tension powerline bisecting the park indicates civilization beyond.

The well-maintained Travertine Springs Trail winds east. Some parts are road-width, but not negotiable by vehicles. At 3.7 miles, deep in a fir forest, you cross the San Lorenzo River rushing beneath a wooden bridge. Beyond the bridge the trail runs uphill under the powerline, with construction debris strewn about. Your route follows the powerline road uphill for 100', then goes right through chaparral. Look ahead for a view of Varian Peak.

Continuing east, the Travertine Springs Trail has a hot uphill section on a south-facing slope. Blue witch (*solanum*, or deadly nightshade) was blooming here in January. At 4.5 miles you hear water running and see the Craig Springs branch of the San Lorenzo River flowing down from Twin Bridges. Groves of bay trees shelter you, and pools in the stream might be nice to cool off in on hot days. Big-leaf maples grow on the creek bank, their giant leaves larger than dinner plates.

Shortly ahead is a junction with the Saratoga Gap Trail, described in Trip 2. Turn left uphill to reach the park gate and then the Saratoga Gap Trail. At 6.8 miles you join the cutoff to the Skyline-to-the-Sea Trail, bearing left now and walking below the road through a forest of madrone trees, with another view down the San Lorenzo River valley.

Soon you pass a junction with the Saratoga Toll Road (Trip 2) and meet the Skyline-to-the-Sea Trail, on which you turn right (northwest) to cross Highway 9. Through a stile you follow the Skyline-to-the-Sea Trail, here road-width, southwest, downhill, paralleling Highway 9 on its north side through madrone woods. The trail passes two gates leading into MROSD's Long Ridge Preserve, and you can take a brief rest on a bench with a westward view. The trail becomes narrow, covered with needles, rocks and moss, and is close to the highway as you walk downhill.

At 8.4 miles the Skyline-to-the-Sea Trail crosses the highway to Sempervirens Point, your starting place.

4

Castle Rock State Park
THROUGH MEADOWS TO AN ANCIENT AND HISTORIC ROUTE

Travel down to join the route used first by Ohlone Indians and then by European-American settlers and lumbermen on their way to the coast.

Distance: 7.9-mile loop

Time: 4 hours

Elevation Gain/Loss: 800'

Trail Notes

From Saratoga Gap drive west down Highway 9 two miles to Sempervirens Point parking area.

After taking in the view at Sempervirens Point (see Trip 3, page 117), start at the northeast end of the parking lot and cross a steep meadow, watching your step because the vistas to the east and south will lure you. A short side trip to your left up an old road/trail leads you to the memorial "McCann-Ginzton Summit Meadows Grove," with a nearby bench. The main Summit Meadows Trail (for hikers only) was a bit hidden in the shrubbery when the authors took it, but it had a sign and is also marked by the sharp-scented vinegar-weed left by former cattle grazing. In summer the meadow is lush with a carpet of flowers: lupine, owls clover, clarkia, blue-eyed grass, California poppies, and larkspur.

Watch carefully for the trail, which beyond the meadow becomes an old road/trail through fir forest, with a few knobcone pines in warm areas.

After a mile you reach the intersection with Highway 9 and cross over to the Skyline-to-the-Sea Trail, on which you turn northeast. There is a large roadside pullout area here, and MROSD property lies north of the highway. No bicycles or horses are permitted on the Skyline-to-the-Sea Trail. This section of it is on a bench above the road, about half a mile long. Reaching Highway 9 again, cross to the southeast side, go slightly left downhill, and bear right on the Saratoga Toll Road Trail, where horses (but not bicycles) are allowed. Yellow Douglas iris greet you as you enter a Douglas fir forest on a gentle downhill grade. This reminds you how busy was Scottish botanist David Douglas to have so many plants in the western U. S. named after him.

This upper (northern) part of the Saratoga Toll Road runs on a park easement through private property (the Indian Rock Ranch subdivision), and occasional views of the houses remind you of human presence. In openings in the forest you will see buckeye trees adorned with tall candle-like blooms in early summer, and yellow woolly sunflowers in meadowy areas. Passing occasional driveways, at 4 miles from your start at Semper-virens Point you reach the State Park boundary, and bear left on the road/trail.

The banks on the downhill side of the trail become very steep, and soon views open up that help you orient yourself. Below to the east are the San Lorenzo River headwaters, the site of the Travertine Springs Trail (Trip 3), the powerline, and Varian Peak and Mt. Bielawski in the distance, at the eastern boundary of the park. All of the Indian Rock Ranch subdivision is visible to your left, the houses perched among the trees and rocks with superb vistas to their south.

At 5 miles is a huge landslide in which the entire hill has slumped down to the left. Follow the re-routed trail straight ahead, although there is another route leading down to the left to join the Travertine Springs Trail (see Trip 3, page 117).

At 5.4 miles you reach a dammed pond and cross the dam, bypassing a derelict bridge. Shortly thereafter is a junction with a road/trail up to the right, the Beekhuis Trail. Two branches here reach the Skyline-to-the-Sea Trail; take the broader road/trail and at 6.3 miles reach the Skyline-to-the-Sea Trail and turn right. You will notice all through the woods on the Saratoga Toll Road Trail that there are remnants of old roads, some with 100-year-old trees growing in their middle. Quiet as these woods now appear, we know they saw much human activity in the past.

Return north on the Skyline-to-the-Sea Trail gently uphill, crossing occasional private driveways, and at 7.9 miles reach the Sempervirens Point parking lot.

Castle Rock State Park
UP THE HISTORIC TOLL ROAD, DOWN THE SKYLINE-TO-THE-SEA TRAIL

Gently climb the San Lorenzo River Valley on an ancient route, return by a modern route.

Distance: 9-mile loop

Time: 4½ hours

Elevation Gain/Loss: 680'

Trail Notes

From Saratoga Gap take Highway 9 six miles south to its junction with Highway 236; park off highway in pullout area.

This trip follows two routes, a 20th century, hand-built trail and a historic road made by teams of horses or oxen in the 19th century.

At the junction of Highway 236 with Highway 9 a private dirt road leads off to the right (north) to the lands of Red Tree Properties, a lumbering company. Active logging operations are in progress, the trees being hauled all the way north on Skyline Boulevard and through San Francisco to mills in Sonoma and Mendocino counties. You can leave your car on the shoulder of Highway 9 or on a small pullout behind a berm on the right (no overnight parking).

The Skyline-to-the-Sea Trail passes this intersection, coming down to the east side of Highway 9 from the Waterman Gap Trail Camp, crossing to the west side, and continuing south up a knoll paralleling Highway 236 on its west side. After only 100' or so this trail descends again, crossing Highway 236 to its east side and continuing south. Here the narrow trail parallels the road through second-growth redwoods and a few old burnt stumps. The understory is fairly clear, with some ferns, and Douglas fir and tanoak grow between the redwoods.

After half a mile you reach a junction: the Saratoga Toll Road Connector comes in from the left and the Skyline-to-the-Sea Trail continues right 8.6 miles to Big Basin Headquarters.

Taking the Connector to the left, you descend steeply down for a short distance, then bear left on an old road heading east. Monkey flowers and honeysuckle can be seen here blooming in July. The redwood thins out and you pass an open, chaparral-covered area on your right. Turning left (north) the trail continues gently downhill under the powerlines that traverse Castle Rock State Park, where the vegetation has been clear-cut. Passing some openings with huckleberry bushes and a few old redwood stumps with "fairy rings" of young trees around them, you descend 5 switchbacks to a bridge over a tiny stream. At 1.4 miles you start gently up, navigating a slide which blocks the trail, and leaving the redwood area.

Highway 9 traffic can be heard below, and at 2 miles from your start you cross the highway (carefully) and bear left to rejoin the trail, following signs saying "Skyline-to-the Sea Toll Road Connector" and "To Toll Road 0.2 mi., no bikes; horses O.K." There is room at the roadside for 3-4 cars. The trail is not easy to find, but eventually you will see a wide junction with a sign: TO SARATOGA GAP 6.8.

Go left on a road with remnants of asphalt paving. You hear a flowing stream to the right—the San Lorenzo River—increasing with the addition of each tiny tributary. This road has powerlines above, with poles by the road; on the left there is a gate to a Division of Forestry yard and private property signs; it is not a wilderness experience. After climbing over a deadfall at the main junction with the Toll Road, you reach a bridge over a tributary stream and a sign telling of the history of the Saratoga and Pescadero Toll Road.

Continuing up the Toll Road you pass several inhabited dwellings, cross a stream, and even dodge a swing hanging in the middle of the trail (not occupied when the authors passed). Here the trail is in an old road bed, but is covered with leaves and no longer has any asphalt. You are hiking in a forest of tanoak and madrone on a gentle uphill grade.

At 3.3 miles you reach the State Park boundary. Sounds of the San Lorenzo River rise from below to your right, and noise of the gun club near Skyline punctuates the air. The trail rises through an open forest toward the northwest, and at 5 miles you emerge from the trees into a chaparral community. In July blooming chamise fills the air with sweetness. Mt. Bielawski looms to the east across the valley.

The Toll Road here has become wider, and you pass an unmarked road to the right, but continue straight. At 5.3 you reach the Beekhuis Road junction (Trips 3 and 4) and go left (northwest) on it. Nearing the ridgetop take the cutoff to the left and emerge from a fir forest into chaparral and meadow with great views. At the Skyline-to-the-Sea Trail junction turn left (south) on the narrow trail and continue through the forest just below Highway 9.

In a chaparral area at 6.3 miles find a good lunch spot, surrounded by blooming monkey flower and yerba santa on a south-facing slope.

Continuing south, the Skyline-to-the-Sea Trail curves past a private driveway and across little wooden bridges over small draws. There is some confusion at 7.8 miles as you cross a paved road leading east with no sign but a private gate. Find the Skyline-to-the-Sea Trail beyond the gate heading downhill through successive groves of redwood, fir, tanoak and hazelnut.

As you near Waterman Gap at 8.2 miles you cross the service road and pass a water tank. Go left a short distance to the Waterman Gap Trail Camp. Here you will find 3 designated campsites with outhouse, garbage cans, drinking water faucet, and a symphony of traffic noise from Highway 9 not far below. Bring ear plugs if you plan to stay overnight.

To complete your trip, start southwest on the trail camp road, which soon becomes a foot trail and rises to the right over a ridge to cross Highway 9 just above its intersection with Highway 236 where you started. You have hiked 9 miles. Cross the highway (carefully), and go left to find your car. From this spot it is 6 miles to Saratoga Gap, 14 miles to the town of Saratoga.

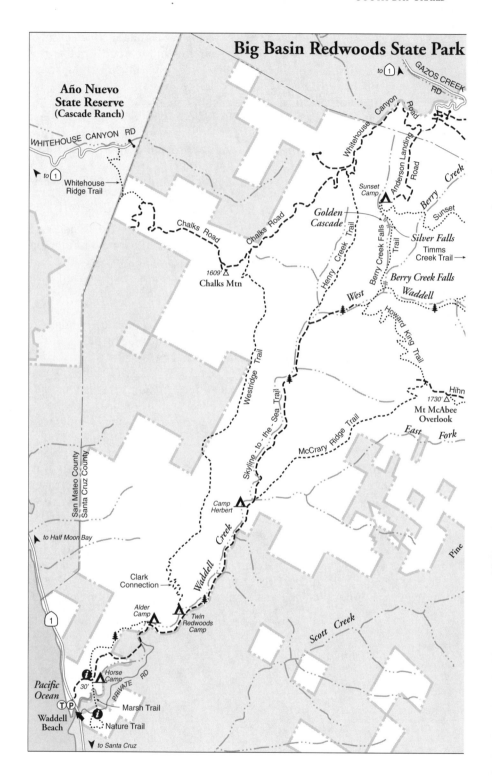

Big Basin Redwoods State Park

to ① ► GAZOS CREEK RD

**Año Nuevo
State Reserve
(Cascade Ranch)**

WHITEHOUSE CANYON RD

► to ①

Whitehouse
Ridge Trail

Whitehouse Canyon Road

Anderson Landing Road

Berry Creek

Sunset
Camp

Chalks Road

Chalks Road

*Golden
Cascade*

Henry Creek Trail

Berry Creek Falls Trail

Sunset

Silver Falls

Timms
Creek Trail →

1609' △
Chalks Mtn

West

Berry Creek Falls

Waddell

Howard King Trail

Westridge Trail

Hihn
1730' △

**Mt McAbee
Overlook**

East Fork

Skyline - to - the - Sea Trail

McCrary Ridge Trail

Camp
Herbert

San Mateo County
Santa Cruz County

► to Half Moon Bay

Waddell Creek

Pine

Clark
Connection

Alder
Camp

Twin
Redwoods
Camp

Scott Creek

①

*Pacific
Ocean*

30'

Horse
Camp

PRIVATE RD

**Waddell
Beach**

ⓣⓟ

ⓘ

ⓘ

Marsh Trail

Nature Trail

► to Santa Cruz

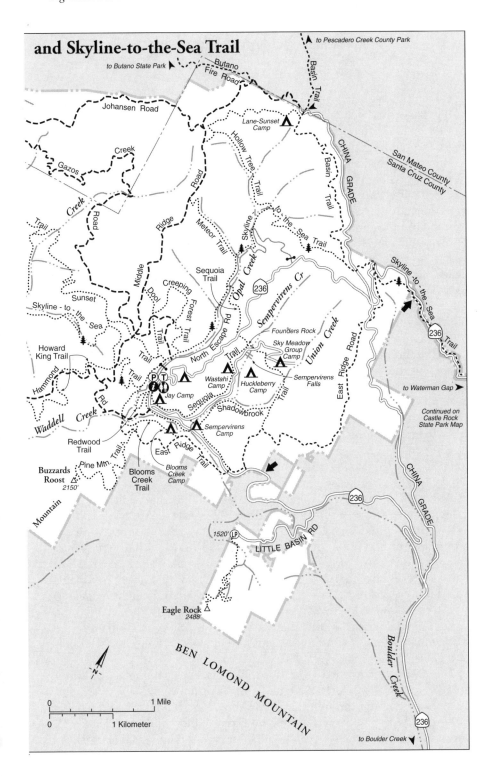

and Skyline-to-the-Sea Trail

to Pescadero Creek County Park

to Butano State Park
Butano Fire Road
Basin Trail

Johansen Road

Creek
Gazos

Creek
Trail
Trail

Lane-Sunset Camp

Hollow Tree Trail

Basin Trail

Skyline

to the Sea Trail

CHINA GRADE

San Mateo County
Santa Cruz County

Road
Ridge
Meteor Trail
Sequoia Trail

Middle
Dool
Creeping Forest Trail

Sunset

Skyline - to - the - Sea

Howard King Trail

Hammond

Trail

Opal Creek
236

Sempervirens Cr.

Founders Rock
Sky Meadow Group Camp

Union Creek

Skyline -to-the- Sea Trail

236

to Waterman Gap

North Escape Rd

Trail

Sequoia Trail

Wastahi Camp

Huckleberry Camp

Sempervirens Falls

East Ridge Road

P T

Jay Camp

Shadowbrook

Waddell Creek Rd

Sempervirens Camp

Continued on Castle Rock State Park Map

Redwood Trail

Pine Mtn.

East Ridge Trail

Blooms Creek Trail

Blooms Creek Camp

Buzzards Roost 2150'

Mountain

236

CHINA GRADE

1520' LP

LITTLE BASIN RD

Boulder Creek

Eagle Rock 2488'

BEN LOMOND MOUNTAIN

N

0   1 Mile
0   1 Kilometer

236

to Boulder Creek

♦ Big Basin Redwoods State Park ♦

Big Basin Redwoods, the first of California's state parks, was purchased in 1902 after a successful campaign led by a prominent San Jose artist and photographer, Andrew P. Hill. Following a fire at a private redwood grove near Felton, Hill was commissioned to photograph the giant trees, but was harassed by the owner, who intended to cut them for lumber. Believing that these beautiful redwoods should be preserved, Hill determined to start a campaign to save them. Enlisting the academic community and prominent civic leaders, including several women's groups, he arranged a meeting at Stanford University in 1900. On May 19th of that year, meeting at the base of Slippery Rock, these far-sighted people established the Sempervirens Club, dedicated to preserving for posterity the redwoods in the valley now known as Big Basin Redwoods State Park. Two years later the State of California's purchase of 2500 acres from the Big Basin Lumber Company and H. L. Middleton's gift of an additional 1300 acres, became the first state park.

Before the park could be opened to the public it was hit by a fire that traveled through all the then-parklands before being stopped just short of the ancient trees along today's Redwood Trail. It took until 1911 before the park was ready for public use.

Today, the park encompasses 18,000 acres and thousands of people come to marvel at the height and girth of the redwoods, to admire its free-flowing creeks and spectacular waterfalls, to walk along its 80 miles of trails, to camp in its redwood groves, or to picnic in the cool forests along Opal Creek.

Although Native Americans probably came to this valley to hunt game, harvest acorns, and collect seeds and berries, they probably did not live in the depths of its forests. The earliest recorded visitors were the group sent out by Gaspar de Portolá to look for Monterey Bay, which they had missed on their fog-enshrouded sail north along the coast. Their party, suffering from fatigue and illness, camped at the mouth of today's Waddell Creek. After a few days here, they were completely recovered and, thanking God for their renewed health and spirits, they named the place Cañada de la Salud—the Valley of Health. A commemorative plaque marks this site on the east side of Highway 1, just inside the present gates.

The basin was formed over the millennia by earthquakes uplifting great rocky blocks to form a circular rim around a central valley eroded by streams running through it. Mt. McAbee, Pine Mountain, and Chalks Mountain, high points on this rim, are accessible by trail. Waddell Creek and those which join it—Opal, Blooms, Berry and many smaller creeks—

empty into the Pacific, just 19 miles north of Santa Cruz. Other creeks—Año Nuevo, Whitehouse, Gazos, and Cascade—rise in the park's highlands, and drain directly into the ocean north of Waddell Creek.

The park is known for its abundance of native plant and animal life that early explorers and Native American tribes knew. Under the shade of the giant redwoods and along its streams the visitor will find delicate spring wildflowers, such as trillium, redwood sorrel, and flowering shrubs, especially the fragrant western azalea. Douglas firs, tanoaks, and madrone trees spring up where a redwood has fallen leaving space for sunlight to help these new trees take hold. On the higher, rocky ridges the typical trees are live oak, knobcone pine, buckeye, and the dense, often scratchy, chaparral plants like ceanothus, magenta-flowered pickeringia, manzanita and fine-leaved chamise. Many Big Basin trails take the hiker from the depths of the redwood forest up to its higher, drier rim populated by the chaparral community.

The best way to know and appreciate Big Basin is to walk along its trails, admire its magnificent trees, watch the spray from the waterfalls, and glory in the profusion of wildflowers that last late into summer. Sighting squirrels and deer, hearing the calls of Steller's jays and quail, and finding huckleberry bushes and clumps of wild iris are special pleasures for an observant visitor. A stay of several days will allow you to fully explore the park's best features. There are 6 campgrounds, 2 of which are for group camping, 5 backpack camps, and several tent cabins.

Included here are 11 hikes—some to high points in the park for glimpses of the ocean, some to its near and distant waterfalls, others to groves of monarch redwoods where the visitor feels dwarfed under their soaring majesty, and still others beside clear streams that ripple over moss-covered rocks between fern-clad banks.

Jurisdiction: State of California

Facilities: Park headquarters, small museum and visitor center; interpretive programs during summer months; central campfire area. 80+ miles of trails: hiking; wide park service roads open to equestrians and bicyclists. 146 family campsites, some accommodate trailers and RVs; 4 group campsites; several walk-in campsites—reservations 800-444-park (7275) or website http://www.cal-parks.ca.gov. Six backpacking trail camps—reservations required—call or visit park office 831-338-8861. Tent cabins, privately run, 800-874-8368. Horse camp at Rancho del Oso, reservations 831-425-1218.

Park Rules: Open year round. Dogs allowed in campsites, must be on leash at all times, not allowed on trails.

Maps: Mountain Parks Foundation *Big Basin Redwoods State Park*; Sempervirens Fund *Skyline-to-the-Sea Trail*, USGS topos *Big Basin, Franklin Point* and *Año Nuevo.*

How to Get There: *By Car:* From Saratoga Gap (west of Saratoga in Santa Clara County) at Skyline Blvd./Hwy. 9 junction take Hwy. 9 to

Hwy. 236 (Waterman Gap) and proceed 9 miles southwest to park head-quarters; or from Hwy. 9 in Boulder Creek in Santa Cruz County turn northwest on Hwy. 236 (Big Basin Hwy), and go 6 miles to park head-quarters.

By Bus: Santa Cruz Metropolitan Transit District buses stop at Big Basin headquarters and at Waddell Beach except during winter—831-425-8600.

Three Short Hikes from Park Headquarters.

Each visits a beautiful stream, encounters great redwoods, includes very little elevation gain and can be done in a few hours.

Big Basin Redwoods State Park
THE REDWOOD LOOP

Meandering among the trunks and stumps of ancient redwoods, some as old as 2000 years, this wide trail offers an introduction to redwood ecology and an inspiration to all who walk here.

Distance: 0.6-mile loop

Time: ½ hour

Elevation Change: Relatively Level

Trail Notes

At park headquarters you can purchase a pamphlet about the trail and walk across the road to the trail's entrance. The pamphlet, keyed to num-bered posts along the route, explains characteristics of redwood ecology. The Father Tree, thought to be 2000 years old and the park's largest, and the Mother Tree, considered the tallest at 329 feet, are marked stops on the route. Spend as much time as you like to marvel and admire these still-living giants. On summer weekends and on special occasions, well-informed and inspiring docents lead walks on this trail. Their knowledge will enrich your stay in the park.

The *Sequoia sempervirens* has a wide-spreading and sensitive, rather shallow root system which depends on surface moisture and the fog that nourishes it from above. Its habitat is restricted to coastal regions in California from south of Monterey to southern Oregon.

When one tree dies, its roots send out shoots that grow up in a circle around the fallen tree, and the new trees bear the parent's same genetic pattern. These circles are known as "fairy rings". If a tree falls in the park, it is left to slowly decompose, thus nourishing the soil where its new trees spring up.

This is a quiet walk, a place to reflect on the wonders of our natural world and to say thanks to Andrew P. Hill, his friend Father Robert Kenna, and the other visionaries who brought Big Basin Park into being.

Be sure to visit the Sempervirens Museum and the Visitor Center to see dioramas of the park, to listen to a presentation on the park's history, and to admire artifacts from its earliest days. All artifacts are protected, as are the plants and living creatures who share this place with you.

Big Basin Redwoods State Park
CREEPING FOREST AND DOOL TRAIL LOOP

Wide paths winding through the forested ridges on either side of Redwood Creek make a good family jaunt before a picnic lunch.

Distance: 3-mile loop

Time: 1¼ hours

Elevation Gain: 500'

Trail Notes

From park headquarters cross the road toward the Redwood Trail, go straight west, cross the bridge over Opal Creek, and turn right. You will be on the Skyline-to-the-Sea Trail heading north. As you follow the top of the creek bank on a pleasant footpath, note the water's milky, opalescent tone. Minerals suspended in the water and decaying plant material give it the lovely blue, lavender and rose hues of the precious stone—opal.

When you meet the Dool/Sunset trails junction, continue beyond it, pass the Gazos Creek bridge and trail and watch closely for the Creeping Forest Trail on your left. Shortly after turning onto this trail, you duck under a huge downed redwood that is resting on its elbow—a strong limb.

Uphill from this trail are picnic areas and restrooms, reached by a loop road off the Gazos Creek Road. But, continuing onward, you climb rather steeply, walk under an arching madrone tree and pass three redwoods whose trunks have fused together. With huckleberry bushes gracing the trailside, you bend sharply left and pass through a head-high cut in a fallen tree.

Where a sign points to Gazos Creek Road cutting off left, you stay right on the Creeping Forest Trail heading toward the Dool Trail, 0.8 mile beyond. Here are immense trees forming fairy rings around craters where ancient monarchs once grew. Part of the charm of this short trip is the many shapes and sizes of the burnt-out cavities of the still-living ancient trees. Redwoods will continue to grow and try to close the cavity as long as the tree retains a living cambium layer between the bark and the wood. Even when dead, trees of tremendous girth with a hollow core will stand for many years.

Children will love this trail, because they can climb into or through the tree cavities, play house in them or make up plays with their own imaginary characters or those from Winnie-the-Pooh or Swiss Family Robinson. On a windy day the small redwood needles fall like rain; on calm days bird calls fill the forest and squirrels can be seen scampering from branch to branch.

After 1.6 miles you descend to a crossing of the upper reaches of Redwood Creek and its marshy surroundings. By climbing steps cut in the roots of a fallen tree you walk on its 4-foot-wide trunk, which serves as a bridge. Wire is laid down to lessen a possible slippery passage in wet weather.

Now veering away from the ravine, at an unmarked junction, you go briefly right (uphill) to parallel Gazos Creek Road, which you then cross and head downhill, left, on the Dool Trail, named for one of this park's first rangers. Pass the Sunset Trail on your right and in less than 0.1 mile you hit the Skyline-to-the-Sea Trail. Follow it right (south), retracing your steps toward park headquarters, less then 0.5 mile from this junction. A stop at the Visitor Center will help you identify some of the flowers, shrubs and animals you have seen on this trip.

Big Basin Redwoods State Park
SEMPERVIRENS FALLS LOOP

A shady hike to the falls and monument commemorating the group that preserved these lands for a state park.

Distance: 4-mile loop

Time: 2 hours

Elevation Gain: 200'

Trail Notes

From headquarters turn south on the paved trail and, just beyond the meadow, pick up the Sequoia Trail on the left and follow it past the Jay Trail Camp. Bearing east, you meander between eight-foot-high hedges of huckleberry, zig-zag around gigantic redwoods, and go through the middle of a ring of redwoods that have grown since the matriarchal tree died. In the early morning or the late afternoon, slanting shafts of light coming through the trees deepen the tone of the red-brown redwood trunks and glisten on shiny-leaved huckleberry bushes.

Passing through lovely groves of stately sequoias, this well-designed trail then bends north beside Sempervirens Creek. Sometimes close to the creek, at others high above it on a narrow trail, you continue to the Wastahi Campground, perhaps named for one of the Native American groups who once frequented the park. Some say that Campfire Girls coined the name for *Water Star Hill.*

Beyond the camp you gradually ascend a trail along the base of a hill above Rogers Road, named for an early logger in this area who built this road on which to haul his wood. Watch for the sign that points to Sempervirens Falls across this road. On the other side a ramp and stairs lead to a viewing platform under a canopy of trees. Here, across from the falls, you are eye-to-eye with a wide band of water splashing into a deep, circular pool bounded by high rock walls festooned with ferns. A narrow ribbon of water cascades over a rocky course above the main falls. If you should be here when the sunlight strikes the waterfalls, it seems to illuminate individual drops of sparkling water.

To continue your hike, go back across the road and walk north a bit farther to see the plaque on the Founders Rock pedestal commemorating the 1902 founding of Big Basin Redwoods, the first California state park. Nearby are boulders and a downed tree that make good seats for lunching in the sun.

Then go left (northwest) on the Sequoia Trail and amble uphill over a vast, rough, mudstone shale slab punctuated by small groves of alders and shrubs, and covered with moss that can be slippery when wet—thus the name Slippery Rock. In spring, water flows over much of the rock, and

it may be necessary to pick your way along the edge of the forest on either side of the rock's uneven surface.

At the top of the slab a sign directs you left across a level area and onto a paved trail up through madrone and oak trees to a crossing of Highway 236, the main road through the park. On the other side of the road, the Sequoia Trail drops steadily down hill on the southwest side of a very steep slope covered with a relatively young redwood forest that is now shading out the tanoak trees that grew up after a forest fire. Traversing such a steep slope puts the hiker at

Sempervirens Falls seen from a viewing platform

mid-height of these redwoods—almost eye-level with squirrels or birds resting there. Towards the bottom of the canyon you come upon a clearing where immense, graceful ferns and shade-loving grasses fill the spaces around a great fallen redwood and several charred, dead, and uprooted redwoods.

Making a sharp left turn you look down on an arm of Opal Creek and then arrive at the North Escape Road bridge. You can take this road back to headquarters, but just on the other side of the bridge lies the Skyline-to-the-Sea Trail, a gentle, mostly downhill route. This trip crosses the bridge to the Skyline-to-the-Sea Trail, which follows the creek, veers around majestic redwoods, and in 0.2 mile it reaches the site of Maddock's Cabin. Here Tom Maddock and his son built their cabin out of a single, felled redwood tree on a 160-acre homestead claim.

Maddock stripped bark from tanoak trees in the surrounding forest and sold it by the wagon-load to a tannery in Santa Cruz. The family lived on their homestead in the present-day park for several years, hunting, fishing, and gathering berries, while also fending off the grizzly bears.

Continuing beside and around redwoods where tall azaleas and graceful ferns arch over the creek, you cross little tributaries of Opal Creek on short plank bridges. In spring lovely white coral bells, creamy wild ginger, and deep red trillium blossom beside the trail. After passing the junction with the Creeping Forest Trail on your right, you can take the Gazos Creek Road bridge (closed to autos, open to horses and bicycles) over to the North Escape Road or you can continue on the Skyline-to-the-Sea Trail for another 0.5 mile to the Redwood Trail where you turn left to reach park headquarters.

An alternate route from Sempervirens Falls to headquarters continues north from Founders Rock for less than 0.1 mile, crosses the bridge over Sempervirens Creek, and then follows the Shadowbrook Trail east toward Sky Meadow Group Camp. If you take this route, you will pass the group camp entrance, bear east to a crossing of Union Creek, and then head south beside it.

You can cross Union Creek on a foot trail to the Huckleberry Campground or follow the south side of Union Creek to another foot trail entrance to Huckleberry Campground on the right. Huckleberry is a beautiful big campground set among stately trees and laid out beside roads that meander in two circles on the north side of a connector road to Rogers Road. There are several tent cabins at this site that can be rented by calling the number listed in this book, page 127.

Now the Shadowbrook Trail turns south, follows the east side of Sempervirens Creek and parallels the Sequoia Trail, which you took north at the beginning of this trip. After almost a mile you pass Sempervirens Campground, then follow its road down to Highway 236 and turn right through thickets of huckleberry bushes. When you get to the Rogers Road junction, you can cross Highway 236 and follow its south side past the

Blooms Creek Campground entrance, turn north beside the highway, and shortly return to headquarters.

Three Trips on the Skyline-to-the-Sea Trail through Big Basin Redwoods

Big Basin Redwoods State Park

WATERMAN GAP TO CHINA GRADE ROAD

An undulating forest walk that makes a gradual elevation gain.

Distance: 4.5 miles one way

Time: 2½ hours

Elevation Gain: 640'

Trail Notes

This last leg of the Skyline-to-the-Sea Trail before the Big Basin Redwoods State Park boundary begins at Waterman Gap, where you may leave a car during daylight hours on the west side of the Highway 9/236 intersection. For a one-way hike, plan for a shuttle car to meet you at China Grade Road.

From Waterman Gap, you continue down the Skyline-to-the-Sea Trail heading generally west, cross Highway 9 to the west side and turn south, paralleling Highway 236. You cross a private logging road which goes north, go up a little knoll, and soon cross to the east side of the highway. Here you contour below the road and pass the junction with the Saratoga Toll Road trail leading uphill back to Castle Rock State Park.

Then gradually climbing, you encounter many huge stumps of redwood trees badly burned in an old fire. Tanoaks and madrones fill the gaps where heavy logging of the redwoods occurred. Their leaf litter makes a soft, mauve cover underfoot. In some places tall huckleberry thickets line the trail.

When you again cross the road to the west side, you wander in and around many more stumps of ancient burned redwoods still bearing the deep horizontal slots made to install springboards that the loggers stood on to cut these huge trees. After rising to the tops of little knolls and dipping down to cross private driveways beside the highway, you then turn back into the forest. Occasionally, you find a stump cut low enough for a seat on which you can pause to enjoy the smells and sounds of the forest.

Rounding a deep ravine, you walk through the center of an immense burned out redwood and turn gently downhill, now bearing west. At the top of the ravine is a cement dam, a spillway and a wooden bridge over the headwaters of Boulder Creek. Here, 4.2 miles from Waterman Gap, is a well-marked junction where you *must* turn sharp right and cross to the north side of Highway 236 if you are to continue on the Skyline-to-the-Sea Trail. If you cross the bridge and go south, you will take a somewhat overgrown but wide trail that ends at a gate to the East Ridge Trail and the south leg of China Grade Road, not the Skyline-to-the-Sea Trail route.

After crossing the highway your route zig-zags uphill through a mixed forest for less than 0.4 mile to reach the Skyline-to-the-Sea trailhead at China Grade Road. Across this road is the next leg of this wonderful 25-mile trail.

Big Basin Redwoods State Park
CHINA GRADE ROAD TO PARK HEADQUARTERS ON THE SKYLINE-TO-THE-SEA TRAIL

For a downhill adventure crossing sandstone outcrops and many creeks, have a friend drop you off at China Grade Road.

Distance: 4.5 miles one way

Time: 2¼ hours

Elevation Loss: 1000'

Trail Notes

Begin your trip on the next leg of the Skyline-to-the-Sea Trail from the south side of China Grade Road, just 0.4 mile north of its intersection with Highway 236. The trail entrance is directly across China Grade Road from the Skyline-to-the-Sea Trail coming from Waterman Gap. Your trip drops quickly to a junction with the hiking/equestrian Basin Trail taking off right for the Lane Camp and on to Portola Redwoods. However, the hikers-only Skyline-to-the-Sea Trail goes straight ahead (west) through chaparral, descending over and around sandstone outcrops. Patches of straggly knobcone pines and a few Douglas firs cast shadows on the trail; in drier areas madrones and tall ceanothus dominate, interspersed with gray-leaved manzanita and pickeringia—a thorny, magenta-blossomed chaparral plant of the pea family.

The most unusual feature of the trip is the immense Butano Sandstone slab which you cross—it covers the entire hillside—extending from just below China Grade Road across this trail and below it. Water channels are etched into the rock, and water, wind, and sand have hollowed out little basins. Several very large sandstone outcrops rise above the trail, one shaped like a large turtle, with head and flippers easily imagined. What shapes do you see?

You will cross tiny rivulets, some still seeping in late summer, several supplied with plank bridges. Where the moisture is plentiful, redwoods are creeping in and shading out the knobcone pines. As you lose elevation, the forest thickens, and you are walking along the top of a knife-edged ridge above the canyons of Opal Creek on either side. In an opening in the forest you can look due south across the valley to one of the high points of Big Basin—2150′ Buzzard's Roost, a knobby outcrop on Pine Mountain (see Trip 9, page 144). Visible too, on a clear day, is Eagle Rock, the tallest of the park's mountains at an elevation of 2488′ (see Trip 11, page 149).

Before long you are in a cool forest of very large redwoods. Your trail swings wide to the south and then turns due north, descending to cross two arms of Opal Creek, one just a small stream trickling musically through a tight ravine, the other, possibly the main branch of the creek, a broad stream with a sturdy bridge. At the junction with the Hollow Tree Trail, 1.8 mile from your starting point, the signs point south to park headquarters, just 2.7 miles farther along.

On a plank bridge over deep pools edged with clumps of tall, graceful, wavy grass you see Opal Creek coursing around lichen and moss-covered rocks. Among tall redwoods and tanoaks yet another branch of this beautiful creek joins the main stem.

While climbing up a side ridge overlooking the creek you may notice numerous fallen trees here, probably from serious storms of recent years. The creek banks are profusely clad with tall ferns, western azalea (come in May or June to see its creamy white blossoms and enjoy its sweet fragrance), slender-stalked, white coral bells, and large, flat heads of cream-colored blossoms of giant-leaved aralia.

Just 0.5 mile from the Hollow Tree Trail junction you meet the North Escape Road on your left and a picnic area on the right side of the creek. The Skyline-to-the-Sea Trail stays on the west side of the road and crosses Rodgers Creek (named for W. S. Rodgers, editor of the Boulder Creek newspaper *Mountain Echo,* who became an ardent proponent of this first California State Park—Big Basin. After passing the Meteor Trail on the right, walk straight ahead (south) on the west side of Opal Creek. Here the creek begins to show its luminescent colors—lavender, blue, rose—caused by minerals suspended in the water which are apparently not harmful to the animals who drink it.

Still descending, you walk around and beside some of the most magnificent trees in the park. At the Maddock Cabin Site you can read the historical plaque and marvel that one man and a boy could fell a huge redwood and build their house here in 1877. Then at the Gazos Creek Road junction you can follow the Skyline-to-the-Sea Trail to the Redwood Trail and thence to park headquarters or you can take the bridge over the creek and follow the paved park road past a very large picnic area set under stately, ancient redwoods, where perhaps your friends await you with a picnic lunch, or carry on a short way to the park office on your left.

Big Basin Redwoods State Park
DOWN TO THE SEA ON FOOT

A great adventure beside the park's major creeks on the Skyline-to-the-Sea Trail from park headquarters to the Pacific.

Distance: 9.9 miles one-way

Time: 5–6 hours

Elevation Loss: 1000'

Trail Notes

Be sure to check with park headquarters before starting this hike. Right after a heavy storm, creek crossings may be impossible. In addition, only the most hardy can do this as a round trip. Therefore, either take two cars, leaving one at Waddell Creek on Highway 1 and driving the other to the park headquarters; or from trail's end at Waddell Beach take the bus to Santa Cruz and transfer to another Metro bus back to your starting point. Schedules are available at the park and at the Santa Cruz Bus Station. You can get permission to leave a car overnight inside the Waddell Creek gate if you plan to camp along the way.

This last and most varied leg of a 25-mile trail from Saratoga Gap to the Pacific Ocean begins at park headquarters and follows Waddell Creek and its tributaries all the way. Just across the road from headquarters, follow the wide path past the Redwood Trail and pick up the Skyline-to-the-Sea Trail on the west side of Opal Creek. Turn left and head south to wind around the stumps of fallen monarch redwoods, pass beside still living giants and marvel at their immense girth and the outreaching roots that keep these trees upright.

Here in late spring the creamy white blossoms of the western azaleas fill the air with a heavenly fragrance. The mosses and ferns collect moisture from the fog, and the resulting water droplets sparkle in the sunlight.

Shortly you pass a foot trail on the left which goes south to connect with Hihn Hammond Road, but you bear right (west) toward Middle Ridge on a circuitous route. Two bridges built at almost right angles take you over and along a vast, steep ravine. Still climbing, you walk through the cavity of a burned-out tree and hit the wide Middle Ridge Road. Eschew the Howard King Trail on the left and bear right (north) on the

Skyline-to-the-Sea Trail. This segment contours pleasantly through a more open forest, curving around little ravines where water trickles down the hillside, even in late summer.

Bear left past the short connector to the Sunset Trail and continue on the Skyline-to-the-Sea Trail, noting a sign that says it is 1.6 miles to the Timms Creek Trail. Heading southwest, you pass the east end of a Kelly Creek alternate trail descending to a little flat beside Kelly Creek to which this alternate will take you. In 0.3 mile you meet the other (west) end of the Kelly Creek alternate and cross yet another bridge.

Consider the maintenance that rangers and volunteers do to keep this trail open. Trees often fall during storms, the bridges wash out during heavy rainfall, and banks give way. The bridge across Kelly Creek had just been replaced when the authors last hiked this route.

Now 2.7 miles from headquarters and in deep shade, you are at a major confluence of creeks—Kelly Creek meets the West Waddell flowing in from the north and then, almost immediately from the south an unnamed stream comes in, which you go over on a narrow bridge. Following the Skyline-to-the-Sea-Trail down the south bank of the West Waddell, you then emerge into a more open forest where sunshine is welcome on a sunny, but cool, spring day.

Descending steps of varying width and height carved into the hillside, you see the West Waddell, descending too, in little cascades over rounded rocks and boulders between pools edged with wavy grasses. A low, wide, wooden bridge takes you across to the other side where Berry Creek tumbles out of its confined canyon after its dramatic 60' plunge over a vertical rock shelf. It is a "must-do" detour up to a viewing platform to admire that silvery thread dropping into a misty basin at your feet. Back at the Waddell pools, there are some convenient rocks and a short plank bench where you can stop for lunch in the sun.

Beyond the confluence of Berry and West Waddell creeks you follow the west side of the Waddell as it descends in cascades and riffles in a widening canyon. At its first crossing (as of this writing), you need to balance on an aluminum I-beam or wade to cross the creek. Shortly you pass the Howard King Trail on the left (see Trip 10, page 147 for description of this trail) and walk on a wide road under a high canopy of alders and Douglas firs. The thimbleberry bushes' large, light yellow-green leaves make a pretty roadside hedge.

Again crossing the creek, this time on a portable bridge, you reach a sandy beach on the far side. Then another crossing, this time on a wide vehicle bridge apparently damaged by storms, goes to the west side of the Waddell. At 4.7 miles into your trip you meet the Henry Creek Trail coming in from the north. The sign here informs you that Waddell Beach is 5.2 miles ahead on your Skyline-to-the-Sea Trail route.

The canyon is more open now and you see many young redwoods among the stumps left from earlier logging days which ended in the

1960s. Storm damage from El Niño is still evident in the tangles of downed trees and broken shrubs. Five redwood trees were lying across the road when the authors walked this trail. Yet, luxurious ferns line the trail and aralia's big flower heads poke out of the creekbed. On a meander of the creek, which has undercut the bank here, you soon pass a grassy flat where new alders are thriving. Young leafy shrubs, sedges, and horsetails grow near the creek and potato vines wind around the underbrush. Great stalks of woodwardia ferns wave in the breeze.

Now walking closer to creek level, after being above it, you meet the McCrary Ridge Trail, a horse trail that descends from the Hihn Hammond Road at the Mt. Mc Abee Overlook. Here also the West Waddell Fork joins the East Fork and the main Waddell's speed and volume pick up. This grand stream, named for the early woodsman who died of injuries inflicted by a grizzly bear, transports the drainage from almost all the Big Basin Redwoods watershed.

Hikers cross the Waddell on a high, arched-steel bridge with wooden planks. Horses must ford the creek. Beyond the bridge in fall is a boulder-strewn island, and the creekbed is more open and wider. Shortly, on the right you find the Camp Herbert sign and a hazelnut-lined path that leads to 6 campsites laid out on little flats separated by tall ferns. Not far from the nearby streambed a huge redwood stump sits in the middle of an opening—a good place for a group to gather. If you are planning to camp along this route, you can make reservations through the park office.

Continuing your trip to the sea, you pass by a crescent-shaped flat covered with a dense green undergrowth of vinca, a plant with delicate blue flowers found in many once-occupied settlements in the Coast Range. Just a little farther downstream is an intriguing sign on your left—Tramway Springs—at a gated road. About a mile farther you reach a second trail camp—Twin Redwoods, its 6 campsites laid out in a tall bay tree forest. Narrow trails through a dense vinca ground cover lead to each site. As in all Big Basin trail camps, no open fires are allowed, but camp stoves can be used. Ask when you make your reservations if there is water in the tanks. Otherwise, carry your own or bring the means to filter out microbial elements from creek water. Campsite #1 is under an immense, spreading, gnarled, multi-trunked bay tree.

You are losing elevation fast—Camp Herbert is at 200' and Twin Redwoods at 100'. For the past mile your way has been through a narrow canyon with high, imposing, steep-sided West Ridge on your right. The Clark Connection to the West Ridge Trail is a horse trail that follows the ridgetops from Chalk Mountain, then zig-zags down the last steep 2 miles.

The next campsite marked on your map, Alder Camp, was completely washed out during El Niño storms, and may not have been replaced. Check with the rangers.

Shortly beyond the Clark Connection and the site of the former Alder Camp is a foot trail that swings out in two semi-circles to the west, bypassing the main road, which is open to equestrians and bicyclists. This foot trail crosses the Waddell on a steel bridge installed in 1987 by the Sempervirens Fund. According to the plaque, this bridge over the Cañon del Oso (no bears in sight) is dedicated to the "Hikers of Big Basin Redwoods State Park." Beyond the bridge the trail goes a bit north and uphill through a Douglas fir forest, then into a conglomeration of moss-draped buckeye trees, berry vines and hazelnut bushes. Eventually the trail heads south, contouring along West Ridge, crossing several little streams (dry in summer), and in an opening looking down on the market gardens and orchards of Rancho del Oso.

Suddenly you round a corner and see the ocean! But you must first cross a little ravine and walk along a high mudstone cliff before descending to the road at the ranger office (open on Saturdays and Sundays from noon to 4 P.M.). After being in the canyons and forests of the park, you now feel the expansiveness of the Theodore J. Hoover Natural Preserve, a wide freshwater marsh. And you can hear the roar of the waves on Waddell Beach. From the ranger station a trail wanders south through the marsh to the Rancho del Oso Nature Center, usually open on weekends.

If you choose to go directly to the beach and the parking areas there, continue down the road to the park gate. Just inside this gate is a bronze plaque mounted on a granite slab which records the rest stop that Gaspar de Portolá's party made here in October 1769. Nourished by the abundant wild berries and small game the sick members made a quick return to health. They named it *Cañada de la Salud*, the Valley of Good Health.

You can cross Highway 1 on the Waddell Creek bridge and visit the long, crescent-shaped beach where pelicans, seagulls, and surfers enjoy its meandering lagoon and sometimes wild waves. While inhaling the fresh sea air, invigorating after your long hike, you can watch the wind-surfers skim over the tops of waves as they head out to catch a ride on the crests of incoming rollers.

Two Trips in the Park's Northwestern Reaches

Big Basin Redwoods State Park
A LOOP TRIP THROUGH THE OPAL CREEK WATERSHED

Discover the Hollow Tree, find an old logging camp, and lunch at a Trail Camp.

Distance: 8.1-mile loop

Time: 5 hours

Elevation Gain: 882'

Trail Notes

Begin this trip from China Grade Road (follow the directions for Trip 5, page 134) on the Skyline-to-the-Sea Trail and continue down to the second Opal Creek crossing, where a sign points right for the Hollow Tree Trail and the Middle Ridge Fire Road. In a forest of Douglas fir and tanoak trees there are many fire-scarred but living redwoods. After passing the Papadopoulos Redwood Grove, you curve around a ravine and there is the still-living, burned-out Hollow Tree which gives this trail its name.

Crossing another branch of Opal Creek you begin to see the results of a very disastrous fire—devastated redwoods. Some are huge, blackened stumps, some are completely burned, fallen trees, and others are craters, where the fire burned the tree roots. Many of the redwoods are still living, though badly scarred.

The newcomer trees—tanoaks, especially, are filling in and their fallen leaves cover the ground, picking up a little light to brighten the morbid scene. As the trail climbs beside the creek around still-living skeletons and moss-covered rocks, you meet and cross several branches of the creek. The side walls of the canyon are very steep, and the creek drops over the joined, burned roots of two giant redwoods. A rickety bridge over a great, rocky fall (almost dry in late summer) takes the hiker onto a nose between two branches of the creek.

After 1.4 miles from the Hollow Tree/Skyline-to-the-Sea trails junction, Middle Ridge Road is just ahead, but you follow the Hollow Tree Trail to the right. At this elevation the terrain is drier, there are San Lorenzo formation outcrops, the manzanita and madrone are prominent, and there is still some evidence of fire damage. As you round the ridge and head back into redwoods, you reach the site of the former Johansen Shingle Mill, built in 1927. Remnants of a large logging operation are visible—boilers, shingles, boards scattered about, loading platforms, and a 1992 memorial bench to R. Bruce Deame by the hiking group Companions of the Trail.

Resuming your hike on the Hollow Tree Trail, you bear east across the upper reaches of Opal Creek where it flows over a sandstone wall—a fine waterfall in spring, but only a trickle in late summer. The dense forest of tall, slender tanoaks is struggling to gain a foothold on the sandstone, and former fire damage is evident. After going into the heads of several ravines and around the shoulders of ridges, you reach an intersection and a sign for Lane Trail Camp, which is back to the left (west). Here are six primitive campsites, several on a high knoll where you could stop for lunch. These sites can be reserved for overnight backpack camping, although you must carry your own water or the means to purify water from creeks you crossed.

After your lunch, return to the Hollow Tree Trail junction. Ahead is China Grade Road and across it is the trailhead for the Basin Trail to Portola Redwoods State Park. On your right is the 3.2-mile Basin Trail, your return route southeast to the Skyline-to-the-Sea trailhead from which you started.

Also known as the Sunrise Rim Trail, the Basin Trail, a horse and hiking trail (no bikes), begins as a narrow path dropping downhill through a fir, redwood, and tanoak forest marked by signs of recent and old fires. Soon you encounter sandstone outcrops and the forest changes to knobcone pines. There are some leather oaks, too, small shrubby trees with leathery, dull-green leaves whose upper surface is curled under and supplied with sharp spines.

Before long you begin a long traverse over the top of the great sandstone slab you crossed at the beginning of your trip. Where shrubs have gained a toehold, there is manzanita. In early summer lovely specimens of two- to five-foot-tall pitcher sage border the trail, recognized by their dull-white to lavender-hued, cup-like blossoms resembling a pitcher. In fall you can usually see the brilliant red-orange California fuchsias tucked into crevices in the rock. At one point above the trail there is a huge, double-trunked redwood with completely burned-out heart. But the predominant tree is the knobcone pine.

Now the trail contours along a very steep hillside, and although no longer on bare sandstone, the soil is sandy and not very deep. Going around more burned-out redwoods, your trail crosses some moist sections where graceful hazelnut bushes thrive. Then, in less than 2 hours from Lane Camp you reach the junction with the Skyline-to-the-Sea Trail and go uphill a few paces to China Grade Road and the end of your loop trip.

Big Basin Redwoods State Park
TRIPLE WATERFALLS HIKE

Try this vigorous hiker's loop trip to visit some of the park's most beautiful features.

Distance: 10.2 miles

Time: 5½ hours

Elevation Gain: 600'

Trail Notes

From park headquarters take the Skyline-to-the-Sea Trail right (north), turn left (northwest) on the Dool Trail, and then almost immediately turn left (west) on the Sunset Trail. Now you begin a most delightful walk on a beautifully built, hikers-only trail that contours up and down in a generally western direction. Here, as on many Big Basin park trails, you will see great hulks of redwoods, badly burned, some still living, others just shells.

In 0.5 mile you cross Middle Ridge Road just below its intersection with Gazos Creek Road. Both these roads, left over from previous logging days and occasionally used by park personnel for routine inspection trips or emergency situations, are used by equestrians and are open to bicyclists as well.

Shortly after the Middle Ridge Road junction take note of a short connector trail to the Skyline-to-the-Sea Trail for your return trip, but outward-bound, continue along the side of a gentle slope, detouring around fallen trees and crossing little rivulets on plank bridges. In some places where a redwood has fallen across the trail, the rangers have cut a big slice out of the tree and hikers can pass through.

Contouring northward you begin to hear water flowing and then you dip down to see it in West Waddell Creek. The creekside is decorated with large leaves of colt's foot and stalks of horsetails; logs, both great and small, lie in and across the creek's course. The authors took this trip in late August and found all the streams running and star-flowers and honeysuckle still blooming.

You descend to a rustic bridge, cross the West Waddell, and begin climbing to meet the Timms Creek Trail, which follows the Waddell down to the Skyline-to-the-Sea Trail. At 3.5 miles from its start, this trip continues westward on the Sunset Trail, but for those who want to return to headquarters on a shorter loop, the Timms Creek Trail is a possibility.

The Sunset Trail is a popular route—you will meet many others who are on their way to or from Berry Creek Falls. A particularly interesting 10-foot redwood stump, devoid of bark, sits beside the trail. With dark spots for eyes and a slit for a mouth it looks like "Old Man Redwood." A mile from the Timms Creek Trail junction, you drop down to cross Berry Creek. Shade-loving plants—pink-flowered redwood sorrel, broad-leaved fetid adder's tongue, and fern-like *Vancouveria*—thrive here, but soon you ascend a ridge where chaparral and sandstone prevail. Light-blue bush lupines blooming in summer are a surprise, and just as you are getting used to some open country, you head back into the trees. Never mind, now you see several specimens of the rather rare California nutmeg tree.

One-half mile from Berry Creek, you come to a junction where a trail takes off right to Sunset Trail Camp. If you want to lunch at this camp, or are planning to spend the night there, take this trail up a short, steep, chalky slot, pass the outhouse, and then descend into the forest, where you will find 10 campsites. An old logging road services the camp and also provides a barrier from the main trail. The campsites, laid out with 6 sites to the right and 4 others to the left, are separated from each other by trees and shrubs, have logs to sit on, and have plenty of space to spread out several sleeping bags. Water is available at the creek above the falls, just 0.2 mile farther along the main trail. All creek water must be purified.

To get to the falls, return to the main trail, turn right, and follow your ears! You can hear the water dropping over the top ledge as you zig-zag down to the upper falls, or Golden Cascade, on West Berry Creek. Under the high canopy of a redwood and Douglas fir forest, the creek drops over a sandstone ledge, tumbles over four more ledges, and then splashes into a pool carved out of golden sandstone.

From this pool draped with five-finger ferns, you begin a precarious descent down slippery rock steps, which are lined with white coral bells and hug the edge of a steep 25- to 30-foot-high wall over which the creek drops—the magnificent Silver Falls. At its base is another little pool, more shallow than the one below Golden Cascade. Then the creek drops through a narrow watergate between mossy boulders and you cross a bridge at the confluence of West Berry and Berry creeks. Evidence of the creek's power can be seen in the trees and rocks which have been dis-lodged and transported by the water.

The trail is now on the west side of the creek, and you descend beside the dramatic 60-foot drop of Berry Creek Falls. High, fern-draped walls enclose this tree-topped canyon; sunshine bores through the trees in silver shafts. Some redwoods cling to the rocky sides, but others have fallen; one tree stands askew at the base of the falls.

It is difficult to appreciate the full power and the beauty of the falls as you descend beside it, but there is a viewing platform and a memorial bench on the north side of the waterfall's base where you can see the wide stream plunge over the shelf, come together in a V, then become a single strand that free-falls to the base of the cliff.

When you've had your fill of the magical water wonders and are ready for your return to park headquarters, walk back to the trail junction at the confluence of Berry and West Waddell creeks, cross the Waddell, and mount the stairs cut into the mossy, damp hillside. You have now rejoined the Skyline-to-the-Sea Trail leading back to headquarters. Here in reverse, is a short description of this trail described in Trip 6.

You climb over huge redwood roots laid bare by traffic and weather, mount more steps, and cross little rivulets emerging from the moist hillsides. In mid-summer you may have the pleasure of seeing the showy deep-pink blossoms of *Clintonia* on a tall stalk above light green, strap-like leaves. Later in summer, its shiny blue berries appear on these stalks, which the deer find very appetizing.

At the confluence of West Waddell and Kelly creeks, you leave the Waddell and walk over several bridges crossing Kelly Creek. After gaining several hundred feet in elevation beyond Kelly Creek along steep side slopes, you reach a trail junction where you have two possibilities—bear south to continue on the Skyline-to-the-Sea Trail or jog a bit north to join the Sunset Trail, on which you started west. Either takes you back to your starting point at park headquarters.

This is a long, fairly strenuous trip, but well-prepared hikers in good condition can do it easily. However, for weather and bridge conditions, plus vagaries of storm damage, check with the rangers before starting, and carry plenty of water, and extra food and clothing.

Three Peak Trips

See the park from its rocky heights.

9

Big Basin Redwoods State Park
TO PINE MOUNTAIN AND BUZZARD'S ROOST

A rocky scramble leads to views of park peaks and South Bay high points.

Distance: 4.4 miles round trip; alternate return—add 2 miles.

Time: 2½ hours; alternate return—add 1 hour.

Elevation Gain: 1150'

Trail Notes

From the park office go across the main road, pick up the trail that roughly parallels the road and turn left (south). Follow this trail for about 0.4 mile until you reach the Blooms Creek Campground road, on which you turn right (south). Go through the gate (open during daylight hours)

Climb Buzzard's Roost for great views

and very soon you take the trail on the left that crosses Blooms Creek. Almost immediately after the bridge, turn right on the Blooms Creek Trail (left goes to the campgrounds), and watch for the Pine Mountain Trail on your left (southeast). If you miss this turn, you will soon intercept the East Ridge Trail (for equestrians), which eventually crosses the Pine Mountain Trail. You will be climbing on either trail, but the more intimate, narrower hiker's trail keeps you in touch with its huckleberry-bush border under a high tan-oak, fir, and redwood canopy.

After crossing the East Ridge Trail, you will begin to see fine specimens of salal, that very shiny-leaved, spreading, low-growing shrub of moist environments that has blossoms similar to manzanita flowers. Another plant of the wet, coastal zones is the western azalea, which you will see on this trip and on several others described in this guide to Big Basin Redwoods State Park.

When a fork of the trail goes off at an acute angle to the left, take it, because both forks come out on the old Pine Mountain Road. Follow the road just around a bend and find the trail resuming on the right. Now about 0.8 mile from the park office, you continue uphill, climbing over some outcrops, and using great arms of tree roots and nearby rocks to help gain elevation.

After you round one of several switchbacks where there is a scattering of young nutmeg trees (flat needles with sharp points distinguish it from Douglas fir needles), the view begins to open up. Off to the northeast you can see the grasslands of Long Ridge Open Space Preserve undulating west from Skyline Boulevard.

Continuing ever upward, you come up to a trail junction. Be sure to go left! The right-hand trail is closed and impassable. Going left will reward you with a short climb up the face of a bare sandstone slab. At its apex is Buzzard's Roost—a knobby, 10'-protrusion with 340° views. The summit of Pine Mountain on the left blocks the ocean view. (If you have soft-soled shoes, hiking boots or sturdy running shoes, the footing is secure on its summit).

Nearly around-the-compass views greet you, with Mt. McAbee directly west (the trail to it is described in Trip 10.) Its almost-vertical face rises abruptly from the canyon of the East Waddell between it and Buzzard's Roost. Even farther west and a bit south you can see the white line of Chalks Road winding down toward the west boundary of the park. Almost due north is the 2000' ridge of Butano State Park, the Butano Fire Trail and China Grade Road on Big Basin's north boundary. Castle Rock State Park's 3000' ridge lies slightly north and east. Due east lie Mt. Umunhum and Loma Prieta, both higher than your position on this mountain. The tallest point in the park, Eagle Rock at 2488', is east and usually visible across the Scott Creek Canyon known as Little Basin. A former lookout, it is accessible by trail through a forest regrown after serious fires of the past. (See Trip 11, page 149 for directions and trail description.)

If the day is clear, you might catch a glimpse of the Pacific sparkling in the sunlight, but the authors found the view better from Mt. McAbee, because the line-of-sight down the Waddell Canyon is more direct. (Densely forested Pine Mountain is just southwest.)

After orienting yourself to these high points, return down the same Pine Mountain Trail to park headquarters. For an additional 2-mile variation, turn right when you hit the Blooms Creek Trail junction and follow the creek northeast through some fine redwood groves to the East Ridge Trail, which eventually crosses Highway 236. On the other side of the highway you meet the Shadowbrook Trail, on which you can turn left (west), pass Sempervirens Campground, and cross the highway again. The trail on the highway's south side soon joins the trail you took from headquarters to start this trip.

10

Big Basin Redwoods State Park
A LOOP TRIP TO MT. MCABEE OVERLOOK

Climb to views down the Waddell canyon and see the sea from the Howard King Trail.

Distance: 3 miles to Overlook; 6 miles, if return on same route; 11 miles, if you descend Howard King Trail and return on Skyline-to-the-Sea Trail

Time: 3–6½ hours, depending on route

Elevation Gain: 730' to Overlook; Berry Creek Falls to HQ 600'

Elevation Loss: 1330' to Berry Creek Falls

Trail Notes

Start from headquarters by crossing the road, pass the Redwood Trail, walk across the Opal Creek bridge and take the Skyline-to-the-Sea Trail left (south). After 0.2 mile a sign points to the Hihn-Hammond Connector, which you do not take. It is the old road, the horse route. Stay on the Skyline-to-the-Sea Trail until you get to Middle Ridge Road (0.9 mile), which you cross and then turn left (southwest) on the Howard King Trail. This trail is named for a fine nature photographer who knows every tree, shrub, creek, and trail in the park. You can see some of his splendid black-and-white photographs of the park in the Visitor Center and in the Sempervirens Room.

On the Howard King Trail you begin an upward pitch on a very narrow, beautiful, hikers-only trail, traverse quiet, steep-sided canyons covered with slim redwoods and tanoaks, and then walk along a knife-edged ridge. After 0.6 mile you come out onto wide Hihn-Hammond Road, walk uphill a few feet and look for an indistinct trail on your right. When you find it across a drainage ditch, you climb abruptly uphill on the northwest side of this ridge. Huckleberries, tanoaks and young redwoods, along with some scruffy knobcones, close in on the trail, which then goes across an old skid road, where you turn left onto Hihn-Hammond Road again. Continue just 0.05 mile and take the trail going off to the left, where you alternately go through stretches of chaparral and forest.

Now on the south side of the mountain, you round a corner and there across the canyon lie Pine Mountain and Buzzard's Roost at 2150'. The buzzards, which are more correctly called turkey vultures, like to soar on the updrafts from the canyon between that mountain and this one (see Trip 9, page 144). When again in the chaparral, you may find multi-colored wildflowers to brighten the scene. The blue lupines, apricot-colored sticky-monkey flower, lavender yerba santa, yellow lotus and magenta pick-eringia were still very showy when the authors were here in October.

Shortly emerging on the wide road again, you find a wooden bench—just right for lunch in the sun with a view of the ocean, broader than the glimpse you had earlier. If the day is very clear, you can see the surf and catch an occasional flash of sunlight reflected off a car window on Highway 1. If you are planning to take the Skyline-to-the-Sea Trail to Waddell Beach some day, here is an aerial view of the canyon and your destination.

This trip continues west on the Howard King Trail, but if you would like to take a shorter return, retrace your steps northeast on the Howard King and Skyline-to-the-Sea trails to park headquarters.

To continue northwest, follow the wide road over exposed, chalky stone slabs around the west end of the ridge for less than 0.5 mile to a junction and bear right (northwest) uphill. At this junction is a veritable forest of chinquapin trees—a chaparral native which has golden-backed leaves and prickly-sided seed pods. (From here the road takes off due south and shortly becomes the McCrary Ridge horse trail, ending at the junction of two forks of Waddell Creek.)

From the junction the Howard King Trail climbs up the ridge—you weren't really on the top of Mt. McAbee when at the Overlook—and eventually you start down on quite a narrow trail. But before you get too deep into the predominantly redwood forest, look out across the Waddell Canyon to Chalk Mountain at 1609' and north to China Grade Road at 2000'.

Your descent on the Howard King Trail is a zig-zag trip down a narrow ridge that loses elevation at every step. The authors found the going quite slippery—we called it a "ball-bearing trail," because little pebbles of bro-ken-up sandstone, oak acorns, and seed cones of redwoods were covered with a deep layer of tanoak leaves and we slid at each step. Toward the bottom of the trail we could hear the sound of the creek and its waterfalls. Here in this moist environment were beautiful specimens of lacy-leaved hazelnut trees.

Turning right at the bottom of the trail, you see a hitchrack for horses and the evidence of an old logging road coming in on the right. Shortly you meet the Berry Creek Falls Trail at its junction with the Skyline-to-the-Sea Trail. If you haven't seen the falls yet, take a quick side trip up to the viewing platform to see Berry Creek's 60' silvery thread drop into a pool at your feet. (See Trip 8, page 142, for a loop trip to all the falls on Berry Creek and find the directions for your Skyline-to-the-Sea Trail return trip to headquarters.)

Big Basin Redwoods State Park
EAGLE ROCK ASCENT

360-degree views reward the hiker who scrambles to the site of a former fire lookout.

Distance: 3.1 miles round trip

Time: 2¼ hours

Elevation Gain: 1328'

How to Get There: From park headquarters take Highway 236 east for 2.7 miles to its intersection with Little Basin Road. Turn right (south) and follow this winding, one-lane road for about a mile to roadside parking outside the gate to Little Basin, a private recreation camp. Do not block this gated road nor the private driveway on the road's east side. Or take Highway 9 past Waterman Gap heading toward Boulder Creek, and turn right (southwest) on Highway 236, and then left (south) on Little Basin Road and proceed as directed above.

Trail Notes

Begin your hike up the private driveway until you see a steel gate. Just before the gate is a foot trail leading uphill on the right. You climb up a forested ridge, cross another unpaved road, and stay on the trail roughly paralleling a tributary of Blooms Creek. You cross branches of this creek many times on this trip, staying for the most part on its western arm. This creek is named for a late 19th century lumberman turned preservationist who became a vice-president of the Sempervirens Club.

The fairly well-defined trail mounts consistently uphill. Many burned-out trees, some still alive, attest to past fires here. At 0.9 mile you cross a deep ravine on a handsome 35-foot, arched wooden bridge, its planks and sides held together with wooden pegs (runnels is the technical term). This "no-nails" Bridge is the handiwork of two ardent Santa Cruz Mountains Trail Association trail builders—Jack Schultz and Bob Kirsch—along with more than 200 association volunteers.

Where the trees are dense and tall on the north side of Eagle Rock, there is very little undergrowth, but as you climb, the forest thins and allows more light to penetrate, and chaparral plants, such as manzanita, chamise, and knobcone pines move in. Climbing over and around large boulders on a trail that narrows as it rises, you come to a spur trail that leads west to a rocky promontory—not the summit of Eagle Rock. Carry on now for another half-mile on the north side of the mountain, switchbacking until you hit the old fire road that will take you along a narrow ridge to the top.

If the day is clear, you will be able to identify many of the mountains and canyons you have visited in Big Basin—Buzzard's Roost, Mt.McAbee and the canyons of the Waddell separating them. To the northeast lie Mt. Umunhum and Loma Prieta and the Castle Rock heights; to the south you may be able to see the Santa Lucia Mountains rising above Monterey Bay; and off to the west lies the Pacific Ocean, perhaps even shimmering in the sunshine!

As you prepare to make your way back down the mountain, think of the fire-watchers who stayed up here to signal early warnings of forest fires. Now new technology has supplanted those individuals, but the little wooden structure still stands as a tribute to their efforts to keep our forests green.

Big Basin Redwoods "Connected"

Over the years after the founding of Big Basin State Park in 1902, efforts continued to enlarge the boundaries of the park to include the entire Waddell Creek watershed. As more lands were added, state, regional and local agencies created trail links to parks in southwestern San Mateo County and northern Santa Cruz County. Listed here are the names and short descriptions of these trail connections.

As noted in the section on the Skyline-to-the-Sea Trail in this book, the oldest connection is between Castle Rock State Park at Saratoga Gap and Waterman Gap. From Waterman Gap to Waddell Beach, a distance of 20 miles through Big Basin Redwoods, was later accomplished to complete the 25-mile trip from the crest of the Santa Cruz Mountains to Waddell State Beach on the Pacific Coast. See Trips 2, 3, 4 and 5 (pages 115-123) in Castle Rock State Park and Trips 4, 5 and 6 (pages 133-139) in Big Basin Redwoods.

A more recent connection, the Basin Trail, links Big Basin with the Pescadero Creek County Park complex and Portola Redwoods State Park, a combined area of over 10,000 acres in southwestern San Mateo County. The Basin Trail leaves China Grade Road just opposite the junction of the Hollow Tree and Basin trails at Lane Trail Camp. Open to hikers and equestrians only (property owner's deed restrictions ban bicyclists), the trail ambles gently up and down through a thriving young forest traversing a 15-foot-wide wide easement. It continues to a scenic overlook where views of Midpeninsula Regional Open Space Preserves along the Skyline ridge open up.

Beyond the overlook this splendid trail switchbacks downhill in Pescadero Creek County Park through a forest where some ancient redwoods survived fires and logging, passes lively cascades on two creeks, and then enters the magnificent forests of Portola Redwoods State Park— a distance of 6.8 miles from China Grade Road.

From Portola Redwoods State Park, the Slate Creek and Ward Road trails lead to MROSD's Long Ridge Open Space Preserve. (See *Peninsula*

Trails by Rusmore, Spangle and Crowder for more detailed descriptions of the park, preserve, and trails.)

A link to Butano State Park was opened in 1999 along the existing Butano Fire Trail. It follows North China Grade Road on the north boundary of Big Basin Redwoods beyond the Lane Camp entrance for about a mile, and passes Johansen Road on the left. From there the Butano Fire Trail continues 1.5 miles due west along an easement across private land closed to bicycles by deed restriction of property owners.

Another trail link connects the 6-mile Big Basin park segment of Gazos

Bright yellow Banana slugs mating

Creek Road to the 8-mile public section of this road at Sandy Point in southwestern San Mateo County. Especially suitable for equestrians and bicyclists, this road leaves park headquarters off of the North Escape Road and leads northwest for 6 miles to Sandy Point. From there trail users can reach Gazos Creek State Beach, the Coastal Trail and the northern Cascade Ranch section of Año Nuevo State Reserve.

Another trail connection from the junction of North China Grade and Johansen roads follows Johansen Road south and then west about 4 miles to Sandy Point, where it meets Gazos Creek Road on the park's northwest boundary.

Another new trail connection, the Whitehouse Ridge Trail, leaves the west end of Chalks Road on the park's western boundary to join the Cascade Ranch section of Año Nuevo State Reserve. This new trail zig-zags downhill through a regenerating redwood, fir and oak forest to the eastern end of Whitehouse Creek Road. Rather narrow and laid out along steep slopes, this trail is suitable for hikers only. It leads to two vista points from which Pigeon Point Lighthouse and Año Nuevo Island, historic points along the southern San Mateo Coast, can be seen.

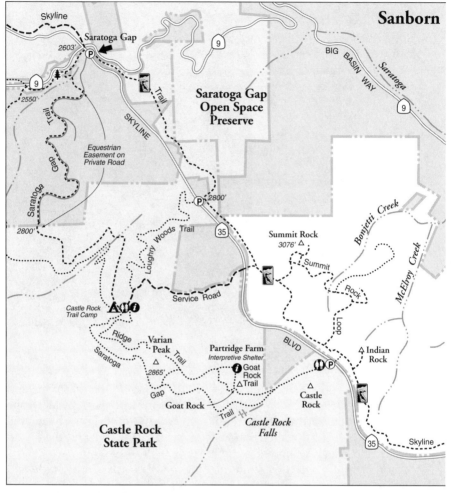

Sanborn

Saratoga Gap
Open Space
Preserve

Saratoga Gap

2603'

Skyline

Equestrian
Easement on
Private Road

2550'

2800'

Summit Rock
3076'

Castle Rock
Trail Camp

Loughry Woods Trail

Service Road

Ridge

Saratoga

Varian
Peak
2865'

Gap

Partridge Farm
Interpretive Shelter

Goat
Rock
Trail

Goat Rock

Trail

Castle Rock
Falls

Castle Rock
State Park

Summit

Rock

Loop

Indian
Rock

Castle
Rock

Skyline

BIG BASIN WAY

Bonjetti Creek

McElroy Creek

BLVD

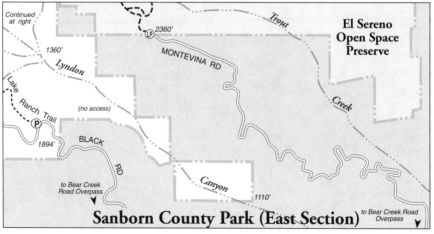

Continued
at right

1360'

2360'

Lyndon

MONTEVINA RD

El Sereno
Open Space
Preserve

Trout

Lake Ranch Trail

(no access)

Creek

1894'

BLACK

RD

to Bear Creek
Road Overpass

Canyon

1110'

to Bear Creek Road
Overpass

Sanborn County Park (East Section)

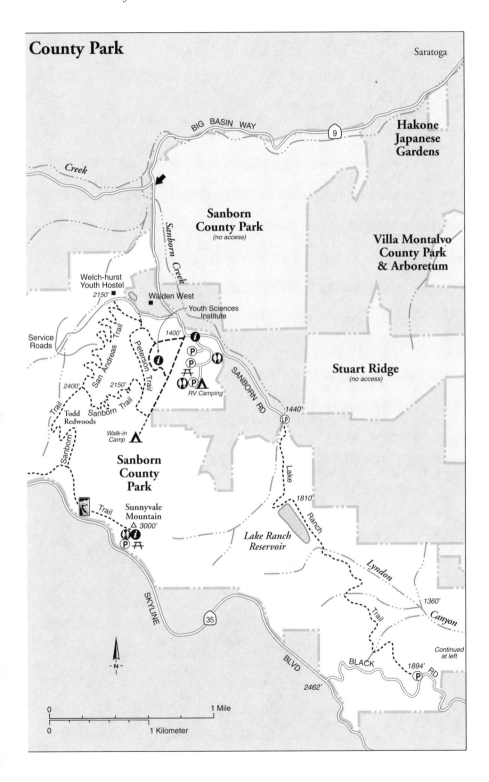

County Park

Saratoga

BIG BASIN WAY

9

Hakone Japanese Gardens

Creek

Sanborn County Park
(no access)

Sanborn Creek

Villa Montalvo County Park & Arboretum

Welch-hurst Youth Hostel
2150'

Walden West

Youth Sciences Institute

1400'

i

P
P

P

RV Camping

Stuart Ridge
(no access)

Service Roads

San Andreas Trail

Peterson Trail

2400'

2150'

Sanborn Trail

Todd Redwoods

Sanborn

SANBORN RD

1440'
LP

Walk-in Camp

Sanborn County Park

Trail

Sunnyvale Mountain
△ 3000'

P

Lake Ranch

1810'

Lake Ranch Reservoir

Lyndon

1360'

Canyon

Continued at left

SKYLINE

35

BLVD

BLACK

1894' RD
P

2462'

–N–

0   1 Mile

0   1 Kilometer

✦ Sanborn County Park ✦

The park's 3600+ acres extend up the heavily wooded canyons of the Santa Cruz Mountains west from Sanborn Road to the Skyline ridge, its steep hillsides cut by a number of year-round creeks. The park stretches for nearly 7 miles along the east side of the ridge, from Castle Rock Park southeast through Lyndon Canyon. A southern corner of the park touches the El Sereno Open Space Preserve (MROSD), and Saratoga Gap OSP is close to the northern boundary of Sanborn, along Highway 9. The Bay Area Ridge Trail runs along the Skyline Trail, at its boundary along Skyline Boulevard (Highway 35). Park headquarters, picnic areas, campgrounds and a hostel are concentrated off Sanborn Road near the park entrance.

For thousands of years this mountainside was frequented by Ohlone Indians, who came from their villages in the valley below to hunt deer and rabbits and gather wild blackberries, strawberries and seeds. The arrival of the Spaniards in the 18th century brought little change. The steep canyons and hills were not suited to cattle grazing and the land was not included in any Spanish land grant. After U.S. acquisition of California, land-hungry settlers came to the Bay Area, and this land was opened to homesteaders. Soon Swiss, Italian and German settlers from Alpine regions of Europe, who felt at home in these hills, were farming the slopes of what is now Sanborn Park.

Redwood tree in Sanborn County Park

The work was hard—clearing, plowing and planting orchards. There were also vineyards and small wineries in every family's holdings. These farms were largely self-sufficient. The early farmers' names survive on creeks and roads—Bonjetti, Taudt (now Todd), McElroy. Kendall Clark Sandborn, an early settler, petitioned for improving a road to Lake Ranch. Although he left these parts soon after, his name remains on Sanborn Road (without the "d").

The demand for lumber to build rapidly growing San Francisco during the Gold Rush brought loggers to the groves of redwoods and Douglas firs. Then came wood cutters, who marketed oak for firewood and tanbark for tanning leather. Large-scale lumbering, however, was over early in this century.

As the Santa Clara Valley was settled, these lands attracted families for excursions to the forests, orchards and mountain streams. Over the dirt roads, which crisscrossed the hills, they came on horseback and in wagons to fish, hunt and enjoy the flower-covered hills that we take such pleasure in to this day.

The great earthquake of 1906 struck the Sanborn County Park area, which is crossed by the San Andreas Fault, with great intensity. Cracks opened up in the ground 5 or 6 feet deep and as long as 100 feet. Though there were few houses here, the quake took its toll on the forests as trees were toppled and split. Spring flows were changed and landslides left cliffs as high as 40 feet. Chaparral and forest now conceal this destruction except from the trained eye of a geologist. The quake also shook down water tanks, all too vulnerable on their wooden foundations, and damaged wineries.

By the early 1900s many landholdings were consolidated. Judge James Welch, a Superior Court Judge of Santa Clara County, purchased the Lotti and McElroy lands. On this 800-acre estate he put up a lodge of redwood logs, which today serves as Welch-hurst, an attractive American Youth Hostel, included in the National Register of Historic Places. It was largely due to Judge Welch's efforts that Skyline Boulevard rights-of-way were acquired.

About this time the holdings of Taudt and Baille, and later Pourroy, were purchased by H.P. Dyer. He engaged a stone cutter to cut building blocks of local sandstone for his house. To safeguard his water supply from Sanborn Creek, Dyer bought Pourroy's holdings upstream. On his estate he cleared land around his house, planting orchards and vineyards. Santa Clara County bought Dyer's land in 1974. We now enjoy this handsome building as Sanborn Park's headquarters and his orchard as the picnic grounds.

Meanwhile Judge Welch's family sold their place in 1950, and it changed hands again when Vernon J. Pick, who had made a fortune mining uranium, bought it. During Pick's tenure he tunneled into the hill to make an elaborate bomb shelter. However, he soon sold the land. In 1976 Santa Clara County purchased the piece.

A master plan for the park, under preparation at this writing, is evaluating trail design and use, which may result in new trails or different alignments. However, 8.4 miles of trail take hikers through forest and meadow, by streams and ponds. Included in the park trails is the Skyline Trail, now a dedicated segment of the Bay Area Ridge Trail. This trail, for hikers and equestrians, follows the Skyline Scenic Corridor, providing important trail connections to parks and preserves to the north and on the west side of the Santa Cruz Mountains. This opens up backpacking possibilities for trips from the Welch-hurst hostel to the Sky-

Wheelchair access to Sanborn Peterson Grove

line ridge and on to the chain of backpack camps extending to the coast. Northward, trails lead to the backpack camp on Monte Bello Ridge and to a trail down Black Mountain to the AYH hostel at Hidden Villa.

Jurisdiction: Santa Clara County.

Facilities: Headquarters and Youth Science Institute exhibits. Trails: hiking, self-guiding nature trail; equestrians (Skyline Trail only); a 0.125-mile paved loop trail providing access to redwood forest and pond environments for people of all abilities; picnicking: family and group by reservation. Camping: 40 walk-in family sites, RV sites and youth-group site by reservation. Phone: 408-867-3654 or 408-358-3751. Youth hostel reservations: 408-741-0166. Fishing at Lake Ranch Reservoir, under State Fish and Game regulations.

Park Rules: Dogs on leash in picnic grounds and R.V. campgrounds. No dogs on trails or in walk-in campgrounds. Bicycles on paved trails only. Hours: 8 A.M. to ½ hour after sunset. Off-season hours as posted. Fees: call 408-358-375l for current rates.

Maps: Santa Clara County *Sanborn Park*; USGS quads *Castle Rock Ridge, Cupertino*; Sempervirens Fund *Skyline-to-the-Sea Trail, Map 1.*

How To Get There: From the town of Saratoga at the intersection of Saratoga-Sunnyvale and Saratoga-Los Gatos roads take Hwy. 9 for 2 miles west to Sanborn Rd. Turn left and go 1 mile to park entrance. For the hostel, turn right at the AYH sign before the park entrance and follow the road 0.4 mile to the hostel.

Sanborn County Park
CIRCLE HIKE TO THE TODD CREEK REDWOODS

A climb up the mountainside on the Sanborn and San Andreas trails takes you to a tall redwood grove on a creek-side flat where ancient redwoods were cut.

Distance: 4-mile loop

Time: 2½ hours

Elevation Gain: 1200′

Trail Notes

The Sanborn Trail leaves the west side of the picnic grounds, going uphill under redwoods on the service road through the walk-in campgrounds. You pass inviting camps scattered under the trees within the sound of Sanborn Creek.

After you leave the campgrounds the route crosses the creek, which cascades into the canyon below. Rounding an open slope of an old clearing, you pass a deer trail, where you often come across deer going down to the creek.

Soon you turn back into fir, madrone and maple woodlands. You will see grapevines left from an old family vineyard growing through the chaparral that edges the road. The road you have followed reaches a small flat and circles the site of an old house that once perched on this hillside. From this point the broad road dwindles to a narrow, steep, rocky way where greasewood crowds the trail. After a few minutes' climb, though, a left turn (south) takes you back into a cool canyon where firs and tanoaks rise above a ground cover of wood ferns. From here a good trail winds up a ridge on an easy grade. You realize how far up the mountain you have come when you see the summer fog drifting over the heights of the Skyline ridge above and feel its cooling breezes.

A long switchback into a canyon and out takes you higher into the forest. Now on a delightful section of the trail, you find the woods are open and the path underfoot softened with the leaves of tanoak and madrone. The duff on the trail reflects the tree cover—pink and gold under madrones and buff under tanoaks. As you go north, the trail appears to fork. Keep left (south); the other trail is a shortcut over a steep, uncomfortable route.

Continuing up and around the ridge, you come to the San Andreas Trail, which has climbed south on the east side of Todd Creek. To reach the Todd Creek Redwoods, continue south on the Sanborn Trail, up a steep slope broken by many sandstone outcrops. The mountain falls away precipitously below the trail.

Just beyond the San Andreas Trail you will see the first of the redwoods that herald the Todd grove. The straight red-brown trunks become more numerous as you near Todd Creek. These second-growth trees are now 2-3′ in diameter. Large stumps with young trees circling around them are signs of old logging.

In 0.25 mile from the San Andreas Trail junction in a little flat crossed by the creek, we reach the largest of the Todd Creek Redwoods. We see 8-10′ stumps of giant old trees that grew where water from the creek was most plentiful. This flat was once dominated by a dozen or so huge trees that had grown for thousands of years along the creek. The flat is now thickly grown with new redwoods and some of the Douglas firs that spring up after a forest is cleared. The creek banks are lined with giant chain fern. The creek, disrupted over a century ago by logging and still clogged with debris of broken limbs and fallen trees, is regaining its fern gardens and its mossy-rocked appearance. A few redwoods of considerable size lend dignity to the grove.

As you stop here, you can imagine the scene when loggers were felling trees in the 1800s. Redwoods were felled uphill to avoid splitting, then cut in 10-20′ lengths. Teams of oxen, chained together, dragged them down chutes along the creek to a mill, perhaps at Saratoga. You can see notches on the stumps, cut by lumberjacks to hold springboards on which they stood while sawing the trees. Lumbermen lived in a camp at the foot of McElroy Creek, but sometimes camped near this grove. Mules carried their supplies over trails you traveled on to get to this grove.

The Sanborn Trail continues uphill through the Todd grove to join the Skyline Trail, the route of the Bay Area Ridge Trail, in 0.3 mile. But to return to park headquarters you can make a loop back on the 1.8-mile San Andreas Trail. This trail may be re-routed upon completion of the park's master plan to avoid some eroded sections.

For now, retrace your steps to the trail junction. The San Andreas Trail goes on switchbacks down a ridge above Todd Creek. Your trail first leads under an airy forest canopy of young madrones where in summer the ground is golden from their leaf fall, then under dark-foliaged firs. Finally the trail descends a hill above the redwood-covered east bank of Todd Canyon. As your trail turns east, it enters the quiet of another redwood forest. Along the way you will see rings of redwood trees. Each ring, marking the site of an ancient tree, long crumbled to duff, is now circled by younger trees. Each young tree, cut in the last century, now in turn has an outer ring of third-generation trees around its stump.

Out of the redwoods the trail descends to a flat and turns east toward park headquarters. For 0.7 mile you go along old roads past the scene of early farming to reach a segment of the Nature Trail, which leads back to headquarters, picnic grounds and parking lot.

Sanborn County Park
LEVEL WALK TO LAKE RANCH RESERVOIR

On a short, level service road through the steep forested water-shed of Lake Ranch Reservoir you wind in and out of ravines to reach the reservoir that was once an important water source for the City of San Jose.

Distance: 3 miles round trip

Time: 1½ hours

Elevation Gain: Nearly level

How To Get There: On Black Rd. go 4 miles west from Hwy. 17 or 1 mile east from Skyline Blvd. At this writing there is room for a few cars by the gated park entrance, which must be kept clear, and room for a few cars in turnouts nearby. Or, continue southeast on Sanborn Rd. past the main park entrance to limited parking at the trailhead.

Trail Notes

This trail starts from Black Road at a green gate on a service road used by the San Jose Water Company. A tiny sign on the post announces Sanborn County Park, and permits hiking, horseback riding, and fishing, and prohibits bicycling, dogs, swimming, fires, cigarettes, guns, cars and motorcycles. Note as you start a large dead fir tree with a giant poison oak vine winding clear to the top.

Trees meet overhead on this level road, making it a cool walk in summer. Along the steep, forested slope, young firs predominate, but with a scattering of very large old firs. On small flats and ridges are oaks and madrones. Thimbleberry, creambush, ferns and wild blackberry form a pale-green understory. In steep ravines where streams tumble down rocky watercourses, small groves of redwoods thrive in the ample moisture, and shoulder-high giant chain ferns grow where they find under-ground water.

From a bend in the road you can see the dry, chaparral-covered hills on the far side of Lyndon Canyon. The road comes out at the reservoir's south end. New construction for bank protection and outflow pipes shows that this reservoir is still part of the Valley's water supply.

The reservoir, dammed at both ends, lies in a saddle between the drainage of Saratoga Creek to the north and that of Lyndon Canyon, flow-ing southeast into Lexington Reservoir. One should not be misled by the USGS topographic map showing the Lake Ranch Reservoir brimful of blue water. The present draw-down of water in summer leaves bare banks and murky green waters.

The San Andreas Fault Zone runs through the reservoir at the head of two narrow canyons. Earth movement here during the 1906 quake was violent. Present concern for the seismic safety of earth dams requires lower-than-designed-for water levels.

The road circles the east side of the reservoir toward the wider, higher dam at the far end, 0.33 mile away. There is no trail on the west side of the reservoir, where tree cover is heavy and banks steep. The southeast hill-side above the lake, part of which is included in the park, is chaparral-covered—predominately chamise which turns bronze in summer. As you reach the far end of the reservoir, two dirt roads turn uphill. On a cool day you can walk up one in the sun for a view of the lake and its forest back-drop.

Shady flats at the north end of the reservoir are appealing on warm, sunny days. From the top of the earthen dam, where several spreading maples give you shade, there is a nice view out over the water. In a grove of tall live oaks west of the dam you will find some remnants of the ranch that was here years ago—fine stone foundations of an old winery, a stone-lined creek channel and fragments of farm machinery. After lingering in the pleasant shade by the reservoir, retrace your steps back to Black Road. If you have done a car shuttle, you can continue half a mile down a steep road to a small parking area on Sanborn Road.

Sanborn County Park
LOOP TRIP TO SUMMIT ROCK AND BONJETTI CREEK

Climb Summit Rock, descend to homesteader Bonjetti's creek and an orchard in the canyon, and then take a side trip to a nearby knoll.

Distance: 1.6-mile loop; additional 1.2-mile side trip to knoll.

Time: 1 hour; add ½ hour for round trip to knoll.

Elevation Gain: 400′

How to Get There: From the Hwy. 35/9 intersection at Saratoga Gap, go 1.9 miles southeast on Hwy. 35 to a turnout on the east side of the road. There is ample parking.

Trail Notes

A loop trip down to Bonjetti Creek and back is good in any season, for the compacted road surface is not muddy in winter and the way is sheltered from winds. In spring, meadows are flowery and irises bloom in the woods. Apple trees blossom in May in the little orchard by the creek.

You start your trip following the old Summit Road route southeast on the well-marked Skyline Trail, also the route of the Bay Area Ridge Trail. At the entrance stile is an old stone wall, possibly a remnant of an old house-site, and an old apple tree. You pass through a fir, oak and madrone forest typical of the mountains east of the Skyline ridge. Sunlight filters through the young fir trees to an understory of pale green, soft-leaved thimbleberry and prickly-stemmed roses. Here and there an old giant of a fir towers above the rest of the forest, its thick gray trunk 5′ or so in diameter.

After 0.5 mile, at a trail junction, a well-worn path turns left off the Skyline Trail. Here you may hear sounds of gunshots on the west side of Skyline, coming from lands of the Los Altos Rod and Gun Club, where members practice Thursday to Sunday; there also is a shooting range on the east side of Skyline operated by the Santa Clara County Sheriff's Department. The well-worn path to Summit Rock leads left here, very steeply uphill, to a huge and lovely Tafoni formation favored by rock climbers. The drop-off on the valley side is alarmingly long. Eroded pits in the rocks make good handholds and footholds for the nimble climber to reach the top. From this vantage point you can look up and down the Santa Clara Valley.

After enjoying the views, descend on a more southerly trail, a bit less steep than the northerly one since it has stone ledges for steps. Turn south along the Summit Rock Loop Trail for 0.8 mile down into the canyon of Bonjetti Creek, one of the wild canyons that furrow the east face of the Santa Cruz Mountains. As you switchback downhill on an old wagon road, you glimpse the valley below through a thick madrone forest, where the papery bark peels off smooth red trunks in late summer. Passing a sloping meadow of bracken fern you reach an old orchard of apples, pears and olives planted by the original homesteader, Bonjetti. The creek named after this settler gurgles through a culvert in a shady flat, where large redwood stumps and some 100-foot-tall second-growth trees remind you of the earlier forest. A few remains of the former Bonjetti homestead are mostly overgrown by trees. In May you could celebrate the blossoming apple trees with a lunch in the sun.

A fine side trip from this little orchard is a 20-minute walk up to a knoll. Take an old, overgrown road left on the south side of Bonjetti Creek below a steep grassland where a few old nut trees cling to the slope, their nuts now harvested only by squirrels. Wind up through young fir forest and some chaparral to the top of the knoll about 2800' high, possibly an old house site, where an oak woodland now flourishes.

To return to the Summit Rock Loop Trail retrace your steps to the last trail sign and go uphill, west. On this shady route through the forest, you climb a narrow ridge between cascading Bonjetti Creek on one side and a waterfall spilling over a 20'-high mossy rock on the other. In winter and spring, the sounds of cascade and waterfall are heard in counter point. Seeping springs keep banks fern-clad, and big-leaf maples flourish alongside the stream.

You soon meet the Skyline Trail, now also signed the Bay Area Ridge Trail, where it passes below the Skyline ridge. Turn right (north). In 0.25 mile the trail rises to a flat ridgetop close to the highway, as you can hear from traffic sounds. Under black oaks and through small meadows, then through a fir forest, you walk for another 0.5 mile to rejoin the Summit Rock Loop Trail. The Skyline Trail bears left (northwest) and you continue on it back to the parking area.

Sanborn County Park
THE SKYLINE TRAIL TO SARATOGA GAP

Follow the old wagon route along the ridge paralleling present-day Skyline Boulevard on a dedicated segment of the Bay Area Ridge Trail. In the shade of madrone woods and fir forests you pass trails taking off to destinations in Sanborn and Castle Rock parks.

Distance: 6 miles one way

Time: 3 hours

Elevation Gain/Loss: 300'/600'

How To Get There: To reach the south end of the trail, drive about 5 miles southeast of Saratoga Gap on Hwy. 35 to Sanborn Park's day-use picnic area, known as Sunnyvale Mountain, on the east side of the road. There is also off-road parking space at the following access points to the trail: at Castle Rock, northern entrance to the Summit Rock Loop Trail and Saratoga Gap.

Trail Notes

Although the scenic and recreation values of the Santa Cruz Mountains Skyline have long been recognized, the ambitious concept of a 100-mile recreation corridor from the Golden Gate Bridge to the Pajaro River has been carried out only in part. Santa Clara County plans for the Skyline have been realized to a large extent in the Skyline Trail, completed in the 1980s and now a dedicated segment of the Bay Area Ridge Trail.

Part of the trail is in Santa Clara County's Sanborn Park, where the trail is open to hikers and equestrians. North of the park the trail goes through Castle Rock State Park. Bicyclists use Skyline Boulevard, which parallels the trail.

This trip is described from the trail's higher south end at Sanborn Park's Sunnyvale Mountain picnic area. The trail climbs gradually for 2 miles to its highest point near Mt. Bielawski, gaining more than 300' in elevation, then slopes down to Saratoga Gap, 600' lower.

You can do the Skyline Trail in short segments, or you can take the whole trip from one end to the other utilizing a car shuttle. With a longer car shuttle, you can leave the Skyline Trail and take the Sanborn Trail down into Sanborn Park.

Begin your trip at the Sunnyvale Mountain parking area at Skyline Trail's southern end, on the east side of Skyline Boulevard. Here you are shaded by huge black oaks, firs and madrone, and nearby picnic tables invite a short pause. A wooden county sign and the blue, red and white logo of the Bay Area Ridge Trail point to the trail heading north on an old ranch road.

Your trail lies west of a grassy meadow under big black oaks. Rounding a bend, you walk through an abandoned pear orchard and come to the site of an old ranch residence. This originally belonged to a sea captain named Seagraves. The house is long gone, but among the domestic plantings to the right of the trail is a mighty oak, at least 6' in diameter. Its giant limbs, once trussed by cables, have now split, yet the tree lives on.

The trail now veers west and from several viewpoints you can look 25 miles south across the western flanks of the Santa Cruz Mountains to Monterey Bay. Farther along, the trail returns to Skyline Boulevard at a point where two picnic tables sit under the shade of a clump of redwoods behind a high stone wall, which suffered some damage in the earthquake of October 17, 1989. Through the old wall was the entrance, now blocked, to the Seagraves homesite.

When the trail forks just beyond here, keep to the upper fork—the lower one deadends at a flat below the main trail. After the trail narrows, you pass through another abandoned orchard in an overgrown clearing. Back in the shelter of the woods, 10-25' sandstone boulders by the trail have been eroded to form niches roomy enough for small children to crawl into. The tree cover of multi-trunked madrones spreads a pink and yellow carpet of spent leaves on the trail.

Around numerous bends and back into ravines, the trail continues through a quiet forest. After 1.8 miles from the starting point you make a wide swing away from Skyline Boulevard, round a bend and descend to the Sanborn Trail junction. From here it is only 0.3 mile down to the Todd Creek Redwoods. Second-growth trees now shade the little flat by the creek where giant redwoods were cut (see Trip 1, page 157).

At this trail junction the county park sign tells you that it is 1.9 miles to the Castle Rock Trail and another 2.0 miles to Saratoga Gap. The forest is deep here and the trail surface is covered with leaves and a light layer of duff—your feet fairly spring off the soft ground. In the tops of Douglas firs, some as much as 4' in diameter, Steller's jays call.

Continuing north on the Skyline Trail, you emerge into a clearing where you may find bright patches of goldenrod blooming beside the trail in the fall, and still a few magenta flowers of farewell-to-spring coming through the grass. Just west of Skyline Boulevard Mt. Bielawski rises to 3231', shielded from your view by the tall trees above your trail, which is only a few hundred feet below its summit. Eastward, the mountainside falls away steeply as your trail passes around the headwall of the canyon of McElroy Creek.

When the trail once again comes out near Skyline Boulevard, you will see a well-used trail going off into the tanoak-madrone forest heading up to Indian Rock. This outcrop, which rises 25–30' above the surrounding

Climbers on Indian Rock

land, is a favorite of rock climbers and picnickers. On the north side the canyon drops off sharply, leaving a surprisingly precipitous rock face.

After your detour to Indian Rock, you soon come to the Castle Rock Trail crossing, where you could again depart from your route to hike on trails through Castle Rock to Waterman Gap and Big Basin. However, if you keep to the Skyline Trail, you will soon descend to the junction from where the Summit Rock Loop Trail goes right, downhill, to reach Bonjetti Creek. This trail is described in Trip 3.

At the junction a prominent park sign points straight ahead to Saratoga Gap on the Skyline Trail, which generally follows the route of old Summit Road. The trail rises to the ridgetop, where small meadows alternate with groves of black oaks and madrones. Not long ago a house stood on a knoll east of the trail. There are the remains of a water tank and abandoned machinery.

Heading north on this stretch of the trail, you come to a junction with the north end of the Summit Rock Loop Trail. From this junction, Summit Rock and the start of the trail down to Bonjetti Creek are only a few minutes' walk away (see Trip 3, page 161). To continue on the Skyline Trail to Saratoga Gap, keep to the left through the forest. In 0.2 mile you emerge at a generous parking area which was left after a realignment of Skyline Boulevard. This parking area is the starting point for the Summit Rock Loop Trail to Bonjetti Creek (see Trip 3, page 161).

The Skyline Trail/Ridge Trail continues just east of the parking area, going through the woods for 0.25 mile to Skyline Boulevard, where you leave Sanborn Park, cross a private drive and enter Castle Rock State Park. At this point, west across Skyline Boulevard the Loughry Woods Trail starts down to the Castle Rock Trail Camp (see Trip 2, page 115, Castle Rock State Park). The Skyline Trail/Ridge Trail now descends below Skyline Boulevard to traverse the steep mountainside on a narrow path through the forest. Newly-acquired MROSD lands lie below to the east.

After veering east close to the Castle Rock Park boundary line, your trail turns back toward Skyline Boulevard and skirts around some fenced private property. Here the trail widens and you are now on the historic Old Summit Road, traveled by wagons and early autos. The old toll-road station was at Saratoga Gap. More than forty years ago this part of the ridge was logged, and you will see signs of old logging roads and skid roads. Young firs are now growing up through the oaks.

For the last 0.33 mile you take a narrow footpath on a steep side slope, open to hikers only. Crossing several bridges built of wooden planks, you tread a route tight against the sandstone cliff.

Soon you come to the parking area at Saratoga Gap, a staging area for many trails. Hikers, bicyclists and equestrians can go northward on the 7.6-mile trail through the Saratoga Gap and the Monte Bello open space preserves to Page Mill Road. Westward the Skyline-to-the-Sea Trail heads down beside Highway 9 toward Big Basin and the coast, and the Saratoga Gap Trail takes off south to the Castle Rock Trail Camp.

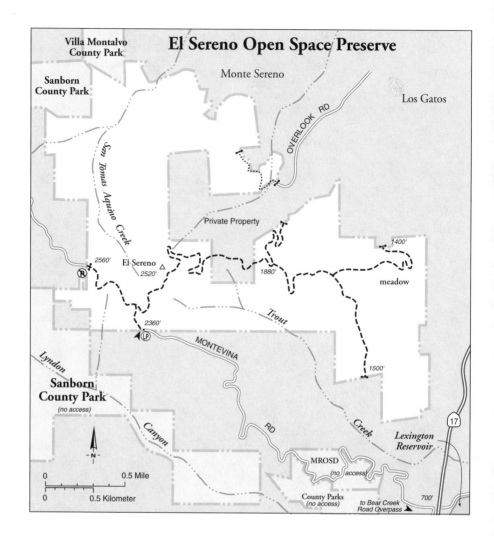

El Sereno Open Space Preserve

◆ El Sereno Open Space Preserve ◆

The mountain for which the preserve is named is the highest point on the ridge west of Los Gatos. The preserve's 1,342 acres, lying at the south end of the Sierra Morena, extend almost to the cleft where Los Gatos Creek and Highway 17 cut through the Santa Cruz Mountains. Though the ridge is mostly chaparral covered, a few hardy live oaks are beginning to come up through the chaparral. Stands of oak, bay and tanoak trees fill the canyons.

Around the turn of the century the land was used for raising hay and grazing cattle and was regularly burned to eliminate chaparral growth. In the '40s a Bay Area industrialist bred horses on the site. Now this 2-mile-long MROSD Preserve is a part of the growing chain of green belts along both sides of the crest of the Santa Cruz Mountains.

The preserve has about 4 miles of dirt roads that traverse the ridgeline. These roads, now used for patrolling the park and servicing the power-lines, act as firebreaks and make fine, wide hiking, riding and bicycling trails. Even in winter their surface is firm, though not paved. This is a place to enjoy on bright, sunny days in winter and spring or in late afternoons of summer and fall.

Jurisdiction: Midpeninsula Regional Open Space District.

Facilities: Undeveloped except for 4 miles of trails.

Preserve Rules: Open from dawn to dusk. No dogs, guns or fires.

Maps: MROSD *El Sereno*; USGS quads *Castle Rock Ridge* and *Los Gatos*.

How to Get There: From Hwy. 17 at the Alma Bridge/Bear Creek over-crossing near Lexington Dam turn right (west), then proceed right (north), paralleling the highway, and turn left on Montevina Rd. At the end of the road, where signs mark the preserve entrance, there is a steep, roughly surfaced roadside shoulder for limited parking.

El Sereno Open Space Preserve
HIKE TO THE MEADOW

A wide, south-facing trail skirts the high plateau above Los Gatos and Saratoga, ending at a sloping meadow edged with spreading oaks and brightened by wildflowers in spring.

Distance: 5 miles round trip

Time: 3 hours

Elevation Loss: 960′

Trail Notes

From the preserve entrance the trail climbs along the spine of the ridge above Lyndon Canyon, which lies in the San Andreas Fault Zone. Looking out over this steep canyon on a clear day, you can see the Pacific Ocean over the tops of the forested western flanks of the Santa Cruz Mountains. Nearby you look down on Lexington Reservoir, where brightly colored sailboats and windsurfing craft dot the waters.

In less than 0.5 mile, as the trail goes through a clump of oaks and madrones, you make a right turn at a junction and start a traverse along the flanks of El Sereno. After a couple of switchbacks the trail turns sharply east. Here on a windblown shelf you can see the benchmarks made when the land was surveyed. Three points are set out in triangular form on this high hill. However, you will not need a land survey to recognize the familiar landmarks of the South Bay—the giant hangars at Moffett Field, the salt ponds along the Bay, the black Pruneyard towers and the distinctive forms of the Diablo Range from Mission Peak to Mt. Hamilton. Southeastward stretches the Sierra Azul, with the tops of Mt. Thayer and Mt. Umunhum most visible.

Now the trail begins a gradual descent along the side of Trout Creek Canyon. With its headwaters in the preserve, this creek flows southeast to empty into Los Gatos Creek just below Lexington Dam. Its banks are densely wooded, making good cover for the deer who freely roam the ridge and its canyons.

About 2 miles from the entrance the trail makes a hairpin turn. After this turn watch for an opening in the bushes where you follow a trail leading off to your left (not to be confused with the gated trail 20 feet west). This trail to a meadow is edged with ceanothus, also known as deer brush. In a very short time you reach a sloping, grassy meadow where you can sit and enjoy the views. At its lower edge are several fine oaks whose spreading branches reach the ground, forming perfect perches for picnickers. Golden poppies, purple owl's clover and deep-blue brodiaea grow up through the meadow grasses.

You may note a 4-5' band of nearly bare ground skirting the grassland at the edge of the chaparral. Experiments at Stanford's Jasper Ridge Biological Preserve have shown that this band is not due, as some had thought, to a sterilizing effect of the chaparral. It is, rather, due to the nibbling of small creatures—field mice, shrews, voles—that make their home in the chaparral. They venture out only a short way from the safety of their cover. From the number of hawks often circling over the meadow, you can see this is a life-saving precaution.

In summer and early fall try this meadow for an early supper so you can enjoy the view and make the uphill return trip in the cool of evening. A recent purchase by MROSD to the north of El Sereno OSP may some day make it possible to connect with Villa Montalvo Park.

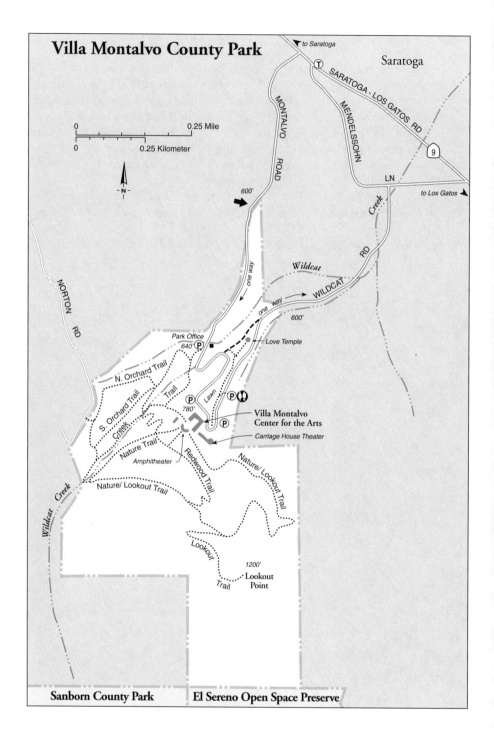

Villa Montalvo County Park

0.25 Mile

0.25 Kilometer

-N-

to Saratoga

Saratoga

T

SARATOGA - LOS GATOS RD

MONTALVO ROAD

MENDELSSOHN

9

LN

RD

to Los Gatos

600'

one way

Wildcat

one way

WILDCAT

600'

Creek

NORTON RD

Park Office
640' P

Love Temple

N. Orchard Trail

S. Orchard Trail

Trail

Creek

780' P

Lawn

P

P

Villa Montalvo
Center for the Arts

Carriage House Theater

Nature Trail

Amphitheater

Redwood Trail

Nature/ Lookout Trail

Nature/ Lookout Trail

Wildcat Creek

Lookout

1200'

Lookout
Point

Lookout
Trail

Sanborn County Park   El Sereno Open Space Preserve

◆ Villa Montalvo County Park ◆

This 175-acre estate is a historical landmark, and was built in 1912 by James D. Phelan, a former mayor of San Francisco who became the first popularly-elected U.S. Senator from California. The Mediterranean-style villa and surrounding buildings were a center of artistic, political and social life in northern California. At Senator Phelan's death in 1930 he left Villa Montalvo to be used as "a public park open under reasonable restrictions" and "as far as possible for the development of art, literature, music and architecture..."

At the present, Villa Montalvo Center for the Arts is an educational and cultural facility with many activities open to the public, such as plays, concerts, recitals, and art exhibits. The grounds are maintained by the Santa Clara County Park and Recreation Department as a county park and wildlife sanctuary, with 3.3 miles of trails on the hillside to the west and south of the arts complex. Information on the activities at the Villa is available from the park administration at 408-358-3741, or from Friends of Villa Montalvo at 408-961-5800.

Villa Montalvo has a network of trails branching from the Villa and beginning along Wildcat Creek, a tributary of larger San Tomas Aquino Creek which enters San Francisco Bay west of Alviso. The park is on a north-facing slope, which gives it protection from the hottest summer sun and allows lush plant growth. There are, at present, no trail connections beyond the park, but recent land acquisitions by MROSD near El Sereno Open Space Preserve may allow for through routes in the future. Because of its small size, we propose only one trip at Villa Montalvo, which might be combined with a visit to some of the cultural displays or events at the villa itself.

Jurisdiction: Santa Clara County Park and Recreation Department.

Facilities: Historical Villa, site of cultural events and displays; grounds available for rent for weddings and other events; 3.3 miles of trails.

Park Rules: Hours 8:00 A.M. M-F, 9:00 A.M. S-S and holidays; closed at 5:00 P.M. Motor vehicles only on roadways; no dogs allowed; no picnicking, fires, firearms or alcohol. Entrance fee.

Maps: Santa Clara County *Villa Montalvo County Park*, USGS quad *Castle Rock Ridge*

How to Get There: From Hwy. 9, 0.25 miles east of Saratoga, turn right on Montalvo Rd. and follow signs 0.5 mile to the villa gate.

Villa Montalvo County Park
LOOKOUT LOOP TRIP

From a shady canyon climb through woods and chaparral to a vista point.

Distance: 2 miles

Time: 1½ hours

Elevation Gain: 200′

Trail Notes

Park at parking lot 2 and take the Creek Trail northwest downhill until it crosses Wildcat Creek on a bridge. You are in an open forest of maple and bay trees, and will notice that the rocks over which the creek runs are gray. Perhaps they contain the limestone that has often been quarried in these hills. Near the creek is an old stone barbecue and some stone steps, shaded by creekside redwoods.

Turning right at the barbecue you switchback uphill, bearing left on the South Orchard Trail. Completely overgrown by native oak and madrone, there is little remaining of the original orchard. Soon you pass a junction on your left with the Creek Trail, but bear right. At an unmarked cutoff on your right you keep left until you meet the North Orchard Trail, which you follow left (south). This trail takes you down again to Wildcat Creek, where there are remains of what must at one time have been a bridge. Scramble across the creek (which is dry except in winter) to reach a somewhat confusing sign for the Nature Trail. This is not marked as such on the County map, but Villa Montalvo's map indicates a one and one-half mile nature trail loop. The authors saw no interpretive markers.

Following the County map, you turn right uphill on the Lookout Trail, a well-maintained trail rising gradually to the southeast. Soon on the right is an outcrop of reddish rock. Could this be the cinnabar for which New Almaden became famous? On the other side of the trail is an unusual pair of oak trees that grew so close together that they actually joined in two places.

You are walking through a young redwood forest, which has probably replaced an earlier old-growth forest, although there are no stumps to indicate previous logging. Pass an unmarked trail on your left (this is part of the Nature loop, labeled Redwood Trail on the Villa Montalvo map), and views to the east soon open up at a level place. You can see some of the roofs of Saratoga and part of the Santa Clara Valley below.

Continue past a trail on the left, the downhill return route of your trip, by climbing right and looping around through the forest. Soon you emerge onto a cleared knoll surrounded by chaparral, and can rest on a bench to enjoy the scenery. The park department has clipped the trees and bushes in order to improve your view. You see Black Mountain to the north with the Kaiser Quarry below it, the landmark hangars at Moffett Field by the Bay to your northeast, and on toward the south the ridge of Almaden Quicksilver County Park with distant Mt. Umunhum beyond.

On your return trip you loop back to the first junction on the right, the downhill return route that curves through the young forest to the north and west. Soon parking lots 3 and 4 and the roofs of the Villa complex come into view and your trail ends at an outdoor amphitheater behind the Villa.

Before returning to your car, pause at the Box Office to investigate the many cultural offerings that are held at Villa Montalvo throughout the year. Walk also through the arboretum near the house to see some of the exotic trees and plants of this beautifully kept estate.

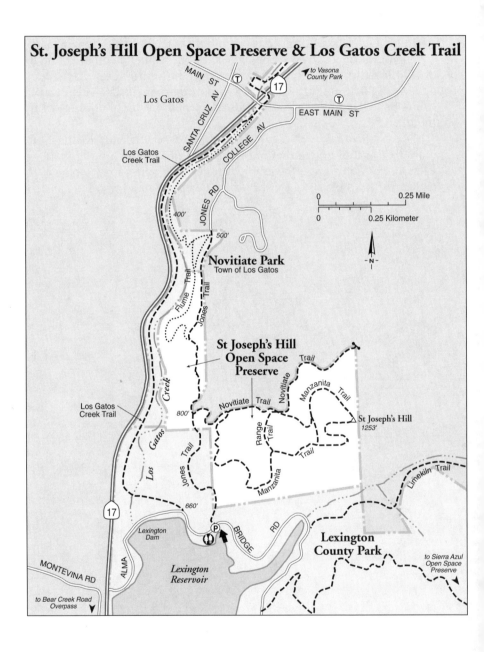

St. Joseph's Hill Open Space Preserve & Los Gatos Creek Trail

◆ St. Joseph's Hill Open Space Preserve ◆

This 270-acre site adjoining the Town of Los Gatos was formerly part of the Jesuit Novitiate. The dominant feature of the site is St. Joseph's Hill, a grassy knoll on the east boundary. The preserve lies between the Santa Clara County parklands around Lexington Reservoir and those of the Town of Los Gatos, thus forming an open-space corridor between the north and south sections of the Santa Cruz Mountains.

Jurisdiction: MROSD.

Facilities: Trails for hikers, runners and bicyclists.

Preserve Rules: Open from dawn to dusk. Dogs allowed on leash.

Maps: MROSD *St. Joseph's Hill Open Space Preserve*, USGS quad *Los Gatos*

How to Get There: Take Hwy. 17 south from Los Gatos, exit at Alma Bridge/Bear Creek roads and go across overpass to the east side of the highway. Re-enter Hwy. 17 going north. Take Alma Bridge Rd. exit, cross dam to parking lot at boat launch area. Going north on Hwy. 17, take Alma Bridge Rd. exit and continue to the parking lot.

St. Joseph's Hill Open Space Preserve
LOOP TRIP TO THE HILLTOP AND BACK BY THE CREEK

A favorite of runners and bicyclists, this trip reaches a knoll above Lexington Reservoir, then follows the route of an old water flume to Los Gatos and returns on the Los Gatos Creek Trail.

Distance: 5-mile loop

Time: 2–3 hours

Elevation Gain: 600′

Trail Notes

Park at the first roadside parking on Santa Clara County property on Alma Bridge Road next to Lexington Reservoir. Here are restrooms and a few picnic tables. Start uphill on a gated road across from the boat-launching ramp and begin climbing on a rough and rocky road-width trail. Glowing through the dry grasses in summer are great drifts of magenta clarkia (farewell-to-spring). As you climb, a chorus of bird song greets you from the tall eucalyptus below the trail and from a mixed oak and chaparral hillside on your left. Through openings in these woods you look west to the steep slopes of El Sereno Open Space Preserve and the new Bear Creek Redwoods Preserve, the latter not yet open to the public. From below, the noise of Highway 17 rises, but as you drop into a shady ravine filled with bays and oaks the sound fades.

You are traversing Santa Clara County parklands for about half a mile, almost until you reach a fork in the trail. Then you are in the MROSD preserve. At the fork a sign offers two options: the Jones Trail going left toward Los Gatos or the Novitiate Trail to the right toward St. Joseph's Hill. Choosing St. Joseph's Hill, you turn right, uphill, to follow the service road along a cyclone fence. Through the fence you see old terraces where once-thriving vineyards produced the grapes from which the Novitiate wines were made. No longer in wine production, this north half of the preserve is under an MROSD and Town of Los Gatos open-space easement, but off-limits to the public at this writing.

You are on serpentine soil here, walking past plants that are characteristic of that nutrient-poor environment: *Quercus durata*, or leather oak, with tightly-curled, prickly leaves, *Garrya elliptica*, or silk-tassel bush, which has long gray-green tassels in winter. Madrone trees grow on your left, and manzanita bushes cover the hillside.

After almost a mile, you reach a junction with the Manzanita Trail, which you take to the right, contouring around a knoll. As you work slowly east uphill, look for native bunchgrasses in shady stream drainages. There are several side trails, some unofficial; you take the Range Trail right through a wide, graded area once used as a shooting range, now restored. Turn left (east) on the Manzanita Trail.

When you have walked nearly 2 miles you reach the knoll that is St. Joseph's Hill. Here you have commanding views out to San Francisco Bay, across the canyon to El Sereno, northwest to forest-clad ridges of the northern Santa Cruz Mountains, and south to the lake behind Lexington Dam. In the near distance is a large scar that is the Limekiln Quarry, one of several such quarries in the Santa Cruz Mountains. East lies the Sierra Azul Open Space Preserve, dominated by the broad flanks of Mt. Umunhum.

Near St. Joseph's Hill itself is a recently planted area called a "mitigation measure," installed by Caltrans at the time the agency built the Alma Bridge Road overpass. The native oaks here soon will grow above the surrounding shrubs and return this hill to the condition it was in before Europeans came. This is an inviting place for a picnic in fine weather.

Retrace your steps to the first junction below the top and turn right for a different route to the Novitiate Trail along the fence line, then take it downhill, left, to the main trail. Here, turn right on the Jones Trail, which follows a historic stage route that once connected Los Gatos with the towns of Lexington and Alma. Both these towns were flooded (and abandoned) when Lexington Reservoir was built in 1952.

The Jones Trail traverses the extremely steep hillside above Los Gatos Creek, alternating between woods of oak and bay trees and chaparral where lavender pennyroyal and purple nightshade edge the trail.

After about 0.33 mile you reach a junction. Hikers can turn left here, on the Flume Trail, while bicyclists and equestrians can either continue north on the Jones Trail to Jones Road in Los Gatos, or return left to Alma Bridge Road parking.

The Flume Trail, with its steep side slopes and narrow tread, follows the precarious route of an old wooden flume that used to carry water to Los Gatos and San Jose. The remnants of this flume were removed when the trail was built, but a section of flume is installed in a local museum.

Switchbacking down the Flume Trail you see Highway 17 below, and looking back get a view of the face of Lexington Dam. At the end of the Flume Trail you reach meadowy Novitiate Park at the edge of Los Gatos and follow a Boy Scout-built trail to the paved road. There is no parking here, so you can either return to your starting point, have a car shuttle waiting at a public parking lot off Main Street in town, or continue the longer loop.

To make the loop trip, continue down Jones Road about 0.25 mile through residential neighborhoods to Main Street and turn west. Just before crossing the bridge over Highway 17, look for the Los Gatos Creek Trail entrance on the left. Follow this trail 1.7 miles upstream to Lexington Dam and back to your car. (See Los Gatos Creek Trail, Trip 3, page 277.)

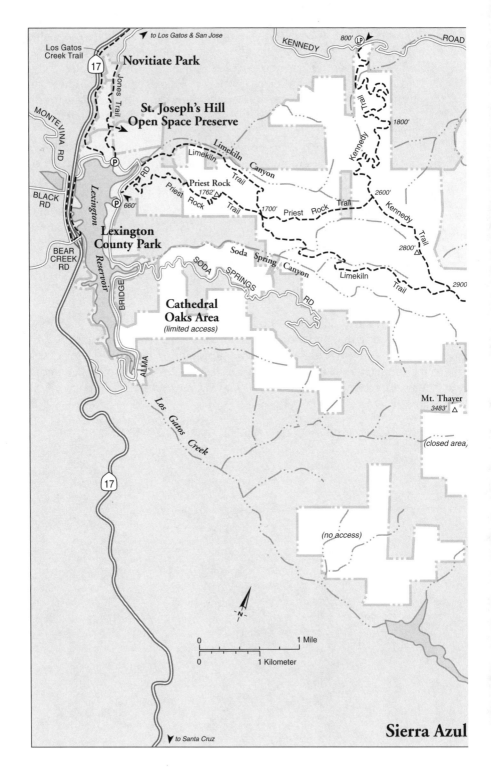

to Los Gatos & San Jose

Los Gatos
Creek Trail

17

Jones Trail

KENNEDY   800' LP   ROAD

Novitiate Park

MONTEVINA RD

**St. Joseph's Hill
Open Space Preserve**

1800'

Kennedy Trail

Limekiln   Canyon

Limekiln
Trail

P

BLACK
RD

RD

Priest   **Priest Rock**
Rock   1762'
Trail

P 660'

2600'

1700'   Priest   Rock   Trail

Kennedy   Trail

**Lexington
County Park**

2800'

BEAR
CREEK
RD

Lexington   Reservoir

Soda   Spring   Canyon

Limekiln

2900

SODA
SPRINGS

Limekiln   Trail

BRIDGE

RD

**Cathedral
Oaks Area**
(limited access)

ALMA

Mt. Thayer
3483'

Los Gatos Creek

(closed area,

17

(no access)

N

0   1 Mile
0   1 Kilometer

to Santa Cruz

Sierra Azul

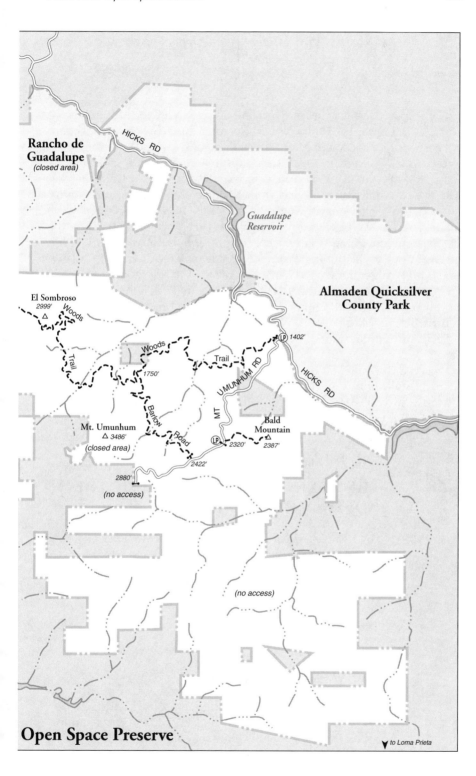

Rancho de
Guadalupe
(closed area)

HICKS RD

*Guadalupe
Reservoir*

El Sombroso
2999'
△

Woods

Trail

**Almaden Quicksilver
County Park**

Woods

Trail

LP 1402'

1750'

Barlow

MT UMUNHUM RD

HICKS RD

Road

**Bald
Mountain**
△
2387'

Mt. Umunhum
△ *3486'*
(closed area)

LP
2320'

2422'

2880'
(no access)

(no access)

Open Space Preserve

▼ *to Loma Prieta*

◆ Sierra Azul Open Space Preserve ◆

The Spaniards called the southern half of the Santa Cruz Mountains the Sierra Azul. In 1983 the Midpeninsula Regional Open Space District chose this name for its collection of preserves in the Sierra Azul's northern section. At this writing the 14,000-acre preserve comprises four areas: the Kennedy Limekiln Area, which includes trails accessible from the east side of Lexington Reservoir and from Kennedy Road east of Los Gatos; the Cathedral Oaks Area; the Rancho Guadalupe Area, not yet open to the public; and the Mt. Umunhum Area where, except for some trails on the east flank, access to the larger part of the preserve is not yet open. Within the areas open to the public, unsurfaced roads make wide trails to the preserve's high ridges. Described here are three trips to ridgetops on the west and north flanks of the Sierra Azul in the Kennedy Limekiln Area and one short hike to a destination on the north side of the Mt. Umunhum Area.

Jurisdiction: Midpeninsula Regional Open Space District.

Facilities: Undeveloped, except for hiking, equestrian and bicycling trails.

Preserve Rules: Open dawn to dusk; dogs on Kennedy/Priest Rock/Limekiln trails only.

Maps: MROSD *Sierra Azul, Limekiln Kennedy Area and Mt. Umunhum Area*, USGS quads *Los Gatos* and *Santa Teresa Hills*.

Sierra Azul Open Space Preserve
THE KENNEDY TRAIL ASCENT OF THE NORTH SLOPES

An 1800-foot climb from Kennedy Road to the heights of the Sierra Azul rewards you with sweeping views, shady canyons and a delightful picnic site halfway to the top.

Distance: 8 miles round trip to fork in trail

Time: 4 hours

Elevation Gain: 1800'

How To Get There: From Hwy. 17 take the East Los Gatos exit and go south to Los Gatos Blvd. Turn left (north) and in 0.2 mile turn right on Kennedy Rd. Go 2 miles to Top of the Hill Rd. An MROSD three-car parking lot on the right is at the entrance to the Kennedy Trail;

additional cars park on Top of the Hill Rd. across from
the preserve entrance.

Trail Notes

This area was part of the Rinconada land grant, later owned by a Mrs.
Mahoney. When the town of Los Gatos needed water for its growing population, it tapped the streams of this mountainside, but the supply was neither dependable nor plentiful. In the 1940s a road was built, now the
Kennedy Trail. A camellia nursery operated at the foot of the mountain.
Subdivisions were talked of, including a 200-home scheme, but the lack of
a good water supply and the steep road grade finally led its investors to
abandon the idea. The unsurfaced road to the proposed subdivision makes
a wide, though sometimes exposed, trail to the heights of the preserve.

On the west side of Kennedy Road look for cement gateposts marking
a driveway. Immediately beyond, go over the stile in the split-log rail
fence to a dirt road going uphill through an old walnut and apricot
orchard. You will see the MROSD preserve map and wildlands sign with
its familiar logo and symbols inviting hikers, bicyclists and equestrians
but barring motor vehicles.

From here you climb steadily but gradually on an east-facing slope to
walk into the first of several deep canyons. As you enter the cool shade of
oaks and bays, the sound of rushing water comes to you in winter and
spring.

After a few more turns around the slopes you come to another ravine
with a stream still running as late as June. These intermittent watercourses
dry up by late summer, but their canyons offer cooler temperatures all year.

Now you head due east again, coming out in chaparral country. Many
plants of the chaparral bloom in summer after spring wildflowers have
faded and gone. Chamise, that small-leaved, scrubby bush that covers so
much of this hillside, produces small, creamy clusters of flowers on the
ends of its branches in June and July. Yerba santa bears pale purple, trum-
pet-shaped blossoms on its 6-8' stems. And all along this trail you will
find the profusely blooming, apricot-colored sticky monkey flower clinging to the banks. After several rainy years its blossoms are spectacular,
lasting late into fall.

In less than two hours you come to a natural bench in the mountainside where the trail enters a lovely oak forest. This is a good place to stop
for a picnic under the trees. Leading off from your trail is a network of old
side roads in the forest, laid out for the subdivision that never material-
ized. In small grassy clearings Indian warrior, Douglas iris and lupines
bloom in the spring where the light reaches them.

To continue, you climb through a heavily wooded hillside graced by
more oaks and madrones. The trail now alternates between chaparral and
woodland as it rises to the 2400' level. From these heights are views in all
directions. Due east and appearing right below you on Los Capitancillos

Ridge is Almaden Quicksilver County Park. South of that ridge rise the flanks of Mt. Umunhum, Mt. Thayer and El Sombroso, The north half of the Santa Cruz Mountains, the Sierra Morena, stretches as far as the eye can see.

Veering sharply east across the spine of the ridge, you then descend to a fork in the trail. Take the right-hand trail to continue west and downhill for 2.5 miles to reach the shores of Lexington Reservoir (see Trip 2 below). However, if you don't have a car shuttle waiting, turn back at the fork. You can make the easy downhill trip in about 1½ hours.

Sierra Azul Open Space Preserve
A CLIMB TO PRIEST ROCK AND THE RIDGETOPS ABOVE LIMEKILN CANYON

Climbing a winding service road on a ridge between Limekiln and Soda Spring canyons takes you from Lexington Reservoir toward the heights of El Sombroso.

Distance: 6.5 miles round trip

Time: 3½ hours

Elevation Gain: 1300′

How To Get There: From Hwy. 17 south from Los Gatos exit at Alma Bridge/Bear Creek roads, go east on the overcrossing and re-enter Hwy. 17 going north. Take Alma Ridge Rd. exit and cross Lexington Dam. Circle around the reservoir, passing the road to Limekiln Quarry and crossing over an inlet from Limekiln Canyon where you see a green gate at the beginning of the Limekiln Trail. There is a county parking lot ahead on your right, with restrooms and a few reservoir-side picnic tables, but you continue about 0.5 mile until you see a second green gate, left, with some pullout parking spaces beside the road. A second parking lot is 0.3 miles further; using it necessitates a walk back on the narrow road.

Trail Notes

This is a trip for the cool weather of crisp fall days or sunny spring days. Much of the steep, chaparral-clad ridge has only occasional trees and is hot in summer.

Cross the stile by the green metal gate and take the service road— which we will now call a trail—uphill. The first mile of this trip traverses lands leased from the Santa Clara Valley Water District by the Santa Clara County Parks and Recreation Department for its Lexington Reservoir Park. The trail climbs a steep hillside, winding through an oak forest with an understory of toyon, manzanita and buckbrush. As you go up, you can, for a time, look directly down through the trees to Lexington Reservoir. When the spring wildflowers are in bloom, you will find blossoms of purple brodiaea and clumps of Douglas iris. In summer graceful, creamy white flower heads of ocean spray hang over the trail.

The path now rises more steeply over chaparral-covered hillsides. After nearly a mile you reach an abandoned road-grader, snugly attached to the ground by encroaching coyote-brush bushes. Shortly beyond you come to a gate with an equestrian stile; you are now on MROSD property, on the Priest Rock Trail. Here is a good place to turn and look back at the view to the reservoir and beyond. Across the valley of Los Gatos Creek are two MROSD preserves, El Sereno and the new Bear Creek Redwoods. Continuing 1.5 miles from the trailhead, the trail bends sharply and comes to a brushy hilltop where a craggy outcrop, Priest Rock, stands above the manzanitas on the left of the trail.

From here at an elevation of 1762' look south down into Soda Spring Canyon. On the north side of the ridge is Limekiln Canyon, on the sides of which you can see the scars of quarrying. Alongside the trail in late spring the prickly chaparral pea blooms a bright magenta, and nearby is a delicate yellow bush poppy.

From here the trail stays more level on the ridgetop, heading east. Shortly (2.4 miles from your starting point) you come to a crossroads, called by the patrol rangers "four corners junction." To your right the Limekiln Trail continues 3.5 miles to El Sombroso (your return route); to your left the Limekiln Trail descends to Alma Bridge Road. Following the Priest Rock Trail straight ahead along the ridge for 1.5 miles you reach the Kennedy Trail junction (see Trip 1, page 182). Turn southeast on the Kennedy Trail and continue over a 2800' knob toward El Sombroso for l.6 miles to another junction. Here the Woods Trail goes east, the Limekiln Trail goes west. These two segments are described in Trip 4.

For your return trip go right on the Limekiln Trail, which skirts the south side of the ridge above Soda Springs Canyon. This is described in Trip 4; your return trip to Alma Bridge Road is 5.5 miles.

A pleasant alternative route for this trip would be the lower segment of the Limekiln Trail, running from Alma Bridge Road (the first green gate you passed) up a shady, if somewhat dusty, canyon for 1.6 miles on the north side of the El Sombroso ridge. Unfortunately at this writing slides had closed this route, as often happens in wet winters.

Sierra Azul Open Space Preserve
BALD MOUNTAIN RAMBLE

This nearly level trail takes you to a grassy knoll overlooking the crest of the Santa Cruz Mountains and across to the heights of the Diablo Range.

Distance: 1.5 miles round trip

Time: 1 hour

Elevation Gain: Nearly level

How To Get There: In southwest San Jose, take Hicks Rd. south from Camden Ave. South of the Guadalupe Reservoir turn west (uphill) on Mt. Umunhum Rd. This road immediately veers left just after the turnoff and continues past a hand-painted sign declaring it a private road. MROSD has access rights to the preserve over this road, but visitors should stay on the road at this time, using only the trail to Bald Mountain. In 2.5 miles park at the roadside by MROSD gate SA07.

Trail Notes

On your way to the junction of Hicks Road and Mt. Umunhum Road be on the lookout for an historical building. At the corner of Arnerich and Hicks roads is the Guadalupe Mine School House, built in the 1880s when the quicksilver mines were flourishing on the slopes north of the road. Restored in the 1980s, and now a private house, it boasts a cinnabar red trim on a tawny gold base, reproducing the color of the mercury-bearing ore and the gold that brought fame and fortune to owners of the Almaden Mines. These tones are seen today in the rocks underfoot and the grasslands beside the trails in Almaden Quicksilver Park and also on some of the trails in Sierra Azul Preserve.

The trail to Bald Mountain, a wide fire road at gate SA07, leaves the left side of Mt. Umunhum Road. Past an MROSD sign you head east on this trail, which traverses a south-facing mountainside just below its 2300' crest. There is very little tree cover, but tall chaparral shrubs overhang both sides of the trail. Although quite hot on a midsummer day, this protected trail is pleasant on a sunny day in winter.

A few sycamores are flourishing on the downslope, probably nourished by hidden springs. The deep canyon on your right drops off abruptly and you can see where its drainage joins Herbert Creek, which then flows east through more steep-sided canyons around the prow of Bald Mountain to reach Almaden Reservoir. These canyons are filled with stands of bay and oak trees, which also crowd the ravines on the opposite ridges.

Dominating your view to the right (south) on the outward leg of this trip is the flattened, antenna-covered top of Loma Prieta. Mt. Umunhum (Native American term for humming bird), surmounted by its formidable, multi-storied structure, looms to the west on the skyline as you return. Between these two peaks, two of the highest in the Santa Cruz Mountains, runs a ridge, almost as high, forming a protective rampart for the Santa Clara Valley against incoming storms and winds.

When the authors took this hike in late June, spring wildflowers—purple brodiaea, orange poppies, yellow daisies and magenta clarkia, were still blooming beside the trail. At the same time, the creamy white flowers of chaparral plants, chamise and toyon, perfumed the air.

Just before reaching the grass-covered knoll that is the top of Bald Mountain, you cross a saddle through which the breeze can blow stiffly, once you are out from the lee of the hill. Grand views open up north and east to a trio of Santa Clara County foothill parks—Almaden Quicksilver, Calero and Santa Teresa, but dominating the vista to the east is Mt. Hamilton, seemingly at your same elevation. You are, however, only at 2387'; Mt. Hamilton is 4209', Mt. Umunhum is 3486'.

When you have identified other familiar landmarks of the South Bay, the East Bay and the southern Santa Clara Valley, continue around the top of the mountain and then retrace your steps back to your car.

Sierra Azul Open Space Preserve
WOODS TRAIL ACROSS SIERRA AZUL PRESERVE

A walk or ride through many plant communities on the northern slopes of Mt. Unumhum.

Distance: 11.4 miles one way

Time: 6 hours

Elevation Gain/Loss: 1800'/2200'

How To Get There: See Trip 3, page 186 route to Mt. Umunhum Rd. This trip requires a car shuttle at Priest Rock Trail on the Alma Bridge Rd.

Trail Notes
Park off the pavement at the junction of Hicks Road and Mt. Umunhum Road, being careful not to block Gate SA06. Take the Woods

Trail through the gate on your right, starting gently uphill. Graded by PG&E for vehicle access to its high-voltage powerlines, this trail is easy walking and relatively shady the first part of the way. Chaparral is low enough for splendid views to your left of the monolith and fire tower on Mt. Umunhum. On your right the canyon of Guadalupe Creek and its tributaries drops off sharply. An amusing remnant of earlier land uses is an old cattle guard with sign reading TRACK LAYERS USE PLANKS. Contouring around a culverted creek, you start uphill past a eucalyptus grove, and then surprisingly see tall pines above on the left. After a mile the trail passes through a meadowy area that has been graded for power pole installation, and Almaden Quicksilver County Park is visible to the northeast. The only human sound that disturbs bird songs is that of a generator on some private property to the south of your trail.

At 2.1 miles you reach Barlow Road on your left, unmarked, leading steeply uphill opposite an abandoned track running into the brush on your right. Barlow Road has some very interesting plants on it, and is worth a side trip of another mile uphill. You will climb 800' in about a mile, and will be rewarded by views of continuing Woods Trail and Mt. Sombroso to the northwest, the Diablo Range and Mt. Hamilton to the northeast, and a panorama of the Santa Clara Valley. You are so close to Mt. Umunhum on this ridge that the monolith is hidden. Several side roads leading to former house sites are blocked off, but you may want to pause at a level place to contemplate the assemblage of plants, and perhaps have a picnic. The ridge above you has a significant grove of gray pines, most commonly found in the Sierra Nevada foothills, and their large cones have fallen on the road around you. Chaparral currant blooms next to Douglas fir, and then a special cluster of California nutmeg (*Torreya californica*) is a real treasure to the left of the trail.

As yet there is no trail connection to make a loop trip back to where you left your car, which would make a good short trip, so you now return downhill to the Woods Trail and continue northwest. The trail contours around upper reaches of Rincon and Guadalupe creeks, sources for Guadalupe Reservoir below, and for the river that flows through the center of San Jose on its way to the Bay. These creeks are in deep canyons with trees on their north-facing slopes, chaparral on the south-facing sides. This part of the Woods Trail is still relatively level and shady, with bay and madrone forest including occasional *torreya* trees. Reflect, as you proceed, how difficult it was for PG&E to string its wires across the wide space canyons to El Sombroso ahead. Did they use helicopters; did they shoot an arrow across pulling a string; had they trained a bird to carry a line?

After crossing Rincon Creek the Woods Trail continues another 2 miles very steeply up to El Sombroso, contouring along a chaparral-covered hillside toward this landmark. As you round sharp curves, your view is of the monolith atop Mt. Umunhum, which together with other abandoned buildings was part of a U.S. Air Force base in the 1940s to 1970s. At the ridgetop there are short roads leading to the PG&E towers, from which you have more spectacular views to the east, south and west, but there is no easy route to the summit of El Sombroso at 2999'. Chaparral covers the ridges, interspersed with grassland where tower construction took place. A continual bloom of orange monkey flower borders the trail, and keep your eyes open for purple asters and succulent Dudleya on the rocky outcroppings. You have now walked 5.7 miles.

It is only 0.5 mile to the junction (right) of the Kennedy Trail; you now leave the Woods Trail and turn left on the Limekiln Trail. From this junction the trail trends steeply down, and re-enters the trees on the side of Soda Springs Canyon. Several side roads are for PG&E tower maintenance; you have paralleled the powerline the whole way. Despite the southern exposure there is water enough from a spring to fill a water trough next to the road.

As you work lower on the slopes you reach a saddle on the ridge at 9.0 miles, the "four corners junction" as the rangers call it, where the Priest Rock and Kennedy trails branch off from the Limekiln Trail. It would be preferable to descend the Limekiln Trail to Alma Bridge Road, 2.4 miles ahead, but if this route is closed by landslides you will take the Priest Rock Trail to the left instead (see Trip 2, page 184).

As you descend the steep Priest Rock Trail, take care not to slide on the "ball-bearing" surface. Views across Los Gatos Creek canyon are splendid, and give you a chance to thank the foresighted people who have preserved so much public land for future generations.

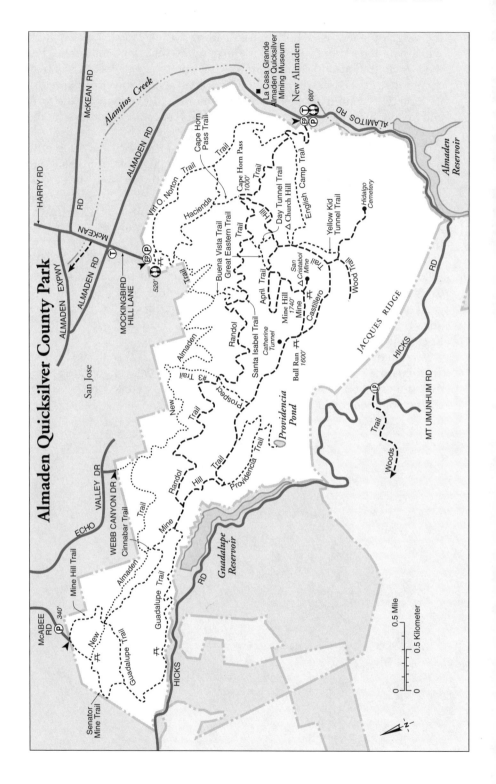

Almaden Quicksilver County Park

✦ Almaden Quicksilver County Park ✦

Almaden Quicksilver County Park's 3977 acres take in most of the 6-mile-long Los Capitancillos Ridge in the lower Santa Cruz Mountains, the site of the once-most-productive quicksilver mine in the western world. Today on 33 miles of trails following old mining roads, hikers, runners, equestrians and bicyclists can explore these lovely hills and imagine New Almaden's heyday when miles of tunnels pierced the hills and more than 500 houses clustered on the ridge.

On the oak-dotted ridge mine tunnels and shafts are now closed off, and at the main park entrance the furnaces of the New Almaden Quicksilver Mining Company have long since been dismantled. English Town, Spanish Town and a Chinese Camp where miners lived are gone. But the hills are still strewn here and there with relics of mining days. Beginning in 1998, crews spread tons of clean soil over the residue known as calcine which was left from "cooking" cinnabar rock into mercury. This soil will prevent the mercury from the calcine from seeping into the near-by creeks and water supply.

The cinnabar ore in these hills attracted Indians long before the coming of the Spanish in the 19th century. They traveled from as far as the Columbia River to get the red ore they used to paint their bodies. A well-worn trail along Guadalupe Creek led from the Ohlone villages near the Bay to a shallow cave on top of the hill where the ore was visible.

As early as 1824 Antonio Suñol of San José, looking for gold in these hills, found red ore, but it was not until 1845 that a Mexican cavalry officer and engineer, Andres Castillero, filed a mining claim to this deposit, and still later that the red ore was confirmed as mercury-producing cinnabar. Meanwhile, the Mexican Governor of California had made grants of two ranches on these hills, one on each side of the ridge, with boundary descriptions so vague as to give rise to violent disputes and years of litigation.

Castillero returned to Mexico, where he met Alexander Forbes, who acquired part of his interest in the mine. Forbes came to California and brought Mexican miners to construct mine workings. He named the mine "New Almaden" after the famous quicksilver mine in Spain and formed the New Almaden Quicksilver Mining Company.

When the discovery of gold in California greatly increased the demand for quicksilver, which was used in the reduction of gold ore, mine operations expanded. Miles of tunnels were built and giant ore-reduction furnaces constructed. The reduction works, known as the "Hacienda" (from one of the Spanish meanings of the term), were built at the foot of the hill near the present Hacienda entrance to today's park.

By 1851 two mines were in operation in addition to the New Almaden—the Enriquita and the Guadalupe, northeast along the ridge. In 1854 the manager, Henry Halleck, began construction of La Casa Grande, a building of 27 rooms and 3 stories, originally planned as a hotel, but used as the manager's house. A village of cottages for the staff was built along Alamitos Creek. A Spanish Town for Mexicans and an English Town for Cornish miners were perched high on the hill near the mines. For a short time there was also a Chinese Camp.

New Almaden became a tourist attraction bringing eminent visitors, including an emissary from the emperor of China, who came seeking purchases of quicksilver. The emperor, pleased by the reception of his emissary, sent back an eight-sided pagoda, which stood on La Casa Grande grounds until 1920. Pillars from the tea house can be seen at the New Almaden Mercury Mining Museum.

By 1870 production at the mine had peaked, but under a new manager, James Randol, mining methods were improved and new bodies of ore found at the Randol shaft, sunk at some distance from the other mines. After Randol left in 1892, the fortunes of the company declined again and by 1912 it was in bankruptcy.

Under different management the Senador Mine at the north end of the ridge, put into operation with modern reduction equipment, produced through 1926, the last large-scale production.

During the Depression the Army Corps of Engineers demolished nearly all the early structures in a program to reduce hazards. Not a single cottage in English Town or Spanish Town remains. The two churches on Mine Hill are gone.

After a brief period of operation during World War II, the mine was shut down and the last furnace was dismantled. Although an 8-year study by the U.S. Geological Survey showed that there is still the possibility of finding ore at New Almaden, mining has ceased. All mine shafts and tunnels have been sealed. However, the entrance to the San Cristobal Mine has been reconstructed so that visitors can look into the tunnel.

In 1974 Santa Clara County purchased 3598 acres of the mine area for a park. New Almaden is now listed as a Historic District in the National Register of Historic Places. The community of New Almaden has been placed under a County Historic Zoning District so that the integrity of this more-than-a-century-old village is protected.

Now at the main park entrance a ranger's office is in place. Here also a reconstruction of the old mine office will some day house an interpretive center. At present, historical markers and interpretive plaques tell the story of cinnabar, a term derived from an ancient Persian word meaning dragon's blood. In a grassy field beside Alamitos Creek another marker recounts the story of an 1880s failed carbonated-water bottling venture.

The county's New Almaden Mercury Mining Museum is now located in the refurbished La Casa Grande at 21570 Almaden Road, which has displays of mining equipment, models, maps and photographs which give you some grasp of the astounding scale of mining operations at New Almaden. Exhibits of household furnishings, clothing and a collection of photographs of the vanished settlements bring to life the busy community of the late 19th century.

A New Almaden Quicksilver County Park Association, a group formed in 1983, supports the protection, restoration and development of this unique site. It sponsors work parties to maintain trails and stages events to encourage community involvement in projects to benefit the park. The association conducts tours in the park to places of special interest and into restricted areas open only on such tours. Guides familiar with the history of the fabled English Town and Spanish Town bring alive for you the park's lively past. You will hear details of the mercury mining operations. There are also occasional docent-led hiking and horseback trips to famous mining sites. Be sure to pick up the association's Walking Tour map of New Almaden which guides you past its historic buildings.

In 1994 Santa Clara County, jointly with MROSD and with a habitat conservation grant, acquired 907 acres on Jacques Ridge near Hicks Road. This important purchase connects Almaden Quicksilver Park with the Mt. Umunhum Area of Sierra Azul Open Space Preserve and provides a valuable wildlife corridor connecting 18,000 acres of open space. Jacques Ridge will be a vital link in the Bay Area Ridge Trail. Santa Clara County owns the 372 acres northeast of Hicks Road and MROSD owns 535 acres to the southwest.

Thirty three miles of trails over the hills of Almaden Quicksilver Park provide easy trips of a few miles and vigorous climbs of 10 miles or more across the 1700' summit of the ridge. This park offers trails that take you away from the urban scene to secluded woods and to restful vistas of the Santa Cruz Mountains. Some of the trails, long popular with equestrians, hikers and runners, are now open to bicyclists. Horsecarts too, now may use the Randol and Mine Hill trails.

Three entrances to Almaden Quicksilver Park offer good choices of trails and a great variety of terrain. Trails from the Hacienda and Mockingbird Hill entrances rise more steeply than those from the McAbee Road entrance. However, all reach fine vista points and visit places once teeming with the mining and processing of the mercury ore.

Jurisdiction: Santa Clara County.

Facilities: Trails: hiking, equestrian, bicycling, and horsecart driving. Park office, water, restrooms at the main entrance on Almaden Road—La Hacienda. Picnic areas, restrooms, potable water, equestrian staging area and horse trough at Mockingbird Hill Road entrance.

Park Rules: Open from 8 A.M. to ½ hour past sunset. Dogs must be controlled on 6-foot leash (or less) at all times. Bicycles allowed on certain marked trails; helmets required.

Maps: Santa Clara County *Almaden Quicksilver Park*; USGS quads *Los Gatos, Santa Teresa Hills.*

How To Get There: *By Car:* (1) Main entrance—Hacienda: Take Almaden Expressway to Almaden Rd. and go 1.5 miles on it to park entrance on west side of road. (2) Mockingbird Hill entrance—From Almaden Expressway, turn right on Almaden Rd. go 0.7 mile and turn right on Mockingbird Hill Lane to park entrance. (3) McAbee Rd. entrance—From Almaden Expressway turn southwest on Camden Ave., then west on McAbee Rd. to its end. Roadside parking only. (4) A new entrance is proposed on Hicks Rd. at Woods Rd. on west side of park.

By Bicycle: An off-road bike path runs south beside Alamitos Creek from Almaden Lake to McKean Rd., on which you turn right and then continue on Mockingbird Hill Lane to park entrance.

By Bus: County Transit to main park entrance.

 Almaden Quicksilver County Park
MINE HILL TRAIL

Hikers, equestrians, bicyclists and horsecart drivers climb the old wagon road past several New Almaden Mine sites, visit English Town, the former miners' settlement, and follow Los Capitancillos Ridge to the mine site at its north end. Bicyclists must turn around at the Randol Trail junction or return on the Randol Trail to the Hacienda entrance.

Distance: 6.5 miles one way

Time: 3½ hours one way. (Requires car shuttle.)

Elevation Gain: 1200'

Trail Notes

On the way to the main park entrance you pass the community of New Almaden, a row of cottages along Alamitos Creek. This village, which once housed the mine staff, is described in a periodical of 1854 as "...a little hamlet of a row of neat houses, enclosed with a paling fence, containing in front a small flower garden with shrubbery." Also remaining from New Almaden's heyday is La Casa Grande, once the superintendent's home and now Santa Clara County's New Almaden Mercury Mining Museum. Next to the park entrance was the now-dismantled massive ore-reduction works called the Hacienda.

Aside from the absence of these works, your trip up the hill cannot be greatly different from a journey on a road somewhat west of the Mine Hill Trail, taken by Mrs. S.A. Downer in the 19th century. She wrote in the magazine *Pioneer* in 1854, "Around the side winds the road, constructed at immense cost and labor for the transportation of the ore from the mountains to the Hacienda below . . . the road, winding and turning up the mountainside, disclosed new beauties at every foot of distance."

As you climb the road now in the spring, the hillsides are covered with brodiaea, lupine, Indian paintbrush, shooting stars and milkmaids. The old road is an easy grade for walking. From the park entrance, woods shade much of the way up the hill, making this a comfortable trip on any but the hottest days. In 0.5 mile you pass the Hacienda Trail on your right and the English Camp Trail on your left, then continue your winding way to Capehorn Pass, a saddle at an elevation of 1000'. Here is a crossroads, where the Randol Trail and a short connection north to the Hacienda Trail take off.

The Mine Hill Trail continues uphill on the way to settlements where Cornish, Mexican and Chinese miners once lived. The well-weathered banks of the old road become flower gardens in spring. Some sections of roadside below English Town, kept moist by springs above, blossom into delightful herbaceous borders—yellow yarrow, blue larkspur, purple brodiaea, with accents of scarlet Indian paintbrush against a background of delicate white flowers of 4' tall Queen Anne's lace.

After an easy walk of an hour you pass an entrance to English Town, now cleared of hazardous materials and open to the public. Here are remnants of trees, including a derelict palm, planted when a community of 500 houses, with churches, school, stores and cemeteries too, covered the southern hillside. Here also is the mile-long Castillero Trail which contours around the south side of the ridge and reaches Bull Run. From the Castillero Trail is a short trail leading southeast to the Hidalgo Cemetery and to the planned trail connection west to Hicks Road.

The road continues uphill past mine tailings and old side roads leading to mines and shafts now tightly covered. One such side road offers a short trip to the Day Tunnel and a picnic site along the trail. A look at the topographic map for this area shows many mines and shafts with names of a romantic ring—Santa Ysabel and St. George shafts, Enriquita and Providencia mines. But there was little romantic about the hard, dangerous work of mining cinnabar, except for the hopes of riches—often realized for those who owned the mines.

Beyond English Town's entrance a trail turns down to make a brief loop trip to the April Trestle, where there is a section of railroad trestle that carried ore cars. On the way is an old brick powderhouse that stored blasting powder.

After a 3-mile climb the Mine Hill Trail comes out on a high grassy meadow close to the 1700' summit of the ridge. Called Bull Run, this high pasture commands views out over the valley and up to the Santa Cruz Mountains. A picnic table under an oak looks out over the canyon of

Guadalupe Creek to the Sierra Azul. Northeast a very short side trail leads to the Catherine Tunnel.

When you leave Bull Run, your trail follows the ridge as it slopes down northwest. In spring the green meadows are dotted with flowers; by May and June yellow mariposa lilies blossom through the turning grass; by late summer the pale oats are a golden contrast to blue skies and dark oaks edging the meadows.

As you lose altitude, ragged serpentine outcrops break the smooth contours of the hills. The magnesium-rich soil of this formation produces the carpets of flowers—goldfields, cream cups and more—so often found in serpentine grasslands. Serpentine is associated with cinnabar and is a common rock type in the California Coast Ranges.

As the track swings west you can see Guadalupe Reservoir below. Along the way you pass the Prospect #3 Trail going east, which provides a convenient connection down to the Randol Trail. Then at a sharp switchback the Providencia Trail takes off south to contour along the hill below Bull Run with fine views across the canyon to the wooded slopes of Mt. Umunhum.

Continuing about 0.75 mile on the Mine Hill Trail, you meet the north end of the Providencia Trail, and then 0.5 mile farther on your right the Randol Trail takes off sharply, on which you could return to the Almaden entrance, thus avoiding the need for a shuttle. However, this trip continues north on the Mine Hill Trail, soon passes the Guadalupe Trail junction, and veers north to traverse a wooded hillside. Easy walking on the broad trail on a gentle grade brings you to shady east slopes. The trail goes under oaks and past groves of buckeyes, so handsome in bloom in May that they are worth a trip to see. Great creamy pink flowers carried on upright panicles as much as 10" long cover the buckeyes' rounded crowns.

After about a mile on this pleasant hillside your trail intersects the north end of the Guadalupe Trail. Here also the hikers-only New Almaden Trail comes in from the southeast and heads straight downhill toward the Senador Mine Trail. The Mine Hill Trail goes east, bends left (north) and goes in and out of woods edging small grasslands. High chaparral lining the trail includes particularly luxuriant growths of poison oak, as well as more welcome wild cherry and elderberry. This cool, northeast-facing, damp side of the hill is crossed by small watercourses and supports a fine stand of live oaks. Late in the day quail calls fill this little canyon, and you may see deer going down to the creek below, or at least hear them crashing through the brush as they become aware of your approach.

About 0.6 mile from the Guadalupe Trail intersection, your trail comes out by the McAbee Road park entrance. With a shuttle car parked at this entrance, you can save the long hike back.

Almaden Quicksilver County Park
RANDOL AND MINE HILL TRAILS LOOP

Passing the sites of mine shafts and tunnels on the wooded east side of Los Capitancillos Ridge this trip returns over the Bull Run summit on the Mine Hill Trail.

Distance: 10.5-mile loop

Time: 6 hours

Elevation Gain: 1300'

Trail Notes

You can start a loop trip that includes the Randol Trail and the upper part of the Mine Hill Trail from either end of the park. However, the trip from the Hacienda entrance is shorter by one mile, and is open to all trail users, so it is the one described here.

Begin on the Mine Hill Trail as in Trip 1. In 1.1 mile you will be at the junction where the Randol and Mine Hill trails and a short connector to the Hacienda Trail meet at Capehorn Pass. The Randol Trail, the middle route, drops off down through chaparral of greasewood and poison oak. In shady bends, blue nightshade blossoms luxuriantly all summer, and here and there are slender stalks of cream-colored Fremont lilies in spring. Around a sharp bend 0.5 mile from Capehorn Pass you see the first tailings from the Day Tunnel spilling down the slopes below the road. The Day Tunnel on the uphill side of the trail is now closed, as are all the tunnels and shafts at New Almaden, but you will see the Great Eastern Trail taking off left uphill to meet the Mine Hill Trail. (For a short excursion—3.75 miles—hikers and equestrians could make a loop on this trail, stop at a picnic table in the trail's shady bend and return to the Hacienda park entrance.)

Beyond the Day Tunnel your trail becomes more wooded as it descends the hillside. Coming out on an open ridge, you see the vast dump of the Randol Tunnel, then turn into a ravine. At a sharp bend in the trail is the start of the 0.4-mile Santa Ysabel Trail, which goes uphill under the trees, passes the Santa Ysabel Mine site and then rejoins the Randol Trail, thus short-cutting a long loop east. But if you bear right at this bend, you can continue instead on the 0.9-mile Randol Trail, for hikers and equestrians only, and at a pleasant little flat pass the site of the Buena Vista Shaft, built in 1881. Old stone and brick walls stand in a tangle of weeds and vines. Topping the walls are massive granite blocks on which was bedded the coal-fired steam-powered pump, with a 24-foot flywheel, which went down 600 feet below sea level, and was used to lift

From the Randol Trail lookout over Santa Clara Valley

water from the Randol Tunnel. However, about the time the shaft was put down, the demand for mercury fell, and no ore was ever hoisted from the shaft.

Today, this sunny flat is a good place to pause while you contemplate the New Almaden mining activity of a century ago. The old road you have been following was busy with miners coming and going to shifts in the tunnel and with wagons carrying ore to the reduction furnaces at the foot of the hill. From here a short footpath descends to the hikers-only New Almaden Trail, which meanders along the base of the hill, both left and right.

From the Buena Vista Shaft the Randol Trail descends into a canyon, rejoins the main trail, and climbs again up a ravine to cross one of several little streams that cascade down this side of the New Almaden hills. You traverse along the side of the ridge, the trail rising and falling, bending in and out of ravines. Small grassy slopes alternate with groves of oaks. In spring, displays of flowers on the road banks include baby blue eyes and Douglas iris, and shady hillsides are golden with great drifts of buttercups.

In 1.2 miles beyond the Santa Ysabel/Randol trails junction, you round a broad, grassy ridge and from this vantage point you see the busy valley below, with homes, schools, shopping centers and industrial plants. Here is a picnic table and a junction with the Prospect #3 Trail, which goes steeply uphill (for hikers and equestrians only) to the Mine Hill Trail, or meanders downhill (for hikers only) to the New Almaden Trail.

For the next mile the Randol Trail winds in and out of ravines, a pleasant jaunt under the trees. Climbing through the underbrush are the vines of native clematis, with creamy white flowers in spidery clusters during the spring. By summer the seed heads are balls of fluff that remain on the plants through the fall.

The Randol Trail finally turns decisively uphill through the grasslands to the sloping ridgetop to meet the Mine Hill Trail, 1.6 miles from the Prospect #3 Trail junction. Here you turn left (south) and follow the Mine Hill route that goes uphill and then down to the Hacienda entrance, where your trip started. (See part of Trip 1 in reverse, page 194.) The north section of the Mine Hill Trail, open to hikers, equestrians and horsecart drivers, goes to McAbee Road, slightly less than 2 miles downhill from here.

3

Almaden Quicksilver County Park
A SHORT BUT STEEP LOOP FROM MOCKINGBIRD HILL ENTRANCE

From the heights of the park's southeastern ridge above Alamitos Creek look across to other Santa Clara County parklands.

Distance: 2.9-mile loop

Time: 2 hours

Elevation Gain: 600'

Trail Notes

This trip, for hikers and equestrians only, leaves the Mockingbird Hill staging area on the Hacienda Trail and returns on the Virl O. Norton Trail. The Hacienda Trail from here is broad, but very steep, and is best taken uphill. Dubbed "Cardiac Hill," its shady route is through a handsome oak-and-madrone woodland, first west and then south up a spur of the ridge north of Capehorn Pass.

As you approach the hilltop, the trail goes along a narrow spine from which you look east over the Santa Clara Valley and west to the Mine Hill and Randol trails cutting across the main Almaden ridge. The trail dips, then makes a final rise to its 1000' summit before descending to the turnoff at Capehorn Pass.

From here you could go south through Capehorn Pass to the Mine Hill/Randol trails junction, but this trip turns left (east), continuing on the Hacienda Trail. In late spring just beyond the junction a south-facing hillside is ablaze with masses of apricot-colored sticky monkey flower. Farther on are riots of blue, yellow and white flowers that clothe the trailside. At one point you pass a series of jagged boulders that look like dinosaur fins, against which tall native grasses wave in the breeze.

A series of precipitous drops followed by steep climbs makes this section of the trail a bit uncomfortable for hikers and equestrians alike— more pleasant when done in the cool of the day. However, wide views open up toward the eastern foothills and the Diablo Range. In the foreground to the northeast are the hills of Santa Teresa County Park. Over a low hill to the east lie Calero County Park's reservoir and miles of trails. It is hoped that trail connections one day will link these three parks.

After passing a few grassy flats edged with spreading oaks that cast shade and offer good picnic places, your trail now rounds a hill and meets the Virl O. Norton Memorial Trail. Here are wider views up to the heights of the Santa Cruz Mountains, down the canyon of Alamitos Creek, and west across to the heights of English Town. After orienting yourself to this viewshed, bear left on the Norton Trail to follow a powerline service road downhill.

The descent undulates up and down through grasslands, occasionally passing under the powerlines, and eventually skirting close to houses on the south side of the hill. A final swing east through oak and bay woodlands takes you back to the Mockingbird Hill park entrance.

For a longer, alternate route (4 miles) from the Norton/Hacienda trails junction you could turn right, continuing on the Hacienda Trail, which makes two long traverses and reaches into deep canyons where small streams cascade in winter and spring. Coming out of the last traverse, the

Randol Trail

trail climbs again to the Mine Hill Trail, 0.4 mile above the Hacienda park entrance.

To complete the loop, turn uphill on the Mine Hill Trail and follow its pleasant grade up to Capehorn Pass. (For this segment see Trip 1, page 194.) A half hour will take you to the pass, where you turn right (north) to meet the Hacienda Trail and return on it to the Mockingbird Hill parking area.

Almaden Quicksilver County Park
SENADOR MINE AND GUADALUPE TRAILS LOOP

A 4-mile loop for hikers and equestrians takes you from the Senador Mine across the ridge through meadows flowery in spring to Guadalupe Creek and past its reservoir, returning on the Mine Hill Trail.

Distance: 4-mile loop

Time: 2 hours

Elevation Gain: 720′

Trail Notes

You go through remote meadows and quiet oak woods where any number of sites invite you to enjoy a leisurely picnic. This trip may be taken in either direction, but is described here starting on the Senador Mine Trail. Much of the route is through woods, making it a good choice for warm weather.

There is room for a few cars to park outside the gated McAbee Road entrance to the park, from where a service road follows a creek canyon to the Senador Mine area. The Mine Hill Trail turns off left immediately beyond the entrance gate, but you continue along the road, which becomes the Senador Mine Trail.

Where the canyon widens, you come to two high concrete towers, a part of the furnace plant left from the days when this mine was producing as much as ten 76-pound flasks of mercury a day. After new management took over operations of New Almaden Quicksilver Mine following its bankruptcy in 1912, the Senador Mine was worked again in the 1920s. A plaque by the towers describes the new processes used then in the reduction of mercury at the mine. By 1926 this operation too had ended.

Beyond the towers, the Senador Mine Trail takes off uphill to the right of a small flat where a picnic table and hitch rack nestle under a stately oak tree. Continuing along an old road, you wend your way around a

Deer in Almaden Quicksilver County Park meadow

wooded canyon to a saddle in the ridge. The Senador Mine Trail ends at a saddle where it meets the Guadalupe Trail. One end of this trail turns uphill around the east side of a ridge, but your route goes west, downhill, toward Guadalupe Creek. At the saddle are a number of places to picnic under the shade of oaks if you are out for only a short walk. The easy half-hour walk from the park entrance makes this spot a good choice for an early picnic supper in summer. Just north beyond the park boundary is the site of the Guadalupe Mine, one of the three main mines operating in the mid-1800s.

Continue from the saddle down the Guadalupe Trail. Ahead the Santa Cruz Mountains come into view, topped by 3500' Mt. Umunhum, easily identified by the tall, blocky structures on its summit, former military installations. As you walk downhill you soon catch the sounds of Guadalupe Creek running below. Along the hillside among the sunny grasses are scattered mariposa lilies, their elegant tulip-shaped blossoms borne on tall stems. Both the intense lemon-yellow lily and the taller white lily with maroon markings are plentiful.

A few turns down the trail take you close to the creek, which is outside the park, so you can't go down to it, but you can enjoy its sycamore- and alder-lined banks. From here it is a lovely walk past flowery meadows and through groves of wide-spreading oaks. Occasional glimpses from the trail reveal the steep heights of Los Capitancillos Ridge. During spring and summer shrubby sticky monkey flower plants cover these slopes with their apricot blossoms.

The trail soon turns uphill away from the creek and climbs to the level of Guadalupe Dam. Below the dam and your trail is the site of the San Antonio Mine; now the only signs of it are some tailings and an old shed.

Little Guadalupe Reservoir is a narrow body of water filling the canyon for 1.5 miles upstream from the dam. Its blue waters are inviting, but swimming, diving and boating are strictly forbidden. The trail soon veers away from the reservoir and climbs to a high open hillside. From here you can see the Mine Hill Trail descending Los Capitancillos Ridge to meet the Guadalupe Trail at a saddle. From this saddle take the Mine Hill Trail, which is open to horsecarts, back to the McAbee Road park entrance, an easy walk of less than an hour (see Trip 1, page 194).

Almaden Quicksilver County Park
NEW ALMADEN TRAIL

Enter this hikers-only trail at its north or south terminus, or make a loop on it using three intermediate trail connections.

Distance: 6 miles one way

Time: 3 hours

Elevation Change: Very little

Trail Notes

Although you can start this trip from either of the eastern entrances to the park, it is briefly described here from the southwest corner of the Mockingbird Hill entrance. This pleasant path, for hikers only, contours north for 6 miles along the lower part of the ridge, joining the Mine Hill Trail near the McAbee Road entrance. The trail goes in and out of canyons, now and then emerging on sunny meadows, and traversing wooded hills without making the kind of climbs found on most other trails in the park. Spaced along this route are three connector trails that provide the opportunity for loop trips with the Randol and Mine Hill trails, described in other trips.

The proliferation of yellow star thistle and the tall Italian thistle in many parklands was particularly uncomfortable on this trail when the authors hiked it. Park authorities are working on eliminating these non-native species. In the meantime, long pants and long-sleeved shirts are advisable.

At several places hikers can perch on clumps of rocks, listen to quail calling, and watch for rabbits and deer in the forest. When the footpath nears the north end, it crosses little streams, meanders through grasslands rich with springtime flowers and then passes the remediation area at the former Senador Mine site. From here it is just 0.2 mile to the McAbee Road entrance.

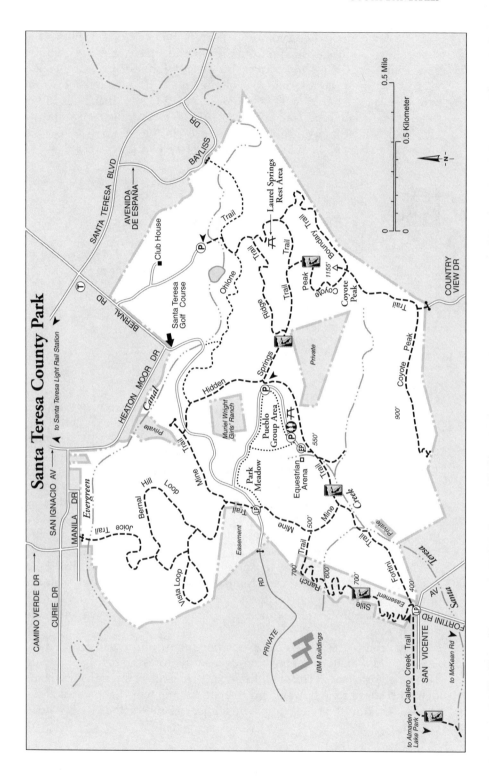

Santa Teresa County Park

◆ Santa Teresa County Park ◆

The rolling hills of 1688-acre Santa Teresa Park rise from the valley floor to 1155' Coyote Peak. The low-lying northeast section is given over to a golf course and an archery range. A broad saddle stretches across the center of the park between Coyote Peak and the hills to the west. In it are picnic tables, barbecues, an equestrian arena and parking. Fourteen miles of trails lead over grasslands, past rugged outcrops and along tree-lined ravines of the Santa Teresa Hills. All trails are open to hikers, equestrians and bicyclists, except for the Ohlone Trail, which is closed to bicyclists, and the Pueblo Trail, a footpath which circles around the Pueblo Picnic Area and crosses back over the big meadow, extends 0.4 mile along the entry road under the shade of young oak and bay trees, and joins the Mine Trail.

The 9646-acre Santa Teresa Ranch was granted in 1834 to José Joaquin Bernal, a native of Spain, and son of a soldier in De Anza's expedition to California, by the Mexican governor of California. Retired from the army at the Presidio in San Francisco, Bernal moved to San Jose and in 1826 moved his family to the Santa Teresa Springs, probably a former Ohlone settlement. Although there were mercury mines in the surrounding Santa Teresa Hills, springs in the hills of Bernal's rancho supplied plentiful water for his large herds and orchards.

Bernal had lived on the ranch for some years before the land grant was made to him at the age of 73. When he died, Bernal left the ranch to his wife and children. Members of this family lived for generations on the ranch, one of whom established various businesses, including a quicksilver mine, and built a home

Stile Ranch Trail looking toward Santa Cruz Mountains

which still stands near the park. The husband of another family member built a ranch house of hand-hewn timbers on original rancho lands, today known as the Joice-Bernal Ranch, situated on the northwest side of today's park. Large orchards, vineyards and cultivated fields that once covered the lower slopes of the hills and fertile flatlands have all but disappeared, replaced by subdivisions and industrial parks.

In Joaquin Bernal's day a French saddlemaker whose work was much valued by equestrians of the time was given an adobe house on the ranch. Today, local equestrians must look elsewhere for saddles, but they find the trails over Santa Teresa's hills good riding.

The park entrance road, realigned to provide access to a research facility just beyond the park's northwestern boundary, crosses the meadow west of the picnic grounds, and bisects the park and the route of the Mine Trail/Hidden Springs Trail Loop. A 6.5-mile segment of the Bay Area Ridge Trail heads west from Coyote Peak on the Coyote Peak, Hidden Springs, Mine and Stile Ranch trails to join the Los Alamitos/Calero Creek Trail, from which roadside trails extend to the Mockingbird Hill entrance of Almaden Quicksilver Park.

Jurisdiction: Santa Clara County.

Facilities: Trails: hiking, equestrian, bicycle. Equestrian arena. Picnic areas and barbecues: family, group by reservation. 18-hole golf course, driving range and clubhouse. Archery range.

Park Rules: Hours: 8 A.M. to ½ hour after sunset. Dogs on 6' leash in picnic areas. Bicycles allowed on all park trails except the Pueblo and Ohlone trails. Phone: 408-225-0225 or 408-358-3741; reservations 408-358-3751.

Maps: Santa Clara County *Santa Teresa Park*; USGS quad *Santa Teresa Hills*.

How To Get There: *By Car:* From Highways 101 or 85 in south San Jose take Bernal Rd. exit going west. Continue uphill into the park and turn left to reach picnic areas, parking and main trails. Or continue on Bernal Rd. past this left turn to limited parking at a turnout before the gate to a research facility. Or, from Hwy. 280, follow Almaden Expressway south till it ends, turn right onto Harry Rd., then turn left onto McKean Rd., continue 1.3 miles and turn left on Fortini Rd. to its end. Turn left onto San Vicente Rd. and proceed to small parking area on road's right side.

By Bus: County Transit 67 and 68 stop at Santa Teresa Expressway and Bernal Rd.

Santa Teresa County Park
COYOTE PEAK CLIMB

A loop trip takes in vistas from Coyote Peak and returns on a traverse across the north-facing hillside.

Distance: 3-mile loop

Time: 2 hours

Elevation Gain: 600'

Trail Notes

Leaving the east side of the Pueblo Group Area, take the Hidden Springs Trail heading uphill (east). In the fall, dun-colored dry grasses are enlivened with the little starry white flowers of tarweed; in the spring some of the hillsides are transformed by wildflowers into seas of color.

The trail rounds the hill, crossing one of the park's year-round streams to meet the Ridge Trail coming in on your left. Continue on the Hidden Springs Trail bearing right (uphill). Climb through woods of buckeye and oaks to come out on a high saddle where your trail meets the Coyote Peak Trail at a three-way junction. Turn right on the Coyote Peak Trail to make the 0.5-mile climb to Coyote Peak, the high point of the park at 1155'.

From the summit (leveled off for communications installations in World War II) one has commanding views southwest of the Sierra Azul and northeast of the Diablo Range, where the white domes of Lick Observatory mark Mt. Hamilton. On the valley floor below, subdivisions have supplanted orchards and field crops that until the '50s flourished on the rich alluvial soil. You can see the electronics plants that now extend down Silicon Valley over the fertile lands that once belonged to the Bernal family. Today, cavalcades of equestrians wearing T-shirts with logos of computer firms canter over these hills on the trails of Santa Teresa Park.

From Coyote Peak you also look down toward the southeast end of the Santa Clara Valley as it narrows between the Santa Teresa Hills and the spurs of the Diablo Range foothills only a few miles away. Through this passage flows Coyote Creek, which drains the rugged ranges of vast Henry W. Coe State Park.

Around the peak great black turkey vultures soar on almost motionless wings, catching the updrafts. Red-tailed hawks circle high over the grass-lands looking for unwary ground squirrels. Earthbound park visitors can meander the heights of Coyote Peak 1.25 miles south and west on the Coyote Peak Trail to ridgetop views of Calero and Almaden Quicksilver county parks.

The Boundary Line Trail descends from the east side of Coyote Peak, but is steep and gravely. So return down the Coyote Peak Trail, and turn right at its intersection with the Hidden Springs Trail. This trail zig-zags 0.5 mile down through scattered trees, coyote bush, poison oak, and elderberry. At a sign marking the Laurel Springs Rest Area, the Coyote Peak Trail makes a steep descent to the lower part of the park, where it meets the Ohlone Trail.

For this trip, turn left into the Laurel Springs Rest Area and cross the creek to a pleasant retreat under tall bay laurels with a picnic table and a tie rack for horses. Trees meeting overhead make a cool canopy on a warm day and a good place to stop for a picnic. A stream from the spring runs in all but the driest years. Coffeeberry and elderberry shrubs grow luxuriantly. Huge burned-out bay trunks fallen by the trail are sending up sprouts to regenerate these hardy trees.

From the rest area take the Ridge Trail, which comes out of the trees on a steep uphill pull, then makes a series of ups and downs. This 0.6-mile leg of the trip goes in and out of groves of oaks and over grasslands, rising and falling on gentle grades. When the Ridge Trail meets the Hidden Springs Trail, turn right and descend 0.2 mile over undulating terrain to the picnic area where you started.

Santa Teresa County Park
THE HIDDEN SPRINGS/MINE TRAIL LOOP

Skirting around the park's central knoll takes you into a remote oak-studded valley.

Distance: 2.5 miles

Time: 1¼ hours

Elevation Gain: 200'

Trail Notes

This trip can be taken in either direction, but is described here starting north on the Hidden Springs Trail. From the Pueblo Picnic Area cross the park's entrance road and turn left (northwest) on the Hidden Springs Trail. Climbing gradually to the trail's summit, you look east across the tree-filled canyons to the sloping grasslands on the east park boundary. A few deciduous oaks offer summer shade; springtime brings bright poppies and delicate lavender brodiaea.

After rounding the central knoll, the trail descends into an oak woodland, crosses the now-closed Bernal Road, passes a turnoff to the Ohlone Trail, and drops abruptly down to the new Bernal Road, 0.6 mile from your start. A crosswalk, flanked by stop signs in both directions, leads you to the Mine Trail on the other side. Your immediate view right is of parking lots, corrals and barns of the former Norred Ranch downhill.

But veering left, you contour through scattered oaks above a wooded swale. You gradually climb west 0.4 mile to the Mine Hill/Bernal Hill Loop Trail junction, from where a bicycle/hiking trail loops around the heights of the park's northwest corner (see Trip 4, page 211). Bear left (west) here on the Mine Trail, which you share with bicyclists, who are required by prominent signs to wear helmets and to control their speed.

Now you are at the highest point of your trip; in the west across the valley loom the dark forested ridges of the Santa Cruz Mountains. Shortly (less than 0.2 mile) you cross Bernal Road again. Note that there is limited parking at a turnout just a few hundred yards up the road, which provides an alternate entry to this trail. As you head down the Mine Trail through rolling grasslands dotted with majestic evergreen and deciduous oaks, you feel far removed from the nearby Silicon Valley scene. The Mine Trail undulates 0.3 mile up and down the hills, then crosses a little reed-lined watercourse that flows south into Arroyo Calero on the park's south side.

Mariposa lilies

Climbing up a last hill, the Mine Trail passes the Stile Ranch Trail on the west, built by volunteers in the early 1990s. Now follow the rising trail 0.2 mile to a small knoll where a sizable clump of small-leaved chaparral oaks thrive. From here you descend 0.2 mile to an old ranch road, now the Fortini Trail. Here you bear left (north), still on the Mine Trail, to ascend through a canyon whose south-facing hillsides, studded with lichen-covered serpentine rock interspersed with straggly gray sagebrush, come ablaze with wildflowers in spring. The wide trail follows tree-lined Santa Teresa Creek for 0.3 mile, passes an old corral, and curves around beside the park's wide, west meadow. Just before the horse arena you can choose the Pueblo or the Mine Trail for 0.3 mile to the parking areas and picnic tables where your trip began.

Santa Teresa County Park
THE HIDDEN SPRINGS/OHLONE TRAIL LOOP

The pleasant Ohlone Trail winds in and out of small canyons above the golf course on the east side of the park, making an easy loop with the Ridge and Hidden Springs Trail.

Distance: 3.8-mile loop

Time: 2 hours

Elevation Loss/Gain: 200'

Trail Notes

Start this trip as in Trip 2 going uphill (north) on the Hidden Springs Trail. After passing the trail's high point, continue downhill through the forest. Just before you reach the trail crossing over the park entrance road, the Ohlone Trail, for hikers only, turns off right. Take this 0.9-mile trail, which contours around the lower east side of the park. Then it leads into a small canyon where a lively little stream emerges from the woods during the wet winter and spring months.

As you bear east around the hillside, your immediate view is of the golf course fairways and clubhouse. The trail passes through a grove of spreading buckeyes and out again onto open slopes. At the next bend you look down on an oval pond, framed by tall poplars, edged with cattails and overhung by willows. Ducks paddle about, shrubs flower in the background and a weeping willow dangles its branches into the water. Unfortunately, this pond is now off limits because it is within the golf course boundaries. The Ohlone Trail goes on ahead into a wooded canyon just above the pond.

If you follow the Ohlone Trail (here a service road) past its junction with the Coyote Peak Trail, you can continue for another 0.33 mile along the hillside, where there are several pleasant transitions from grasslands to wooded canyons. In spring the pathside is sprinkled with blue-eyed grass, poppies, johnny jump-ups and lupines. In summer you will want to linger in the shade of oaks and bays.

Then the Ohlone Trail continues another 0.4 mile to the park boundary. This section crosses the old Alamitos Canal, no longer used by the Santa Clara County Water District, though it often holds some water in winter. Here a park road leads southeast to an archery range and you turn around, looking west to the oak-studded hill in the center of the park.

On the return leg of this 3.8-mile loop you bear left (east) at the Coyote Peak Trail junction, following this steep, uphill trail 0.2 mile to its intersection with the Ridge Trail. Turn right (southwest) on it, meet the Hidden Springs Trail, bear right (west) and return to your starting point. (These last two trails are described in Trips 1 and 2.)

Santa Teresa County Park
A LOOP FROM THE PARK'S WEST ENTRANCE

A vigorous climb past serpentine rocks leads to lush meadows and a loop around the park's northwest corner.

Distance: 5.5 miles

Time: 2½–3 hours

Elevation Gain: 400'

Trail Notes

From the small, west-side parking area on San Vicente Road, take the Stile Ranch Trail uphill on a zig-zag course over rocky terrain. In spring this hillside is resplendent with masses of wildflowers of every hue. As you round one switchback after another, the variety and color change from brilliant yellows to deep blues and purples.

Approaching the summit you will see off to the left a fine old stone wall backed by a barbed-wire fence. On the fence posts are nesting boxes for western bluebirds, which you can recognize by the male's striking blue back and wings and rusty-red chest. At the top of the ridge stand several boulders splashed with orange and chartreuse lichen. Beyond lie the

Gilia on serpentine

high peaks of the Diablo Range with Mt. Hamilton's white observatory domes glinting in the sunlight.

On a long, easy descent in late spring swaths of "farewell-to-spring" (clarkia) cast a magenta haze on this hillside. The trail reaches a wide swale and plank bridges straddle a couple of streams. Fine old valley and live oaks cast welcome shade on a summer day.

Mounting a small rise, you meet the Mine Trail and turn left on it to traverse a quiet glen set between a woodland on the west and a low hill on the east. In 0.33 mile you come to Bernal Road near a turnout for limited parking. Cross the road and follow the Bernal Hill Loop Trail as it swings wide around the top of the hill for 0.75 mile. Circling the north side of the hill, this trail passes the Joice Trail, which descends through a little glen for 0.6 mile to the north boundary of the park. Access to the historic Joice-Bernal House here and the Santa Teresa Springs nearby is by permit only.

Therefore, this trip continues 0.4 mile on the Bernal Hill Loop and then takes the 0.3-mile Vista Loop around the most northwestern point in the park. Here you see over to the research facility and beyond to the wooded flanks of Los Capitancillos Ridge in Almaden Quicksilver Park.

After completing this short loop, return to the Mine Trail and retrace your steps through the glen toward the Stile Ranch Trail. But you stay on the Mine Trail, bearing left up a wide, chalky trail over the top of a low hill. The hillside on your left is punctuated with lichen-encrusted igneous rocks surrounded by silvery sage. In spring the spaces between rocks come alive with glorious blue brodiaea, orange poppies and magenta clarkia.

Watch for the Fortini Trail on your right and follow it beside Santa Teresa Creek as it ripples along under a canopy of numerous fig trees and native willows. This is a rather narrow, multi-use 0.8-mile trail that contours along an east-facing hillside. It passes the former Rossetto property, the former site of the Fortini family's mid-century recreational center known as the 14 E Club. Veering west, you then descend to the parking area at San Vicente and Fortini roads, where this trip began.

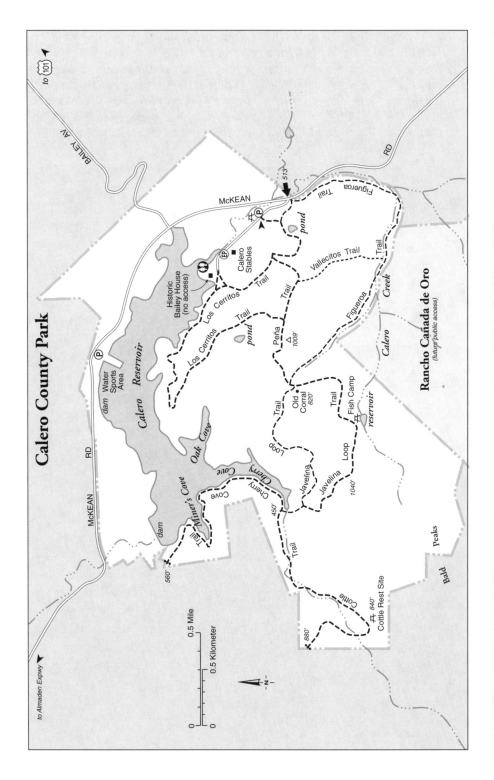

Calero County Park

◆ Calero County Park ◆

Calero County Park's 2400 acres include rolling hills and wooded ridges that are the backdrop for a reservoir open to boating. Miles of trails for hikers and horsemen lead beside creeks to sheltered valleys and to hilltops with sweeping views. An adjacent property of 2400 acres, Rancho Cañada de Oro, was acquired in 1999 by Peninsula Open Space Trust (POST), of which about 1100 acres will be added to Calero Park and the remainder will be managed by the Santa Clara County Open Space Authority. Connections to Almaden Quicksilver County Park to the north are planned for the future.

In 1935 the Santa Clara Valley Water Conservation District constructed a dam on Calero Creek, one of five dams completed that year, in a major effort at water conservation and flood control for the valley. When brimful after winter rains, the reservoir covers 349 acres. Boat-launching ramps and lakeside picnic tables make it popular for water sports, although no swimming is allowed. But by the end of summer the reservoir's water level is likely to be low, especially in dry years.

Park trails into the backcountry take you to hidden glens that seem far removed from the nearby suburbs and make fine trip destinations for any season. You can enter a world little changed over the past 150 years since cattle from Mexican ranchers ranged these hills.

Within the park's boundaries are parts of 2 vast ranches granted in 1835 by José Figueroa, the Mexican Governor of California: the Rancho Ojo de la Coche and the Rancho San Francisco de las Llagas. Both of these ranches were later acquired by Martin Murphy, an Irishman who crossed the Sierra in 1844 with Elisha Stephens and eventually came to own 50,000 acres in and around the Santa Clara Valley. Murphy's holdings were soon broken up, and Boanerges R. Bailey bought a piece by Calero Creek, where he built a house in 1865. The road from Highway 101 bears his name, and his house still stands. The house, now within the park's boundaries, serves as headquarters for the Calero Stables.

Now more than 14 miles of trails through Calero Park offer a variety of trips—easy, level strolls beside creek or reservoir, vigorous climbs over ridges, hikes to spectacular wildflower displays, walks to picnics by wooded coves, and expeditions to the old Cottle ranch house site. Many trails that follow wide ranch roads, now park service roads through open grassland, are quite warm at midday in summer. A master plan for this park, now in draft form, may affect trail design and use.

South of the valley now filled by the reservoir, a ridge runs northwest-to-southeast, rising to an elevation of 1000'. Another ridge extends toward the 1800' heights of Bald Peaks at the south end of the park. Beyond, a succession of steep, wooded ridges leads to the summit of the Santa Cruz Mountains, crowned by Mt. Umunhum and Loma Prieta, and lends a feeling of remoteness to many of Calero Park's trails.

Jurisdiction: Santa Clara County

Facilities: Hiking and equestrian trails. Rental and boarding stables (408-268-2567). Equestrian staging area. Water sports area, launching ramps, catch-and-release fishing, and picnic tables.

Park Rules: Hours: 8 A.M. to ½ hour after sunset. No bicycles, no dogs on trails. Phone: 408-268-3883 or 408-358-3751.

Maps: Santa Clara County *Calero Park* map; USGS quad *Santa Teresa Hills.*

How to Get There: From Hwy. 101 take the Bernal Rd. exit, go south 1 mile, and at Santa Teresa Blvd. go left for 3 miles; at Bailey Ave. go right to McKean Rd. Boating facilities are to the right on McKean Rd.; main park entrance is 1.5 miles to the left (south); entrance and parking on the right.

Calero County Park
CLIMB TO THE RIDGE AND RETURN ALONG THE LAKE

On this loop you ascend the park's central ridge, then ramble down an oak-dotted savanna with views over the lake.

Distance: 3.5 mile loop

Time: 1¾ hours

Elevation Gain: 400'

Trail Notes

From the staging area cross the entrance road to find the Figueroa Trail which leads up to the Los Cerritos Trail, and turn right (north) on it. Springtime finds these open hills thickly scattered with yellow johnny jump-ups for which this park is famous, coming through the short new grass. Pale green leaves are unfolding on the spreading valley oaks. Ground squirrels scurry through the grass searching for seeds to store against the dry seasons ahead, and overhead hawks ride the currents watching for such prey.

Shortly, on a gentle rise, your trail comes to one of several small reservoirs in the park. This stock pond, used by the ranch operations below, is also frequented by great blue herons and white-tailed kites, which comb its shores for frogs and dive into its depths for fish. A sentinel oak by the pond shades an observation platform and picnic table.

Calero Reservoir

To continue toward the ridge, stay on the trail below the reservoir's dam, then climb over a low hill and follow this old road in and out of the next small ravine. At the next outer bend in the road is the junction of the Peña and Los Cerritos trails. This trip turns left on the Peña Trail and climbs steeply for 0.5 mile through grasslands dotted with impressive valley oaks.

Turn to look east across McKean Road at the new private golf course and housing development spreading across the opposite hillside, and reflect how lucky we are to have this public park to hike and ride in.

Passing the narrow Vallecitos Trail on the left (for hiking only), you reach a second junction with the Los Cerritos Trail, which you take to the right (north) at an acute angle. Wider views open up over the lake and north across it to the Santa Teresa Hills. Now on a broad, grassy ridge, punctuated by stately oaks with branches sweeping the ground, you drop into little valleys, then ascend more hills. Steadily heading down, you look north over the reservoir to the boat-launching area by McKean Road. On a fine day the reservoir is blue in the sunshine. Motorboats skim the water and skiers swing back and forth in the wake of the boats.

Before reaching the lake shore, the wide service road veers right and curves around the east side of the ridge. Broader views open up north across the lake and beyond it to the Santa Teresa Hills. Tall blue brodiaea peeks out of the grasses, and the hairy roots of soap plant poke through the dust of the trail. Passing a couple of small peninsulas topped by jumbles of rocks, you wind around little coves, never very close to the lakeshore.

Back at the junction of the Los Cerritos and Peña trails, take the Los Cerritos Trail straight ahead. It goes up and down the hills above the horse stables and paddocks, past the pond and to the turnoff (left) for the parking area.

2   Calero County Park
BY CALERO CREEK TO THE OLD CORRAL

A "get away from it all" trail following Calero Creek around the ridge at the south end of the park leads up to the Old Corral. This can be a short, level walk, stopping beside one of several creek crossings for a picnic, or it can be a loop trip, returning from the corral over the central ridge.

Distance: 4 miles round trip

Time: 2 hours

Elevation Gain: 250′ to the Old Corral; 410′ to the ridgetop.

Trail Notes

Cross the road from the parking area to reach the Los Cerritos Trail, as in Trip 1; then after only 0.1 mile the trail becomes the Figueroa Trail, heading south. In 10 minutes you have left behind the traffic noise from McKean Road and have passed the backyards of houses on the other side of the creek, outside the park. Your trail, an old ranch road, soon reaches Calero Creek. With only the sounds of the creek, you walk under oaks and through flower-filled meadows.

The trail crosses the creek several times as it follows the fence line marking the park's boundary. In the wet season you may have to take off your shoes to wade across, but by summer crossing is easy. On the far side of the first creek crossing is a good-sized meadow. White-barked sycamores edge the creek, and the grass is filled with the johnny jump-ups so prevalent in this park. If you are quiet, you may catch sight of some of the many deer in these hills.

About a mile from your start, following the creek through woodlands and small clearings, you cross the creek again and enter a broad meadow. The open grassy slopes to the right extend to the central ridge that separates us from the park entrance. Here you pass a junction with the narrow Vallecitos Trail. Keep your eyes peeled for a coyote that the authors saw here.

Leaving the meadow, still on the Figueroa Trail, you climb through an oak forest, gaining 80′ in the next 0.5 mile as your trail keeps close to a fence line and a branch of the creek. Grassy clearings alternate with oak forest as the trail approaches the Old Corral, a low point in an oak grove between hills. This is a trail crossroads with routes leading from it to all parts of the park.

The route you have taken is a good beginning for trips farther into the park—around and over the manzanita-crowned ridge to the south on the Javelina Loop, or down the hill to Cherry Cove, an arm of Calero Reservoir, and on to the Cottle Rest Site (see Trips 3 and 4).

You have the choice of retracing your steps, all downhill on the Figueroa Trail by Calero Creek, or returning over the central ridge on the Peña Trail with a 160' gain in elevation. Both routes reach the parking area after approximately the same distance.

At any rate, you will want to stop awhile to enjoy the little valley by the corral, where oaks tower over grassy slopes, and you can glimpse the hills beyond the reservoir in Rancho Cañada de Oro.

3 Calero County Park
JAVELINA LOOP TRIP FROM THE OLD CORRAL TO A HIDDEN RESERVOIR

Have lunch by the reservoir, then climb past a rocky ridge for spectacular views and carpets of wildflowers in season.

Distance: 2.3-mile loop plus 4 miles round trip on Figueroa Trail.

Time: 3½ hours

Elevation Gain: 480'

Trail Notes

From the Old Corral, reached by the Figueroa Trail along Calero Creek described in Trip 2, take the Javelina Loop Trail left, just south of the corral, which goes up a slight rise through an oak glade. A climb of 100' in elevation past small meadows brings you to a plateau where the trail bends west. From here you see rounded, grassy Bald Peaks, which rise to 1800' at the south park boundary. Southeast, you look down Calero Creek canyon to catch a glimpse of the summit of El Toro in Morgan Hill.

The trail continues around the bend, turning into a little valley. Rising steeply above the trail on the right is the rocky ridge around which your return trail will circle. Meadows alternate with ravines shaded by oaks and bays.

The small reservoir and its surroundings in a hidden valley, cut off from the rest of the park by low hills, is known as Fish Camp. Picnic here by the water to savor the seclusion or take a trail over the dam to the shade of a wooded hillside.

When you explore the site, you will find a flaw in this little paradise. During the wet season, springs on the hillside above saturate the meadow and the trail. Then the turf is torn up and at times is so muddy as to be almost impassable—the work of a herd of wild pigs that give this loop its Spanish name, *javelina*. A large and growing herd of feral pigs has taken a fancy to this reservoir. They are rarely in sight and will avoid you, but if you see them leave them alone, particularly boars, which are equipped with formidably long tusks.

The road continues on the west side of the pond. You can escape the springtime mud by clinging to the steep hillside above the road at a drier point. The Javelina Loop Trail leaves Fish Camp, departing from this lush valley into dry sagebrush. After a steep climb of 160' you arrive at the ridgetop.

The Javelina Loop Trail makes a 400' descent through chaparral on hot dry slopes, then ducks into oak-madrone woodlands before reaching a junction with the other leg of the Javelina Loop Trail. Here, in a little ravine under a dense tree canopy, you turn right for a 2-mile uphill trek to the Old Corral, described in reverse in Trip 4.

Your return to the staging area can be on the Figueroa or the Peña Trail, the former being a gentle, downhill trip. However, if you choose the Peña Trail, you will climb to the heights of the park with fine views around the compass.

Calero County Park
TO CHERRY COVE AND COTTLE REST SITE

After passing the Old Corral, stroll through lush meadows along wooded north-facing slopes to the western shores of the reservoir where you have choices east and west. This makes a long but lovely expedition in spring when flowers line the way.

Distance: 8 miles

Time: 5 hours

Elevation Gain: 680'

Trail Notes

Follow directions to the Old Corral in Trip 3. Leaving the corral on the ranch road that leads to Cherry Cove, the Javelina Loop Trail goes northwest up a slight rise, then curves west along the hillside, descending gradually toward this cove on the south end of Calero Reservoir. Where your trail dips into ravines, you cross small streams that are dry by late summer. Yet this trip is shaded and relatively cool, especially if you continue to the Cottle Rest Site.

About ½ hour from the corral you come to a broad meadow edged with great valley oaks. During the wet season this meadow is seeping with moisture from springs above—a muddy crossing. However, goldfields, buttercups and mallow fill the meadow, making it a flowery destination. By June the grass is drying and is speckled with mariposa lilies—pale cream with maroon markings—and lavender brodiaea. From the meadow look north across

Equestrians descend the Javelina Loop Trail

Cherry Cove, from which come sounds of motorboats.

Beyond the meadow you drop down into another ravine with a running stream. Then in a grove of deciduous oaks you meet the other leg of the Javelina Loop Trail, on your left. Bear right and continue downhill on the Cherry Cove Trail. Under the trees are the lavender-and-white blossoms of Chinese houses and small-petaled baby blue eyes. Even in summer yellow mimulus blooms beside the trail in seeps from hillside springs.

The trail descends rapidly to the banks of Cherry Creek where it enters an arm of Calero Reservoir, Cherry Cove. White-barked sycamores overhanging the creek are sometimes standing in water when the lake floods the cove. After crossing Cherry Creek, which is in a big double culvert, you reach the junction of the Cottle Trail on your left.

Turning right takes you along the shores of Cherry Cove, on a woodsy path with flower-covered banks, 1.4 miles to Miners Cove. Short of the Calero dam the trail is gated to prevent further access. Along the lakeshore you can watch boaters picnic in springtime or spin by on their water skis.

If you choose the Cottle Trail westward from the Cherry Creek crossing, you follow a broad service road through grasslands enclosed by tall,

Calero's trails are shaded by oaks

rolling hills. For 0.5 mile you stay on the north side of the tree-lined creek until you cross a double culvert high above the creek. Once on the east side of the rocky streambed you go through an open gate that marks the boundary of the former Cottle property, and begin to climb through oak woodlands. After crossing a tributary stream, you are under a high canopy of trees with a lush understory of ferns, poison oak and toyon, making your way uphill and away from the creek. Look along here in summer for a brilliant fireweed (*Epilobium*, or evening primrose) with spoon-shaped petals and bright red pollen.

At the crest of the hill begin to look on your left for an opening in the old fence leading to a large meadowy area. The authors saw a dainty California gray fox duck into a hole in the bank here. Take the path diagonally through this meadow to the Cottle Rest Site, where the Cottle family house once stood. Now a picnic table, hitching rack and horse watering trough invite man and beast to relax—a welcome reminiscent of the hospitality early ranch families extended to wayfarers in these remote hills. Deciduous and live oaks rim the meadow, and remnants of once-domestic willows and watsonia grow near the homesite. You have now walked 5 miles from your start.

Above the rest site is another clearing where you can see over the tree-tops across the Almaden Valley to the Santa Teresa Hills and on to the heights of the Diablo Range. Northwest are chaparral-covered hills through which the Cottle Trail continues to the end of the park's property.

Reflect that some day from near this point a trail may connect north and west to Almaden Quicksilver County Park.

When you are ready to retrace your steps, cross the meadow to rejoin the Cottle Trail. Your route goes right, downhill all the way to the creek crossing at Cherry Cove, then across the creek and right for an uphill return. At the intersection of the two legs of the Javelina Loop Trail you can choose either one, as they both are about the same length and they meet the Peña and Figueroa trails at Old Corral. All these routes are described in Trips 1-3 of this chapter.

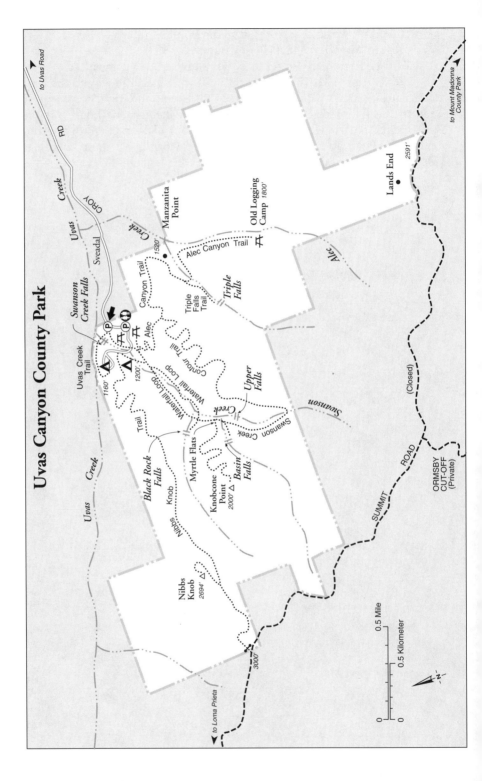

Uvas Canyon County Park

◆ Uvas Canyon County Park ◆

You reach Uvas Canyon Park by way of backcountry roads, a beautiful trip through grasslands, rolling hills and oak woodlands. Wildflowers are abundant by the roadside in spring. Going west on historic Croy Road, you follow pretty Uvas Creek, lined with alders, maples and redwoods all the way.

As you approach the park you pass Sveadal, a Swedish vacation retreat, where Swedish flags still fly and the blue of Sweden's colors trims its balconies. You enter Uvas Canyon Park in a heavily wooded canyon near the junction of Uvas and Swanson creeks. The shaded picnic grounds are close to the entrance, and campsites sit in little flats between the two creeks.

The 1200-acre park extends to the Skyline ridge over typically steep, rugged Santa Cruz Mountain terrain, cut by three creeks and their canyons. Most of the canyon of Uvas Creek is north of the park's boundary, but this beautiful watercourse runs for 0.25 mile through a corner of the park.

Swanson Creek and its two tributaries descend in deep canyons from the Skyline ridge. Alec Creek enters the park from the southwest, flowing down a redwood-filled canyon. Alec Canyon, the site of logging in the second half of the 19th century, is now shaded with second-growth redwoods of good size.

South-facing sunny ridges are chaparral-covered. Here and there, stands of knobcone pines have sprung up after fires of recent years. It was the forests that attracted early settlers to Uvas Canyon, and also the plentiful water from its streams and springs. Not only was the redwood valuable, but the oak, madrone, tanoak and fir were in demand for building and for firewood. Demand for lumber of all sorts for New Almaden, only a day's drive away, sparked lumber operations that continued through the second half of the 19th century.

The Homestead Act of 1862 allowed citizens to file claims for 160 acres of land and receive ownership if they had lived on the land for five years and made certain improvements. Rich soil in the lower canyon here and ample water drew dozens of homesteaders.

But the canyon and the streams were also attractions in themselves, and nearly 30 families filed for homesteads before the end of the century. Bernt and Anna Martin, of Scandinavian extraction, settled down to farm near the confluence of Uvas and Swanson creeks. As they cleared the land with a steam engine, they built a rock wall which you still see by the road as you drive to the park. Their house, set back by a wide lawn, was surrounded with flower beds, vegetable gardens, a vineyard and orchards.

The Martins sold lumber to New Almaden. They also ran Martinholm, a summer hotel, and shot game, caught fish, and raised fruits and vegetables for their guests.

It was this and neighboring properties that were eventually bought by the Swedish American Patriotic League in 1926, to become Sveadal. Crown Prince Gustav and Princess Louise of Sweden got the colony off to a royal start by attending the dedication ceremony that year. Settled by members of the league for a retirement community and summer recreation area for Swedish people of the Bay Area, it continues to serve as a favorite retreat.

The old logging roads through the hills have become park trails. This mountain park of wooded slopes has some easy creekside trails through quiet redwood groves. For the energetic there are steeper trails and a dramatic 1800' climb up a fire road to the Skyline ridge.

Spring is a favorite time to walk along Swanson Creek to enjoy its cascading waters. In summer and fall the trails under the trees appeal to hikers and picnickers as a cool retreat from the valley heat.

Jurisdiction: Santa Clara County.

Facilities: Headquarters. Trails: hiking, nature. Picnic areas: family, group. Camping: family on a first-come basis; youth groups by reservation.

Park Rules: Hours: 8 A.M. to ½ hour after sunset. Dogs on leash in picnic areas and campgrounds. Amphitheater near Madrone picnic area. No dogs on trails. No horses or bicycles on trails. Vehicle and camping fees collected. Group reservations 408-358-3751. Park phone 408-779-9232.

Maps: Santa Clara County *Uvas Canyon Park;* USGS quad *Loma Prieta.*

How to Get There: From Hwy. 101 in south San Jose turn west on Bernal Rd. At Santa Teresa Blvd. turn left and in 3 miles turn right on Bailey Ave. At McKean Rd. turn left (south) beside Calero Park. This road then becomes Uvas Rd. At Croy Rd. turn right (west) and drive to park entrance.

Uvas Canyon County Park
UVAS CREEK TRAIL

A short walk from picnic and camping areas along the tree-lined banks of Uvas Creek.

Distance: 0.5 mile one way

Time: ½ hour—though you could spend all day beside this beautiful creek.

Elevation Loss: 40′

Trail Notes

This trail follows Uvas Creek for its 0.25-mile stretch through the park. The headwaters of Uvas Creek and its tributaries are about 3 miles northwest on the slopes of Loma Prieta. From the park, the creek flows south out of Santa Clara Valley to join the Pajaro River, which empties into Monterey Bay.

This trip is described downstream from the campgrounds, although you can start this hike from either picnic area near the park entrance or the Family Camping area by walking toward the creek. Prominent trail signs mark the paths down to the creekside. Stay on the trails to avoid eroding the fragile banks of this canyon.

From the kiosk in the campgrounds, go down the broad Uvas Creek Trail to the creek, passing from an oak-madrone woodland to the damp, cool canyon of Uvas Creek. Tall alders, huge sycamores and big-leaved maples hug the banks and cast shadows on the waters. The trail stays above summer water level, following the creek as it cascades over boulders. Western dogwood hangs gracefully over the creek on the far side. Where a tributary pours over mossy boulders into Uvas Creek, patches of light-green-leaved thimbleberries grow on the banks.

As the canyon widens, the trail leaves the creekside to start up the steep bank. A carpet of spent leaves in hues of browns and golds covers the trail and the hillside, and in damp weather bay leaves underfoot give off their pungent fragrance.

You follow the trail uphill and step onto a wooden bridge across a side creek. Here you see Swanson Falls tumbling into a rocky pool surrounded on three sides by steep banks. After heavy storms in 1986, these falls were badly eroded, reducing the vertical drop by half.

After crossing the bridge you climb along a steep vine- and fern-covered bank on big rock steps until you come to a junction. One fork continues straight along the banks of Swanson Creek back to the campgrounds; the other goes left to the Family Picnic area. This picnic site on a spacious flat is in the dense shade of large madrone trees, whose deep-red trunks contrast with the shiny, large green leaves. This cool retreat is a popular picnic place for residents of the hot valley below. In this shady environment there is now a new amphitheater.

Uvas Canyon County Park
LOOP TRIP TO WATERFALLS ON SWANSON AND ALEC CREEKS

Going up the Waterfalls Loop Trail, you cross three falls on Swanson Creek and two on its tributaries, then on the Contour Trail visit Triple Falls. Spring is the time for these falls; the little streams often disappear in summer.

Distance: 3.25-mile loop

Time: 2 hours

Elevation Gain: 600'

Trail Notes

Start your trip from the Black Oak Group Area, which is the first picnic area on the left side of the park road. Then walk uphill past the end of the parking area to find the Swanson Creek Trail and head upstream. Continue past the Alec Canyon Trail going off left and shortly you cross a sturdy vehicle bridge, built by conservation crews following the 1986 storm damage, and reach the north side of the creek.

In a few minutes take the steep stairway on your left, cross the creek again and follow the 1-mile Waterfall Loop, a narrow footpath close to the creek. Alders, tanoaks and maples provide shade in summer, and ferns line the canyon banks where the clear, rushing stream cascades over its rocky bed.

From here the Waterfall Loop winds upstream past numbered posts marking interesting native plants and trees. (Ask the ranger for an explanatory leaflet.) After crossing the creek several times, the Waterfall Loop goes over a lovely cascade and climbs a little knoll to reach a park service road on the creek's north side.

Walk a few steps downstream to a Swanson Creek tributary, and to Black Rock Falls, where the waters tumble over dark stones. A narrow trail climbs the creek's west bank to a small observation platform above the dramatic drop of water over black boulders in a narrow, shady canyon.

Returning to the main trail you can walk 0.1 mile farther upstream to a wide opening in the forest. Just 200' to the right you will find Basin Falls dropping into a shallow, oval pool tucked away in a moist, rocky niche.

Alders along Swanson Creek

Back on the main trail near Myrtle Flats you begin to see signs of past habitation. Myrtle, the sprawling, blue-flowered ground cover, also called periwinkle, common in old gardens, has taken over the hillside. Ahead is an old cement dam and above the creek on a shady terrace is a picnic table.

You may want to explore a path that branches west from Myrtle Flats to Knobcone Point. A homestead once stood on the hill above, one of the many agricultural enterprises scattered through these hills. Olive, fig, and cypress trees along the way were planted by the family that tried to cultivate a vineyard on these hills.

You will find another waterfall, Upper Falls, on the main channel of Swanson Creek, a few feet upstream. In 1986 and again in 1998 storm waters swept down Swanson Creek leaving tangles of toppled trees and displaced boulders in their wake. At Upper Falls you see the impressive effects of the storm's force. A jumble of boulders and fallen trees lying above the falls was cleared to facilitate crossing Swanson Creek.

Walk along the Swanson Creek Trail on the west bank, then cross the rock-strewn creek bed to the Contour Trail. There is no bridge here, so hop across on the rocks and climb the far bank. In summer, this is a delightfully cool place to sit on the rocks, watch the dragonflies' flight and listen to the birds calling in the forest.

To continue this trip on the Contour Trail, follow it out on a broad ridge, climbing gently through a young oak forest interspersed with dense growth of madrones. Toyon, manzanita and ceanothus crowd openings where trees have fallen or young ones haven't shaded them out.

The number of knobcone pines growing here suggests that there must have been a fire in the not-too-distant past. Before long your trail starts turning into shady ravines, winding past small watercourses where Douglas firs grow to lordly heights, making a deep, quiet forest. The stillness is broken only by scolding Steller's jays.

An Eagle Scout project in 1981 built a plank bridge, still intact, to take you dry-footed across the head of the third and last ravine on this trail. At the intersection with the Alec Canyon Trail you can turn left (north) on an old logging road. At an opening at a bend in the trail you can rest on a bench and look out over the valley. Then in less than 0.5 mile you are back at the picnic ground where you started.

By turning right on the Alec Canyon Trail, you can make a short side trip to Manzanita Point and Triple Falls. The old logging road you climb brought redwood logs from Alec Canyon to lumber mills in the flats of Uvas Canyon. Manzanitas cover this dry hillside, but at Manzanita Point you look over them to a view of the Diablo Range. On clear days you can make out Mt. Hamilton's white observatory domes.

From Manzanita Point the trail goes south through high chaparral, dominated by pungent purple-flowered yerba santa. Buckeye trees below the trail here hold their leaves late in the spring, suggesting ample underground water. At the first drop of the water table in spring, buckeye leaves dry out, then hang lifeless until blown off in the fall. You are soon in the shade of redwoods beside an intermittent creek, where second-growth trees now make a tall, handsome forest.

At the Triple Falls Trail make a right turn to see this three-tiered waterfall. Five minutes up the narrow trail beside this tributary of Alec Creek will bring you to the 40-foot-high cascades.

Returning to the trail junction, make a right-hand turn and in 0.4 mile you will be at the old logging camp on Alec Creek. A picnic table on a small flat on the west side of the creek makes a fine, shady destination for lunch in the redwoods. Sounds of the creek tumbling over boulders and bird-song in the trees add to the pleasure of a stop in this remote part of the park. Signs on the far side of the creek forbid access beyond this point.

Thick stands of virgin redwoods drew settlers and loggers to this canyon in the 1800s. At one time the hillsides were dotted with loggers' cabins and woodcutters' huts. However, disastrous fires in the canyon in 1909 and again in 1924 erased nearly all signs of logging activity except a network of old roads and this site upstream, the Old Logging Camp.

For the return trip, retrace your steps on the Alec Canyon Trail back to the picnic grounds. The descent under madrones and oaks is an easy end to your trip.

Uvas Canyon County Park
FIRE TRAIL HIKE TO NIBBS KNOB AND SUMMIT ROAD

A steady uphill climb on the ridge between the Uvas Creek and Swanson Creek canyons takes you to views from Nibbs Knob and on to the Skyline ridge.

Distance: 5 miles round trip

Time: 3½ hours

Elevation Gain: 1560' to Nibbs Knob; 1760' to Summit Road

Trail Notes

Best taken in cool weather or as an early-morning summer hike from a campsite in the park, this trip gains almost 1800' elevation in less than 2 miles. The first and last stretches cling to north-facing slopes, while the middle, longer section stays just below the ridgetop on its south side. This is a good hike on which to orient yourself to the peaks and foothills of the South Bay, especially the Diablo Range from Mission Peak south.

Start your hike from the west end of Upper Bench Youth Camp where a fire trail begins beyond a big brown gate. The admonition to carry water, clearly printed on the trail sign, you should surely heed. On a hot day the sun beats relentlessly on the mountainside. However, the first part of the trip goes up the north side of Uvas Canyon in the shade of fir, tanoak, madrone, bay and oak trees. The understory is thick with ferns, honeysuckle, ocean spray and annual flowers. From the first shining white milkmaids of early spring to the yellow blossoms of bush poppies in summer, there are flowers beside the trail.

The sound of the creek in the canyon below mingles with the laughter of children playing, the call of birds in the trees, and sometimes the crashing of deer in the forest. For a while the trail takes all your attention, as it ascends steeply, carved out of this precipitous mountainside. At the second switchback, the footing is more comfortable, and you will be able to peer over the side of the trail down into Swanson Creek Canyon to the park's campgrounds and picnic tables.

At the next switchback you can look across Uvas Canyon to the main Skyline ridge and to 3791' Loma Prieta. The tallest mountain in the Santa Cruz Mountains, its heights are crowned by an array of antennas and microwave towers.

After the fourth switchback, you begin a long, straight ascent on the last north-facing, wooded section of the trail before you come out of the woodland onto the south-facing chaparral-covered slope. From here you see the Skyline ridge, its broad shoulders stretching down to the valley below.

On the ridgetop you will see a thick growth of young pines growing up among the manzanitas; they are the new knobcone pines sprouted from seeds that the heat of a 1961 forest fire released from the previously closed cones. This is one of California's three "fire pines," adapted to sprout after fires and reclothe the burned-over land.

Your trail goes steadily upward through thickets of blue-blossomed California lilac, chaparral pea, and pungent-smelling pitcher sage, topped by an occasional foothill or knobcone pine. On cool winter and early spring days the southern sun is welcome, but in summer the hiker seeks the shade of an occasional bay, scrub oak or pine tree along the way.

Overhead hawks circle lazily on the updrafts, and band-tailed pigeons fly swiftly over the hills, high above the canyons. Hidden in the chaparral, wren-tits sing their distinctive descending-scale call.

Just before the trail re-enters forest, it levels off at a saddle. Watch for a sign on your right marking the turnoff for Nibbs Knob. Don't miss this side trip. In a short 0.2-mile rise you pass the remains of an olive orchard, planted here many years ago by Henry Knibb. Little is known about this man, other than that he was granted a patent to this homestead in 1891, and he spelled his last name with a "k."

You circle around the knob through a forest of big Douglas firs, knobcone pines and madrones to emerge on the flattened top of the mountain, where, quite alone in a small clearing, sits a single picnic table. If the day is cool, this is a good place to have your picnic lunch.

Take time to explore this hilltop. Little remains but a few fences and more olive trees, but the views through small openings between the second-growth fir trees stretch north to Loma Prieta, directly west above you to the Skyline ridge and east to the Diablo Range. On clear days one can see Half Dome in Yosemite from here. Smog often fills the summer sky now, but Henry Knibb must have had unobstructed views.

Now retrace your steps to the junction and start the last stretch of trail up to Summit Road on the Skyline ridge. This is fine walking under a canopy of trees. The trail is covered with bay and oak leaves, only a little more golden than the fine sandstone pebbles of its surface.

You may be surprised to see grapevines climbing up the toyons and wild cherries. These vines, too, were planted by the industrious and adventurous pioneer who laid out the olive orchard in its neat circles around his Knob. From one of the switchbacks you can look back and see the cone shape of that knob, crowned with tall fir trees. Many brave souls tried their luck homesteading such high slopes in the late 1800s, only to find that water and good soil were too scarce and the climate too difficult.

You soon see the park's brown metal gate and a sign marking the limits of the park. Unpaved Summit Road is closed to motor vehicles, except for residents' cars, at this writing. But some day non-motorized traffic may be able to enjoy this mountaintop road with its 360° views. It is a direct, ridgetop route from upper Uvas Canyon Park to Mt. Madonna Park. It is hoped that a trail will soon lead west to Nisene Marks State Park.

When you have enjoyed the shade at trail's end, start back on the Nibbs Knob Fire Trail. There is a sign NO HORSES ALLOWED. The trails in Uvas Park are for hikers only. You soon begin the steep descent back to the canyon bottom. On the upward journey you had time to look around, because you needed to pause for breath. But the return trip requires close attention to your feet on this extremely steep trail.

In less than an hour you are back at the campground, exhilarated from the hike and the wonderful views from the top.

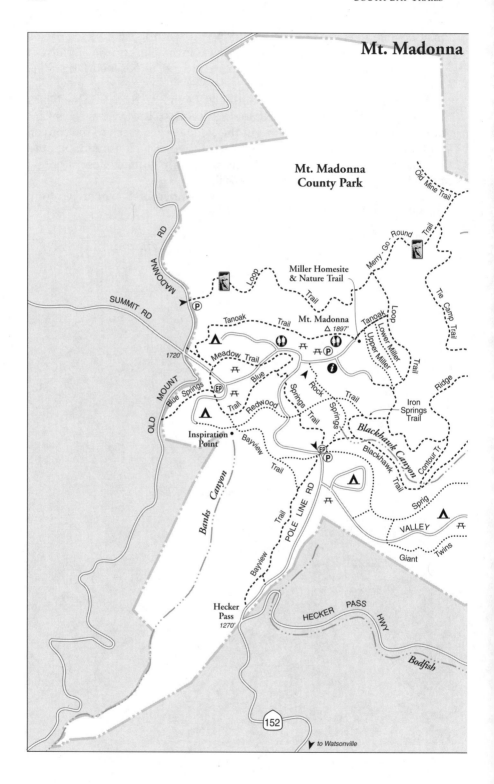

Mt. Madonna

Mt. Madonna County Park

Old Mine Trail

Merry - Go - Round Trail

Miller Homesite & Nature Trail

Tie Camp Trail

Loop Trail

MADONNA RD

SUMMIT RD

P

Tanoak   Trail

Mt. Madonna
△ 1897'

Tanoak

Loop

Upper Miller

Lower Miller

Trail

Ridge

1720'

Meadow Trail

Blue Springs

Blue

Redwood

Springs Trail

Rock

Trail

Springs

Iron Springs Trail

Contour Tr

Blackhawk Canyon

OLD MOUNT

Trail

Inspiration Point

Bayview Trail

EP
P

Blackhawk Trail

Banks Canyon

POLE LINE RD

Sprig

VALLEY

Twins

Giant

Bayview Trail

Hecker Pass
1270'

HECKER   PASS   HWY

Bodfish

152

▼ to Watsonville

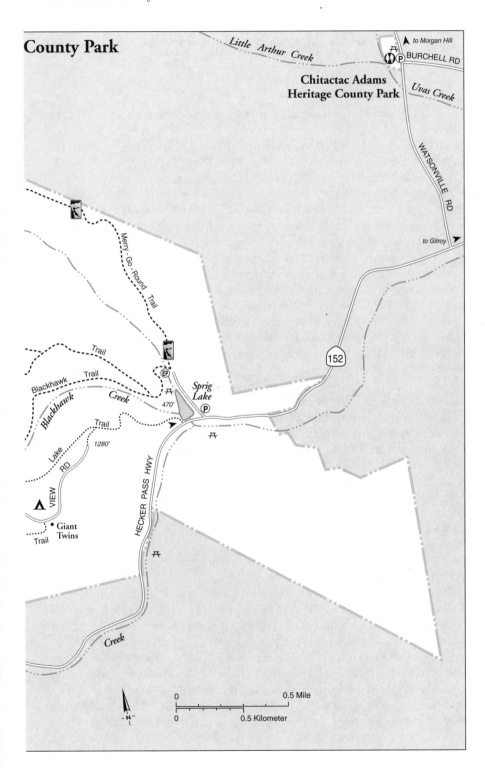

County Park

Little Arthur Creek

to Morgan Hill

BURCHELL RD

**Chitactac Adams
Heritage County Park**

Uvas Creek

WATSONVILLE RD

to Gilroy

Merry - Go - Round   Trail

Trail

Blackhawk   Trail

Blackhawk   Creek

470'

Trail

1280'

EP

Sprig
Lake

152

HECKER PASS HWY

Lake   RD

VIEW

Giant
Twins

Trail

0   0.5 Mile

0   0.5 Kilometer

- N -

• Mt. Madonna County Park •

Mt. Madonna Park surrounds the 1897′ southernmost high point of the Santa Cruz Mountains. From viewpoints on its 3219 acres one can see Monterey Bay and the Pajaro and Salinas River plains on the west and the Santa Clara Valley on the east. On clear days the views stretch south to the Santa Lucia Mountains and east to the Diablo Range.

In several deep canyons that crease the sides of the mountain, streams thread their way over boulders, fallen logs and tree roots. Dense redwood, madrone and tanoak forests cover the coast-facing slopes and the mountaintop. As the slopes descend toward the east, vegetation changes to oak woodlands, then to dense chaparral and grassy meadows.

Bird and animal life abound in the park. You will often see Steller's jays and raccoons boldly picking up remnants of picnickers' lunches. You may see a black-tailed deer on a forest trail or hear it crashing through the underbrush. The chatter of squirrels in the trees overhead is often raucous, but the shy shrew and the silent opossum are seldom sighted and never heard. White fallow deer restricted to a large hilltop pen are on view all the year.

A visit to Mt. Madonna Park in spring or early summer will reward you with sights of bright wildflowers in the grasslands and along the trails. However, at any time of year the display of fine wildflower photographs in the park office is well worth a visit to see the variety of blossoms you can find in the park. Here also are some stuffed specimens of park wildlife.

Remnants of Native American culture have been found in the area, attesting to its use as a hunting and fishing site, as well as a place to gather acorns. Today, many artifacts gathered from here are displayed at the Chitactac Adams Heritage County Park situated along Uvas Creek on Watsonville Road, just 1 mile north of Highway 152. Not to be missed is the interpretive trail which features petroglyphs, bedrock mortars, Ohlone buildings, and the Chitactac Village.

When Henry Miller was lord of a vast cattle domain in central California, he sought out the cool summit of this mountain for a summer retreat. Here he built a fine home and cottages for his two children. He set out orchards and vineyards and planted elaborate gardens. Expert craftsmen using stone quarried on the mountain constructed the foundations and the rock walls enclosing its garden walks. Italian woodcutters employed by Miller affectionately called the mountain "Madonna," which became its official name. Another version credits the poet Hiram Wentworth with naming the peak after the Italian term for the Virgin Mary.

Serving as Miller's summer headquarters high above his main ranch, Bloomfield Farm, in the hot valley near Gilroy, this retreat had views far out over his extensive lands in central California. It has been said that every acre of land he could see from here belonged to him. When he died in 1916, he owned one million acres of land and one million head of cattle, worth an estimated 50 million dollars.

Eventually his heirs sold the land on this mountain to Santa Clara County for a park. One of the houses was removed and reassembled on the Watsonville Road and the others were sold for salvage. Now only the foundations and fragments of walls remain, further damaged by the 7.1 earthquake of October 17, 1989. Tanoaks and redwoods 12" or more in diameter grow within the former walls.

Today, you can take a self-guided walk around the ruins and enjoy picnicking and camping on the mountaintop retreat of California's 19th century cattle baron. Spacious campgrounds and picnic areas shaded by tall second-growth redwoods, the park office, a playing field, a pen of fallow deer and an amphitheater share the mile-long plateau on the ridgecrest.

Beside the Hecker Pass Road on the park's east flank is Sprig Lake, a fishing pond exclusively for children 5–12 years and a family picnic place. A horse-staging area beyond the pond in the lower park is convenient to the equestrian trails. And archery enthusiasts will find a range in mid-park.

A trail network on old logging roads, powerline service roads and foot-paths covers the park north of Hecker Pass (Highway 152). On 20 miles of trails hikers and horsemen can explore its mountainsides, creek canyons and open grasslands. Some trails connect the camping and picnic areas, many begin near the park office, and several take off from Sprig Lake. A few trails through environmentally sensitive areas are restricted to foot traffic. Bicycles are not allowed on Mt. Madonna trails.

Jurisdiction: Santa Clara County.

Facilities: Park office houses small museum. Trails: 20 miles hiking, 13 miles equestrian. 100 picnic sites and 117 campsites for families; groups by reservation. Fishing at Sprig Lake. Archery range and amphitheater.

Park Rules: Hours: Open all year for day use from 8 A.M. to sundown. Fishing at Sprig Lake for children 5–12 years only, from late April through June. Dogs and pets on 6-foot leash only; no pets on trails. No bicycles on trails. Entry fees collected daily year-round; fees required for camping and for group picnic and group camping areas year-round. Call 408-358-3751 for group reservations and 408-842-2341 for park ranger and visitor center.

Maps: Santa Clara County *Mt. Madonna Park*; USGS quad *Mt. Madonna*.

How to Get There: (1) Main entrance—From Hwy. 101 in Gilroy or Hwy. 1 in Watsonville take Hecker Pass Hwy. 152, turn north on Pole Line Rd. (2) Sprig Lake entrance—on east side of park turn north off 152.

Mt. Madonna County Park

CIRCLE TRIP THROUGH BANKS AND BLACKHAWK CANYONS

Visit the major stream canyons on the east and west sides of Mt. Madonna's ridgetop to see flowers in spring and ferns in summer.

Distance: 2-mile loop

Time: 1¼ hours

Elevation Gain: 420'

Trail Notes

From the park office go west along the road a few hundred yards, pass the amphitheater and turn left, downhill on the Rock Springs Trail, for hikers only. At first you are in a shallow-soil, dry zone where chinquapin, knobcone pine and manzanita thrive. In spring the manzanita's bell-shaped flowers hang in clumps from its shiny-leaved branches. In summer the tall, yellow-flowered bush poppies and magenta-blossomed chaparral peas brighten the wide trail cut for powerline maintenance.

Keep heading downhill, staying east of the road until you come to the Redwood Trail junction. You turn right here, cross Pole Line Road, and step onto a narrower, shady foot trail which trends gently downhill 0.3 mile through the redwood forest. After crossing the head of Banks Canyon, your woodland way dips down to the creek bed. Sword ferns grow shoulder-high along the hillside and boulders line the streambed. Although this canyon was logged years ago, some second-growth trees are now 2 or 3 feet in diameter and over 100 feet tall.

As the Redwood Trail rises out of the canyon, it meets the Bayview Trail close to the park's west boundary. Here you turn left. Through an opening in the forest you can see out to the waters of Monterey Bay on a clear day, but in summer the coastal fog at times closes in and hangs on the southwest face of the Santa Cruz Mountains. Caught by the redwood's leaves, fog drips to the ground below, watering its shallow roots.

The Bayview Trail dips down into Banks Canyon again, makes several switchbacks and then ascends beside Pole Line Road for 0.29 mile. If you go left here for 0.13 mile, you will come to a major trail junction at a clearing across Pole Line Road. Instead, this trip proceeds a little farther on the Bayview Trail for its sweeping vistas southwest to the Pajaro Valley and the Santa Lucia Mountains.

After continuing on this more open section of the Bayview Trail for 0.22 mile, look for the sharp left uphill turn that will take you on the horse trail and back to the trail junction at Pole Line Road.

When you reach the junction, you are at the head of Blackhawk Canyon. You can choose any of the three springs trails—Blue, Rock or Iron—that traverse the upper canyon of Blackhawk Creek. At this writing some of these trails are unmarked, but each leads back up the mountain to the park office. To take the Iron Springs Trail, follow the wide Blackhawk Trail east down a shady canyon beside the creek. In a few minutes you arrive at the Iron Springs Trail and make a sharp left turn, keeping to the trail along the right slope. The rust-colored soil to the left of the trail shows the seepage from Iron Springs.

Walking through this canyon, one might think of a spacious forest reception hall, the high, leafy roof supported by tall columns of bare tree trunks. The springs and rivulets of this canyon feed Blackhawk Creek. In less 0.2 mile on the Iron Springs Trail you meet the Redwood Trail, on which you turn left and go uphill.

Shortly you reach the Redwood/Rock Springs Trail junction. A right turn on the Rock Springs Trail, for hikers only, leads back uphill to the main road, where you turn right again. En route you pass the amphitheater, often the scene of wedding festivities under the trees. If the park office is open, stop in to see the exhibits of Mt. Madonna's history and its plant and animal life.

Mt. Madonna County Park
AN ECOLOGICAL SAMPLER

A circle trip from the Miller homesite goes through a broadleaf evergreen forest to chaparral country and into redwoods on the mountain's east slope.

Distance: 3.5-mile loop

Time: 2 hours

Elevation Gain: 300'

Trail Notes

Go east past the park office to the old Miller homesite at the end of the road, where the broad, gated Tanoak Trail leads off to the northeast. Take this trail downhill through the filtered light of a broadleaf evergreen forest. Underfoot a carpet of fallen creamy pink and tan leaves from madrone and tanoak trees makes pleasant walking. Wild honeysuckle vines and poison oak compete with red-berried toyon shrubs for light and space under the trees. In early spring the upper leaves on foot-high Indian warrior plants turn deep red at the base of the trees.

After passing a couple of trails going off right, at the Loop Trail you turn left and continue through the forest for a short stretch. The woods thin out as you approach the Merry-Go-Round Trail, and you then turn right, downhill, on it. Soon you are out in chaparral, where manzanita, chamise, toyon and ceanothus predominate. Hiking here is best in winter or very early on a summer day.

The chaparral, a miniature forest, supports many birds, including the scrub jay, easy to recognize by his bright blue feathers and his raucous call. You may also see a small gray bird with a black hood hopping into the bushes. This bird—the Oregon junco—is quite at home in California too.

In about 0.5 mile you'll find the junction with the Tie Camp Trail, where you turn right. In the railroad's heyday, redwood ties were made at Tie Camp, south of here. For the next 0.5 mile the trail goes through chaparral and oak woodlands, with some foothill pines here and there on the hillside. Then as the trail turns into a ravine, it enters a deep redwood forest.

The trail has been following an old road on a gentle grade. At a second ravine you leave the road for a narrow trail and begin switchbacks up the mountain through open woods. The Tie Camp Trail widens as it meets the Ridge Trail, where you turn right and continue uphill through oak wood-land for 0.5 mile. You are now on an old logging road under second-growth redwoods that clothe the hillside.

Still in the woods you see the Contour Trail going off left, but to con-tinue on the Ridge Trail, veer right toward the Iron Springs and Loop trails. You head uphill through the trees, where now madrones and oaks meet overhead. Perhaps you will notice spiral ridges on the limbs of some madrones. The tree twists toward the light as other trees grow above it, blocking full sunlight. In 0.3 mile the Iron Springs Trail goes straight ahead, but you turn right on the Loop Trail. Steadfastly bear north, uphill, on this wide trail. Now out in open brushy country, only scattered euca-lyptus trees and electric powerlines rise above you. After 0.3 mile on the Loop Trail you turn left (the trail sign at this intersection was missing when the authors hiked it) to wend your way uphill through remnants of overgrown orchards, vineyards and gardens that circle the hillside below Miller's summer home. The empty stone-and-cement pool you pass was the estate's old fountain, once graced by a statue.

When you reach the wide carriage road below the basement founda-tions, all that remain of Miller's house, bear up through the ruins and walk right to the park road where you started. If you have time, a histor-ical and nature-trail guide, available at the park office, will help you explore more of this hilltop site, which once looked out over the vast domain of cattle baron Henry Miller.

3

Mt. Madonna County Park
ROUND TRIP FROM SPRIG LAKE TO THE RIDGE

This circle hike climbs up the ridge beside Blackhawk Creek and then descends gradually on a narrow foot trail through oak woodland, chaparral and beautiful redwoods back to the lake.

Distance: 4.2 miles round trip

Time: 3 hours round trip

Elevation Gain: 1100'

Trail Notes

On hot days start this trip early, even though the Blackhawk Trail goes through forest most of the way. You will gain 800' in the first 1.1 miles. After that the grade becomes gentler as you approach the upper ridge beyond the Contour Trail junction.

From the Sprig Lake parking area, go up the dirt road, pass the horse staging area and turn left, uphill, on the Blackhawk Trail. This wide trail, once a wagon road used for hauling logs, mounts steadily, rounds several spurs of the mountain and passes through small grassy openings in the oak-madrone woodlands. Fluffy panicles of cream bush overhang the trail in early summer, and blue-eyed grass puts out its yellow-centered, deep-blue blossoms in shady places beside the trail.

On some bare banks in the forest you may find little "villages" of 3–6-inch "skyscrapers," known as "hoodoos" by geologists. These occur when large raindrops fall from the trees and erode away soil, leaving little columns protected by a hard capstone.

About halfway up the mountain the trail paralleling Blackhawk Creek becomes a shady route among redwoods. Tall woodwardia ferns line the banks, and bright white milkmaids blossom in early spring. The Blackhawk Trail through the cool redwoods and firs follows the year-round stream. Pink-blossomed sorrel carpets the ground, and tall ferns grow by the creek side. This trip up the beautiful canyon crosses the creek several times, and in stormy winters there may be downed trees and mud underfoot.

Big pools have formed where boulders and fallen trees temporarily interrupt the creek's flow. Past the Contour Trail the route climbs more gradually, and before long you come to the big sand filters and pump-house, once part of the park's auxiliary water supply, fed by the springs you pass on the last leg of Trip 1.

After passing the Iron Springs Trail taking off right, uphill, you enter a wide opening in the forest, a junction of many trails beside Pole Line Road. If the day is cool, this sunny space may be a welcome rest stop.

When you are ready to start your downward trek, look for the Sprig Lake Trail and campground signs on a post on the south side of the opening. This narrow trail, for hikers only, curves around the side of one ravine and then another under beautiful tall redwoods dripping with a feathery moss. Noting a side trail going right to the Valley View Campgrounds, perhaps for a future camping trip there, you pass it and go left.

In a section of the mountain where crews have cut a wide swath for powerlines, the vegetation changes to manzanita, knobcone pines, a few madrones and plentiful huckleberries bushes. The authors found many ripe berries on the bushes in early October.

Not so plentiful are the chinquapin, a near relative of the oaks, and the knobcone pine, a tree found occasionally on the east slopes of the Santa Cruz Mountains. You can tell the chinquapin by its gold-backed leaves and prickly burrs. The knobcone pine has whorls of short, stubby cones that remain closed and on the tree until a fire comes along. Then the cones open, letting the seeds fall.

When you pass the trail to Giant Twins (two redwoods) on the right, signs tell you that Sprig Lake is 1.9 miles away and no horses, bikes or vehicles are allowed on the trail. Descending over occasional patches of sandstone you drop down out of the chaparral and come upon a huge burned redwood stump. The trail angles left below it, narrows, and traverses a steep side slope above Blackhawk Canyon.

More charred redwood stumps, which attest to a former forestry practice of burning slash, now illegal, stand beside the trail as you descend on long traverses. Where sunlight penetrates the bigleaf maple, oak and tanoak forest, thimbleberry thickets abound. Even in July the authors found little purple-throated white violets here. In spring the purple iris stand in thick clumps beside the trail. After rounding a few sharp turns over damp ravines, your way descends past an old skid road, crosses the little creek that empties into Sprig Lake and drops down rapidly to the west side of Sprig Lake.

The vigorous, 1100' climb followed by this long, cool descent is a good stimulus to a hearty picnic supper at the lakeside tables.

Mt. Madonna County Park
DOWNHILL HIKE FROM REDWOODS TO LAKESHORE

Skirting the park's northeast boundaries on the Loop and Merry-Go-Round trails, this gentle hike traverses dense redwood forests, crosses grassy knolls and terminates at Sprig Lake—if you have a car shuttle. This trip is also the route of the Bay Area Ridge Trail, the 400-mile trail that follows the ridgetops around San Francisco Bay.

Distance: 3.4 miles one way

Time: 1½ hours

Elevation Loss: 1080'

Trail Notes

Some of your party could do this hike on the last day of a camping trip in Mt. Madonna Park, arranging to be picked up at Sprig Lake as your car heads back to the valley.

Starting from the ridgecrest at the Summit and Old Mt. Madonna roads intersection, drive 0.3 mile north on the unpaved section of Old Mt. Madonna Road. Once the main road from Gilroy to the Pajaro Valley, now this seldom-used backroad winds quietly through a shady redwood canyon. You could safely walk down this road to the beginning of the trail. However, there is room for several cars to park near the trail entrance.

Walk around the logs barring vehicular traffic and begin your forest walk on the Loop Trail. The forest is very quiet, except for the song of birds and the chatter of squirrels. First the trail dips into a little ravine where a stream still flows in the summer of wet years, and in five minutes you come upon some of Henry Miller's work—a big water tank and pump house backed by a 15' moss-covered stone wall. Miller dug back several hundred feet into the steep hillside here to tap the spring and then piped its flow into the tank, from which with a steam engine he pumped it hundreds of feet uphill to his home. Today this water is used as a back-up water supply for fire suppression.

From the water tank your way continues on a gentle grade, curving back into canyon heads, rounding little knobs or going far out on a mountain shoulder. Always in the shade, this is a delightful, cool leg of the trip. In spring the blooms of the shade-loving forest wildflowers—deep-rose trillium and yellow-green fetid adder's tongue—punctuate the shadows of the tree-covered slopes.

The stumps of some very large redwoods have notches where the lumberjacks inserted boards to stand on while sawing the tree. The loggers always felled a tree uphill, because the longer fall downhill would have splintered it.

Now that logging has ended, the redwoods are growing large again. Redwood needles and tanoak leaves carpet the trail, making pleasant underfooting. The rivulets and streams from the steep sides of Mt. Madonna's north slope feed charming Little Arthur Creek in the valley below.

At the junction of the Loop and Merry-Go-Round trails, you could turn right and follow the Loop Trail 0.8 mile back to the park office. However, with a shuttle arranged you continue downhill to more open country on the Merry-Go-Round Trail. The trail is on sandstone, and as the forest gives way to chaparral the grade becomes steeper.

In 0.5 mile you come to a turnoff to the Tie Camp Trail, but your walk continues through scrub oak, ceanothus and manzanita country to the grasslands just 10 minutes down the trail. Here the views are lovely. On a clear day you can see across to the ridges of the southern Diablo Range. Above you to the south lie the forested flanks of Mt. Madonna. Bands of dark-green trees mark the major canyons where Blackhawk and Bodfish creeks flow eastward through the park. These boulder-strewn, grassy meadows with their long views would make delightful picnic stops on a sunny winter or early spring day. Even in summer, the authors found the shade of occasional oaks, tall elderberries or toyon comfortable places to enjoy the open meadowlands.

Turning south, the trail swings away from the park boundary and drops into an oak woodland, where it crosses a creekbed several times. Back out on a ridge with woods on either side, the trail then winds down into a deep redwood-and-bay-tree forest with an understory of tall wood ferns, wild blackberries and poison oak. The creek is joined by several tributaries on its journey to Sprig Lake. When you come to the horse-staging area, go around the log gate and head down the hard-surfaced road to the popular picnic and fishing area.

The little lake is stocked by a Gilroy sportsman's club and the Santa Clara County Fish and Game Commission. Fishing is restricted to children between 5 and 12 years, with a limit of 5 fish per day. Eager youngsters line the lakeshore, while parents and older children applaud the catch.

◆ Creekside Park Chains ◆

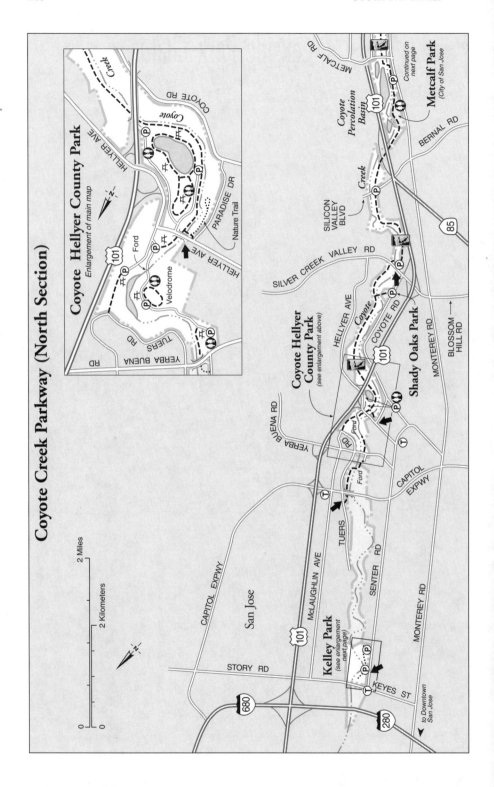

Coyote Creek Parkway (North Section)

Coyote Hellyer County Park
Enlargement of main map

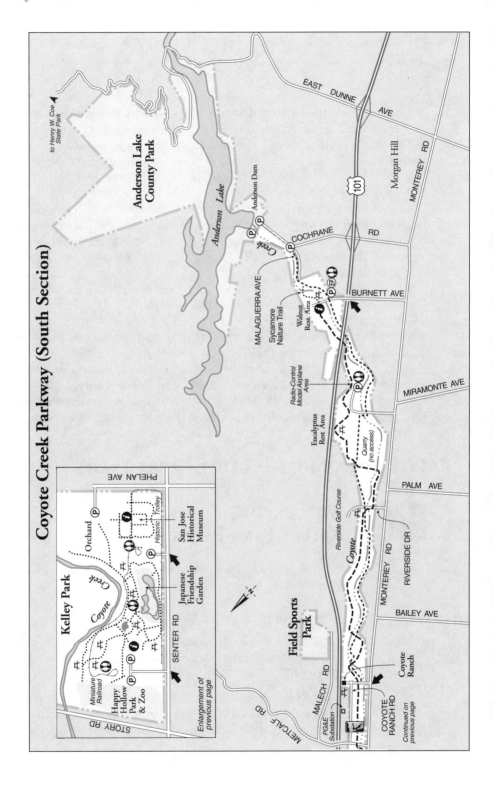

Coyote Creek Parkway (South Section)

Anderson Lake County Park

to Henry W. Coe State Park

Anderson Lake

Anderson Dam

Creek

COCHRANE RD

EAST DUNNE AVE

Morgan Hill

MONTEREY RD

US 101

MALAGUERRA AVE

Sycamore Nature Trail

Walnut Rest Area

BURNETT AVE

Radio-Control Model Airplane Area

Eucalyptus Rest Area

MIRAMONTE AVE

Quarry (no access)

Riverside Golf Course

PALM AVE

Coyote

RIVERSIDE DR

MONTEREY RD

BAILEY AVE

Field Sports Park

MALECH RD

METCALF RD

PG&E Substation

COYOTE RANCH RD

Coyote Ranch

Continued on previous page

Enlargement of previous page

PHELAN AVE

Kelley Park

Orchard

Historic Trolley

San Jose Historical Museum

Japanese Friendship Garden

Creek

Coyote

SENTER RD

STORY RD

Miniature Railroad

Happy Hollow Park & Zoo

◆ Coyote Creek Parkway ◆

Coyote Creek, the longest of Santa Clara County's watercourses, flows year-round, still relatively untrammeled for most of its tree-bordered route to San Francisco Bay. From its headwaters in the rugged Diablo Range it flows through Henry W. Coe State Park, then is impounded at Coyote and Anderson dams. From the dam it flows north 60 miles to the Bay.

Nearly all of the creekside land is in public ownership from Anderson Dam to downtown San Jose. County parks border the creek for nearly 20 miles and then San Jose's Senter, Kelley and William Street parks preserve large sections of land on both sides of the creek. From there until it reaches the Wildlife Refuge, the creek passes by a public golf course, an airport, and three small parks.

Long-range plans envisage trails along Coyote Creek from Anderson Dam to San Francisco Bay in a creekside park chain. Paths along Coyote Creek are part of the San Francisco Bay Area Ridge Trail route. A short connector from the Bernal Road creek crossing will join the existing Ridge Trail route in Santa Teresa Park.

At this writing paths border the creek in Kelley Park, and parklands extend southeast to Yerba Buena Road, through Coyote Hellyer Park, and upstream along the creek to Burnett Park below Anderson Dam. Described here are three trips in parklands beside this beautiful creek.

CITY OF SAN JOSE—COYOTE CREEK TRAILS

Coyote Creek Parkway
KELLEY PARK PATHS

Stroll through a San Jose creekside park to picnic areas, a zoo and a historical museum.

Jurisdiction: City of San Jose.

Facilities: Japanese gardens, miniature railroad, zoo, picnic areas, historical museum. Wheelchair accessible. Phone: 408-277-4192.

Park Rules: Hours: 8 A.M. to ½ hour after sunset daily. Japanese Friendship Gardens 10 A.M. to sunset. Happy Hollow 10 A.M. to 5 P.M. Monday–Saturday, Sunday 11

A.M.–6 P.M. (last admission 5 P.M.). Phone: 408-277-4193.
San Jose Historical Museum 10 A.M. to 4:30 P.M. Tuesday
through Friday, 12 to 4:30 P.M. Saturday and Sunday.
Admission fees for Happy Hollow, San Jose Historical
Museum. Parking fees collected.

Map: City of San Jose *Kelley Park.*

How To Get There: *By Car:* From Hwy. 101 take
Story Rd. west to Senter Rd. Turn southeast to the
park entrance on the northeast side of the road.

By Bus: Santa Clara County Transit.

Trail Notes

The first formal trail upstream from downtown San Jose begins at
Kelley Park, where the city's 156 acres beside Coyote Creek offer enter-
tainment for the whole family as well as trails enough for an hour's stroll.
Children find fun and adventure at Happy Hollow, with its Baby Zoo,
puppet shows and a scaled-down railroad.

After a quiet walk through the flowery Japanese Friendship Garden
past carp-filled ponds and over zig-zag bridges you can stop at the tea-
house for a cup of tea and
a snack. Picnic tables and
barbecues are scattered
under the trees through-
out the park.

Adults and children as
well take pleasure in San
Jose's Historical Museum,
where old homes and
businesses are restored or
authentically reconstructed. Among them is the
Victorian cottage of An-
drew P. Hill, founder of
the Sempervirens Club.
O'Brien's Candy Store,
for fifty years an institu-
tion in downtown San
Jose, awaits with ice
cream sodas to end your
trip.

Coyote Creek near Fontanoso Bridge

SANTA CLARA COUNTY—COYOTE CREEK TRAILS

For the next 3.5 miles from Kelley Park upstream to Coyote Hellyer Park, Coyote Creek flows through a broad band of publicly held lands. However, except in San Jose's Senter Park, which borders the creek for 0.25 mile, there are no established trails as far as Capitol Expressway. Upstream from this busy road a trail meanders through a broad band of flood plain between subdivisions to Yerba Buena Road.

Jurisdiction: Santa Clara County

Facilities: Trails: 14 miles hiking, bicycling, and equestrian; wheelchair accessible in part. Visitor Center. Picnic areas and barbecues: family, groups by reservation. Children's playground. Volleyball court. Velodrome. Fishing, boating. Phone: 408-358-3751.

Park Rules: Hours: 8 A.M. to ½ hour after sunset. No swimming. Dogs on 6-foot leash; not permitted on trails. Vehicle fees collected. Seniors free.

Maps: Santa Clara County *Coyote Hellyer Park*, USGS quads *Morgan Hill, Santa Teresa Hills, San Jose East* and *Milpitas*

How to Get There: *By Car*: (Trip 2) From Hwy. 101 southeast of I-280 interchange take Hellyer Ave. west 0.5 mile to park entrance. Metcalf Rd.: From Hwy. 101 take Bernal Rd. exit, go south to Monterey Hwy. (82), go left (southeast) for 1 mile, make a U-turn at Metcalf Rd. and go north 0.25 mile to parking area on right. (Trip 3) To Burnett Ave. From Monterey Hwy. (82) go southeast on Burnett Ave. to parking near trail.

Coyote Creek Parkway

COYOTE HELLYER PARK TRAILS SOUTH TO METCALF ROAD

Walk or bike along tree-shaded paths.

Distance: 6.1 miles one way

Time: 3 hours hikers; bicyclists and equestrians much less

Elevation Gain: Very little.

Trail Notes

South of Yerba Buena Road the trail passes pretty picnic areas and convenient parking places, and then uses the park road on to the velodrome. South of the velodrome the multi-use trail continues on the east side of the creek past more picnic areas set amid broad lawns and thence on to the central area of Coyote Hellyer Park at Hellyer Avenue.

In 223-acre Coyote Hellyer Park, on the banks of Coyote Creek, an 8-foot-wide paved trail starts from Hellyer Avenue and extends through

One of only a few orchards remaining beside Coyote Creek Trail

the park all the way upstream to Metcalf Road. In the park, set among tall cottonwood and sycamore trees, are picnic tables and barbecues on little knolls beside the creek. At the Visitor Center is a small natural-history exhibit. A velodrome for bicycle races is north of Hellyer Avenue is an added attraction. A stocked lake draws anglers to its shores.

You can enter this trail from several locations within Coyote Hellyer Park as well as at Silver Creek Valley and Metcalf roads south of the park.

Leave your car at one of the northern picnic areas in the 223-acre park and walk over to the creek's edge. The paved pedestrian and bicycle path starts at Hellyer Avenue and continues through the park on the creek's east side. Generally it stays close to the water, passing picnic areas shaded by tall cottonwood trees. It is continuous south all the way to the percolation ponds at Metcalf Road. Although there is no formal equestrian trail until after Metcalf Road, certain sections are used by local equestrians.

After the trail goes under the Hellyer Avenue bridge, squeezed between a cyclone fence and the bridge abutments, high above the creek, it shortly returns closer to creek level, skirting the parking and picnic areas. At low water the stream is very narrow, but after winter rains, this creek can be a deep, racing watercourse, to be treated with respect. The stream banks are fragile and easily eroded. Users are encouraged to remain on the trails.

Soon the trail leaves the creek and heads around Cottonwood Lake, where more picnic tables and barbecues are placed under a canopy of trees. Anglers line the shores of the lake, often bringing in catches of trout and bluegill. On the far side of the lake are a children's playground and nearby a parking area.

Beyond the lake the trail dips under the concrete span of Highway 101 and enters a woodsy stretch where the gravelly creek bed is wide and wild blackberry bushes grow in mounds on the banks. This is the coolest section of the trip. In summer the cottonwood and sycamore trees shade the trail.

As the trail heads south, passing a new industrial park on your left, you come to the end of Coyote Hellyer Park. For the next mile the trail lies in a narrow strip of publicly owned park land by the creek.

As you continue, the tree border changes to oaks with an understory of toyon, poison oak and elderberry bushes. Some of the oaks must be two hundred years old, their huge branches arching over the trail to make a leafy green canopy. If you pause for a while in their shade, you can hear woodpeckers hammering on dead tree trunks or quail calling in the bushes.

One and a half miles from the highway undercrossing a handsome bridge arches over the wide riparian corridor. Cross it to the City of San Jose's Shady Oaks Park, where acres of turf and benches under ancient oaks make a pleasant rest stop.

Then return to the trail and continue upstream past a few farms now being replaced by an industrial park. In 0.5 mile a bridge on Silver Creek Valley Road vaults over the creek. The trail passes under this bridge and bears right on the old Fontanoso Avenue bridge to the west side of the creek. Use caution during the rainy season—the trail could be flooded.

On the west side of the creek is a generous staging area and the trail itself descends to creek level, shaded by rangy sycamore trees with white and gray-mottled trunks. One could park a car at the Silver Creek Valley Road trail entrance and walk along the creek in either direction for several miles, a pleasant stroll on a sunny winter day. In summer, it is a delightful late afternoon or early evening walk, since there are some fine big oak trees shading the way.

You stay close to the creek, where there are a few orchards between you and the freeway. Passing a section where new houses fill the former farmlands, the creek makes a wide arc to the left. The paved trail also bends left, but borders a percolation pond next to the creek. Farther on there are still some farms, but subdivisions and industrial parks are taking the place of row crops. This fertile valley is rapidly being taken over by housing and industrial development. Fortunately, the Santa Clara Valley Water District and Santa Clara County had the vision to preserve Coyote Creek and wide sections of its banks for water conservation, flood protection and recreation. The creek and trail wind through this open land before coming to the Silicon Valley Boulevard crossing.

Just south of Silver Creek Valley Road on your right is a 24-acre mitigation site. Here Caltrans created and planted a riparian habitat to mitigate the destruction of all wetlands destroyed in the course of completing Highway 85 in this area. Beyond this site the trail follows the creek closely, often in sight of the freeway—in fact, the trail goes right under the freeway where it bridges the creek. You find a pleasant stream here, with alders and willows growing on the creek banks and reeds, blackberries and poison oak forming a dense undergrowth. Where the trail is high above the creek, the grandeur of the giant oaks reminds one that these may be the same magnificent trees Captain George Vancouver described so glowingly when he traveled through this valley from Monterey in 1792.

About a mile past Silver Creek Valley Boulevard the paved trail comes to a weir across the creek. The trail climbs to the top of the levee, and here begins a series of percolation ponds extending all the way to Metcalf Road. This is the largest freshwater marsh in the county, attracting a great variety of birds, including grebes, cormorants, kestrels, kingfishers and, of course, seagulls.

To the west of the ponds the trail passes a subdivision and then for a short open stretch offers views of the Santa Clara Valley foothills. Westward you can see the rounded hills of Santa Teresa County Park, where eventually an existing 6.5-mile segment of the Bay Area Ridge Trail will be connected to this trail. Southeast lies the low range of hills where Coyote Creek's waters are impounded behind Anderson Dam before they resume their journey to the Bay.

From the last half-mile of trail you can look out over the Parkway Lakes where fishermen line the banks and members of a water-skiing club practice jumps and fancy maneuvers. Ducks and coots search the waters for food, while hawks patrol the skies for rodents that venture from their holes.

Coyote Creek Trail
METCALF ROAD TO BURNETT AVENUE

Several shady rest stops add interest to this creekside trip.

Distance: 7.9 miles

Time: 4 hours

Elevation Gain: 350'

Trail Notes

The levee trail crosses the Metcalf Road bridge over the creek and continues south on a paved hiking and bicycling path and parallel equestrian trail to wooded 3-acre Burnett County Park on Coyote Creek just below Anderson Dam. Officially dedicated in May 1992, this southern leg of the Coyote Creek Parkway meanders through public lands where the

Fishing near Metcalf Road in Coyote Lakes

lush creekside environment of evergreen oaks, rangy sycamores, graceful willows and an understory of berries and shrubs is preserved.

At three rest stops you can enjoy this quiet scene while eating your lunch at one of the tree-shaded picnic tables. The first is about one mile south of Metcalf Road and east of the trail near Coyote Ranch. When you return to the trail, it crosses the creek; the paved trail veers south away from the creek; the horse trail stays nearer its west bank.

Two-and-a-half miles farther south is another picnic area just west of the Riverside Golf Course—the Sycamore Rest Area. After crossing the creek, the paved trail makes a sharp turn east to avoid the quarry and then in 1.7 miles reaches the Eucalyptus Rest Area.

About a mile farther south you may notice a buzzing noise. Soon, you will see model airplanes taking off and landing at their very own airport. Here you will find a public phone and restrooms.

The last leg of this parkway trail bends east, staying close to the creek, and then passes under Highway 101 before reaching the ranger office at Burnett Avenue. Here are parking spaces, restrooms, and a telephone. Across the creek are the Walnut Rest Area and a path under lovely oak and sycamore trees, a favorite place for anglers trying their luck from the creek bank.

You can walk right up to the base of the dam where a well-fenced spillway sends out a roaring arc of water from Anderson Dam. Here too is a generous parking area accessible from Cochrane Road and from a bike path beside Malaguerra Avenue, where subdivisions are creeping up to the creek parkway. If you started on a bicycle from Metcalf Road, Coyote

Hellyer Avenue, or any of the streets in between, you will have a down-hill-all-the-way return. Those on foot may want a shuttle car to meet them at the end of this beautiful 14+ mile trip along the meandering course of Coyote Creek.

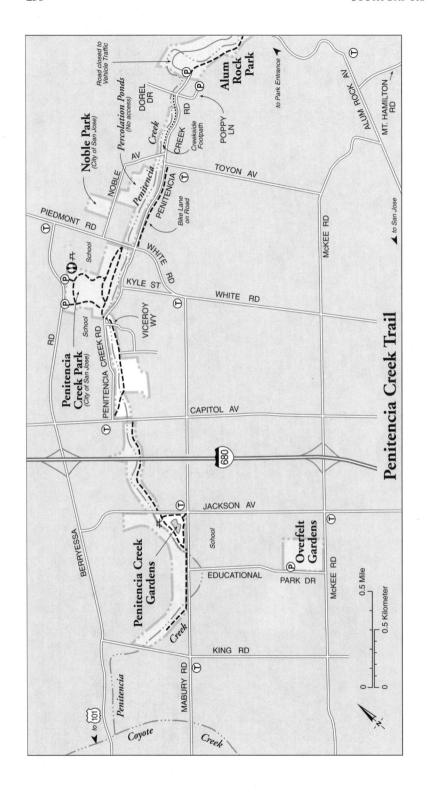

Penitencia Creek Trail

◆ Penitencia Creek Trail ◆

Penitencia Creek originates high in the hills east of Alum Rock Park. Its waters are impounded in Cherry Flat Reservoir, then flow down to enter a steep-sided canyon near the park's eastern boundary. After cascading over falls, the creek is joined by the smaller Arroyo Aguague to become the centerpiece of Alum Rock Park. Leaving the park, it flows through residential neighborhoods, still retaining much of its stately tree border.

The creek has long been recognized as one of the county's loveliest watercourses and recent public acquisition of creekside lands now makes it possible for us to walk beside its waters downstream from Alum Rock Park. Santa Clara County and San Jose City plans call for a Penitencia Creek Park Chain from Alum Rock Park to the Coyote Creek confluence at Berryessa Road, a project that now is almost completed.

Jurisdiction: Santa Clara County, Santa Clara Valley Water District

Facilities: Trails: 3 miles hiking, bicycling. Penitencia Creek Park: picnic tables and play area. Some sections wheelchair accessible.

Park Rules: Hours: 8 A.M. to ½ hour after sunset. No dogs on trail.

Maps: *Northern San Jose* street map; USGS quad *Calaveras Reservoir.*

How to Get There: *By Car:* From Freeway 101 or I-680 in east San Jose take McKee Rd. exit and go east to Jackson Ave. Turn north and go 0.75 mile to Penitencia Creek Park at Mabury Rd.

By Bicycle: From bike lanes on Berryessa Rd. and Capitol Ave. enter the midsection of the trail and go east or west on the trail.

Penitencia Creek Trail

A STROLL OR SPIN ON THE PENITENCIA CREEK TRAIL

Follow the tree-lined creek for 3 miles to Alum Rock Park.

Distance: 6 miles round trip

Time: 3 hours

Elevation Gain: 220′

Trail Notes

Try this walk or bicycle ride on a sunny winter day or in the late afternoon in summer. Old sycamores, oaks and walnuts shade your way on the banks of Penitencia Creek. This trip is described going upstream from

Penitencia Creek County Park Gardens at Mabury Road and Jackson Avenue to Alum Rock Park. Although some sections of the trail are not yet complete, sidewalks along Penitencia Creek Road fill in the gaps for the moment. Along the way the trail passes through small parks, beside several public schools and on top of levees beside percolation ponds.

The Santa Clara Valley Water District manages the creek from Alum Rock Park west. Weirs and valves divert the water to percolation ponds, impound it behind small check dams or release it to flow freely.

Start at Penitencia Creek County Park at the corner of Mabury and Jackson streets, at an area called Penitencia Creek Gardens. Here is a water percolation pond with a central fountain, surrounded by native plants demonstrating the original meadowland habitat of the valley.

At the Jackson Avenue end of the park, cross the street to a center-striped path that meanders above the creek by Mossdale Way. At Gateview Drive the paved path veers left and ducks under the 680 Freeway. You emerge on the other side of the underpass where highway construction re-channeled the creekbed. Reeds and grasses now cover the banks, but you see the route of the old channel marked by a line of tall sycamores and valley oaks curving off to the south.

Now continue along the fenced bicycle and pedestrian trail above the creek to Capitol Avenue. Turning left on a bridge sidewalk and crossing the street takes you to a wide, paved trail winding through broad fields that alternately border an old orchard and the local streets. Never far from the creek, this path is well-used by local residents on foot, on bicycle or on roller skates. Near here the Girl Scouts have leased a 2.9-acre plot that is fenced and used for summer overnight adventures.

Soon you cross a footbridge to the north side of Penitencia Creek Road at Viceroy Way and continue on the levee trail under tall shade trees past the spacious playing fields of a city/county park adjoining a school.

When you reach Piedmont Road the official Penitencia Creek Trail comes to an end at the entrance to an area used by the Water District for percolation ponds. From Piedmont Road to Noble Avenue a formal, paved, separated path was not finished at this writing. There are bike lanes on the south side of Penitencia Creek Road, and a sidewalk between Bard Street and Toyon Avenue. You can in this area also use an informal creekside path as far as Dorel Drive/Poppy Lane, where the path beside the stream ends.

You can retrace your steps back to Penitencia Creek Park where there are picnic tables by the creek with views of the eastern foothills. Or you can continue to Alum Rock Park, by making your way 0.2 mile along the edge of Penitencia Creek Road and past an abandoned quarry to the park's west entrance. From there the Creek Trail takes you in 0.5 mile to the Quail Hollow Picnic Area.

Back at the park where you started, you might want to cross Mabury Road to the 33-acre Overfelt Gardens. Miss Mildred Overfelt gave this

Penitencia Creek Trail winds along past subdivisions

land in honor of her parents, San Jose pioneers. In the tradition of two other women benefactors of the people of Santa Clara County, Josephine Grant and Sada Coe, Miss Overfelt wanted her gift to become a place where one could find peace and solitude. The lovely gardens can be viewed from paths that meander past lakes, an amphitheater, a Chinese Cultural Center and a camellia garden. The gardens are open daily from 10 A.M. to sunset.

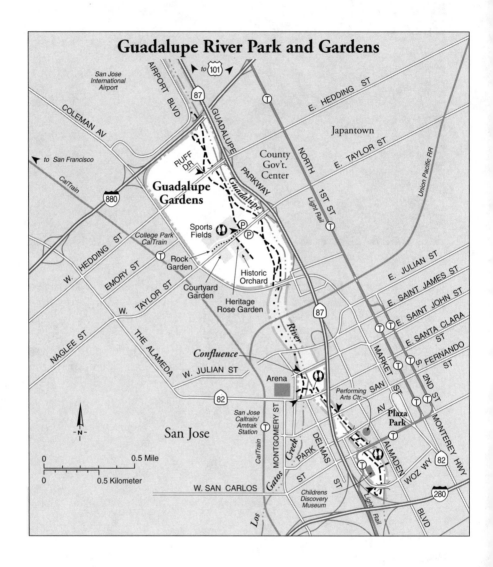

Guadalupe River Park and Gardens

• Guadalupe River Park and Gardens •

A quite extraordinary riverside park lies right in the heart of San Jose, the center of "Silicon Valley". Twining along the Guadalupe River, this chain of greenery provides recreation, visual relief from concrete, and a display of history and art that is inspiring to visitors and employees of the adjacent modern buildings.

From Mt. Umunhum to San Francisco Bay this year-round stream threads its way down steep hillsides, over gravely flats, past suburban housing, through downtown San Jose and along the industrialized bay-side to the marshes and sloughs of the Bay, entering just north of Alviso.

Indians had three large villages beside the Guadalupe, and they followed it upstream to dig cinnabar in the Almaden Hills. They ground this red ore to paint their bodies and to barter with other coastal tribes.

The first Spanish settlers built the Pueblo de San José close to the river banks, but they were flooded out and had to seek higher ground. Their final site for the pueblo, near today's downtown, proved to be more desirable. The Anglos extended the town to both sides of the river. In 1850 San José became the first capital of California.

The waters of the Guadalupe irrigated the early orchards in the Santa Clara Valley, but they flooded homes too. In 1935 the Guadalupe Dam was built to protect farmlands, and small dams and percolation ponds served to build up the groundwater storage. Although tamed by the dam upstream, the Guadalupe still flows in its tree-bordered river bed relatively free of concrete and riprap.

Let us think of the Guadalupe River in several sections: 1) Mt. Umunhum (in Sierra Azul Open Space Preserve to Almaden Lake, undeveloped); 2) Los Alamitos/Calero Creek Trail and Almaden Lake sections, described on pages 267 and 268; 3) Alamitos to I-280, undeveloped; 4) Woz Way to St. John Street, described below; 5) St. John Street to Coleman Avenue, undeveloped; 6) Coleman Avenue to I-880 and Guadalupe Gardens, described below, but beyond the Gardens existing trails may be closed doe to construction; 7) I-880 to Highway 101 and on to the Bay at Alviso has no formal trails at present, although some access to the river levees is permitted by the Santa Clara Valley Water District (call 408-265-2600 for information).

You can start your tour of the Guadalupe Parkway in the center of San Jose. The San Jose Redevelopment Agency has transformed downtown San Jose in the last 25 years, and the area along Guadalupe River is the centerpiece of this urban renewal. Important buildings such as the Center for Performing Arts, the Arena, the Children's Discovery Museum, the Technology Museum of Innovation, and the McEnery Convention Center were designed by noted architects, and are surrounded by high-rise buildings of well-known business and technology companies. The center-piece knitting these edifices together is the Guadalupe River Parkway, about 0.5 mile of which is already developed.

The river trail corridor eventually will connect with the Guadalupe Gardens, a regional park about a mile north in an area where buildings have been removed beneath the airport approach zone. Between the two sections flood control schemes are being developed, and freeway con-struction is in progress, so one must drive between the two areas. Most of the riverwalk is in place from Woz Way by the Children's Discovery Museum to St. John Street. Some day these paths for pedestrians and bicy-cles will be a part of a riverside trail system from the Guadalupe Dam to San Francisco Bay, creating a recreation facility worthy of this beautiful river.

Jurisdiction: City of San Jose.

Maps: San Jose Regional Parks Dept.: *Guadalupe River Park and Gardens.* 408-277-2757

How to Get There: From I-280 exit at Almaden Blvd., go left (north) to Woz Way, go left to parking lots (fee).

Guadalupe River Park and Gardens
RIVERSIDE PATH IN DOWNTOWN SAN JOSE AND PATHS IN GUADALUPE GARDENS

A path on the east bank of the Guadalupe River provides a recre-ational resource for workers in nearby offices and visitors to the city; open space along the river and a rose garden provide room to run as well as education.

Distance: Parkway: 1 mile round trip; Gardens: 1 mile loop

Time: 1 hour for each walk

Elevation Change: Level.

Trail Notes

From the parking lot under Highway 87 cross Woz Way to the Chil-dren's Discovery Museum. Situated next to a huge lawn area where visit-ing children can let off steam, this museum will fascinate children of all ages with its hands-on displays. Shaded picnic areas are enhanced with climbable animal sculptures, while adults can watch the VTA Light Rail trolleys trundle past. Somewhat blighting the scene is heavy traffic noise from 87 to your west and pervasive roaring from jets coasting to a landing at the airport to your north.

The Guadalupe River is east of the Discovery Museum; you can cross it on a fancifully-designed footbridge and look below (in summer) at the slow-moving stream. In winter the river is quite a different animal; raging full of runoff from the Santa Cruz Mountains, it historically floods its banks every few years. Note that the riverbed is lined in many places with wire-held rocks, or gabions, which also protect the banks in many places. Ranks of cement bags also stabilize the banks.

Descend a ramp to the paved riverside walk, going north. As you follow this path, you will sometimes cross under the cross-streets, sometimes be forced to climb up and walk across the streets where the undercrossings have not been completed. Riparian vegetation has taken root among the gabions along the river, providing welcome shade. Attractive landscaping, some provided by the Parks Department, some installed by the adjacent businesses, is interspersed with fountains and sculptures along the way. As you go north you will be walking underneath Highway 87, but when you emerge at Santa Clara Street cross the road to the San Jose Parks Department Visitor Center. Perched above the river as though waiting for high waters, this building has leaflets and other information about the Parkway and the Guadalupe Gardens. To your west from the Visitor Center the trail crosses a footbridge to the Arena, venue of San Jose sporting events, and the Arena Green, site of a children's playground and a handsome merry-go-round (or carrousel).

You have just crossed Los Gatos Creek, running out of Lexington Reservoir higher up in the Santa Cruz Mountains, a short distance above its confluence with Guadalupe River. The enlarged stream continues north, but the Parkway has not been completed beyond St. John Street, so your trip must return to the starting point at Woz Way. Before turning south walk east on St. John Street to see an area of small, historic houses that will be restored as part of the redevelopment project.

Try to cross the river as often as possible on your way back. At the Park Avenue bridge be sure to notice several wiley bronze coyotes, an eagle, and a hummingbird which commemorate the aboriginal Muwekma/ Ohlone people who first settled this area. On the southeast side of Park Avenue you will find a bittersweet Veterans' Memorial with white memorial flags and a display featuring quotations from servicemen's letters from all U S. wars, and shadowy photos of long-gone patriots. In front of the Performing Arts Center are a fountain and a fine Bufano bear sculpture. Various other sculptures grace the pathway as you walk south. Keep looking as you walk for other treasures: a group of three dancers; a footbridge with animals and birds; a samurai with his dog, bird and monkey with a sword in his belt and tablet in his hand.

Gardens at Guadalupe River Park

To walk in Guadalupe Gardens you must drive north, most easily done by going east from Woz Way on San Carlos Street then left (north) on First Street to Taylor Street which crosses Highway 87 (under construction at this writing) and the Guadalupe River and you find yourself in a 200-acre area devoid of buildings. It is surprising to see this "urbanly-renewed" area where formerly stood a thriving neighborhood, now demolished for safety because of the landing pattern of the nearby airport. Along the abandoned streets are curb-cuts showing where homes once stood.

Park anywhere to explore Guadalupe Gardens. There is a network of paths winding through Guadalupe Gardens, one on the north side of Taylor Street with native plantings and interpretive signs, and others on the south side leading to an orchard with historic fruit trees, a "courtyard garden", and an extensive rose garden. An active group of volunteers works in this garden, with support from the City of San Jose and various other sponsors.

You can walk a mile or more in Guadalupe Gardens, enjoying the open space, but deploring the noisy planes overhead.

At this writing, extensive construction to improve traffic flow on Highway 87 and Guadalupe Parkway and to install flood control measures have disrupted the trail northward along the Guadalupe River. Some areas with paved paths are retained but not open at this writing for walking or bicycling. Plans call for a collaboration between Caltrans, the U.S. Army Corps of Engineers, the City of San Jose and the Santa Clara Valley Water District. Eventually the Guadalupe River Parkway will extend the length of the river from the heights of Mt. Umunhum to San Francisco Bay at Alviso, there to meet the Bay Trail.

Beyond Bayshore Freeway the Santa Clara Valley Water District levees along the Guadalupe River, rebuilt in 1983 for flood control, could provide a trail route to Alviso and connections with Baylands trails and those of the Don Edwards San Francisco Bay National Wildlife Refuge near Alviso. There are as yet no formal trails on these levees, but the Water District may allow recreational use of these routes if some governmental body takes the responsibility for operating and maintaining them.

The river north of Bayshore Freeway passes through industrial parks and small subdivisions. Historic buildings along the way—James Lick's mansion and John Wade's house and barns—are close to its banks. North of Montague Expressway the river passes Agnews State Hospital and a municipal golf course. And a few bends before the river reaches the Bay in Guadalupe Slough it is bordered by a trail in Sunnyvale Baylands.

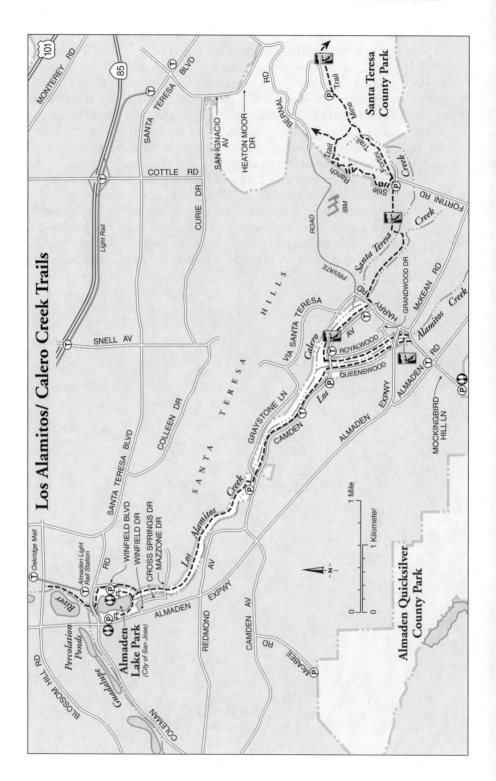

Los Alamitos / Calero Creek Trails

• Los Alamitos and Calero Creek Trails •

In the Almaden Valley the Los Alamitos Creek Trail, south of popular 65-acre Almaden Lake, follows levees upstream to the confluence of Los Alamitos and Calero creeks. Upstream along Calero Creek are paved trails beside Camden Avenue as far as Harry Road, from where a path continues up the creek and into Santa Teresa Park. Beyond the confluence, where Los Alamitos Creek trends southwest, a paved trail continues on its east bank almost a mile to McKean Road. On the west bank is a wide horse and hiker trail.

These trails will some day be important links in a continuous trail system that will join Almaden Quicksilver, Calero and Santa Teresa county parks. The Los Alamitos Creek Trail will be extended downstream around Almaden Lake to join the Guadalupe River Park Chain. This Almaden Valley trail will thus be a link in the City and County regional trail system. From Almaden Lake commuters on foot and by bike can follow the trail north to the light-rail station on Coleman Avenue at Winfield Boulevard.

Jurisdiction: City of San Jose, Santa Clara County and Santa Clara Valley Water District. Mailing Address: 6099 Winfield Blvd., San Jose, CA 95120-1535.

Facilities: Paths for pedestrians, bicyclists and equestrians. At Almaden Lake are picnic areas, small boat rentals, playgrounds, a swimming beach and paths that circle ¾ of the lake.

Almaden Lake

An egret looks for prey on Los Alamitos Creek

Park Rules: Park open 8 A.M. to ½ hour after sunset. No glass containers or alcoholic beverages allowed on the beach, in the swim area, in the park play area or the tot lot. Swimming only allowed in designated areas and while lifeguards are on duty. Parking fees collected daily from April through September.

Maps: City of San Jose *Los Alamitos Creek Trail* and *Almaden Lake*, USGS quad *Santa Teresa Hills.*

How to Get There: *By Car:* From Almaden Expressway south of Coleman Ave. turn into the West Entrance Station or from Winfield Blvd. turn into the East Entrance Station. Trails on levees east of the Graystone Lane bridge are reached from Camden Ave.

By Bus: Santa Clara County Transportation Agency serves the park with light rail and bus. Call 408-321-2300.

Trail Notes

You can walk up and down lovely Los Alamitos Creek on this trail for 3.9 miles. Ancient sycamores grow by the water's edge, their twisted white limbs hang over the creek and shade your way. On the banks are willows and maples, and live oaks line the creek corridor. Occasional picnic tables set under the oaks and sycamores offer resting places with views of the creek. Fitness buffs can use the challenging stations along the trail; commuters on bicycles find the trail very convenient for access to light rail and buses.

The grassy Santa Teresa Hills rise steeply above the northeast banks of the creek. Immense boulders at the base of the hills are outcrops of the same sandstone cut from quarries here to build Stanford University and the San Jose Hall of Justice. Near the trail the historic little Pfeiffer Stone House, built in 1875, housed tools for the quarry. As the creek meanders along its tree-bordered course, it widens into ponds, then narrows. About a mile from the lake, near Pfeiffer Ranch Road on the trail's uphill side, are the fruit-drying sheds left from the period when apricot and prune orchards clothed this valley.

The City of San Jose's development of this lake and creekside trail emphasizes the natural riparian habitat, using native plantings. Interpretive plaques highlight the values of such creek systems, calling attention to the importance of maintaining the riparian corridor for animal life and for human enjoyment. For Almaden Valley residents the parallel pedestrian, bicycle and equestrian paths link small parks, playgrounds and community facilities along this winding year-round stream.

Beyond the confluence of the two creeks at Villagewood Drive, trails continue upstream. Beside Los Alamitos Creek are existing parallel paths—an asphalt path for hikers and bicyclists on the east levee, and an unpaved pedestrian and equestrian path on a shelf along the west side of the creek. At the McKean/Harry roads junction a proposed equestrian and hiker trail will go west to the Mockingbird Hill entrance to Almaden Quicksilver Park.

By Calero Creek are an existing equestrian trail and a bike/pedestrian trail beside Camden Avenue. Santa Clara County's unpaved trail continues upstream past Harry Road for 1.5 miles, passing handsome sycamores and willows and lush creekside undergrowth. It then joins the Stile Ranch and Fortini trails into Santa Teresa Park. These trails through the Almaden Valley are expected to become links between the Bay Area Ridge Trail and the Bay Trail.

Los Gatos Creek (North)

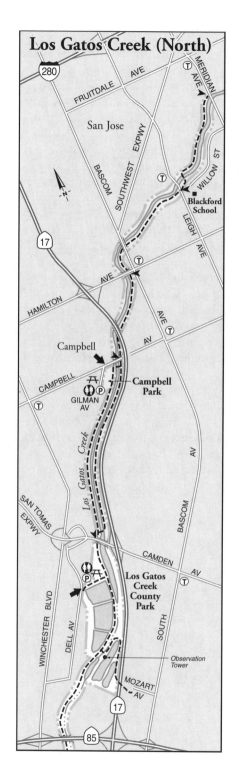

Los Gatos Creek (South)

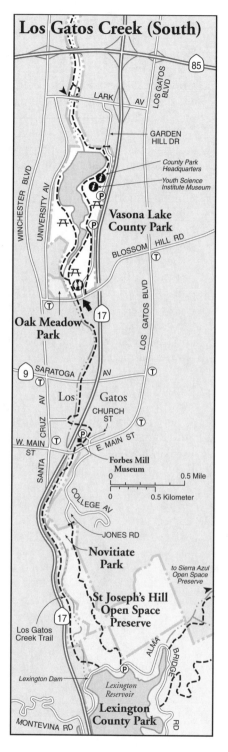

◆ Los Gatos Creek Trail ◆

Los Gatos Creek originates on the south side of Loma Prieta, drains the western flanks of the northern Sierra Azul, and flows northwest in a beautiful canyon to Lake Elsman, a San Jose Water Company dam. After escaping the dam, it travels several miles to its impoundment at Lexington Reservoir. From the spillway of this reservoir it continues through parks, percolation ponds, and residential and commercial areas to its confluence with the Guadalupe River in central San Jose.

The Santa Clara County Trails Plan proposes almost 20 miles of trails along Los Gatos Creek's banks. Existing trails now meander more than 14 miles along its banks downstream from Lexington Reservoir through Vasona Lake Park and Los Gatos Creek Park in Los Gatos, through Campbell City Park, and then follow the creek downstream to Meridian Avenue in San Jose. All of these trails are paved for bicycling, hiking, skating, and jogging. Included here are three trips along this lively, perennial stream.

Many jurisdictions have cooperated to create this linear recreational parkway, including the cities of Los Gatos, San Jose and Campbell, Santa Clara County, the Santa Clara Valley Water Conservation District, and the State of California.

Jurisdiction: Parks—City of Campbell, Santa Clara County; Trails—Santa Clara County, City of Campbell, Town of Los Gatos, City of San Jose.

Facilities: Trails: hiking, jogging, bicycling, skating. All parks have picnic and barbecue areas. Family groups by reservation. Playgrounds, restrooms, parking. Other facilities: (1) Campbell Park—parcourse. (2) Los Gatos Creek Park—lake for windsurfing, model-boat sailing, fishing; observation tower. (3) Vasona Lake Park—lake for sailing, paddle boats and row boats, boat launch ramp and storage facility, fishing pier; turfed activity area; miniature railroad; Youth Science Institute Museum.

Park Rules: (1) Campbell Park Hours: 7 A.M. to 10 P.M. Group reservations for picnic areas at City Hall. Phone: 408-866-2100. Dogs on leash. (2) Los Gatos Creek and (3) Vasona Lake Park—Hours: 8 A.M. to sunset. Trail open 7 A.M. to sunset. Dogs on leash in designated areas only. No swimming. Fees: Vehicle entrance fees collected year round. Phone: Ranger—408-356-2729 or Reservations—408-358-3741.

Maps: City of Campbell, *Campbell Park*, Santa Clara County, *Los Gatos Creek Trails*, *Vasona Lake and Los Gatos Creek Parks*, and *Lexington Reservoir*; USGS quads *San Jose West* and *Los Gatos*.

How to Get There: *By Car:* (1) Campbell Park—From Hwy. 17 take Hamilton Ave. exit and go west on it to Winchester Blvd., where you turn left. At Campbell Ave. turn left, turn right at Gilman Ave. and then go to the park entrance on your left. (2) Los Gatos Creek Park—From Hwy. 17

take Camden Ave./San Tomas Expwy. exit and go west on it. In less than 0.25 mile turn right at the first exit onto Dell Ave. which curves around south under Camden Ave./San Tomas Expwy. past Sunnyoaks Ave. to a small lane on your left which leads to the park. (3) Vasona Lake Park—From Hwy. 17 take Lark Ave. west, turn left on University Ave., and left on Blossom Hill Rd., on which you continue to a left turn into the park.

By Foot and Bicycle: Pedestrians and bicyclists can enter the parks' trails from several city streets.

By Bus: County Transit serves Campbell Park, Los Gatos Creek and Vasona Lake County Parks.

Los Gatos Creek Trail
UPSTREAM FROM CAMPBELL PARK TO VASONA LAKE AND ON TO FORBES MILL

Join hikers, joggers, bicyclists, skaters and bird-lovers on miles of creekside trails. Convenient trail entry points at Los Gatos Creek and Vasona Lake parks and at major street crossings allow for short loops or trips of any length.

Distance: 6.1 miles one way with shuttle

Time: 3 hours

Elevation Gain: A slight rise upstream 230'.

Trail Notes

Try these paved level paths upstream from Campbell Park on a sunny winter day with the creek a torrent of storm waters, with winter-migrating waterfowl bobbing at its edge, and with a few dark clouds gathering over the distant mountains. You will have plenty of company—joggers, serious walkers, bicyclists and rollerbladers. The busy scene is reminiscent of promenades on the banks of European rivers.

The native trees, alders, oaks and sycamores, planted when the trail was new, now branch overhead, and the shrubs screen adjoining businesses and Highway 17. Wild fennel, willows and cattails grow along the creek banks.

Starting at Campbell Park on the west side of the creek a parcourse invites you to add a series of exercises to your walk or run. Prescribing stretching and bending movements at 18 stations, the course uses the trail on both sides of the creek.

Heading southwest, you are soon at the first dam. When the creek is running full, water pours over in a glistening sheet to break with a mighty roar below. From a convenient bench you can watch the spray and let the sound of falling water mask the presence of the nearby freeway. In summer, a limited amount of water goes over the spillway, and the stream, much tamed, is only inches deep.

If you are following the parcourse or are ready to return to Campbell Park, a bridge crosses the stream just below the spillway. Wooden benches on the other side invite the casual stroller to pause and watch the ducks that fly up and down the stream. When you reach Campbell Avenue, cross the bridge and go down the stairs to Campbell Park's picnic tables, green lawns and playground under the trees, a pleasant finish to a 3.5-mile round trip.

If you continue upstream past the dam, the

Los Gatos Creek Park dam

trail goes under Camden Avenue and passes the relatively new casting pond where avid fly fishers can hone their skills in an enclosed area. In 0.25 mile you reach the hub of Los Gatos Creek Park. This park is especially appealing for its water-oriented sports. If the breeze is up, the windsurfers' brightly colored sailing craft on the pond will catch your eye.

Anglers lining the banks of this first pond near the parking area actually catch fish—it is stocked with rainbow trout. Black bass, blue gill and carp are also caught. If you plan to fish, look into the licensing requirements, as a State Fish and Game warden patrols the area.

Continuing upstream on the paved levee path between the creek and the three large western ponds, you pass the model-boaters' pond. You look across the creek to other percolation ponds edged with plantings of native shrubs that give food and shelter to many birds. Reportedly 100 species have been counted here.

To make best use of your bird book to identify the waterfowl, come during the spring nesting season when their plumage is brighter and more like the pictures. In winter, you will find migrating and resident ducks. But in any season you will recognize the handsome 20-30-inch-tall white egrets as they fly above you, their long legs stretched out behind.

Near the end of the third percolation pond you can cross the creek to the Observation Tower by taking the path to the left. (A wooden ramp makes the covered hexagonal deck wheelchair-accessible.) From here you have a long view east to the Diablo Range and west to the Santa Cruz Mountains. On a clear day you can see the observatory buildings on Mt. Hamilton. And on the creekside paths below, joggers, strollers and bicycle riders provide an almost continuous passing parade.

Retrace your steps to the main paved trail heading south toward Vasona Lake Park. The stream banks, though rock-lined against floods, support blackberries, coyote bushes, alders, willows and some ancient sycamores. On your right the urban scene encroaches. However, development ordinances in the towns of Los Gatos, San Jose and Campbell required installation of trail segments according to an adopted plan, with plantings to grace the way.

After passing under the wide expanse of Highway 85, the trail continues uninterrupted another half-mile on the west side of the creek. Where the path forks, take the left fork to follow the meandering creek to Lark Avenue, then cross the creek on the Lark Avenue bridge to a paved path on your right. Now your way passes close to backyards but borders the creek where alders, sycamores and cottonwoods line the bank. In 0.5 mile you will hear, especially in the rainy season, the sound of water thundering over the dam that impounds Vasona Lake. At the foot of the dam immense alders and oaks spread their roots out over the creek bank. The 30-foot-high dam, completed in 1935, was one of a half dozen conservation dams constructed at this time for flood protection and for restoration of Santa Clara Valley's rapidly falling water table.

When you have taken in the splashing waters of the spillway in winter or enjoyed the cool, leafy creekside in summer, follow the trail to the top of the dam. You will see Vasona's lakeside trails curving around to the picnic tables scattered through the park. The authors' favorite spot is on a slight rise under some of the park's magnificent oaks.

Boating on the lake, fishing piers, playgrounds for children and turfed activity areas attract large weekend crowds to this park at all times of the year. If children have accompanied you, a sure-fire treat is the miniature railroad that leaves from Oak Meadow Park on the northwest corner of Vasona Lake Park. A visit to the Youth Science Institute will intrigue nature-lovers, both young and old.

If you return to Campbell Park from the dam, it is a gentle downhill trip, and a round trip of 4.5 miles. However, to continue to Forbes Flour Mill in Los Gatos, descend to the well-marked lakeside trail through Vasona Lake Park. The ducks and geese are almost as populous as the park visitors. Prominent signs prohibit feeding all waterfowl. A pamphlet explains the harmful effects of artificial feeding of wild waterfowl—over-

Los Gatos Creek Trail skirts Vasona Lake, a popular boating area

population, avian disease, interbreeding with domestic species, and consequent change from native migratory patterns.

After passing an arched span to the other side of the lake, the trail follows the creek in its natural course graced by huge native sycamores, oaks, and alders. Soon you parallel the miniature train tracks, then cross them just east of a path to the train station in Oak Meadow Park. Here are more picnic tables for families and groups. Beyond is a stretch where the creekside vegetation is quite dense, but glimpses of the watercourse and the sound of its musical flow make its presence known.

Soon you pass under Blossom Hill Road and then under Roberts Road. Here the winding path is tucked between the top of the creek bank and adjacent housing. Huge sycamores and creekside vegetation add shade and charm to this innovative solution to the trail's completion. As the creek makes a wide meander, the trail is protected from Highway 17 by a thick, high, masonry wall. Beyond are gates that close the trail in the park at sunset—open at 7 A.M.

For a short stretch the highway noise is intense, but shortly the new oaks and underbrush mask it and you find mounds of Himalayan blackberries gone wild—tempting when ripe. Beyond is a half-mile, straight stretch beside the east bank of the creek, which is now confined to a narrow, concrete-sided channel. New young oaks are almost touching overhead and will soon provide welcome shade, which you can also find at Balzer Field's baseball diamond on the east side of the trail. Restrooms and low spectator benches under large oaks are welcome trailside amenities.

Shortly beyond the ball field you cross the creek on a wide metal bridge with wooden planks and continue on an elevated trail to the west side of the creek in Los Gatos. Adjacent to the creek trail on your right are shops, restaurants and parking on University Avenue.

But to continue to Forbes Flour Mill turn sharply left at the Forbes Mill Footbridge, where a charming youth mural decorates its entrance and more student art work adorns the bridge metal panels. This footbridge spans the year-round creek and four lanes of Highway 17 speeding traffic. But when you get to the other side, the stone Forbes Flour Mill Museum sits peacefully among tall sycamores where the mill was erected by James Alexander Forbes in 1854. See Trip 3 to continue to Lexington Dam.

2

Los Gatos Creek Trail
DOWNSTREAM FROM CAMPBELL PARK TO MERIDIAN AVENUE

This wide, paved trail attracts local residents and park visitors.

Distance: 4 miles round trip

Time: 2 hours

Elevation Loss: A small loss

Trail Notes

From Campbell Park you can make a 2-mile trip downstream along Los Gatos Creek. Leave the parking area at Campbell Park, cross the Campbell Avenue bridge and go right, down the ramp. Turn right again and walk under the bridge on a cantilevered wood-plank path with a yellow center stripe. This elaborate and expensive structure hanging over the creek demonstrates the City/County commitment to a continuous regional creekside trail system.

The trail passes inns and industrial and office buildings, with side trails leading to neighborhood streets and major shopping areas. The one to the Pruneyard, on a steep pitch, slows down-coming bicyclists with a maze of zig-zag fencing. Up and down the path go roller skaters, bicyclists young, old and just learning, skateboarders, joggers and of course those on foot. The traffic is heavy and it pays to be observant.

All the while the creek is just below the trail, flowing steadily between its banks to join the Guadalupe River. From the fenced trail are varied vistas of the creek corridor—sometimes a narrow channel enclosed by high side walls, sometimes a tree-canopied watercourse, and elsewhere a subdivision-lined creekside, where the path is bordered with fledgling trees and native shrubs.

Crossing under Highway 17, Hamilton and Bascom avenues, you follow the paved path edged with subdivisions that are set back from the creek's wide banks. Here are parallel paths, one paved for bicyclists, skaters and baby strollers, and another unsurfaced for joggers, pedestrians and dogs. Strict rules apply to dogs—they must be on leash at all times and their owners must pick up after them. This is stated on the prominent signs at trail entrances.

At Leigh Avenue, the trail ducks under the street and continues to Blackford School. Here a bridge over the creek takes trail users to its north side where a wide trail continues to Meridian Avenue in San Jose.

This lovely creek continues its course toward the Guadalupe River and their combined passage to the Bay. As development occurs along this stretch, new creekside trails will be built. Someday you will be able to hike, bike, or skate your way to the Bay. In the meantime, turn around at Meridian Avenue and retrace your steps along with the multitudes of recreational travelers on this popular creekside trail.

3 Los Gatos Creek Trail
FORBES MILL TO LEXINGTON DAM

A wide trail through Los Gatos Creek's narrow canyon follows part of a historic route to the coast. Now modern joggers and strollers frequent the way used by Indians and early settlers.

How To Get There: *By Car:* (1) Forbes Mill entrance: From Hwy. 17 take the East Los Gatos exit and go to Los Gatos Blvd. Turn right. This becomes Main Street. Turn right on Church Street and go past shops and condominiums downhill to Forbes Mill Museum and parking. (2) Lexington Dam entrance: From Hwy. 17 south of Los Gatos take Bear Creek Rd. exit. Cross over Hwy. 17 and rejoin it going north. Turn east on Alma Bridge Rd. to parking lot at boat launch area and find trail entrance on left.

By Bicycle: Bike lanes on Los Gatos Blvd. and Main St. lead to Church St. and Forbes Mill Museum. Bike overcrossing of Hwy. 17 from Lundy Lane in West Los Gatos terminates at museum.

By Bus: VTA buses to Los Gatos

Distance: 3.4 miles round trip

Time: 2 hours

Elevation Gain: 300'

Trail Notes

Take this trail midday in winter months, when you can enjoy the creek racing down its channel, or in early spring, when you can look out over the delicate greens of budding alders and sycamores lining the canyon. In summer the sun makes the trail warm for much of its length, so walk it in early morning or in late afternoon when the sun is behind the hills.

Though this trail is accessible from either end and combines with trails in St. Joseph's Hill Open Space Preserve, starting the round trip from Forbes Flour Mill takes advantage of a downhill return. First-time walkers should plan a trip when the attractive museum at the mill is open Wednesdays through Sundays, 12 noon to 4 P.M.

The old Forbes Flour Mill was built by James Alexander Forbes in 1854, when he brought water to his grinding stones in a wooden flume from a mile up the creek. Photographs in the museum show an imposing four-story building of gray sandstone. After years of disuse only one story remained. Now rebuilt as a museum, it contains well-displayed photographs and artifacts of Santa Clara Valley history.

Scottish-born Forbes, who came to California already fluent in Spanish and experienced in business, became mayordomo for Mission Santa Clara. He took out Mexican citizenship and was granted Rancho Potrero de Santa Clara.

In 1850 Forbes acquired 2000 acres of Rancho Rinconada de Los Gatos on the creek and beside the mission trail between Santa Clara and Santa Cruz. When he built his mill with machinery ordered from New York, a delay in delivery resulted in losses that led to his bankruptcy. Although the mill eventually proved successful, he lost his mill and his fortune. Forbes then turned to horticulture, planting orchards and vineyards in the valley.

Through this narrow canyon beside Forbes Flour Mill centuries of travelers have passed. Undoubtedly it was an Indian route to the coast. Then it became the Mission Trail between Santa Clara and Santa Cruz. Later, a stage line ran through the canyon, meeting morning trains from San Francisco at the San Jose station, stopping for lunch at the Lyndon Hotel in the Town of Lexington and then going on to Santa Cruz.

Next, the Southern Pacific Company completed a railroad in 1888. Soon after the building of the Los Gatos/Santa Cruz Highway in 1935, the railroad was abandoned. Now, on a modern four-lane road, routed around Lexington Reservoir, a torrent of cars and trucks pours over the summit of the Santa Cruz Mountains, linking populous San Jose and Santa Cruz. Today, on foot, we have come full circle as we walk here for pleasure and exercise.

To begin this walk take the marked trail entrance left of the museum. This Town of Los Gatos trail goes under Main Street and out between the concrete-channeled creek and Highway 17. The sounds of traffic will lessen as the highway climbs above and away from the creek. Soon oak trees spread shade over the trail and alders grow by the creek, no longer confined to a trapezoidal ditch. Beside the trail under arching oaks is a huge pipe carrying water to thirsty San Jose from Lake Elsman. On shady banks bright yellow buttercups bloom by the path in spring, contrasting with the various blue blossoms of Douglas iris, larkspur and lupine.

As the trail gains elevation, the canyon opens up. Around a bend, Lexington Dam comes into view, rising nearly 200' above the creek bed. This rolled-earth dam, completed in 1955, flooded the little communities of Lexington and Alma and a lovely valley.

Soon the trail bears left and comes out at a bridge crossing the spillway. Far below in the canyon you see a few remnants of the old road. Then the paved trail makes a diagonal sweep across the dam's concrete face. Encased in a chain link fence, the trail rises gradually, yet steadily, to the dam's crest. When winter rains swell the lake behind the dam, water pours out in torrents from the 50-inch outfall pipe. The last push up the steep side of Lexington Dam is challenging. Downhill bicyclists must obey the signs to walk their bikes.

From the dam's crest you are rewarded by views of the reservoir and the heavily wooded hills of the Santa Cruz Mountains. The 1.5-mile-long lake is popular for windsurfing, fishing and boating, but swimming is not allowed. You can watch the action at the lake or take Alma Bridge Road to the lakeside Miller Point Area for a picnic under the trees.

If you are going to take the loop trip, walk along Alma Bridge Road 0.25 mile to St. Joseph's Hill Open Space Preserve and take the Jones Trail to Main Street in Los Gatos. The preserve entrance is on your left. See St. Joseph's Hill, page 176.

The trip back on the Los Gatos Creek Trail is an easy one, downhill all the way. If you have time, take the pedestrian overcrossing by the museum, the Forbes Mill Footbridge, to Old Town Los Gatos with its antique stores, shops, and old buildings. With Phyllis Butler's *The Valley of Santa Clara Historic Buildings, 1792-1920*, you can spend a fruitful day discovering the old town built around Forbes Mill, Forbestown, which was eventually renamed Los Gatos.

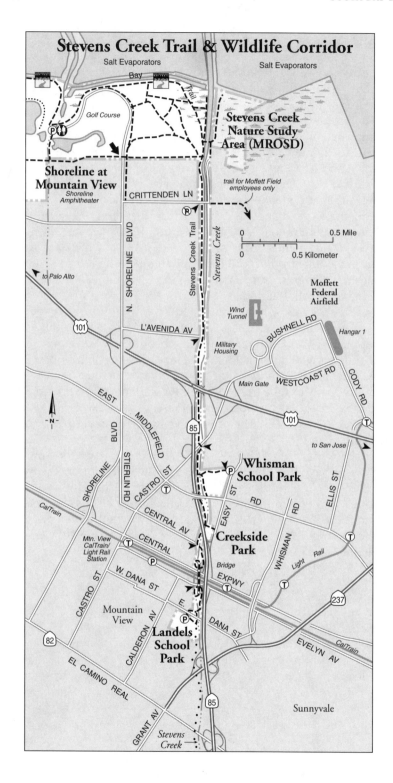

Stevens Creek Trail & Wildlife Corridor

◆ Stevens Creek Trail and Wildlife Corridor ◆

Stevens Creek rises in the Santa Cruz Mountains, flows south through public parklands of Monte Bello Open Space Preserve and Upper Stevens Creek County Park, turns east to meander through Stevens Creek County Park, is temporarily held back in the Stevens Creek Reservoir and then makes its way past subdivisions, schools, and four cities to San Francisco Bay at Mountain View. This creek, bordered by a busy freeway, crossed by numerous bridges carrying thousands of vehicles daily and adjoined to backyards, schools and shopping malls, was ignored for many years.

Today, a vigorous citizens' committee and the City of Mountain View have built a 3.7-mile trail along the creek that stretches from the salt ponds of Shoreline at Mountain View south to Landels Park, in the area between the Central Expressway and Highway 237 in Mountain View. Another 0.3-mile segment in Mountain View is funded and will extend out over the creekbed to make the trail wide enough for users. Design studies are under way for another reach as far as El Camino Real. The final segment in Mountain View will someday extend to Mountain View High School, making a total of 6 miles in the City of Mountain View.

The City of Cupertino has funded studies to determine the location and feasibility of extending the trail southward along its creekside.

Stevens Creek was named for Elisha Stephens, the leader of the Stephens, Murphy, Townsend Party that crossed the Sierra in 1844 (before the fateful journey of the Donner Party). Stephens (whose name was later shortened) settled on Cupertino Creek and set out vineyards there. Sometime after 1860, he left his lands and moved on to less "heavily populated" areas. Today, a busy thoroughfare is named for him and Cupertino Creek is known as Stevens Creek.

Nowadays, walkers, hikers, joggers, rollerbladers, and recreational and commuting bicyclists throng the creekside paths and wildlife corridor that Stevens once trod.

Jurisdiction: City of Mountain View, Santa Clara Valley Water District

Facilities: Wide trail with center line, benches, bridges over main arterials, and access to neighboring parks, main thoroughfares and public transportation.

Rules: Trail open from 6 a.m. to ½ hour after sunset. Keep to the right, speed limit maximum 15 miles per hour, observe posted lower speeds; dogs on leash at all times; no skateboards, alcohol, fires, camping or weapons.

Maps: City of Mountain View *Stevens Creek Trail and Wildlife Corridor*, USGS quad *Mountain View*.

How to Get There: *By Car* (1) Shoreline at Mountain View: see page 320. (2) Whisman Park: From Hwy. 101 or Central Expwy. take Shoreline Blvd, turn east on Middlefield Rd., north on Easy St. and continue to parking at Whisman Park and School. Trail is accessible from north side of park. (3) Landels Park: From Hwy. 101 or Central Expwy., take Shoreline Blvd. south, turn west on Dana St., cross bridge and turn left into Landels School parking area on south side of street.

Stevens Creek Trail And Wildlife Corridor
A WALK, SPIN OR SKATE ALONG STEVENS CREEK

From Bay to parkside, enjoy this wide, leafy corridor in the mode of your choice.

Distance: 3.7 miles one way

Time: 1½ hours

Elevation Gain: 97'

Trail Notes

Starting at the east end of the Bay Trail in Shoreline, turn right (south) to rise up to the levee on the west side of the creek. Wide and slow-moving except after heavy storms, the brackish water here supports numerous bird species, especially dabbler and diving ducks, egrets and great blue herons. On little islands surrounded by reeds many waterfowl rest and nest. Early in the morning and toward sunset, flocks of red-winged blackbirds will serenade you with their trilling song. With a bird book in hand, you soon can recognize the different species by their size, leg length and shape of bill.

Continuing upstream, you will pass acres of high-tech plants and parking lots, as well as a large nursery. High above are powerlines that follow the creek upstream for your entire trip. Trail-users of every persuasion pass by, often smiling or calling "hello," all seeming to appreciate the chance to enjoy the creek, its wildlife and the native plantings on the stream banks that shade the way.

Just before the Highway 101 undercrossing, the creek drops suddenly, and artificial barriers in the concrete surface work to slow the flow. (The trail can be closed here when there is danger of floods.) As you duck under the highway, you may be startled by the whirr of pigeon wings as these birds fly swiftly to and from nests under the wide span.

Shortly you reach the path and bridge to Whisman Park and the plaque that commemorates the opening of this stretch of trail. At the school are broad playing fields, restrooms and water, and many pieces of innovative play equipment for young children. Summer vacation brings families and neighborhood groups cycling up and down the trail from their homes in this neighborhood. Bicyclists, commuting from nearby hi-tech plants and Moffett Field, whiz by, carefully passing on the left.

Continuing on south, you tread a leafy way accented by attractive displays of native wildflowers and flowering shrubs. Bring your native plant book and look up the names of those you'd like to plant in your own garden.

A handsome bridge spans the busy traffic lanes on Middlefield Road and then you cross the creek on a wide bridge flanked by stone pillars at the charming little Creekside Park on Easy Street. Young children, ages 2–5, enjoy the brightly painted play equipment while mothers visit and sun themselves. Here there are picnic tables shaded by tall trees and an innovative awning of deep blue, metal slats suspended on taut cables. This could make a pleasant stop for lunch on your way up or down the trail.

Another fine bridge spans the divided traffic lanes and the railroad lines of Central Expressway. This bridge, like the one over Middlefield Road, is painted a deep blue-green, is 12 feet wide, and is reached by stairs and ramps. A narrow-gauge, chain-linked, plastic-covered screen covers the sides and top of the bridge. Here walking and bicycling commuters can exit to reach the train or buses that frequent this corridor.

When the authors hiked this trail in June, the creek was almost dry, yet we knew this to be a perennial stream. The answer was found on signs posted by the Santa Clara Valley Water District: to improve conditions for the endangered steelhead trout, the District is retaining more water upstream in deep, cool pools where these fish can avoid the warmer water of the creek's lower reaches.

Continuing upstream on the creek's west side under a high, leafy canopy of oaks and alders, you pass landscaped trail exits to neighboring streets. Then, leaving the vine-clad banks of Stevens Creek, take the next path west to Landels School and Park, the trail's temporary terminus. More segments are in the works.

It appears that this trail and wildlife corridor is proving desirable for today's trail-users as well as for the descendants of birds, fish and animals who inhabited it when Elisha Stephens walked here.

Palo Alto Baylands

◆ The Baylands ◆

Over millennia San Francisco Bay has gone through many cycles of change. During the ice ages, when sea level was some 300 feet lower than it is now, the Bay was a valley. As the last ice age ended, the Bay was flooded until it reached approximately its outline about 5,000 years ago.

As sediments from the surrounding mountains filled the depths of the South Bay during the past 200 years, the salt marshes, once narrow strips, broadened. In 1850 bay marshes covered over 300 square miles. Now 80 percent of this area has been lost by filling and diking.

The South Bay, as Spanish explorers found it, was a narrow body of water bordered by broad salt marshes through which meandered sloughs carrying waters from the surrounding mountains.

When Gaspar de Portolá's expedition of 1769 approached the southern arm of San Francisco Bay, it had to keep inland to skirt impassable marshes. In 1776 Juan Bautista de Anza, Pedro Font and Jose' Joaquin Moraga, setting out to explore the east side of the Bay, left camp on the Guadalupe River and met with a network of sloughs and marshes. Along Coyote Creek where it turns west, they were forced "to twist their way to higher ground at the foot of the hills." Traveling in late March, they went past level country "green and flower-covered," crossing five arroyos before coming to Alameda Creek.

Just upland of the marshes, these explorers came across Indian villages near sloughs where fish, shellfish and waterfowl were plentiful. In canoe-like balsas made of bundles of tules, Indians traveled down the sloughs and out into the Bay to spear fish and to net waterfowl.

Soon after the founding of Mission Santa Clara and the Pueblo of San José, Alviso became the main port at this end of the Bay. Over the next 100 years landings ringed the South Bay at the heads of navigable waters on its sloughs. After completion of the railroad from San Francisco to San Jose in 1864, these ports diminished in importance.

Sweeping changes in the South Bay came later, with the diking of its broad marshes to make salt-evaporator ponds, which began in the late 19th century. By the 1940s much of the cordgrass had been eliminated by construction of salt ponds. Only a small fraction of marshland remained—along sloughs and in patches near their outlets. The value of the extraordinarily productive cordgrass is now recognized, and the remaining areas of it are protected. The shallow salt ponds do serve a function for wildlife, having become feeding grounds for myriad resident shorebirds and migrants. Some levees are now important nesting grounds for several bird species.

Looking over Palo Alto Baylands to East Bay Hills

Here and there South Bay marshes were filled in the first half of the 20th century. Only since World War II, however, have our marshes, tidelands and flood plains in the South Bay come to be viewed as real estate, to be filled to make acreage for industry and houses to serve the surging populations of Santa Clara and Alameda counties.

The Bay's edge has been used not only for salt ponds but more recently for dumping garbage and sewage and also for industry. As more creeks have been dammed, spring runoffs have decreased and so has their flushing action in the Bay.

By the 1950s public clamor against pollution, degradation and filling of the Bay grew into a campaign to "Save the Bay." Biologists, naturalists, ornithologists and botanists who had long recognized the damage being done were joined in the 1960s by a groundswell of conservation activists. Led by such crusaders as Lucy Evans and Harriet Mundy in the South Bay, and the indomitable Helen Kerr, Sylvia McLaughlin, and Esther Gulick in Berkeley, the Save the Bay organization was born. Legislation passed in 1968 created the Bay Conservation and Development Commission, which has controlled development within 100 feet of the shoreline.

The commission has had considerable success in reversing the trend of pollution and fill. Parks, preserves and wildlife refuges around much of the South Bay now allow frequent public access to the shoreline. Regulations of the Army Corps of Engineers now afford some protection to seasonal wetlands.

Today, in parks and preserves around the Bay trails draw hikers, bicyclists, runners, birdwatchers, and nature buffs to the marshes, sloughs, and salt ponds by the Bay. At visitor centers and museums and through workshops and conducted tours, the public is learning about the ever-changing tidelands, marshes, mudflats and sloughs that were once out of sight and out of mind.

For a deeper understanding of the South Bay, its natural history and its wildlife, the authors heartily recommend Diane Conradson's *Exploring Our Baylands*, the revised and expanded third edition of 1996. It will enrich any trip by the Bay. The Santa Clara Valley Audubon Society's *Birding at the Bottom of the Bay* gives novice and expert alike a good idea of what birds are found in our Baylands.

◆ The San Francisco Bay Trail ◆

After many years of planning and effort, a system of trails around the South Bay is taking shape. The concept of a Bay trail was included in Santa Clara County plans as early as 1973 and by 1983 Palo Alto had a Bayfront Trail.

Further impetus to Bay trails came from the Bay Trail legislation of 1987, requiring the Association of Bay Area Governments to prepare a recreation trail for hikers and bicyclists ringing San Francisco and San Pablo bays. A Bay Trail plan, prepared with advice of citizen committees and local officials, is now being implemented with the cooperation of federal, state and local government agencies.

Today many miles of trail are open to hikers and bicyclists from Palo Alto to Alviso, and more miles down the eastern shores from Coyote Hills to Newark are now in place. Palo Alto's Bayfront Trail continues past its flood-control basin and joins Shoreline at Mountain View's Bayfront Trail. A bridge across Stevens Creek to the Midpeninsula Regional Open Space District's Stevens Creek Nature Study Area takes the trail down to Moffett Field.

Although Moffett Field still presents a trail-routing problem, an easement runs south of there through industrial land to Sunnyvale's Bay-

San Francisco Bay Trail along Bayview Trail heading south to San Francisco Wildlife Refuge

lands. The City of Sunnyvale opened nearly 4 miles of trail around levees bayward of its water-treatment plant. The adjoining Sunnyvale Baylands Park is a wetlands preserve with trails at its perimeter and a wide trail along its southern boundary which continues beyond the park on a paved route. It passes the thriving Tom Harvey Marsh, crosses bridges over Calabasas and San Tomas Aquino creeks, and the Highway 237 on- and off-ramps to reach Alviso at Gold Street.

From Alviso, by an as-yet-undecided route, the trail will go to Dixon Landing. However, there are sidewalks along some sections of Gold Street in Alviso and walkers and bicyclists can follow its streets to the Don Edwards San Francisco Bay National Wildlife Refuge's Environmental Education Center at the end of Grand Avenue on Triangle Marsh. Just north is a 2-mile stretch of existing Bay Trail through marshes and Coyote Creek Lagoon. From there routes are under discussion, at this writing, for a link to the Don Edwards San Francisco Bay National Wildlife Refuge at Newark. Refuge trails join Coyote Hills Regional Park trails, reaching all the way to Alameda Creek, thus completing the part of the Bay Trail around the South Bay.

The plan for this regional Bay Trail also provides for connections to existing parks and creeks and to existing and proposed transportation facilities. Wide aprons above both San Tomas and Calabasas creeks appear to be usable for hiking at this writing.

Public agencies are making progress in filling the gaps in the South Bay. Persistent trail enthusiasts and planners from four counties, a half dozen cities, the National Wildlife Refuge and the Midpeninsula Regional Open Space District, with the cooperation of flood-control districts, public-works departments and special districts, have already put together miles of bayside trails. It may be some years before you can bicycle or walk completely around the South Bay, but an impressive start has been made.

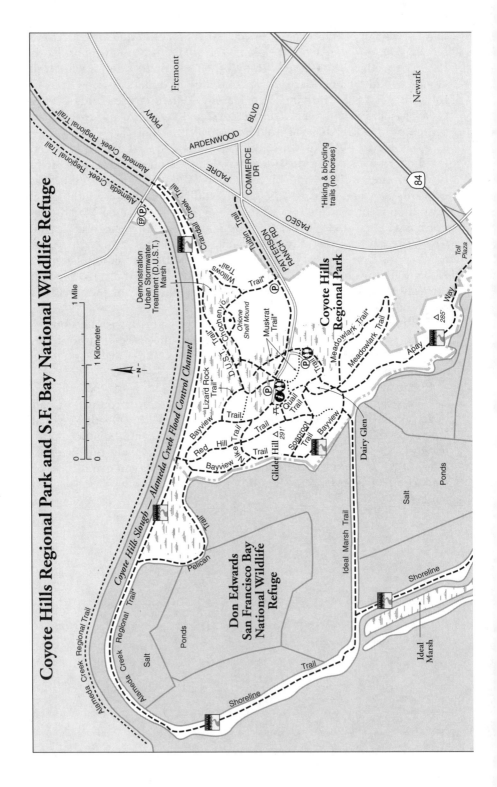

Coyote Hills Regional Park and S.F. Bay National Wildlife Refuge

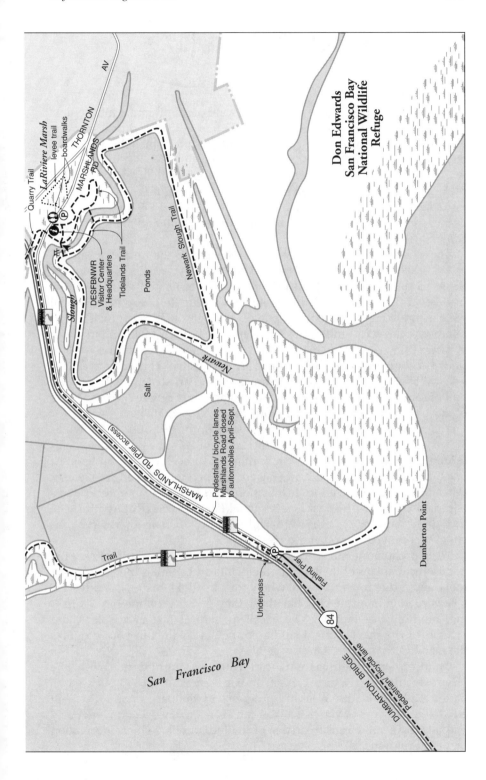

Don Edwards
San Francisco Bay
National Wildlife
Refuge

Dumbarton Point

THORNTON AV

Quarry Trail

LaRiviere Marsh

levee trail

boardwalks

MARSHLANDS RD

DESFBNWR
Visitor Center
& Headquarters

Tidelands Trail

Slough

Ponds

Salt

Newark

Newark Slough Trail

MARSHLANDS RD (Pier access)

Pedestrian/ bicycle lanes.
Marshlands Road closed
to automobiles April-Sept.

Trail

Underpass

Fishing Pier

84

San Francisco Bay

DUMBARTON BRIDGE
Pedestrian/ bicycle lane

◆ Coyote Hills Regional Park ◆

In this park are approximately a thousand acres of gentle hills, brackish and salt marshes, and the site of an Indian village and its 2300-year-old shellmound. The park is a sanctuary for wildlife, which the visitor can observe at close hand from park trails and boardwalks.

The Coyote Hills are a rocky miniature range, rising from an alluvial plain. Juan Bautista de Anza's party, when exploring this side of the Bay, looked out from the lower East Bay hills and mistook these hills for islands, perhaps seeing some of the surrounding land and marshes flooded at high tide.

The marshes attract a great variety of birds and the upland meadows provide habitats for songbirds, small animals and even a herd of deer. Bayward of the park are the salt ponds, levee trails and marshes of the Don Edwards San Francisco Bay National Wildlife Refuge, where you can walk at the edge of the Bay by one of its largest salt marshes. The salt ponds are haven to a multitude of waterbirds, both resident and migrant.

These hills were home to Ohlone Indians. Their village by the Willows Marsh is gone, but their shellmounds are still visible. Through archeological investigations of the site, facsimiles of Indian structures have been built. Programs centered on the Indian village site bring to life the culture of those who lived here for thousands of years.

The Spanish grant of these hills and surrounding lands was known as *Potrero de los Cerritos*—"Pasture of the Little Hills." Since that time, dairy farming, truck farming and duck hunting have been carried on here. At one time a thousand ducks a week were shipped to San Francisco restaurants. More recently military installations and research laboratories have occupied the hills. The East Bay Regional Park District acquired this site in 1967. Today this park, a wonderful wildlife sanctuary, is reserved for environmental education and recreation.

To help you understand the site, stop in at the Visitor Center to see the handsome displays of the Indians, the plants and animals they used, their tools, and a diorama of the site where they lived. Here too, is a full-scale reconstruction of a tule boat like those they paddled on the Bay for fishing, hunting and trading. The excellent natural history displays and exhibits of the plant and animal life in the park will help you recognize the marsh plants and uplands vegetation.

Children and their parents can learn through doing with the "Discovery Boxes", which contain Indian games and tools, as well as nature exploration kits. Weekend programs by the park's naturalists will add to the pleasure of your visit. You can even join a weekend work party and take part in the reconstruction of the Indian village. For information on park programs call the center at 510-795-9385.

At the Visitor Center one can see a 14-minute videotape, shown on request, highlighting the park's features—a fine introduction to Coyote Hills. Videos on the Indians and the salt marshes are also available.

More than 16 miles of trails take visitors through the park's hills, marshes and salt ponds. There is a connection for hikers and bicyclists to the Alameda Creek Regional Trail, which extends 8.5 miles to Niles and 3 miles to the edge of the Bay. Within the park, the Bayview Trail is open to bicyclists. You can continue on the Don Edwards San Francisco Bay National Wildlife Refuge's Shoreline Trail, on an outer levee, to the Dumbarton Bridge approach. Now the Apay Way joins Coyote Hills to trails at the Wildlife Refuge Visitor Center.

Jurisdiction: East Bay Regional Park District. Park address: 8000 Patterson Ranch Road, Fremont, CA 94536

Facilities: Visitor Center. Trails: hiking, bicycling, equestrian, nature. Picnic areas and barbecues: family and group. Group camping, day and overnight, by reservation. Many of the trails and programs are suitable for the physically limited. Phone: 510-795-9385.

Park Rules: Hours: 8 A.M. to posted closing hour. Visitor Center hours: Thursdays to Sundays, 9:30 A.M. to 5 P.M. Dogs must be on leash at all times. No dogs allowed in marsh areas or on levee trails. Fee: $2/car on weekends and holidays. Dog fee: $1, collected daily.

Maps: EBRPD *Coyote Hills Regional Park*; USGS quad *Newark*.

How to Get There: *By Car:* From Hwy. 84 turn north on Paseo Padre Pkwy. Turn west on Patterson Ranch Rd. 0.6 mile and go to park entrance gate.

By Bicycle: Take the Alameda Creek Regional Trail from the east or Dumbarton Bridge bike lanes from the west, or the Tuibun Trail paralleling Patterson Ranch Rd. from Paseo Padre Pkwy.

Coyote Hills Regional Park
BAYVIEW TRAIL

Hikers and bicyclists circle a hill for a bird's-eye view of the park and its surroundings.

Distance: 3.5-mile loop

Time: 2 hours

Elevation Gain: 50'; 200' if you go to the hilltop.

Trail Notes

Start through a gate on the road north of the Visitor Center parking lot and continue out around the north end of Coyote Hills. The Bayview Trail goes along the hillside through open grassland. Looking east over the fresh-water marsh, you will usually catch sight of some white egrets. You will easily identify this large, long-legged wading bird, over 30" tall, which hunts fish, frogs and other small animals in the marshes. In flight its neck forms an S curve; its cry is a low croaking sound. As you go up the hill, you may startle a ring-necked pheasant into noisy, whirring flight. This spectacular bird, with its long, pointed tail, was introduced from China as a game bird, and now is spreading over much of the western U.S.

Continuing around the hill, the trail keeps to an elevation about 50 feet above the Bay. Below, where once was marsh, are the salt-evaporator ponds in the Don Edwards San Francisco Bay National Wildlife Refuge. The Alameda Creek flood-control channel goes along the northern boundary of this park. Take the short trail on your right to join the bicycle and hiking trail on the south side of the channel. Just opposite this trail you can go uphill (south) and walk the length of Red Hill Trail for broad views of the Bay.

But this trip on the Bayview Trail continues around the bend, where you can take the stairs down to the Pelican Trail, which skirts a marsh and continues to the Shoreline Trail. (See Trip 4, page 297.)

Returning to the Bayview Trail, you can enjoy the view over the salt ponds to the far levee and its fringe of marsh and, beyond, the Peninsula hills. Birds fill the shallow ponds, particularly in fall and winter when resident birds are joined by migrants. Stop a while to listen to the fine chorus of their calls and cries.

Where the trail starts to turn away from the Bay, you pass the Ideal Marsh Trail, which follows a levee to the Shoreline Trail at the Bay's edge. The Bayview Trail now turns east through a low saddle toward a fresh water marsh on the east side of Coyote Hills. The Meadowlark Trail Loop turns south here, but you veer toward the Visitor Center and go around a bend above Dairy Glen, a reservation camping and picnic area.

The Bayview Trail turns south and then continues east but this trip turns off left (north) on the Quail Trail, just a few feet beyond the Bayview/Soaproot Trail junction. After 0.25 mile on the Quail Trail you are looking down on the lawns, trees and tables of the picnic grounds at the Visitor Center—and the end of your trip.

Coyote Hills Regional Park
BOARDWALK AND MUSKRAT LOOP TRAIL

Take a walk over ponds and marsh and along the tule-bordered Muskrat Trail to one of the finest birding areas around the Bay

Distance: 1.5-mile loop

Time: 1 hour; more if the birding is good

Elevation Change: Level. Wheelchair access.

Duck pond along the Coyote Hills Muskrat Trail

Trail Notes

From the Visitor Center, walk across the main entrance road and veer right to the boardwalk. Here you enter the special world of a marsh teeming with life. The boardwalk follows a labyrinthine course over small ponds, through narrow passages between shoulder-high cattails, and out to larger bodies of water. You can look down into algae-rich shallows where decomposing reeds are a nourishing breeding ground for myriad insects and microorganisms and darting schools of tiny fish. Dragonflies skim the surface, and waterfowl in great variety feed here.

Convenient benches let you rest and take in the scene around you. The boardwalk is a birder's delight—from it many a rare bird can be sighted. If you take one of the naturalist's bird walks here, you will soon be checking off species on the park's handy bird list.

Soon after the boardwalk ends, you turn south on the Muskrat Trail, which leads through the higher and drier parts of the marsh. During winters of heavy rainfall this whole marsh area can become a vast lake, sometimes submerging the trail. As the water level drops in spring, new growth comes out on the tules and cattails. A desk copy of the Muskrat Trail guide is available for loan at the Visitor Center desk.

Turn to look over the expanse of cattails and tules, and you can understand what an inexhaustible supply of material they offered the Indians, who used them to make mats and thatching for their houses and to build the boats (balsas) that carried them out into the Bay.

The Muskrat Trail continues through seasonal wetlands, crosses the park entry road and then turns north back to the Visitor Center. On the way back you pass Castle Rock, an imposing outcrop of Franciscan chert, formed from minerals and the shells of tiny marine animals and uplifted from an ancient sea floor.

Coyote Hills Regional Park
CHOCHENYO TRAIL

A walk into the past takes you through marsh uplands to the site of an Indian village.

Distance: 3-mile loop

Time: 1½ hours

Elevation Change: Level. Wheelchair access.

Trail Notes

This trail extends north from the park entrance on Patterson Ranch Road to the fenced-off village site, circles it, and turns down to the Visitor Center. You can start from either the park entrance or the Visitor Center.

Starting from the Visitor Center, you can use the boardwalk through the marsh or go due north on the Chochenyo Trail. Turn east on the D.U.S.T. Trail and then make a short jog south to continue east on the Chochenyo Trail. When you come to the village site, on a small rise surrounded by willows, go around to the far side, where you can look through a chain-link fence at some of the village reconstruction. For a better view, most Sundays at 2 P.M.—weather permitting and by reservation—you can meet the park naturalist and join in a walk to the village. Sitting by the excavation, you can hear about the Ohlone Indians who lived here. Or you can take part in one of the park's programs on Indians at the Visitor Center learning some of the skills the native Americans used in their everyday lives. You have a chance to try your hand at making string or shaping an arrowhead, and to see how a fire is made without matches or flint and steel. For information call the Visitor Center.

As you walk this trail in summer or fall, you can make out tracks of many small animals in the dust of the path. You may even catch sight of a deer bounding through the tules. It is not hard to imagine how easily this land could support the Ohlones of this village. When they lived here, there were waterbirds and game animals in vast numbers. Fish filled the creeks, and free for the gathering were little spiral-shelled California horn snails, which grew abundantly in mud flats and on rocks. The shells of this snail, a staple of the village diet along with oysters, fill the mounds that have been excavated at the park.

Coyote Hills Regional Park
MEADOWLARK LOOP TRAIL

This trip takes you to high grasslands where meadowlarks sing and along remote inland fresh-water marshes.

Distance: 3-mile loop

Time: 1 to 2 hours

Elevation Gain: 200′

Trail Notes

Start off west on the foot trail beside the Visitor Center to reach the Quail Trail and go south over the rise ahead and downhill for about 0.25 mile. Veer right on the Bayview Trail and pass the Dairy Glen Day Camp. When you reach the saddle between Red Hill Top and the southern ridge of Coyote Hills, there are several trails. This trip starts on the level trail closest to the marsh, for hikers and bicyclists only, and returns on the ridgetop trail.

From the Bayview Trail junction, walk a few paces due south, then veer left on a wide trail that lies in the lee of the ridge. This is a good trip for those windy days in spring, when you and the birds seek the warm, protected grasslands. Watch the red-winged blackbirds fluttering from cattails to reeds, catching insects for their young.

Winding along beside the marsh on this unpaved trail, you may come across one of the huge black-tailed jackrabbits that live in the grass. It may try to escape your notice by lowering its long ears and huddling close to the ground or it may bound away in 10-foot leaps.

The almost-level Bayview Trail circles the park's periphery

Listen for the meadowlarks. These robin-sized birds, bright yellow beneath and mottled brown above, nest in the grass. Hearing their loud and lovely flute-like song is one of the pleasures of walking over open hills. As their grassland habitat is reduced by encroaching development, however, their song is becoming rarer.

In about 0.75 mile you meet a graveled road turning sharply uphill toward the top of the ridge. Go right on it and follow it past fields of fennel and remnants of former military installations. At the ridgetop you meet the paved Meadowlark Trail, the return leg of your loop. But first take in the commanding views of the Bay and the sweep of East Bay hills. From here too, you look down on the bright blue waters of the many sloughs, hidden behind the reeds as you walked by earlier. From these heights you can grasp the extent of these marshes and seasonal wetlands, once home to the Ohlone Indians.

Turn right and head downhill past chert outcrops, a few scattered shrubs and flowers blooming in the grasslands. The way is lined with a veritable forest of fennel that lends an aromatic flavor to Bay breezes. The miles of paved trail in this park, accessible to nearby city-dwellers by off-road trails, are ideal for bicyclists.

At the bottom of the hill turn right to retrace your steps to the Visitor Center.

Coyote Hills Regional Park
THE APAY WAY TO THE WILDLIFE REFUGE

Walk the route of the Bright Moon to reach the Don Edwards San Francisco Bay National Wildlife Refuge. Or ride your bicycle and pedal the levee trails beside the salt ponds.

Distance: 3.5 miles

Time: 2 hours

Elevation Gain: Nearly level.

Trail Notes

Start this trip as in Trip 4, but continue on the Bayview Trail past both the Meadowlark Trail junctions. Turn right (south) on the Apay Way. *Apay* is a Native American word meaning a bright moon pathway. You skirt the salt ponds, winding in and out of little coves close to the water.

On one of the windless, warm days by the Bay that sometimes come in spring and fall (and occasionally throughout the year), this segment of the San Francisco Bay*Trail is a choice route that will tempt you to linger and picnic along the way on a small peninsula extending out into the water. The grassy hillsides blossom in spring with poppies and mustard. Here and there small eucalyptus groves mark the sites of early homes.

There are deer here, too, which find cover in the scant brush or the tall stands of fennel growing so plentifully. At the south end of the hill, a quarry is still in operation. Past its excavations, fenced off from the trail, you veer right to reach the overcrossing of the Dumbarton Bridge toll plaza, which makes it possible for you to cross safely. Then take a trail that winds through toyon, ceanothus and fremontia to the base of the hill where you see the Wildlife Refuge Visitor Center.

Coyote Hills Regional Park
SHORELINE LOOP TRAIL
(Operated by Don Edwards San Francisco Bay National Wildlife Refuge)

A bracing walk on the levees to the edge of the Bay and to the Ideal Marsh gives you open views of the North Bay and its bird life along the salt ponds.

Distance: 7.5-mile loop, plus 1.5-mile trip along Ideal Marsh

Time: 4 hours

Elevation Change: Level, except for small rise from levee.

Trail Notes

Start your trip from the Visitor Center on the Bayview Trail. After it rounds the northern tip of Coyote Hills leave it for the Pelican Trail. Stop at the overlook, from which stairs lead down to the levee. Explanatory panels here introduce you to the life in salt ponds and marshes. Since the levee trail must be rebuilt at intervals, it becomes rough and impassable for a year or two at a time.

The Pelican Trail jogs around a stretch of marsh by the channel of Patterson Creek, then joins the outer levee trail by Coyote Slough and the Alameda Creek flood-control channel. This graveled path on the levee takes you past salt ponds that change color as the evaporation process increases salt concentration. The growth of algae turns the water greenish; then, as brine shrimps proliferate, the water becomes pinkish.

Fall and spring bring flocks of migratory birds along the Pacific Flyway, but any time of year there are white egrets and great blue herons. A novice will have no trouble identifying both of these long-legged birds, standing 3–4' tall. Fall finds the ponds lively with more varieties of ducks than the inexpert can distinguish. Distinguish them or not, anyone can take pleasure in watching the flight patterns, plumage, distinctive gaits and feeding habits of the many species of visiting and resident birds. Join some of the weekend bird walks with a bird field manual and your binoculars, and you will soon be telling a canvasback from a pintail and an avocet from a godwit.

When you reach the western side of the levee, about 2 miles from land, the outboard side of the trail is edged with a remnant of natural marsh. Tall cordgrass, green in spring and brown in fall, is washed by daily tides. The changing edge of marsh erodes in heavy winter storms but tends to build up again with deposits of dead cordgrass.

As your trail comes to the Ideal Marsh, it turns back east. This is the largest area of marshland left in this part of the Bay. Even if you do not want to take the 1.5-mile side trip, it is worth going down this marsh a little way before you turn back to the hills. A century ago more than 300 square miles of tide-washed cordgrass marsh like this fragment ringed the Bay. Today 80% of it has been filled or diked. Sloughs from creeks and streams draining into the Bay meandered through these vast green expanses, their muddy banks at low tide a rich source of food for myriad shorebirds.

South of Ideal Marsh, you can continue about two miles on the levee trail to the south side of the Dumbarton Bridge approach. You can reach this levee trail from the south side of the bridge approach, where a paved road, the continuation of Marshlands Road, is open to vehicles for access to this trail and parking for a popular fishing pier. Here, too, is the beginning of the bike lanes that span the Bay on the Dumbarton Bridge.

To return to Coyote Hills, retrace your steps to the north end of Ideal Marsh, then turn east for a 1.5-mile walk on the Ideal Marsh Trail beside the salt ponds to the Bayview Trail.

• Don Edwards San Francisco Bay •
National Wildlife Refuge

See maps on pages 290-291

The 22,350-acre Don Edwards San Francisco Bay National Wildlife Refuge encompasses many of the South Bay's marshes, salt ponds, sloughs, mud flats and open waters and provides a unique opportunity to experience this bayland environment on many miles of trails. The largest urban refuge in the National Wildlife Refuge system, it was established "for the preservation and enhancement of highly significant wildlife habitat . . . for the protection of migratory waterfowl and other wildlife, including species known to be threatened with extinction, and to provide an opportunity for wildlife-oriented recreation and nature study."

The handsome Visitor Center building on a promontory on the south end of the Coyote Hills, near the eastern approach to the Dumbarton Bridge at Newark, houses lively displays of Bay natural history, including a boardwalk trip simulating the mudflats and marshes you can visit across Marshlands Road. A book sales area and an information desk at the entrance to the center offer maps and information about interpretive programs. These programs, planned to interest visitors of all ages, range from elementary bird walks to slough trips by canoe. A docent program enlists and trains volunteers who assist the refuge in expanding its information and education programs. A trip to the Visitor Center at refuge headquarters will open your eyes, challenge your mind and entertain your children.

Miles of trails will take you on levees beside marshes and sloughs. The Refuge has developed a "do-it-yourself" trip around its headquarters, with information panels explaining the dynamics of tidelands, their wildlife and some local history. In addition, more than 30 miles of trails along the Bay shore and out onto levees surrounding salt ponds are currently open to hikers and bicyclists. From these trails visitors can see tidal action at close hand in the marshes, watch shorebirds feeding in the salt ponds and look for birds migrating along the Pacific Flyway. Birding is best from late fall to spring.

A recently restored tidal salt marsh on the east side of Marshlands Road opened during the celebrations marking the Refuge's 25th anniversary. Named for longtime volunteers and ardent advocates of the Refuge, Florence and Philip LaRiviere, it is now the LaRiviere Marsh. Already migratory birds are stopping there and new pickleweed and marsh grasses are flourishing. Watch for a new kiosk with explanatory plaques to be built here. For a bird's eye view of this salt marsh take the 1-mile walk on two short boardwalks over the LaRiviere Marsh which connect to a levee trail along an arm of Newark Slough.

The trails around Refuge headquarters connect with the Apay Way Trail at the south end of Coyote Hills Regional Park by a foot-and-bicycle bridge over the Dumbarton Bridge toll plaza. (See Coyote Hills Trip 5, page 298.)

The Refuge no longer conducts tours into the historic town of Drawbridge due to extremely unsafe conditions there. A new section of the Bay Trail goes through the Refuge's Coyote Creek Lagoon near the Warm Springs District of Fremont.

At Alviso the Environmental Education Center on the edge of a marsh carries on research and teacher-training programs in its laboratories, library and observation tower. The center is open and free to school classes and organized groups. It is also open on weekends to the general public. Nearby, 9 miles of trail circle salt ponds and marshes.

The Refuge owns thousands of acres of salt-evaporator ponds that are still in use for salt production. By agreement, the Cargill Salt Company can continue its salt operations as long as it wants if it uses its present methods of solar evaporation and does not fill in any open water areas. The levees, made of dredged mud, deteriorate and must be rebuilt at intervals, a process that leaves them rough for a year or two. Because most of the refuge's trails utilize levees, trail routes will change from time to time as levees are closed for repairs. Trails are rerouted until the surface has consolidated. And some levees are closed during the season that waterfowl use them for nesting grounds.

Fishing is permitted from the outer levees north and south of the Dumbarton Bridge east approach and from fishing piers at the east end of the old Dumbarton Bridge. These areas also provide good birdwatching. Waterfowl hunting is allowed on some levees and from boats in some of the refuge's salt ponds, sloughs and open waters. Although you may see boats with hunters and their dogs near the Visitor and Environmental Education centers, hunting is forbidden in these areas.

Jurisdiction: U.S. Department of the Interior, Fish and Wildlife Service.

Facilities: Visitor Center, Environmental Education Center. Trails: hiking, bicycling, self-guided nature. Picnic tables. Hunting and fishing in designated areas. Handicapped facilities: call or write for further information.

Park Rules: Stay on the trails to protect yourself and the refuge resources. Pets, allowed only on the Tidelands Trail, must be leashed at all times; not permitted elsewhere in refuge. Hours: Visitor Center, daily 10 A.M. to 5 P.M.; closed on Thanksgiving, Christmas and New Year's Day. Trails open every day during daylight hours. Parking lot locked at 5 P.M. Marshlands Road between Visitor Center and fishing pier closed during nesting season, April 1–August 31; call 510-792-0222 for weekend bus shuttle reservations to fishing pier. For weekend programs at Alviso Environmental Education Center, call 408-262-5513.

Maps: *DESFBNWR Wildlife Refuge*; USGS quad *Milpitas.*

How to Get There: *By Car:* From Hwy. 84, go south on Thornton Ave., turn right on Marshlands Rd. to Refuge Visitor Center.

By Bicycle: From bike lanes on Dumbarton Bridge take Marshlands Rd. or from Apay Way in Coyote Hills Regional Park cross over bridge toll plaza and take Quarry Trail to parking area.

Don Edwards San Francisco Bay National Wildlife Refuge
Tidelands Trail

On this short, self-guiding nature trail you can walk beside a marsh and tidal slough, stop for a picnic in a former salt company pumphouse, hide in an old duck blind to watch the birds and, along the way, learn about the plant and animal life of the South Bay.

Distance: 1.33-mile loop

Time: 1 hour allows time to read the information panels.

Elevation Loss: 150'

Trail Notes

This trail, designated a National Recreation Trail by the Department of the Interior, begins opposite the main entrance of the Visitor Center. It takes you to a hilltop for a view of the Newark Slough and the Bay and down to a salt-pond levee where a series of information panels describes the scene around you.

From the parking lot take the path uphill to the Visitor Center and start your trip at the overlook opposite the main entrance. Information on the Bay and its tides is here. Then go left (uphill) to a knoll, the high point of the hill. Be sure to stop at the crow's-nest observation platform, fenced against strong Bay winds, for a commanding view of the salt ponds and the Bay. You will be able to trace the course of Newark Slough first north, then west around the salt pond, then bending south to meander out to the Bay. On a clear day you can see ships and sailboats against the backdrop of the Santa Cruz Mountains on the far shore.

By the crow's nest is a picnic table protected from the breezes, with views toward the East Bay hills. Now a trail for the physically limited built by the Boy Scouts reaches the summit of this hill. This is a good place for an early lunch at the start of your trip or to return to after your tour of the levees.

From here the trail leads downhill past other enlightening information panels to the level of the marshlands. An overlook at the edge of the marsh bears an account of the busy water traffic that once headed up

Hunters cabin now a picnic area

Newark Slough. A landing here was the embarcadero of Mission San José, 8 miles east. In the mid-1800s travel across the Bay by boat was easier and more direct than long journeys over bad roads. Hay barges and schooners loaded at what became known as Jarvis Landing. However, in the late 1800s railroads and improved roads began to take the place of water traffic, and a severe land subsidence due to pumping water from nearby wells caused flooding of warehouses at the landing. The landing was not used after World War I.

Along the trail, in a craggy serpentine outcrop, grow century plants and aloes, not native to this region, but doing well at this writing. Around the bend at another overlook you learn about marshland inhabitants and their adjustment to the ebb and flow of tides.

From here a short trail continues northwest on this level back to the picnic tables below the Visitor Center, but the Tidelands Trail descends on a switchback down to a handsome bridge crossing Newark Slough.

At the far side of the bridge, you come to the levee trail. Keep right on the Tidelands Trail, which is also a leg of the Newark Slough Trail. Going left will take you south on the 5-mile Newark Slough Trail. Along the levee trail you have marsh and a tidal slough on your right, a salt-evaporator pond on your left.

A salt marsh, an intricate natural system converting the sun's energy to plants and animals, is a place of incredible productivity, sustaining a rich variety of life. Salt ponds, though designed to produce salt, have become adopted homes for many bird species that feed on the brine flies and brine shrimp living in the shallow waters. Some levees have become nesting grounds for resident and migrating species.

As you continue along the levee, you come to an old duck-hunter's cabin at the edge of the slough, furnished as it was in former duck-hunting days. The story of waterfowl hunting is told here, from the life-sustaining ways of the Indians and early duck shooting by the Anglos through the destructive mass commercial hunting at the turn of the century to today's controlled sport hunting. At a nearby duck blind you can crawl inside and shoot birds with your camera.

Your trail back goes right past a small building with picnic tables, then crosses a footbridge over Newark Slough. Note the landing for boats and canoes from halfway across the bridge. Refuge personnel lead an occasional canoe trip on a "bring your own canoe" basis. A trail from the bridge leads to more picnic tables on the level below the Visitor Center and to the last of the information panels. Above you is the Visitor Center and the end of your trip.

Don Edwards San Francisco Bay National Wildlife Refuge
NEWARK SLOUGH

> *The loop trail around the slough is an invigorating walk for bird-watchers and all who enjoy open marshland and salt ponds in the Bay's many moods.*

Distance: 5-mile loop

Time: 2½ hours

Elevation Change: Level

Trail Notes

From the refuge parking lot take the path around the north side of the headquarters building and find the gravel trail to your right, heading downhill to the bridge that crosses Newark Slough. The Newark Slough Trail, on a salt-pond levee, follows the slough around north, then west to the far side of the pond, then south to where the slough meanders out to the Bay. Then it leaves the slough, heads east, and goes north again to complete the loop.

At the far side of the bridge are two old buildings. The one on the right, the Pavilion, is an old pump house converted to a picnic shelter. Nearby is the Newark Slough Learning Center with an amphitheater and classrooms, donated by local service groups and businesses. Your trail passes the pump house and turns right by the marsh-edged slough. This is a place of open sky, wide horizons and seemingly limitless space. The subtle colors of salt ponds and marshes change with the seasons. The muted pinks of the ponds are accented by pickleweed as it turns reddish in the fall; in the winter the cordgrass and salt grass in the marsh are brown. The ponds reflect clouds on still days, and the dark skies of winter make a dramatic contrast with white gulls resting on the ponds.

An old hunting blind remodeled into birdwatching blind, useful to photographers and birders, is welcomed also by those who just like to sit by the trail and enjoy the expanse of water (today somewhat lessened by incessant traffic noise on the Dumbarton Bridge). From fall to spring the ponds are filled with migrant birds stopping on their way up or down the Pacific Flyway. Throughout the year a large population of gulls, avocets, stilts, willets and many others is in residence. Flocks of stilts far out in the pond stand with only their feet under water, a gauge of how shallow and level the pond is. In summer the migrant birds have left and resident birds prefer the marsh edges to the salt-encrusted ponds.

You may be startled by the flap of a northern harrier hawk's great wings as it flies out of the marsh. Formerly called a marsh hawk, and now renamed, this brownish bird with a black-and-white striped tail and a white rump patch soars with its wings (spanning almost 4') in a shallow V like those of the British fighter plane named for its European relatives.

In contrasting scale, a scampering of sandpipers busy themselves in the mud along the pond's edge, searching for food. Out in the pond a flotilla of gulls turns and moves away a little at the approach of hikers on the levee, but does not take flight.

Between the 2-mile and 3-mile posts an expanse of marsh by the Newark Slough broadens as the levee trail turns south. At high tide the marsh floods, making pools here and there that attract common or white egrets searching for fish and rodents. It does not take an expert to recognize these stately creatures, standing 3' tall on their long legs. With slow dignity they stalk their prey of insects, small animals and fish. Head moving forward, long neck outstretched, they advance one foot with deliberation and then gather their bodies forward. With a swift dart, they catch a fish or a mouse with their long beak.

Less frequently you will see the much smaller snowy egret, with a black bill and yellow feet, and in nesting season tufted plumage on its head and breast. Also less frequently seen is the great blue heron, which stands 4' tall and flies with slow sweeps of its great wings. Halfway around the loop a small bird blind for photographers and birdwatchers looks out over the marsh to the west—a good place for two or three people to sit for lunch while watching ducks landing in a pond and egrets looking for food.

Beyond this point your trail turns east to return to the Visitor Center. You are now close to the 10'-diameter Hetch-Hetchy pipelines, carrying water from the Sierra to Crystal Springs Lakes. To the east high-tech offices and rows of houses sit at the head of Newark Slough.

As you continue east, the low hills at the refuge headquarters loom larger, and you finally come to the east end of the salt pond. Going through a stile by a gate across the levee, you turn back, left, toward the Visitor Center. The path now follows a bend in Newark Slough, and soon it meets the upstream reach of the slough, close to the site of the old Jarvis Landing. Go through a second stile and follow the slough to the left until you come to a bridge. Here you can cross the bridge and complete your trip along the hill back to the Visitor Center, or continue on the levee trail to the northern bridge from which you started. As you cross the slough, check the difference three hours has made in the tide level.

Fremont/Warm Springs Bay Trail

A two-mile segment of the San Francisco Bay Trail takes bicyclists, anglers and birdwatchers out to tidal marshes and wetlands and along flood-control channels from a small Bay access park at Fremont Boulevard near West Warren Drive in Fremont. The trail goes through the 300-acre Coyote Creek Lagoon, now a part of the Don Edwards San Francisco Bay National Wildlife Refuge.

At a small landscaped Bay access park are a few tree-shaded picnic tables and parking. Just past a massive industrial building a gravel-surfaced levee trail takes off, heading out along a channel lined with cordgrass, arcing toward Coyote Slough's meanders. In summer the vast expanse of breezy marsh is a refreshing contrast to the sun-baked East Bay hills that rise abruptly from the Bay plain.

The levee trail veers south, passing below the bulk of the Newby Island landfill. Where the trail turns back to the east is a fishing spot popular with anglers who catch sturgeon, bass and salmon here.

At the southern end of the trail is another little access park at Fremont and Lakeview boulevards. You find young trees, a stretch of lawn, parking and a ramp for wheelchair access to the trail. Picnic tables offer a dramatic view of 2517' Mission Peak that will tempt you to overlook the usual marsh breezes and stop for lunch here.

A proposed section of Bay Trail continues south, skirting the Fremont Airport for a few miles to Dixon Landing.

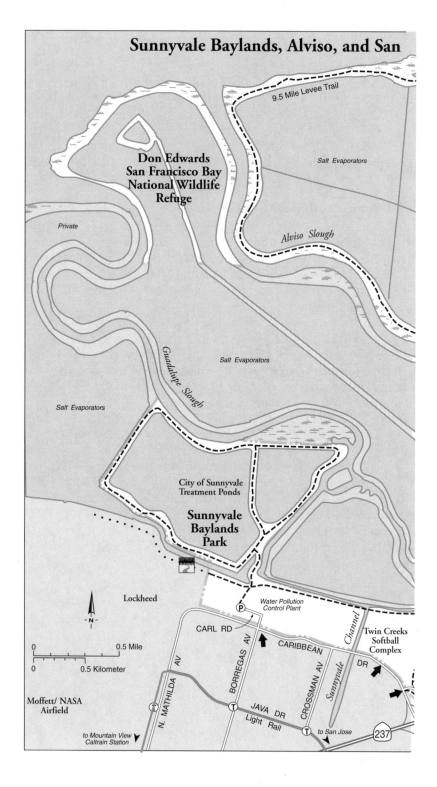

Sunnyvale Baylands, Alviso, and San

9.5 Mile Levee Trail

Salt Evaporators

**Don Edwards
San Francisco Bay
National Wildlife
Refuge**

Private

Alviso Slough

Guadalupe Slough

Salt Evaporators

Salt Evaporators

City of Sunnyvale
Treatment Ponds

**Sunnyvale
Baylands
Park**

Lockheed

- N -

0   0.5 Mile

0   0.5 Kilometer

Moffett/ NASA
Airfield

to Mountain View
Caltrain Station

CARL RD

Water Pollution
Control Plant

N. MATHILDA AV

BORREGAS AV

CARIBBEAN

JAVA DR

Light Rail

CROSSMAN AV

Sunnyvale Channel

DR

Sunnyvale

Twin Creeks
Softball
Complex

to San Jose

237

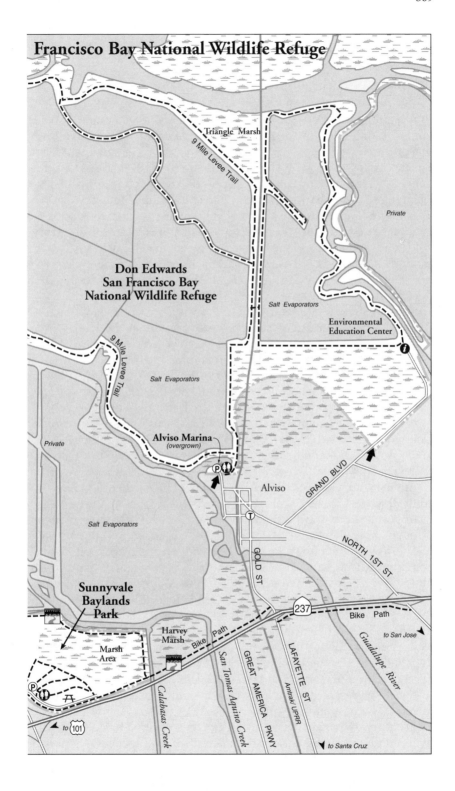

Francisco Bay National Wildlife Refuge

Triangle Marsh

9 Mile Levee Trail

Private

Don Edwards
San Francisco Bay
National Wildlife Refuge

Salt Evaporators

Environmental
Education Center

9 Mile Levee Trail

Salt Evaporators

Private

Alviso Marina
(overgrown)

Alviso

GRAND BLVD

Salt Evaporators

NORTH 1ST ST

GOLD ST

Sunnyvale
Baylands
Park

237

Bike Path

to San Jose

Harvey
Marsh

Bike Path

Marsh
Area

San Tomas Aquino Creek

GREAT AMERICA PKWY

LAFAYETTE ST

Amtrak/UPRR

Guadalupe River

to 101

Calabasas Creek

to Santa Cruz

◆ Alviso ◆

Adjoining the Don Edwards San Francisco Bay National Wildlife Refuge is the historic town of Alviso, named for Ignacio Alviso, the mayor-domo of Santa Clara Mission, who was granted the 6352-acre Rancho de los Esteros by Governor Alvarado in 1838. He took up residence at Alviso two years later. The port of Alviso soon supplanted Santa Clara Mission's embarcadero, nearby on Guadalupe Slough.

A flourishing trade in hides and tallow, exchanged for goods from Yankee vessels, made Alviso an important port. After the discovery of gold, trade with San Francisco so increased that regular steamer runs from Alviso carried produce and manufactured goods. Stagecoaches coming from San Jose met the steamers at Alviso. The town prospered, and docks and warehouses were soon built by the Alviso Slough.

Completion of a railroad from San Francisco to San Jose in 1864 diminished Alviso's importance. However, such families as the Wades and the Tildens remained, as did their houses, which you can see today. The modest house of Henry Wade and his more impressive brick warehouse, built in the early 1860s, stand in the center of town. The handsome Italianate Tilden house, for years occupied by members of the same family, is near the marina on Elizabeth Street, beautifully kept up, as always.

An attempt to revive the port in the 1890s by building a "New Chicago," which was to be the port for the South Bay and the largest city of the West, was a failed dream. The name is now applied to a marsh next to the Environmental Education Center.

Another flurry of activity at Alviso came in 1906, when Tom Foon started the Bayside Cannery, which processed food crops from the fertile lands nearby and from the Sacramento River Delta. The cannery operated through the 1920s.

The town is experiencing another rejuvenation, occasioned by the boom in "Silicon Valley" around San Jose. New industrial and research buildings are spreading north from San Jose along Gold and North First streets, and new, much larger houses are being built. Many buildings of the early days remain, and the port of Alviso is included in the National Register of Historic Places. This designation gives some legal protection to some of the town's historic buildings. The largest remaining old cannery building is owned by the Fish and Wildlife Service. Its walls are now covered with murals by local artists, depicting Alviso's past and present.

A visit to present-day Alviso is an adventure, combining as it does elements of the past and the future. Because of withdrawal of water in the 19th century to irrigate the orchards that then covered Santa Clara Valley, the ground in Alviso has subsided many feet, and the town now is protected by levees from Bay water encroachment. You can climb the levee by the 1896 Yacht Club (note the explanatory sign placed by E. Clampus Vitus) to savor the feel of a peaceful slough near the mouth of the Guadalupe River, with some local boats moored by the wharf. Meadowlarks and blackbirds call from the reeds, and you may glimpse a black-crowned night heron.

In 1979 the Wildlife Refuge's Environmental Education Center, was built about 2 miles east of the town at the end of Grand Boulevard. This attractive building has nature displays and a tower several stories high from which you can view the marshlands for miles around. It is open to classes and groups by reservation, and contains a lab with teaching tools for school classes (call 408-262-5513). Both the center and the marsh trails are open to the public on weekends.

Adjoining the Environmental Education Center is the New Chicago Marsh, accessed by a boardwalk, from which you can take a levee walk along Mallard Slough.

Today Alviso is busy on weekends with history buffs, shutterbugs, birders, hikers and bicyclists—and people just seeking a good seafood dinner at one of its restaurants. This old port itself is well worth a stroll, to see the record of its past that still stands in a half dozen of its buildings. Among the earliest are Wade's brick warehouse on Hope Street and his modest house next door.

Jurisdiction: Town of Alviso: City of San Jose. *Alviso Slough Trail*: SFB-NWR.

Facilities: At the Santa Clara County marina: picnic tables, restrooms, at DESFBNWR: Environmental Education Center, observation platform, trails on DESFBNWR levees.

Maps: SFBNWR *map*. USGS quad *Milpitas*.

How to Get There: Exit Hwy. 237 at N. First St., go northwest to Gold St., right (north) to Elizabeth St., left to Hope St., right to end. Park at Alviso Marina.

1

Alviso
A WALK ON THE ALVISO SLOUGH TRAIL

From this historic town a 9-mile trip along Alviso Slough and Coyote Creek takes you to one of the finest birding opportunities and one of the largest bits of natural marsh in the South Bay.

Distance: 9-mile loop

Time: 4-5 hours

Elevation Change: Level

Trail Notes

This trail uses levees to circle a group of salt ponds between Coyote Creek and Alviso Slough. Reaching the end of the Bay, it passes Triangle Marsh, one of the largest bits of natural marsh left in this area. The trip on the west side of the loop beside Alviso Slough is the most rewarding part, if the whole 9-mile loop is longer than you wish to take. For birders, a morning trip here at low tide during fall or winter will yield the highest bird count.

Start from the east end of the Alviso marina, where a Wildlife Refuge sign points the way through a hiker/bicyclist gate. This marina is no longer usable for boats, as the silted-up marsh has encroached over the original docks and walkways. Take the first trail to the left (west) around the marina and down the levee by Alviso Slough. Another levee trail heading north is the returning end of your loop trip.

Fragments of the marsh remain along both sides of the slough. At low tide you will find avocets, stilts and dowitchers picking their way on the muddy banks, searching for food. Ruddy ducks and coots paddle in the water. You may startle into flight from the cordgrass one of the northern harrier hawks, identified by its 4' wingspread and the white patch on its rump. At high tide look for the shy, big-footed, chicken-sized clapper rail, an endangered species now making a comeback in the protected marshes.

A brisk walk down the levee trail is breezily invigorating. The characteristic northwest wind blows down the Bay in summer. Winter days are often still and mild. On clear days, when smog has been blown off by a storm, this trip brings into view the East Bay hills—emerald green or golden, according to season.

This is a good place to get the feel of South Bay geography. West are the dark, wooded Santa Cruz Mountains. Northeast of the levee is a salt pond stretching almost as far as the eye can see. You pass levees on your right that dike off salt ponds but are closed to hikers for habitat protection. Some of these are resting areas for egrets and pelicans. In migrating season the ponds are often dotted with thousands of birds—many species of ducks and gulls.

After about 4 miles you come to the mouth of Alviso Slough and the open Bay. The trail turns east along Coyote Creek, paralleling a narrow band of marsh for another mile. On the opposite bank of the creek is Station Island, crossed by the Southern Pacific Railroad. Here the little town of Drawbridge thrived in the early 1900s.

From the mouth of Coyote Creek, the trail may follow a levee close to Triangle Marsh or take a more winding route somewhat inland, depending on which levees are currently open to hikers. The marsh along the creek is brackish, where salt water intrudes on the fresh water flowing from the creek.

When the trail reaches the railroad, you are headed toward Alviso. Looking back, you can see directly up the Bay to the gleaming piles of salt at Newark. This is the end product of the process you have seen in the evaporator ponds beside you. It begins at Cargill Salt Company's number-one pond off Shoreline at Mountain View, where water is admitted from the Bay at the time of its highest salinity, in summer. From there brine flows by gravity down a succession of ponds, each an inch lower than the previous one. As water evaporates, the color of the pond changes, first becoming greenish with algae growth, then pinkish with the growth of a red bacterium and the tiny brine shrimp that take on this color.

At the lower end of the Bay, water still at its greenish stage is then pumped for further evaporation to a series of ponds up the East Bay shores. As the concentration increases, the water becomes almost purple. These are the colorful ponds one sees from the air. In late spring, as a final stage, a heavy concentration of brine called "pickle," is pumped into crystallizer ponds to a depth of 1-2'. By fall a 6" layer of sodium chloride crystals has formed at the bottom. Then the top layer, called "bittern," rich in magnesium, bromine and potassium, is drained off, and the salt is ready for harvest. Before the rainy season it is piled in the white pyramids you see on the east side of the Bay.

As you continue on the trail by the railroad tracks, you are on the last leg of this trip and only about 0.5 mile from Alviso. The marsh by the tracks has been drained, as has much of the nearby marshlands that were to be the "New Chicago". The route you follow is subject to some change because of trail closings for levee repair and for habitat protection during nesting. After a few bends in the trail you complete the loop and are back at the marina. The last part of your way blooms with yellow daisies of grindelia, a shrubby, salt-tolerant plant that brightens marshlands above the tides.

From the Environmental Center a shorter levee loop around New Chicago Marsh soon will be available. At this writing, however, recent dredging in Mallard Slough has left the levee walk closed; check with DESFBNWR for its opening.

◆ Sunnyvale Baylands Park and Trails ◆

See maps on pages 308 and 309.

This 220-acre park is managed by the City of Sunnyvale in cooperation with Santa Clara County, which owns the land, on a long-term lease to the city. Recently developed with protected seasonal wetlands, nature trails, picnic areas, and recreation areas, Sunnyvale Baylands is one of the most popular and attractive parks near San Francisco Bay. The adjacent Twin Creeks softball complex has its own entrance and parking area, and is managed commercially. At the park's north end are the SMRT transfer station, from which garbage is taken to Kirby Canyon east of Morgan Hill, and the Sunnyvale Water Pollution Control Plant. Two diked areas along Guadalupe Slough (into which flow Calabasas and San Tomas Aquino creeks) serve as treatment ponds. Their enclosing levees are circled by a 4.5-mile trail.

Park Notes

The City of Sunnyvale facilities at Bay's edge extend roughly from Lockheed Martin's complex south of Moffett Field to the Tom Harvey Marsh just northwest of Alviso. The Sunnyvale Baylands Park was developed largely with county funds as a mitigation for the baseball complex. The park has both protected wetlands for wildlife habitat and "uplands" landscaped with native plants to give a natural effect. Trails in the park lead to an amphitheater on a knoll (from which you get a good view of the whole park and of the East Bay on a clear day). You also can walk toward the Bay along a "wave walk" which rises and falls to simulate waves on the Bay and is bordered by native grasses, leading to a seasonal wetland/dryland. In this area, protected by fencing, burrowing owls may be seen perched on long legs above their underground nests. Attractive display signs with drawings interpret the natural features.

A transition between natural and more manicured sections of the park leads you to a children's play area, with imaginative animal sculptures to be climbed on, and picnic areas. The group/family picnic areas further east have shade structures and are separated from the children's area by a ditch lined with bullrushes.

Close to the industrial parks along Caribbean Drive, this trail is popular with workers enjoying runs on the levee, as well as bird-watchers and family groups out to catch the fresh Bay breezes.

Two centuries ago these busy industrial lands along Caribbean Drive were the lambs' pasture of Mission Santa Clara. Beyond were vast salt marshes through which curved Guadalupe Slough. In 1842 the Rancho Pastoria de las Borregas ("lambs' pasture") was granted to a Spaniard named Estrada. After United States rule in California began, part of the land was patented to Mariano Castro and part to Daniel Murphy. Castro's holdings centered on what we know as Castro Station; Murphy's land empire soon covered a good part of Santa Clara Valley. What remains of the lambs' pasture is the name of Borregas Avenue.

At the height of Bay commerce, McCubbins Landing, on a bend of Guadalupe Slough that borders the levee trail, was one of many landings on the navigable waters of sloughs around the South Bay. But when schooners and steamers could no longer compete with the railroad, which stopped at nearby Castro Station, and the Bay began filling up with sediment washed down from gold mining in the Sierra Nevada, the landing was abandoned. Early in this century the Leslie Salt Company diked the marsh and operated salt evaporators west of Guadalupe Slough. In the mid-1960s, the City of Sunnyvale bought the ponds for aerating waste water before its final, tertiary treatment.

Today the trails around the treatment plant ponds continuing past the Softball Complex and the Baylands Park provide exceptional views of Guadalupe Slough as well as being fine tracks for runners. Beginning at the treatment plant, the San Francisco Bay Trail is designated as part of the regional Bay Trail for hikers and bicyclists. North, a connection is planned to extend around the Bay side of Moffett Field to reach Shoreline at Mountain View. South, the Bay Trail now connects to Alviso via Gold Street. Eventually it will follow Grand Boulevard around the south end of the Bay to reach the Don Edwards San Francisco Bay National Wildlife Area in Newark.

Sunnyvale Baylands Park's play structures for children

Jurisdiction: City of Sunnyvale

Facilities: Recreation areas, access to the San Francisco Bay Trail, commercial softball diamonds and clubhouse, group and family picnic areas, nature areas, restrooms, children's play area, ranger station and parking.

Maps: City of Sunnyvale *Baylands Park*, Association of Bay Area Governments *San Francisco Bay Trail* (ABAG, 510-464-7909), USGS quad *Mountain View.*

Park Rules: No dogs or other pets, no balloons, entrance fee May-October.

How to Get There: Take Caribbean Drive north off Hwy. 237. The park is the first drive on your right; the softball complex is the second drive on the right.

1

Sunnyvale Baylands Park and Trails
A LEVEE TRAIL PAST CALABASAS/ SAN TOMAS AQUINO CREEKS AND GUADALUPE SLOUGH

This trip takes you past a healthy marsh in the company of flocks of birds and armies of runners.

Distance: 4.5-mile loop

Time: 2 hours

Elevation Change: Level

Trail Notes

Start from the parking area on Borregas Avenue and follow the signs to the Bay Trail. Turn left (west). Your trip goes around the sewage treatment ponds and one of the many salt evaporation ponds that fill the South Bay. At noon and early evening the course is popular with employees from nearby industrial parks. Waterbirds in numbers have adapted to these ponds, the largest fresh or brackish ones in the South Bay. You will find birds by the thousands and of many species, arriving, departing, riding the water, or congregating on the levees.

Toward the outer levee of the trail you approach the oxbow bend of Guadalupe Slough, bordered by a broad band of marsh. You may see a great blue heron flying out of the reeds with slow sweeps of its wings. In the slough, pintail ducks dip for food. Coots, black-bodied with white bills, dive under the water for fish. Willets take off and land with flashes of their black-and-white wings. Anyone can enjoy the sight of the many birds feeding here, each in its own manner dabbling, diving, dipping or picking its way along the muddy banks. On the levee trail are benches at intervals. Knowledgeable birders find these marshes particularly rewarding, and they welcome a place to watch the engrossing activities of the birds.

Due north on a clear day the East Bay hills seem close. Mission Peak and Monument Peak rise abruptly from the Bay plain to 2500' heights, their tawny reflections filling the pond on the still days of fall. In spring the green slopes seem a continuation of the marshes in the foreground.

As you circle landward, Moffett Field's massive hangars and NASA's Ames Research Station wind tunnels stand out in pastel shades against the dark background of the Santa Cruz Mountains. The air and the ponds are filled with gulls that challenge you to work at identifying them. The most numerous species is the western gull, a Bay Area resident that appears in great numbers at refuse dumps; adults are snowy white with dark gray wings and back. Many other species visit at certain months or alight on their way up or down the Flyway.

Your trail returns landward near the treatment plant. When the current NASA planning process concludes, the Bay Trail will continue north from Sunnyvale Baylands Park to Shoreline at Mountain View.

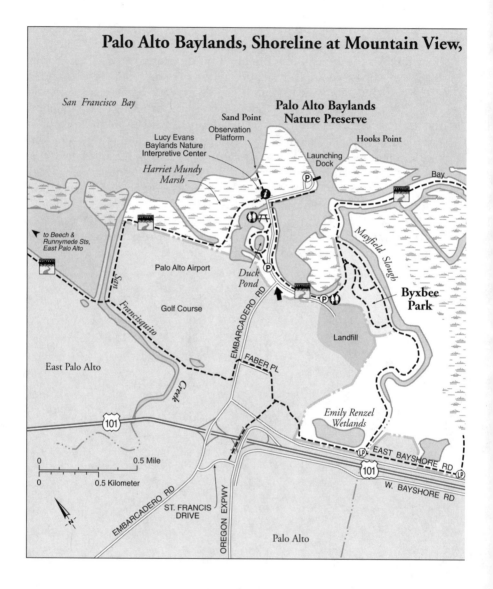

Palo Alto Baylands, Shoreline at Mountain View,

San Francisco Bay

Palo Alto Baylands Nature Preserve

Sand Point

Observation Platform

Lucy Evans Baylands Nature Interpretive Center

Hooks Point

Launching Dock

Harriet Mundy Marsh

Bay

to Beech & Runnymede Sts, East Palo Alto

Mayfield Slough

Palo Alto Airport

Duck Pond

Byxbee Park

San

Golf Course

EMBARCADERO RD

East Palo Alto

Landfill

Creek

Francisquito

FABER PL

101

Emily Renzel Wetlands

0   0.5 Mile

0   0.5 Kilometer

EAST BAYSHORE RD

101

W. BAYSHORE RD

N

EMBARCADERO RD

ST. FRANCIS DRIVE

OREGON EXPWY

Palo Alto

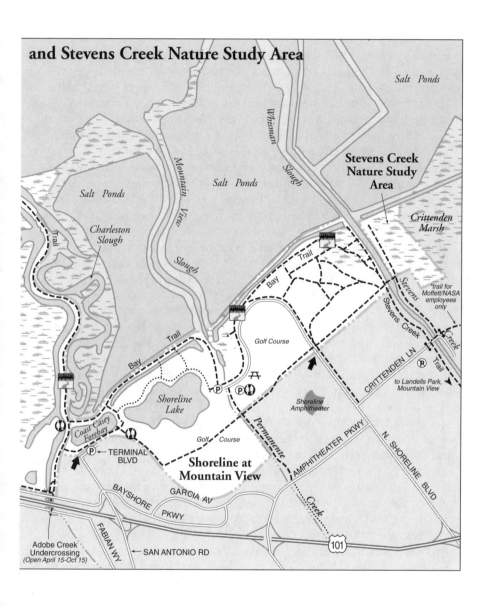

and Stevens Creek Nature Study Area

Salt Ponds

Whisman

Slough

Salt Ponds

Stevens Creek Nature Study Area

Crittenden Marsh

Mountain View

Salt Ponds

Salt Ponds

Trail

Charleston Slough

Slough

Bay Trail

Stevens Creek

*trail for Moffett/NASA employees only

Trail

Bay Trail

Golf Course

Stevens Creek

CRITTENDEN LN

to Landells Park, Mountain View

Bay Trail

Shoreline Lake

Shoreline Amphitheater

CRITTENDEN LN

N. SHORELINE BLVD

AMPHITHEATER PKWY

Permanente

Coast Casey Forebay

Golf Course

Golf Course

TERMINAL BLVD

Shoreline at Mountain View

BAYSHORE PKWY

GARCIA AV

Creek

FABIAN WY

Adobe Creek Undercrossing *(Open April 15-Oct 15)*

← SAN ANTONIO RD

101

✦ Shoreline at Mountain View ✦

In the summer of 1983 the City of Mountain View opened its Shoreline. By the early 1990s the yearly attendance had reached a million people. Strollers, hikers, runners and bicyclists enjoy over 7 miles of paved paths along bayfront, sloughs and marshes. Observation platforms and benches attract birdwatchers. A 50-acre lake for canoeing, small boating and windsurfing now has a boat house. Shoreline offers picnicking on meadows by its shores and an 18-hole golf course and clubhouse.

Shoreline's 544 acres, built on gently rolling terrain over mountains of revenue-bringing sanitary landfill from San Francisco, have been sculpted to create meadows, the lake and the golf course. Fittingly, methane gas is now piped back to San Francisco, providing further revenue.

Trail connections north to Palo Alto's Bay Trail and the trail along Charleston Slough expand opportunities for hikers, runners and bicyclists to explore more of the Bayland scene. Two boardwalks south over the Shoreline's tidal marshes and a bridge over Stevens Creek bring bird enthusiasts and ecologists to the Stevens Creek Nature Study Area of the Midpeninsula Regional Open Space District (MROSD).

As you drive in the main entrance along Shoreline Boulevard, you pass an 18-hole golf course and pro shop and parking. Past the golf course on the left stands the historic Rengstorff house, now restored as a museum and quarters for park administration. Henry Rengstorff built this handsome 16-room house in 1866, with pillared portico and classic pediment over its doorway. Rengstorff came to California during the Gold Rush but chose instead of mining to work on a steamer plying between San Francisco and Alviso. He soon had money to buy a farm and build a warehouse at his pier at the end of Shoreline Boulevard.

The main parking lots are in the center of Shoreline near the lake and golf course. Trips are described from there. The route of the regional San Francisco Bay Trail follows the Bay Trail through Shoreline. Bicycle trails on Shoreline Boulevard and along East Bayshore to Adobe Creek also give access from the cities nearby.

Jurisdiction: City of Mountain View.

Facilities: Trails: hiking, bicycling. Wheelchair access. Lake for small boats, windsurfing, canoeing, boat rental. Marshland nature-study area. Golf course.

Park Rules: Hours: gates open sunrise to dusk. No dogs.

Maps: City of Mountain View *Shoreline.* USGS quad *Mountain View.*

How to Get There: *By Car:* From Hwy. 101 turn east on Shoreline Blvd. and go 1 mile to park entrance. Parking lots on main road near lake. Or park at the end of San Antonio Rd. at Terminal Ave. to access the Coast Casey Forebay Trail.

By Bicycle: Bike lanes on Shoreline Blvd. Palo Alto's Bayfront Trail along East Bayshore Rd. enters the north end of Shoreline at Adobe Creek.

Shoreline at Mountain View
SHORELINE'S BAY TRAIL TO THE CHARLESTON SLOUGH FOREBAY

A walk by Mountain View Slough to the water's edge by a salt pond and along Charleston Slough forebay with a loop trip back by the lake.

Distance: 3-mile loop

Time: 1½ hours

Elevation Change: Nearly level

Trail Notes

From the parking lot near the lake, find the Bay Trail heading bayward along the west side of Mountain View Slough, where you can watch the ebb and flow of the tides, and the avocets, dowitchers and willets feeding on the muddy banks. On the shoreward side of the trail are grassy meadows for picnicking and playing.

Your trail turns west away from the slough, following the edge of the salt pond below. Short trails lead from your trail up through shrubs and grasslands over a low ridge to the lakeside, but you continue ahead toward Charleston Slough.

The expanse of water you look out over is the Cargill Salt Company's number-one salt-evaporator pond, where water is admitted in summer at its highest salinity. San Francisco Bay is one of the few places in the country suitable for making salt by solar evaporation. (See Alviso Slough Trail Notes for a description of the process.)

A few duck blinds, still used, dot the salt pond. Their ownership has been handed down in families for 75 years. All blinds are at least 500 yards from shore, so you are safely beyond range of buckshot. Duck hunting, under state and federal license, is permitted during three winter months.

After a half-mile stroll along the path where you look across the pond to the levee bordering Charleston Slough, you turn down to its forebay on Shoreline's boundary. The path circles the forebay and its fresh-water marsh and islands. Along the path information panels describe the great variety of birds resting and nesting here.

322   SOUTH BAY TRAILS

You will find good birdwatching in the marshes. Stately egrets often pick their way along muddy banks or search through pickleweed for small animals. Avocets sweep the shallow waters with their upturned bills. Meadowlarks, blackbirds, burrowing owls, song sparrows and many others find enough dry land in the nearby flood-control basin for nesting.

You reach a junction with Palo Alto's 6-mile loop trail around the city's flood-control basin and Charleston Slough, a northward extension of the Bay Trail. To return to the parking lot in Shoreline at Mountain View, complete the circle around the forebay and take the Lake Trail eastward, paralleling Shoreline Lake. Young trees frame lake vistas, and green lawns invite picnickers. On weekends bright-sailed windsurfers skim the waters, and golfers beyond breathe fresh air as they pursue their balls.

2 Shoreline at Mountain View
SHORELINE WALK SOUTH TO THE MARSH

For birdwatching and a breath of salt air, walk past Mountain View Slough at the edge of a salt pond to a marshland nature-study area by Stevens Creek.

Distance: 3.5 mile loop

Time: 2 hours

Elevation Change: Level

Trail Notes

This trail, hard-surfaced for easy bicycling, goes east past marshlands to Shoreline's edge along a salt pond and to a vista point at the marsh, then loops back around the former landfill. It is very popular with employees at nearby industrial plants for a noon-time run or in-line skating. Start east from the parking lot around the Mountain View Tidal Marsh, and at the first junction go left on the levee at the edge of Pond A-2, still a functioning salt production pond. Imagine the scene as it was a hundred years ago. Then you would have been standing at about the edge of the Bay's upland marsh, where cordgrass gave way to pickleweed and salt grass. Up sloughs through marshes like this came boats from the Bay to Rengstorff's Landing. Grain and hay from fields nearby and wine from Cupertino vineyards, loaded from Henry Rengstorff's warehouses, sailed on schooners and steamers for San Francisco.

Earlier still, Indians harvested shellfish and netted birds from these sloughs. The site of the largest of their shellmounds in the South Bay is a few miles away, at Castro Station. Further back in time, during the

Pleistocene Epoch, mastodons, sloths and camels roamed the valley that was here before ocean waters flooded it. Their fossils have come to light in excavations nearby.

Returning to the present, continue on the trail as it curves right (south), paralleling Stevens Creek Marsh, which is on your left. When breezes blow away the smog, the East Bay hills look close, and the dark Santa Cruz Mountains fill the western skyline. Numerous benches invite a pause, and excellent interpretive signs explain the marshland habitat along your route.

Turning to the tidal marsh below, you will find in any season shore and water birds that rest and nest in the marsh and ponds. Wintering coots, slate-colored with ivory-white bills, bob as they swim in the pond, diving for vegetable matter in the shallow water. Resident ducks will be joined in winter and spring by many migrant species.

A bridge over Stevens Creek leads to the Stevens Creek Nature Study Area, described below.

To complete your trip in Shoreline at Mountain View, take the trail to the right leading to "Gatehouse." This traverses the former landfill and you have a good view of Shoreline Amphitheater, a striking structure with twin tent-like peaks, visible for many miles. Built on another section of the former landfill, this venue hosts large concerts and other events all summer.

◆ Stevens Creek Nature Study Area ◆

See maps on pages 318 and 319.

The narrow strip of marshland along the east side of Stevens Creek set aside as a nature-study area has kept much of the character of such Baylands before the South Bay was diked and filled. The 54-acre Midpeninsula Regional Open Space Preserve lies across the creek from Shoreline at Mountain View at the northwest corner of Moffett Field. The MROSD acquired the preserve in the 1970's to provide public access to this unique marshland for study and research.

Crittenden Marsh occupies about three fourths of the preserve. The marsh is not subject to tidal flow from the creek but receives fresh-water drainage from adjacent Moffett Field, making brackish marsh of particular interest for research. However, the nearby wetlands at Shoreline at Mountain View do receive tidal waters in channels from the creek.

Although the preserve does contain salt-tolerant plants, some of its vegetation is that of a fresh-water marsh. Consequently, birds and other wildlife of a fresh-water marsh are found here, along with the array of species that frequent the ponds and salt marshes nearby. The preserve is a nesting area for waterfowl and shore birds and a resting place for migrating birds in winter.

Jurisdiction: MROSD

Facilities: The study area has a compacted surface trail along the creek levee but is otherwise undeveloped.

Preserve Rules: Hours: 7 A.M. to dusk when Shoreline at Mountain View is open. Stay on the trail. No dogs. No hunting.

Map: USGS quad *Mountain View.*

How to Get There: Access is through Shoreline at Mountain View, reached from Hwy. 101 via Shoreline Blvd. Either park at the golf course and walk east around it for about a mile, then go left to the bridge over Stevens Creek, or, alternatively, from Shoreline Blvd., turn right on Crittenden Lane to the end. Here is another bridge over Stevens Creek, for pedestrians, bicyclists and service vehicles; you may find an undeveloped piece of ground nearby to leave your car. The industrial plants warn you not to use their paved parking lots.

Trail Notes

A levee trail parallels the east bank of Stevens Creek heading north for about 0.5 mile, then has a short bend to the east. Visitors must not trespass further on the levee system of salt pond trails. As you return to the bridge, look up to Black Mountain on Monte Bello Ridge in the west, behind which are the headwaters of this creek. Named after Elisha Stephens, captain of the Stephens wagon party that crossed the Sierra Nevada in 1844 with some of the earliest immigrants to California, the creek's spelling has been altered since this settler died in 1884. High in MROSD's Monte Bello Open Space Preserve Stevens Creek begins its circuitous 23-mile journey to the Bay. After flowing southeast in the San Andreas Fault canyon, it bends north around the end of Monte Bello Ridge through Stevens Creek County Park, where it is dammed. The Stevens Creek Trail follows the lower course of the creek (for map of Stevens Creek Trail, see page 280).

Environmental study groups find these marshes fruitful for their investigations. The area is a birder's paradise for species whose habitat is freshwater marsh, and a patient birder with a scope might add a new species to his or her list. Ducks in variety are here, as are migrating waterfowl in season. Above, the northern harrier hawks find perches high in the utility towers that cross the preserve.

The huge hangars at Moffett Field now are under the control of NASA (National Aeronautic and Space Administration). NASA has just begun a planning process that will lead to future development of the former Naval Air Station. These plans will include completion of the San Francisco Bay Trail around the north side of the complex, where it will complete the link between Shoreline at Mountain View and Sunnyvale Baylands Park. Planned to be on the existing levees, this long has been a dream of Bay Trail advocates.

◆ Palo Alto Baylands Nature Preserve ◆

See maps on pages 318 and 319.

The City of Palo Alto preserves, in its Baylands, 120 acres of salt marsh and slough as a wildlife sanctuary. The adjacent 600-acre flood-control basin extends south to Charleston Slough and Shoreline at Mountain View. The San Francisco Bay Trail runs north through Palo Alto Baylands from Runnymede Street in East Palo Alto to Shoreline at Mountain View to the south.

The striking Lucy Evans Nature Interpretive Center in the Baylands, designed by William Busse, stands on pilings by a levee at the edge of the marsh. A glass wall faces Bayward to changing scenes of marsh and water. Timely displays, meeting rooms, a library and an open laboratory make this building a lively focus of activity for visitors. Programs on Bay ecology, slide shows, movies and children's workshops are scheduled throughout the year. Weekend walks conducted by the center's naturalists are an inspiring introduction to the special world at the edge of the Bay. The Lucy Evans Nature Interpretive Center and the Harriet Mundy Marsh surrounding it honor two women who crusaded in the 1960s and 1970s for Baylands preservation and were instrumental in securing this sanctuary for our education and enjoyment.

Marshland near the former yacht basin is being restored and a new pier has been built near the Charleston Slough channel at the east end of Harriet Mundy Marsh for launching small watercraft. Trails along levees, boardwalks over marshes, and even a display of modern sculpture in Byxbee Park on a restored section of the city's landfill give you a representative sample of Baylands environments.

Jurisdiction: City of Palo Alto.

Facilities: Nature Interpretive Center, boardwalk and observation platform, pier for launching windsurfing craft, duck pond. Trails: hiking, bicycling. Naturalist programs.

Wheelchair access to Interpretive Center. 14 miles of trails.

Park Rules: Hours: trails, sunrise to sunset; Interpretive Center, Tuesday through Friday, 2-5 P.M., Saturday and Sunday, 1-5 P.M.; Dogs must be on leash at all times. Phone: 650-329-2506.

Maps: Palo Alto *Baylands Nature Preserve*. USGS quad *Mountain View*.

How to Get There: *By Car:* From Bayshore Freeway (Hwy. 101) go east on Embarcadero Rd. 0.7 mile to sign for Baylands, turn left to parking lots along road.

By Bicycle: Take bicycle/pedestrian bridge over freeway from Oregon Ave., cross East Bayshore Rd. and follow bike/path to Faber Place. Turn north on Embarcadero Rd. bike lanes east to preserve.

Palo Alto Baylands Nature Preserve
BOARDWALK TO BAY VIEW

A short exploration of the Baylands takes you on the boardwalk to an observation platform on the edge of the Bay.

Distance: 0.23 mile one way

Time: ½ hour

Elevation Change: Level.

Trail Notes

If this is your first trip to the Baylands, be sure to allow at least an hour to visit the Interpretive Center. Pick up the informative booklets describing plants and animals of the marsh and the self-guiding Nature Trail for a boardwalk tour. Now, armed with your guides to tidelands, binoculars at the ready, start from the Interpretive Center. Walk around the deck to the Bayward side of the building and follow the wide boardwalk across the marsh. Cordgrass, pickleweed and salt grass are right below you, just waiting to be identified. The colors of the marsh vary by the season, changing from the fresh green of cordgrass in spring to gold and brown as it dries in fall, then enlivened by an edging of the rusty red of pickleweed in winter. On boardwalk benches you can pause and watch for birds feeding in the marsh. If you are very lucky, you may glimpse the rare clapper rail pecking about in the mud. About the size of a small chicken, this poor flyer has an orange bill and un-webbed feet, and somewhat resembles the famous New Zealand kiwi bird.

If the tide is very high, the water may be up to the middle of the pickleweed, but at low tide even the stems are out of water. The different plants of the marsh are adapted to varying degrees of salt concentration in water and soil. They also tolerate different periods of submergence by the tides. Salt grass and pickleweed live just above all but the highest tides; cordgrass grows where it is partly submerged at each tide. Pickleweed keeps salt in vacuoles, or cavities, in its stems, whereas cordgrass absorbs salt water and exudes little crystals of salt on its leaves.

Continue out the boardwalk in the Harriet Mundy Marsh to the viewing platform at the edge of the Bay. This vantage point offers a chance to see many species of shore birds, each feeding at the water level to which its legs and bill are adapted. Even the untrained observer can note the difference in bill lengths and in the motions the birds make in seeking their food. For example, the avocet uses its long, upward-curving bill to sweep the shallow waters and disturb small invertebrates for its meal. The short-legged and short-billed sandpipers find their food at the receding water's edge. The long-billed curlew is easy to spot by its downturned bill and its habit of feeding with its head down in the water as it probes for clams and worms.

The marsh from a distance seems an unbroken stretch of cordgrass. At close hand from the walkway, however, you see it in its complexity, broken by little sloughs, muddy-banked at low tide or brimming with water at high tide. Look down at the banks of mud 3-4' thick, composed of layers of silt washed down from the hills, and now rich enough to grow cordgrass, one of the world's most productive land plants as measured by yield per acre.

Palo Alto Baylands Nature Preserve
WALK TO SAN FRANCISQUITO CREEK

A bird-watching trip takes you along the lagoon and around the airport to San Francisquito Creek on the San Francisco Bay Trail, then on a loop around the golf course.

Distance: 3 miles loop

Time: 2 hours

Elevation Change: Level. The first 0.25 mile is suitable for wheelchairs.

Trail Notes

For this trip take the levee path north from the Interpretive Center that leads beside the lagoon, with its population of anglers, birds and birdwatchers. On the bayward side of the path, the Harriet Mundy Marsh extends to the Bay. You are now on a segment of the San Francisco Bay Trail, which is projected, when complete, to run 400 miles around the shores of San Francisco Bay. The segment within Palo Alto now is complete.

At any tide you will see in the lagoon some of the birds that reside in these Baylands. In fall and winter, especially in the early mornings and evenings, or when low tides expose mud flats in the lagoon, this levee walk is a birder's delight. Snowy egrets stalk the waters; flocks of willets alight and take off with a flash of black-and-white wings; muddy banks are alive with scampering least sandpipers.

Northern pintails, the commonest of California ducks, dot the waters or fly off in a haphazard V. You may see a flight of white pelicans, their immense white wings catching the light as they turn in perfect formation. Mallards, which are Baylands residents, will usually be in sight. And always there are gulls of many species taking off, alighting and wheeling in the air on their way to and from the nearby garbage dump.

Even experienced birders may pick up a new find for their lists. The rank amateur will soon be able to identify a good many birds with the help of the illustrated leaflet from the Center. Shore and waterbirds, in general, are easier to identify than the modest little birds of the woodlands, which are so quick to dart out of sight into the trees. In contrast, birds of sloughs and marshes congregate in numbers, often stand still and have bold markings—and most are of good size.

A conducted bird walk with a Baylands naturalist will have you confidently checking off your list on your next visit. Ask at the Interpretive Center for the walk schedule. Even on your own, however, you are bound to enjoy the sights and sounds on this fringe of the Bay.

Your trail continues beyond the lagoon on a straight levee between Palo Alto's airport and marshlands. The sight and sound of planes are constant and quite distracting on this trail. You cross the outlet flow from the Water Quality Control Plant, where tertiary-treated sewage from Palo Alto and Stanford is discharged into the Bay.

In spring, watch the edge of the path for pygmy blue butterflies, pale blue and fingernail-sized, the smallest butterfly in North America. You will find them clustered on the foot-high Australian saltbush, which has been naturalized here. At any time of year you will see California ground squirrels scurrying from the weeds to their burrows.

Peninsula Baylands slough

Cattails and tules grow near the trail, attesting to the existence of a fresh-water marsh. In a little over 0.5 mile the trail reaches the San Francisquito Creek Channel and continues along its levee to a bridge over the creek. Gathering waters from the eastern flanks of the Santa Cruz Mountains, this creek is one of the largest on the Peninsula, forming the boundary between San Mateo and Santa Clara counties. The course of the creek was altered in the 1950s from its original channel into the Bay east of Harriet Mundy Marsh. Along this straight, reconstructed creek channel the trail is on a levee until reaching the bridge over the creek. The Bay Trail continues north along the levee in San Mateo County as far as Runnymede Street in East Palo Alto. There are plans, not yet implemented, to extend this section of the Bay Trail to MROSD's Ravenswood Preserve and thence to the Dumbarton Bridge.

Your route, however, turns left (southeast) following the creek on one side and the golf course on the other, to the Baylands Athletic Center ballfield. From here your return route is along Geng Road and Embarcadero Road sidewalks 1.8 miles back to the Interpretive Center (or you can return the way you came).

Palo Alto Baylands Nature Preserve
DUCK POND

Give your children a few scraps of dry bread, and the waterfowl in the Duck Pond will provide an exciting adventure, which you can follow with a walk around the pond's perimeter to a picnic area by the slough.

Distance: 0.75 mile

Time: ½ hour

Elevation Change: Level

Trail Notes

You need no guidebook to bring the ducks and geese to you begging for food. The year-round residents wait for handouts and jostle one another fighting for scraps. As early as February young mallards are hatching, and soon they are paddling after their mothers on the pond. Your young charges may be more interested in the action of the birds than in identifying the species, but you might enjoy the leaflet on ducks from the Interpretive Center.

After the bread is gone and the children need a romp, take the short path that circles the east end of the Duck Pond. In less than 0.5 mile you will find a picnic table set among remnants of plantings from a former dwelling. In spring birds nest in the undergrowth here, so it is best to stay on the walkway.

The path circles back to the Duck Pond, from where you can continue east along the road to the Interpretive Center. If time and attention allow, many of the displays there, such as mounted birds and a harbor seal, are interesting to small children.

Palo Alto Baylands Nature Preserve
A LOOP AROUND THE FLOOD-CONTROL BASIN

A trip around Palo Alto's flood control basin takes you to the bracing breezes at the Bay's edge and birdwatching along Charleston Slough.

Distance: 7-mile loop

Time: 3-4 hours

Elevation Change: Level

Trail Notes

There are two good starting places for a circuit around Palo Alto's Flood Basin: the parking lot on East Bayshore Road 0.5 mile northwest of Adobe Creek, and the Lucy Evans Interpretive Center described above. This trip begins at the Interpretive Center, near which you can leave your vehicle.

Start walking south across the culvert under Embarcadero Road, just beyond the gate to the Interpretive Center. Your trail, on the left (east) side of the road, soon passes by the old Sea Scout building, the Chester Wrucke, named after an early supporter of the Scouts. The yacht club and docks once were in this same area, but were removed at the time the marsh restoration began, in the late 1970s. The yacht harbor has silted up since the days when San Francisquito Creek flowed across the Palo Alto Baylands to the Bay. In the 1950s Palo Alto decided to build an airport and golf course, and legislation was passed that allowed the city to move not only the creek bed but the county line westward, shrinking the size of the future East Palo Alto and increasing Palo Alto's acreage. The Sea Scout building is in poor repair, subject to flooding in high tides, and its ultimate fate is undecided.

Continuing south you walk on a section of trail covered with crushed oyster shells, installed in early 2000 to fill in a missing segment of the Bay Trail. Coyote brush shields you from the garbage trucks on Embarcadero Road as you curve around toward Byxbee Park. On your right is the mas-

One example of an earthwork sculpture along a side trip from the Bay Trail

sive, rust-colored complex of buildings known as the Regional Water Quality Control Plant (read "sewage treatment plant"), from which the tertiary-treated effluent flows in pipes to divulge into the Bay west of the lagoon by the Interpretive Center.

Just beyond this facility is the Recycling Center, which Palo Alto hopes will eventually largely replace the old landfill area (the dump) which rises in front of you. A large section of the dump already has been "capped" with soil, and planted with grass and trees, and is called Byxbee Park after an early Palo Alto landowner. If you would like a side trip, walk around this interesting mound to look at the various sculptures and other displays of art works. Vistas across the Bay are splendid from the hilltop. Methane gas still is being piped out of this former landfill and is used to generate electricity. A fenced-off area contains the gas-operated generating facility.

Passing the interesting displays at Byxbee Park, you curve around on a levee toward the northeast at the mouth of Mayfield Slough. To your right now is the Palo Alto Flood Basin, which is impounded by levees controlled by tidal gates. During times of heavy winter rain the gates remain closed, so that high tides cannot enter and back the flood waters into the city. At other times of year the gates open and close to let the Bay water flow in and out, maintaining a salt-water-marsh environment.

As you continue on this levee, signs of earlier Bay fill projects are visible, but in general the marsh is restoring itself. There was a duck-shooting club in this area up to the late 1970s; the levee trail was closed by a sign and a flag was raised whenever the hunters were shooting. Catwalks and blinds are slowly disappearing.

Your trail turns south and west beyond a massive set of new flood gates, and you reach a series of excellent interpretive signs as you parallel Charleston Slough, created by the outlet of Adobe Creek. You may wish to stop at one of the numerous benches on a sunny day to watch birds in the slough around you. Soon the Bay Trail heads left (southeast) to Shoreline at Mountain View, but your route continues straight toward Bayshore Freeway (Highway 101), past Mountain View's Coast Casey pumping station.

When you reach the paved path along Bayshore take it to the right (north) and walk parallel to the freeway to a small parking lot on your right. A trail leading 0.25 mile out into the flood basin is popular with bird-watchers. Dogs (which are allowed on-leash in all Palo Alto's Baylands) may not use this trail during the nesting season between March and June.

Past the animal shelter and the municipal service area you reach Gate F on your right, from where a trail leads north between the Emily Renzel Marsh, a freshwater habitat, and Matadero Creek and the Mayfield Slough, a tidal saltwater habitat. The freshwater marsh is named for Emily Renzel, long an environmental activist and a former Palo Alto Councilwoman. For a mile and a half you walk on a levee or on remains of the dump, along the east shore of Byxbee Park, to reach the Bay Trail on which you started. Turn left (northwest) to return to the Interpretive Center.

Appendix A: Guide to Choosing a Trail

Trails for Different Seasons and Reasons

SPRING FLOWERS

Ed R. Levin Park	Los Coches Trails
Joseph D. Grant Park	San Felipe Trail
	Hall's Valley Trail
	Los Huecos Trail
Henry W. Coe State Park	Corral Trail to Arnold Field
	Frog Lake Trail to Coe Monument on Pine Ridge
	Loop Trip to Kelly Lake
	Northern Heights Route to Miller Field
Calero Park	Figueroa Trail
	Javelina Loop to Fish Camp
	Cherry Cove Trail to Cherry and Miner's coves
Big Basin Redwoods State Park	China Grade Rd. to Park HQ
	Sempervirens Falls Loop

SUMMER STROLLS—*Cool canyons, shady streams, breezy Baylands*

Alum Rock Park	Creek Trail—upstream
Sanborn-Skyline Park	Skyline Trail
Calero Park	Figueroa Trail
	Cherry Cove Trail to Cottle Rest Site
Uvas Canyon Park	Swanson Creek Trail—1st part
	Uvas Creek Trail
Mt. Madonna Park	Redwood Trail
	Blackhawk Trail
Coyote Creek	Trail through Coyote Hellyer Park
Baylands Trail for Bay Breezes	
Big Basin Redwoods State Park	Redwood Loop
	Creeping Forest/Dool Trail Loop
Castle Rock State Park	Sandstone Formations
	Loop Through Center of Park

FALL COLOR

Alum Rock Park	Creek Trail
Henry W. Coe State Park	Poverty Flat
	The Narrows
	Gill Route on Orestimba and Red creeks
Almaden Quicksilver Park	Guadalupe Trail
Calero Park	Figueroa Trail along Calero Creek
Uvas Canyon Park	Uvas Creek Trail
Mt. Madonna Park	Blackhawk Trail

Big Basin Redwoods State Park To Pine Mtn. and Buzzard's Roost
Sempervirens Falls Loop
Castle Rock State Park Saratoga Gap Trail
Sempervirens Point through Meadows

WINTER WALKING ON SURFACED PATHS BETWEEN SHOWERS

Alum Rock Park Creek Trail
Coyote Creek Trails Coyote Hellyer Park to Burnett Avenue
Kelley Park
Penitencia Creek Trail
Palo Alto Baylands Boardwalks to observation platform
Los Alamitos Creek Villagewood Drive to Harry Road
Los Gatos Creek Trails Entire trail
Mountain View's Shoreline
Coyote Hills Regional Park Bayview Trail and Boardwalks
Don Edwards San Francisco
Bay National Wildlife Refuge Tidelands Trail
Fremont/Warm Springs Bay Trail
Guadalupe River Park
Sunnyvale Baylands Park
Big Basin Redwoods State Park Redwood Loop

WINTER HIKES ON SUNNY SLOPES

Mission Peak Regional Preserve Peak Trail
Alum Rock Park North Rim Trail to Eagle Rock
Joseph D. Grant Park Hotel Trail to Eagle Lake
Henry W. Coe State Park Corral and Springs trails to Manzanita Point
China Hole to Mahoney Meadows
Sierra Azul Open Space Hike to Priest Rock
Preserve Loop on Priest Rock Trail to Kennedy Road
junction and PG&E service road
Bald Mountain Ramble
Almaden Quicksilver Park Mine Hill Trail to Bull Run
Uvas Canyon Park Fire Trail Hike to Nibbs Knob and Summit Road
Coyote Hills Regional Park Bayview Trail
Castle Rock State Park Saratoga Gap Trail

From Short Walks to Long Hikes

EASY LEVEL STROLLS—*Walk as far as you wish*

Alum Rock Park Creek Trail
Joseph D. Grant Ranch Hotel Trail—1st part
Sanborn-Skyline Park Skyline Trail/Bay Area Ridge Trail to Saratoga Gap
Lake Ranch Reservoir Trail from Beach Road
Calero Park Figueroa Trail along Calero Creek
Mt. Madonna Park Loop Trail—1st mile from Old Mt. Madonna Road
All Baylands and Creek trails

SHORT TRIPS—*Less than 5 miles round trip*

Ed. R. Levin Park	Los Coches Trails
Alum Rock Park	South Rim Loop
	Circle Hike to Eagle Rock
Joseph D. Grant Park	Trails in Hall's Valley
	The Lake Loop
	Hike to Park's East Ridge
Henry W. Coe State Park	Lion Spring Jaunt
	Climb to Coe Monument
Sanborn-Skyline Park	Circle Hike to Todd Redwoods
	Loop Trip to the Hilltop and back by the creek
St. Joseph's Hill Open Space Preserve	A Loop Trip to the Hilltop and back by the creek
Sierra Azul Open Space Preserve	Bald Mountain Ramble
Almaden Quicksilver Park	Senator Mine and Guadalupe Trails Loop
Santa Teresa Park	All trips in this park
Calero Park	Climb to the ridge and return along the lake
	Figueroa Trail by Calero Creek to the Old Corral
Uvas Canyon Park	Loop Trip to Waterfalls
Mt. Madonna Park	Circle trip through Banks and Blackhawk Canyons
	Ecological Sampler
Los Gatos Creek	Campbell Park to Vasona Lake Park—one way
	Forbes Flour Mill to Lexington Dam
El Sereno	Hike to the Meadow
Big Basin Redwoods State Park	Redwood Loop
	Creeping forest/Dool Trail Loop
	Sempervirens Falls Loop
	Waterman Gap to China Grade Road
	China Grade Road to Park HQ
	To Pine Mtn. and Buzzards Roost
	Eagle Rock Ascent

LONG TRIPS *From 5 to 10 miles roundtrip*

Mission Peak Regional Preserve	The Three Trips to the Peak
Ed R. Levin Park	Monument Peak Trail
Joseph D. Grant Park	Dutch Flat Trail to the West Ridge
	Cañada de Pala Trail on the East Ridge
Henry W. Coe State Park	Loop Trip to Middle Ridge via Frog Lake
	Poverty Flat Circle Hike via Middle Ridge
	Circle Hike along Springs and Forest Trails
	2 Loop Trips from Manzanita Point
Sanborn-Skyline Park	Skyline Trail/Bay Area Ridge Trail to Saratoga Gap —one way with shuttle
Sierra Azul Open Space Preserve	Kennedy Trail Ascent of the North Slopes
	Loop hike to Priest Rock
Almaden Quicksilver Park	Mine Hill Traik—one way with shuttle

	Randol Road and Mine Hill Trails Loop
Calero Park	To Cherry Cove and Cottle Rest site
	Javelina Loop Trip
Uvas Canyon Park	Fire Trail Hike to Nibbs Knob and Summit Road
Coyote Creek Trail	Coyote Hellyer Park to Emado Avenue—one way with shuttle
Coyote Hills Regional Park	Shoreline Loop Trail
Don Edwards San Francisco Bay National Wildlife Refuge	Newark Slough Trail
	Alviso Slough Trail
Palo Alto Baylands	Loop Hike around Flood-Control Basin
Castle Rock State Park	Saratoga Gap Trail
	Center of Park Loops
	Historic Toll Road Loop

EXPEDITIONS—*Trips of more than 10 miles*

Mission Peak Regional Preserve	Ohlone Wilderness Trail to Del Valle Regional Park
Joseph D. Grant Park	Washburn Trail to Deer Valley
Henry W. Coe State Park	The Big Loop
	Mahoney Meadows Loop from Park Headquarters
	Loop Trips to Mississippi, Kelly and Coit Lake
	Trips into Orestimba Wilderness
	The Big Loop
	Loop Trip to Kelly Lake from Coyote Creek Entrance
	Loop Trip to Redfern Pond
Almaden Quicksilver Park	Mine Hill Trail roundtrip
Calero Park	Miner's Cove via Figueroa Trail and Javelina Loop
Coyote Creek	Coyote Hellyer Park Upstream to Metcalf Road or Emado Avenue roundtrip
Sierra Azul Open Space Preserve	Woods Trail one-way
Big Basin Redwoods State Park	Triple Waterfalls Hike
	Down to the Sea on Foot
	To Mt. McAbee Overlook Alternate

BACKPACK TRIPS TO TRAIL CAMPS

Mission Peak Regional Preserve	Ohlone Wilderness Trail to Backpack Camps enroute to Del Valle Regional Park
Sanborn-Skyline Park	Skyline Trail to Trail Camps in:
	Castle Rock State Park
	Big Basin State Park
	Monte Bello Open Space Preserve
Henry W. Coe State Park	Loop Trip to Kelly Lake from Coyote Creek Entrance
	Loop Trip to Redfern Pond

Castle Rock State Park Saratoga Gap and Ridge trails
to backpack camps

DOWNHILL ALL THE WAY—*With a car shuttle*
Joseph D. Grant Park Cañada de Pala and Hotel trails from
Mt. Hamilton Road to Park Office
Sanborn-Skyline Park Skyline and Sanborn Trails to Park Office
Mt. Madonna Park Downhill Hike from Redwoods to Lakeshore on
Loop and Merry-Go-Round trails
Blackhawk Trail to Sprig Lake
Los Gatos Creek Trail From Lexington Dam to Forbes Flour Mill

Trails Suited to Different Travelers

FOR EQUESTRIANS—*With horse staging area—H*
Mission Peak Regional Preserve Trails from Stanford Avenue—H
Ed R. Levin Park—H
Alum Rock Park North Rim Trail
Joseph D. Grant Park—H Trails to East and West ridges and Bay Area
Ridge Trail
Henry W. Coe State Park—H Trails from Hunting Hollow and Coyote Creek
entrances
Sierra Azul Open Space Kennedy Road Trail
Preserve Woods Trail
Almaden Quicksilver Park—H
Calero Park—H
Santa Teresa Park—H
Mt. Madonna Park—H
Coyote Hills Regional Park—H Alameda Creek Regional Trail to Niles (north side)
Big Basin Redwoods State Park Sandy Point—Gazos Creek Road entrance
Basin Trail
Certain sections of the Skyline-to-the-Sea Trail

PAVED PATHS FOR BICYCLISTS
Alum Rock Park Creek Trail
Park entrance road and old park road from Alum
Rock Avenue entrance
Los Gatos Creek Meridian Avenue to Lexington Dam
Coyote Creek Coyote Hellyer Park to Burnett Avenue
Coyote Hills Regional Park Bayview Trail
Alameda Creek Regional Trail to Niles (south side)
Dumbarton Bridge Bike Lane
Shoreline at Mountain View Bay Trail
Palo Alto Baylands Bay Trail
Sunnyvale Baylands Bay Trail

PARKS PERMITTING MOUNTAIN BICYCLES ON CERTAIN DESIGNATED UNPAVED TRAILS
Mission Peak Regional Preserve
Alum Rock Park
Ed. R. Levin Park
Joseph D. Grant Park
Henry W. Coe State Park
El Sereno Open Space Preserve
St. Joseph's Hill Open Space Preserve
Sierra Azul Open Space Preserve
Santa Teresa Park

WHEELCHAIR RAMBLES

Alum Rock Park	Creek Trail
Kelley Park	
Los Gatos Creek	Meridian Avenue to Los Gatos Creek Park to Forbes Flour Mlll
Coyote Hills Regional Park	Muskrat Trail
	Chochenyo Trail
Don Edwards San Francisco Bay National Wildlife Refuge	Phone for information on access
Shoreline at Mountain View	Bay Trail
Palo Alto Baylands	Boardwalk to observation platform
	Walk to San Francisquito Creek
Big Basin Redwoods State Park	Redwood Loop
Sunnyvale Baylands	Bay Trail
	Trail from Sunnyvale Baylands to Alviso
Coyote Creek Trail	Coyote Hellyer Park to Burnett Park
Stevens Creek Trail	Entire trail

RECOMMENDED FOR RUNNERS—*Training runs on hills and levees and beside creeks*

Alum Rock Park	Rim Trails
Almaden Quicksilver Park	Mine Hill and Randal trails
Sierra Azul Open Space Preserve	Kennedy Road Trail
	Woods Trail
Santa Teresa Park	Coyote Peak Climb
	Hidden Springs/Ohlone Trail Loop
Mt. Madonna Park	Merry-Go-Round Trail
Coyote Creek	Coyote Hellyer Park upstream
Penitencia Creek Trail	
Guadalupe River Park and Gardens	
Los Gatos Creek	Meridian Avenue to Vasona Lake Park
Coyote Hills Regional Preserve	Bayview Trail
	Alameda Creek Regional Trail

Don Edwards San Francisco
Bay National Wildlife Refuge   Newark Slough Trail
                               Alviso Slough Trail
Sunnyvale Baylands Trail
Shoreline at Mountain View
Palo Alto Baylands   Loop Trail around the Flood-Control Basin
Sierra Azul Open Space   Priest Rock Trail
Preserve   Woods Trail

Special Destinations

PEAK CLIMBS

Mission Peak Regional Preserve   The three trips to Mission Peak
Ed R. Levin Park   Monument Peak Trip
Henry W. Coe Park   Hobbs and Blue Ridge roads to Mt. Sizer
                    Loop Trip to Redfern Pond with side trip to
                       Vasquez Peak
Uvas Canyon Park   Fire Trail to Nibbs Knob and Summit Road
Santa Teresa Park   Coyote Peak Climb
Big Basin Redwoods State Park   To Mt. McAbee Overlook
                                To Pine Mtn. and Buzzards Roost
                                Eagle Rock Ascent

LUNCH BY THE LAKE—*Short walks to picnic places*

Ed R. Levin Park   Sandy Wool Lake
Joseph D. Grant Park   Grant Lake
                       The Lake Loop
                       Eagle Lake Loop
Calero Park   Climb to the Ridge and Return along the Lake
Los Gatos Creek   Los Gatos Creek Park percolation ponds
                  Vasona Lake Park
Mt. Madonna Park   Sprig Lake

SECLUDED SITES—*Get away from it all*

Joseph D. Grant Park   Deer Valley
                       Eagle Lake
Henry W. Coe State Park   Madrone Soda Springs
                          Skeel's Meadow
                          Poverty Flat
                          Orestimba Wilderness
Sanborn-Skyline Park   Bonjetti Creek
                       Todd Redwoods
Sierra Azul Open Space   Bald Mountain
Preserve
Calero Park   Cottle Rest Site
              Old Corral
              Fish Camp

Santa Teresa Park	Laurel Springs Rest Area
Uvas Canyon Park	Nibbs Knob
	Triple Falls and Old Logging Camp
Mt. Madonna Park	Banks Canyon
	Miller's Spring on Loop Trail
Castle Rock State Park	Trips through Center of the Park
Big Basin Redwoods State Park	Loop Trip through Opal Creek Watershed
	Triple Waterfalls Hike

BAYLANDS TRIPS TO THE SPECIAL WORLD OF SALT MARSHES

Coyote Hills Regional Park	Shoreline Trail to Ideal Marsh
Don Edwards San Francisco	
Bay National Wildlife Refuge	Newark Slough Trail
	Alviso Slough Trail to Triangle Marsh
Shoreline at Mountain View	Walk South to the Marsh
	North Bayfront Trail to Forebay
Stevens Creek Nature Study Area	Crittenden Marsh
Palo Alto Baylands	Boardwalk
Sunnyvale Baylands	Tom Harvey Marsh

HIKES INTO HISTORY—*Early ranchos, logging, and historic sites*

Mission Peak Regional Preserve	
Ed R. Levin Park	
Alum Rock Park	
Joseph D. Grant Park	
Henry W. Coe State Park	
St. Joseph's Hill Open Space Preserve	
Almaden Quicksilver Park	
Calero Park	
Mt. Madonna Park	Chitactac
Coyote Creek	Kelley Park San Jose Historical Museum
Los Gatos Creek	Forbes Flour Mill Museum
Big Basin Redwood State Park	Logging, homesteading Maddock's Cabin Site
	Rancho del Oso Nature Center
	Museum at Park HQ
Castle Rock State Park	Saratoga Toll Road

NATURAL HISTORY AND SCIENCE—*Interpreted at Visitor Centers*

Alum Rock Park	
Joseph D. Grant Park	
Sanborn-Skyline Park	
Almaden Quicksilver Park	New Almaden Mercury Mining Museum
Mt. Madonna Park	
Coyote Hellyer Park	

Children's Discovery Museum
at Guadalupe River Park
Vasona Lake Park
Coyote Hills Regional Park
Don Edwards San Francisco Bay
National Wildlife Refuge
Palo Alto Baylands Alviso
Big Basin Redwoods State Park Museum and Visitor Center
Castle Rock State Park Interpretive Shelter

Special Occasions

CHILDREN'S OUTINGS—*Short walks, playgrounds, zoos, picnic tables*
Alum Rock Park
Ed R. Levin Park
Mt. Madonna Park
Coyote Creek Kelley Park
Coyote Hellyer Park
Los Gatos Creek Campbell, Los Gatos Creek and Vasona
Lake parks
Coyote Hills Regional Park
Don Edwards San Francisco Bay
National Wildlife Refuge
Palo Alto Baylands

LET'S GO FISHING—*In lakes and streams*
Ed R. Levin Park Sandy Wool Lake
Joseph D. Grant Park Grant, Bass and McCreery lakes
Henry W. Coe State Park Middle Fork of Coyote Creek
China Hole
Kelly Lake
Mississippi Lake
Sanborn-Skyline Park Lake Ranch Reservoir
Mt. Madonna Sprig Lake for children 5-12 only
Coyote Creek Cottonwood Lake at Coyote Hellyer Park
Parkway Lakes at Metcalf Road
Los Gatos Creek Los Gatos Creek Park percolation ponds
Vasona Lake Park

CAMP IN THE PARK—*Out early on the trail*
Joseph D. Grant Park
Henry W. Coe State Park
Sanborn-Skyline Park
Uvas Canyon Park
Mt. Madonna Park
Big Basin Redwoods State Park
Castle Rock State Park Backpack Camp

GROUP GATHERINGS—*With site reserved ahead, hike before lunch*
Ed R. Levin Park
Alum Rock Park
Joseph D. Grant Park
Sanborn-Skyline Park
Santa Teresa Park
Uvas Canyon Park
Mt. Madonna Park
Coyote Creek Kelley Park
              Coyote Hellyer Park
Los Gatos Creek Campbell, Los Gatos Creek and Vasona
                 Lake parks
Shoreline at Mountain View
Sunnyvale Baylands
Big Basin Redwoods State Park.

Many Santa Clara County Parks are served by the Valley Transportation Authority: see phone numbers in Appendix B

Appendix B: Information Sources on Parks, Preserves, Trails and Trail Activities

Public Agencies

Don Edwards San Francisco Bay National Wildlife Refuge
P.O. Box 524
Newark, CA 94560
510-792-0222
http://desfbay.fws.gov

CA Department of Parks and Recreation
Santa Cruz Mountains District
600 Ocean St.
Santa Cruz, CA 95060
408-429-2859
www.parks.ca.gov

Big Basin State Park
831-338-8860

Castle Rock State Park
408-867-2952

Henry W. Coe State Park
P.O. Box 846
Morgan Hill, CA 95038
408-779-2728
http://www.coepark.parks.ca.gov

ABAG/S.F. Bay Trail Project
101 Eighth St., P.O. Box 2050
Oakland, CA 94604
510-464-7900
http://baytrail.abag.ca.gov

Bay Area Ridge Trail Council
26 O'Farrell St., #400
San Francisco, CA 94108
415-391-9300
www.ridgetrail.org

East Bay Regional Park District
2950 Peralto Oaks Ct.
P.O. Box 5381
Oakland CA, 94605
510-635-0135
www.ebparks.org

Midpeninsula Regional Open Space District
330 Distel Circle
Los Altos, CA 94022
650-691-1200
www.openspace.org

Santa Clara County Parks and Recreation Dept.
298 Garden Hill Drive
Los Gatos 95030
408-358-3741
www.parkhere.org

City of Mountain View Parks Department
500 Castro St., P.O. Box 7540
Mountain View, CA 94040
650-903-6326
www.ci.mtview.ca.us

City of Palo Alto Recreation, Open Space and Science Division
250 Hamilton Ave.
Palo Alto, CA 94301
650-329-2261
www.city.palo-alto.ca.us

Lucy Evans Baylands Nature Interpretive Center
2775 Embarcadero Road
Palo Alto, CA 94301
650-329-2506

City of San Jose Regional Parks
333 W. Santa Clara Street
San Jose, CA 95113
408-277-5531
408-277-4191 (reservations)
www.csj.gov

City of Sunnyvale Parks Department
456 W. Olive, P.O. Box 3707
Sunnyvale, CA 94086
408-730-7350
408-730-7709 Baylands Park
www.ci.sunnyvale.ca.us

Organizations Supporting Parks, Sponsoring Hiking, Equestrian, and Bicycling Activities, Environmental Classes, and other Volunteer Activities

American Youth Hostels
P.O. Box 59024
San Jose,CA
408-293-3787
www.hiayh.org

Sanborn Hostel
408-741-0168

Hidden Villa Hostel
650-949-8848

Almaden Cycle Touring Club
P.O. Box 7286
San Jose, CA 95150
www.actc.org

Audubon Society, Santa Clara Valley Chapter
2221 McClellan Rd.
Cupertino, CA 94086
408-252-3747
www.scvas.org

Big Basin Trail Watch Volunteer Program
Linda Yule, Coordinator
Big Basin Volunteer Trail Crew
1210 Garbo Way, Apt. 1
San Jose, CA 95117
408-242-4245
830-338-3238

California Native Plant Society, Santa Clara
Valley Chapter
P.O. Box 19232
Stanford, CA 94309
www.cnps.org
or: *www.stanford.edu/~rawlings/blazcon.htm*

Coe Park Mounted Patrol
c/o H.W.Coe State Park
P.O. Box 275
San Martin, CA 95046
www.coepark.parks.ca.gov

Community Colleges
see local phone listings

Friends of Anderson/Coyote Creek Park
408-268-6541

Friends of Ed. R. Levin County Park
408-946-3333

Friends of Santa Teresa County Park
408-258-2705

Los Gatos Horseman's Association
P.O. Box 1735
Los Gatos, CA 95033
408-354-2307

**Midpeninsula Regional Open Space
District**
130 Distel Circle
Los Altos, CA 94022
650-691-1200
www.openspace.org

**Mountain Parks Foundation
(Big Basin)**
525 North Big Trees Park Rd.
Felton, CA 95018
831-338-7032
mpfslv@yahoo.com

**New Almaden Quicksilver County
Park Association**
408-268-6541

**Peninsula Conservation Center
Foundation**
3921 E. Bayshore Rd.
Palo Alto, CA 94303
650-962-9876
www.pccf.org

Peninsula Open Space Trust (POST)
3000 Sand Hill Rd.
Menlo Park, CA 94025
650-854-7696
www.openspacetrust.org

Pine Ridge Association
P.O. Box 846
Morgan Hill, CA 95038
408-779-2728
www.coepark.parks.ca.gov

Quicksilver Endurance Riders Inc.
P.O. Box 45
New Almaden, CA 95142
408-997-0368
or 408-285-0839

**ROMP (Responsible Organized
Mountain Pedalers)**
P.O. Box 723
Campbell, CA 95005
info@romp.org
www.romp.org

San Martin Horseman's Association
P.O. Box 275
San Martin, CA 95046
www.smhorse.com

**Santa Clara County Horsemen's
Association**
20350 McKean Rd.
San Jose, CA 95031
408-268-6155
www.horsemens.com

**Santa Clara County Parks and
Recreation Dept.**
Joun Heenan, Volunteer Coordinator
408-846-5761

**Santa Cruz Mountains Trail
Association**
P.O. Box 1141
Los Altos, CA 94023
650-988-1984
www.stanford.edu/mhd/trails

Sempervirens Fund
2483 Old Middlefield Way
Mountain View, CA 94040
650-968-4509
www.sempervirens.org

Senior Centers
see local phone listings

Sierra Club, Loma Prieta Chapter
3921 E. Bayshore Rd.
Palo Alto, CA 94303
Sections: Day Hiking, Black Mountain
Group, Guadalupe Group, Family
Outings, Sierra Singles, Singleaires
650-390-8411
www.sierraclub.org/chapters/lomaprieta

Summit Riders
27495 Miller Hill Rd.
Los Gatos, CA 95033
408-353-1466

Trail Center
3921 E. Bayshore Rd.
Palo Alto, CA 94303
650-725-0280
www.trailcenter.org

Western Wheelers
P.O. Box 518
Palo Alto, CA 94302
www.westernwheelers.org

Youth Science Institute
296 Garden Hill Drive
Los Gatos, CA 95032
408-356-4945
www.ysi.ca.org

Appendix C: Recommended Readings

Bay Area and California

Brewer, William H. *Up and Down California in 1860-1864: The Journal of William H. Brewer.* Berkeley, CA: University of California Press, 1974.

Butler, Phyllis Filiberti. *The Valley of Santa Clara—Historic Buildings,* 2nd ed. Novato, CA: Presidio Press, 1981.

Fleming, Robert. *The Natural World of the California Indians.* Berkeley, CA: University of California Press, 1983.

Goodrich, Teddy. *Indians of Henry W. Coe State Park.* Morgan Hill, CA: Pine Ridge Association, 1996.

Gudde, Erwin G. *California Place Names.* 4th ed. Berkeley, CA: University of California Press, 1998.

Hoover, Mildred B. and Hero Eugene Rensch (revised by Douglas Kyle). *Historic Spots in California,* 4th ed. Stanford, CA: Stanford University Press, 1994.

Johnson, Kenneth M. *The New Almaden Quicksilver Mine.* Georgetown, CA: Talisman Press, 1963.

Loomis, Patricia. *Milpitas, The Century of "Little Cornfields" 1852-1952.* Cupertino, CA: California History Center, Local History Studies, 1986.

Margolin, Malcolm. *The Ohlone Way, Indian Life in the San Francisco — Monterey Bay Area.* Berkeley, CA: Heyday Books, 1978, 1981.

Marinacci, Barbara and Rudy Marinacci. *California's Spanish Place-Names.* 2nd ed. Houston, TX: Gulf Publishing Company, 1997.

Payne, Stephen M. *Santa Clara County, Harvest of Change.* Northridge, CA: Windsor Publications, 1987.

Pierce, Marjorie. *East of the Gabilans.* Fresno, CA: Valley Publishers, 1971.

Sanchez, Nellie Van de Grift. *Spanish and Indian Place Names of California,* 2nd ed. San Francisco, CA: A. M. Robertson, 1922.

Sepeda, Dolores De Moro. *Hills West of El Toro.* Ann Arbor, MI: Braun-Brumfield Inc., 1978.

Waddell Creek, the Environment around Big Basin, Santa Cruz Mountains. Editors Barry Hecht and Barbara Rusmore. Santa Cruz, CA: Sempervirens Fund and U.C. Santa Cruz Environmental Studies Office, 1973.

Water in the Santa Clara Valley: A History, Volume 27. Cupertino, CA: California History Center, DeAnza College Local History Studies, 1981

Natural History
Alden, Peter. *National Audobon Society Field Guide to California.* Washington: National Audobon Society, 1998.

Bakker, Elna S. *An Island Called California.* Berkeley, CA: University of California Press, 1971, 1984.

Birding at the Bottom of the Bay, 2nd ed. Cupertino, CA: Santa Clara Valley Audubon Society, 1990. www.scvas.org

Burt, William H. and Richard P. Grossenheider. *A Field Guide to the Mammals, North America, North of Mexico,* 3rd ed. Boston, MA: Houghton Mifflin Company, 1980.

Conradson, Diane R. *Exploring Our Baylands,* 3rd ed. Newark, CA: San Francisco Bay Wildlife Society, 1996. *www.sfbws.org*

Crittenden, Mabel, and Dorothy Teller. *Wildflowers of the West.* Blaine: Hancock House Publishers, 1992.

Dunn, Jon L. *Field Guide to the Birds of North America,* 3rd. Washington: National Geographic Society, 1999.

Lyons, Kathleen and Mary Beth Cuneo-Lazaneo. *Plants of the Coast Redwood Region.* Los Altos, CA: Looking Press, 1988.

Murie, Olaf J. *A Field Guide to Animal Tracks,* 2nd ed. Boston, MA: Houghton Mifflin, 1998.

Peterson, Roger Tory. *A Field Guide to Western Birds.* Boston, MA: Houghton Mifflin Co., 1990.

Petrides, George A. and Roger Tory Peterson. *A Field Guide to Western Trees.* Boston, MA: Houghton Mifflin Co., 1998.

Schoenherr, Allan A. *A Natural History of California.* Berkeley, CA: University of California Press, 1995.

Sharsmith, Helen K. *Flora of the Mt. Hamilton Range of California.* American Midland Naturalist, Vol. 34, No.2. Special reprint: September 1945. Berkeley, CA: California Native Plant Society, 1982.

Sharsmith, Helen K. *Spring Wildflowers of the San Francisco Bay Region*. Berkeley, CA: University of California Press, 1965.

Sibley, David Allen. *The Sibley Guide to Birds —Field Identification, Audobon Society Nature Guides*. New York, NY: Knopf Publishing Group, 2000.

Stebbins, Robert C. *A Field Guide to Western Reptiles and Amphibians of the San Francisco Bay Region*, 2nd ed. Boston, MA: Houghton Mifflin Company, 1998.

Thomas, John Hunter. *Flora of the Santa Cruz Mountains of California: A Manual of the Vascular Plants*. Palo Alto, CA: Stanford University Press, 1961.

Trail Guides

Backpacking California. Edited by Paul Backhurst. Berkeley, CA: Wilderness Press, 2001.

Heid, Matt. *101 Hikes in Northern California*. Berkeley, CA: Wilderness Press, 2000.

Margolin, Malcolm. *East Bay Out*. Berkeley, CA: Heyday, 1974, 1988.

Perry, John and Perry, Jane Greverus. *The Sierra Club Guide to the Natural Areas of California*. San Francisco, CA: Sierra Club Books, 1983, 1997.

Rusmore, Jean. *The Bay Area Ridge Trail*, 2nd ed. Berkeley, CA: Wilderness Press, 2001.

Rusmore, Jean, Betsy Crowder and Frances Spangle. *Peninsula Trails*, 3rd ed. Berkeley, CA Wilderness Press, 1997.

Weintraub, David. *East Bay Trails*. Berkeley, CA: Wilderness Press, 1998.

Weintraub, David. *North Bay Trails*. Berkeley, CA: Wilderness Press,1999.

Periodicals

Bay Nature. Editor, David Loeb, Publisher, Malcolm Margolin. Berkeley, CA: Clapperstick Institute. This new quarterly magazine is "dedicated to the intelligent and joyful exploration of the natural places of the San Francisco Bay Area and the species that inhabit them." Contact *Bay Nature* at *baynature@baynature.com* or call for a subscription: 925-372-6002.

Index

Numbers in boldface refer to the primary entry for that area.

Acknowledgments

We enjoyed the company of our families and many friends, especially the Walkie Talkies, our women's hiking group, in exploring these trails. To them, and to all those who helped and encouraged us during the preparation of this third and expanded edition of *South Bay Trails*, we extend our gratitude.

We are especially grateful for the assistance of the staffs of the public agencies whose trails we describe: Don Edwards San Francisco Bay National Wildlife Refuge, Marge Kolar, superintendent, and Jon Steiner, ranger; California Department of Parks and Recreation; Henry W. Coe State Park, Kay Robinson, superintendent and Barry Breckling, ranger; Castle Rock State Park, Miles Standish, ranger; Big Basin Redwoods State Park, Elizabeth Burko, supervising ranger and Steve Oka, former supervising ranger; Santa Clara County Parks and Recreation Department, Lisa Killough, acting director, and Mark Frederic, planner; Midpeninsula Regional Open Space District, Ken Miller and Phil Hearing, rangers; East Bay Regional Park District, Steve Fiala, planner; City of Palo Alto, Greg Betts, open space and parks director.

To many other enthusiasts of parks and trails—representatives of advocacy groups, trail users, historical researchers, and to those working for future public acquisition of our fine valleys and mountains, we give our thanks.

We are especially grateful for the patience and forbearance of the Wilderness Press staff, Tom Winnett, Caroline Winnett, Mike Jones, and Jannie Dresser, during the prolonged preparations of the manuscript. To our map-maker, Ben Pease, our computer assistant, Mary Lyn Villaume, and our index assistant, Paula Tuerk, we offer our sincere thanks.

—*Jean Rusmore, Betsy Crowder and Frances Spangle*

357

Read This

Hiking entails unavoidable risks that every hiker assumes and must be aware of and respect. The fact that a trail is described in this book is not a representation that it will be safe for you. Trails vary greatly in difficulty and in the degree of conditioning and agility one needs to enjoy them safely. On some hikes routes may have changed or conditions may have deteriorated since the descriptions were written. Also trail conditions can change even from day to day, owing to weather and other factors. A trail that is safe on a dry day or for a highly conditioned, agile, properly equipped hiker may be completely unsafe for someone else or unsafe under adverse weather conditions.

You can minimize your risks on the trail by being knowledgeable, prepared and alert. There is not space in this book for a general treatise on safety, but there are a number of good books and public courses on the subject and you should take advantage of them to increase your knowledge. Just as important, you should always be aware of your own limitations and of conditions existing when and where you are hiking. If conditions are dangerous, or if you're not prepared to deal with them safely, choose a different hike! It's better to have wasted a drive than to be the subject of a rescue.

These warnings are not intended to scare you off the trails. Millions of people have safe and enjoyable hikes every year. However, one element of the beauty, freedom and excitement of the outdoors is the presence of risks that do not confront us at home. When you hike you assume those risks. They can be met safely, but only if you exercise your own independent judgment and common sense.